BEST PRACTICES IN WRITING INSTRUCTION

SOLVING PROBLEMS IN THE TEACHING OF LITERACY
Cathy Collins Block, *Series Editor*

Best Practices in Writing Instruction

Edited by
STEVE GRAHAM
CHARLES A. MACARTHUR
JILL FITZGERALD

THE GUILFORD PRESS
New York   London

KH

©2007 The Guilford Press
A Division of Guilford Publications, Inc.
72 Spring Street, New York, NY 10012
www.guilford.com

Printed in the United States of America

This book is printed on acid-free paper.

Last digit is print number: 9 8 7 6 5 4 3 2

Library of Congress Cataloging-in-Publication Data

Best practices in writing instruction / edited by Steve Graham, Charles A. MacArthur,
Jill Fitzgerald.
      p. cm. — (Solving problems in the teaching of literacy)
   Includes bibliographical references and index.
   ISBN-13 978-1-59385-432-4 ISBN-10 1-59385-432-3 (pbk. : alk. paper)
   ISBN-13 978-1-59385-433-1 ISBN-10 1-59385-433-1 (cloth : alk. paper)
   1. English language—Composition and exercises—Study and teaching (Elementary)
   2. English language—Composition and exercises—Study and teaching (Secondary)
   I. Graham, Steve, 1950– II. MacArthur, Charles A. III. Fitzgerald, Jill. IV. Series.
   LB1576.B487 2007
   428.0071—dc22
                                                                    2006102550

7/29/08

For a Star Who Fell from the Sky

This book is dedicated to Michael Pressley,
who passed from us in May of 2006.

He was an unforgettable friend and colleague.
While our memory will not fade,
the sky will not shine as brightly.

About the Editors

Steve Graham, EdD, is the Currey–Ingram Professor of Special Education and Literacy in the Peabody School of Education at Vanderbilt University. Prior to moving to his current position in 2005, he taught at the University of Maryland for 23 years and before that at Purdue and Auburn Universities. Most of Dr. Graham's research focuses on identifying the factors involved in writing disabilities and examining the effectiveness of specific prevention and intervention procedures for enhancing writing development. He is the editor of *Exceptional Children* and the former editor of *Contemporary Educational Psychology.* Dr. Graham is the author or editor of more than 200 publications, including the *Handbook of Writing Research, Writing Better, Making the Writing Process Work,* and the *Handbook of Learning Disabilities.* He is coauthor, with Dolores Perin, of *Writing Next,* a meta-analysis of the writing intervention literature in grades 4–12, funded by the Carnegie Corporation of New York. Dr. Graham has received the Council for Exceptional Children's Career Research Award, the Samuel A. Kirk Award from the Division of Learning Disabilities, and the Distinguished Research Award from the Special Education Interest Group of the American Educational Research Association.

Charles A. MacArthur, PhD, is Professor of Special Education and Literacy in the School of Education at the University of Delaware. A former special education teacher, he teaches courses on literacy problems, writing instruction, and assistive technology. Dr. MacArthur is the author or editor of more than 80 publications, including the *Handbook of Writing Research,* and has presented widely. His major research interests include writing development and instruction for students with learning disabilities, applications of technology to support reading and writing, development of self-regulated strategies, and adult literacy. He is coeditor of the *Journal of Special Education* and serves on the editorial boards of several other journals, including *Exceptional Children, Journal of Educational Psychology, Journal of Learning Disabilities,* and *Learning Disability Quarterly.*

Jill Fitzgerald, PhD, is Senior Associate Dean and Professor of Literacy Studies at The University of North Carolina at Chapel Hill, where she has taught since 1979. A former primary-grades teacher and reading specialist, she has taught courses in reading and writing at the undergraduate and graduate levels. Dr. Fitzgerald has published more than 70 works and been an invited speaker at national and international research and professional conferences. Her current research interests center on literacy issues for multilingual learners and early literacy development in relation to literacy-instruction reform efforts. Dr. Fitzgerald has won the American Educational Research Association's Outstanding Review of Research Award and (with George Noblit) the International Reading Association's Dina Feitelson Award for Research. She currently serves on the editorial boards of several national and international journals, including *Journal of Educational Psychology, Reading Research Quarterly, Contemporary Educational Psychology,* and *Review of Educational Research.* She has also served extensively on national and international literacy and educational associations through committee work.

Contributors

Steve Amendum, MEd, School of Education, The University of North Carolina at Chapel Hill, Chapel Hill, North Carolina

Stan Bird, MSc, Division of Applied Psychology, University of Calgary, Calgary, Alberta, Canada

Pietro Boscolo, PhD, Department of Developmental and Socialization Psychology, University of Padua, Padua, Italy

Stacey Boster, MEd, College of Education, The Ohio State University, Columbus, Ohio

Robert C. Calfee, PhD, Graduate School of Education, University of California, Riverside, Riverside, California

David Coker, EdD, School of Education, University of Delaware, Newark, Delaware

Susan De La Paz, PhD, Department of Education, Santa Clara University, Santa Clara, California

Lauren Fingeret, MA, Department of Teacher Education, Michigan State University, East Lansing, Michigan

Jill Fitzgerald, PhD, School of Education, The University of North Carolina at Chapel Hill, Chapel Hill, North Carolina

Carmen Gelati, PhD, Department of Developmental and Socialization Psychology, University of Padua, Padua, Italy

Steve Graham, EdD, Peabody College of Education, Vanderbilt University, Nashville, Tennessee

Karen R. Harris, EdD, Peabody College of Education, Vanderbilt University, Nashville, Tennessee

Ronald L. Honeycutt, PhD, Department of Curriculum and Instruction, North Carolina State University, Raleigh, North Carolina

Marya Jarvey, MSc, Calgary Catholic School District, Calgary, Alberta, Canada

Rachel Karchmer-Klein, PhD, School of Education, University of Delaware, Newark, Delaware

Susan Koukis, MA, College of Education, The Ohio State University, Columbus, Ohio

Charles A. MacArthur, PhD, School of Education, University of Delaware, Newark, Delaware

Ann McKeough, PhD, Division of Applied Psychology, University of Calgary, Calgary, Alberta, Canada

Roxanne Greitz Miller, EdD, School of Education, Chapman University, Orange, California

Lindsey Mohan, BA, Department of Teacher Education, Michigan State University, East Lansing, Michigan

George E. Newell, PhD, College of Education, The Ohio State University, Columbus, Ohio

Jaime Palmer, MSc, Division of Applied Psychology, University of Calgary, Calgary, Alberta, Canada

Dolores Perin, PhD, Teachers College, Columbia University, New York, New York

Michael Pressley, PhD (deceased), Department of Teacher Education, Michigan State University, East Lansing, Michigan

Ruie J. Pritchard, PhD, Department of Curriculum and Instruction, North Carolina State University, Raleigh, North Carolina

Lisa Raphael-Bogaert, PhD, College of Education, University of Illinois–Chicago, Chicago, Illinois

Kelly Reffitt, MA, Department of Teacher Education, Michigan State University, East Lansing, Michigan

Bruce Saddler, PhD, Department of Educational and Counseling Psychology, University at Albany, State University of New York, Albany, New York

Bob Schlagal, PhD, Department of Language, Reading, and Exceptionalities, Appalachian State University, Boone, North Carolina

Contents

xi

PART III. SPECIAL POPULATIONS

Introduction

Best Practices in Writing Instruction Now

STEVE GRAHAM, CHARLES A. MACARTHUR,
and JILL FITZGERALD

We designed this book to help teachers become more effective at teaching writing. It provides evidence-based practices for enhancing the writing of students at all levels—elementary through high school. It also presents effective strategies for teaching writing to multilingual students and those with special needs.

The practical, research-based best practices methods included in this book will be useful to experienced and inexperienced teachers as well as language arts and content-area teachers. They can be used in language arts and writing instruction courses as well as staff development workshops that focus on writing and literacy development, and they should be of value to school principals, writing specialists, and others involved in administering or delivering writing instruction to children and adolescents.

Our decision to develop this book was based on the belief that students deserve the best writing instruction possible. The need for such instruction is based on four interrelated principles.

1

PRINCIPLE 1: WRITING IS ESSENTIAL

Writing is a powerful tool for getting things done. Even young children sometimes recognize the power of writing. Glenda Bissex (1980), in her case study of her 4-year-old son's literacy development, tells a story about him. She was reading and did not respond when her son tried to engage her. A few minutes later he returned and handed her a written message, "R U DF?" It worked. She turned away from her reading and went to talk with him. One of the most important features of writing is that it lets us communicate with others, allowing us to maintain personal links with family, friends, and colleagues who are removed by both distance and time. The advent of e-mail, text messaging, and other forms of electronic text have made writing an even more flexible communication tool.

Writing's power also resides in its ability to convey knowledge and ideas (Diamond, 1999).Writing makes it possible to gather, preserve, and transmit information widely with great detail and accuracy. Even everyday tasks such as cooking a microwaveable dinner involve following written directions.

Another contribution of writing is embodied in the novelist E. M. Forster's question, "How can I know what I think until I see what I say?" Writing provides a useful tool for refining and extending one's knowledge about a particular topic (Applebee, 1984). Its permanence makes ideas readily available for review and evaluation. Its explicitness encourages the establishment of connections between ideas, and its active nature promotes the exploration of unexamined assumptions.

Writing can also be used as a means for persuading others. Examples range from Thomas Paine's pamphlet *Common Sense* to an employee who solved an irritating problem at work by replacing an ineffective sign, "Alarm Will Sound If Door Opened," with the sign "Wet Paint." This written placard had the desired effect of keeping people from using the emergency exit (Hines, 2000, p. 54).

Writing also provides a means for self-expression. People use writing to explore who they are, to combat loneliness, and to chronicle their experiences. Writing about one's experiences or feelings can have beneficial effects, reducing depression, lowering blood pressure, and boosting the immune system (Swedlow, 1999).

While students use writing for all of these purposes (i.e., to communicate, share knowledge, learn, persuade, and explore feelings and beliefs), their mastery of it influences their success in one other important way: Writing is the primary instrument that teachers use to evaluate academic performance (Graham, 1982). In some instances, the amount of writing involved is minimal (e.g., spelling tests, fill-in-the-blank activities, and short-answer questions). With other assessments, the writing demands are considerable and may include essay tests, book reports, research papers, and state competency tests.

The power of writing resides in the many ways in which it can be used. It is essential to school success and has increasingly become a central component of daily life in industrialized societies.

PRINCIPLE 2: WE NEED TO DO
A BETTER JOB TEACHING WRITING

Despite the importance of writing, many students do not write well enough to meet grade-level demands in school. Findings from the two most recent writing assessments conducted by the National Assessment of Educational Progress revealed that an alarmingly high proportion of youngsters are not developing the competence in writing needed at their respective grade levels (Greenwald, Persky, Ambell, & Mazzeo, 1999; Persky, Daane, & Jin, 2003). Despite small improvements over a 4-year period, the writing of approximately two thirds of students in elementary, middle, and high school was below grade-level proficiency. Moreover, one in five first-year college students requires a remedial writing class, and more than half of new college students are unable to write a paper relatively free of errors (Intersegmental Committee of the Academic Senates, 2002). The National Commission on Writing (2003) bluntly concluded that the writing of students in the United States "is not what it should be" (p. 7).

Youngsters who do not learn to write well face many obstacles. They are less likely than their more skilled peers to benefit from the use of writing activities designed to enhance content learning (writing-to-learn activities). Their grades are more likely to suffer, particularly in classes where writing is the primary means for assessing progress. If they do not become competent writers, they are unlikely to realize their educational, occupational, or personal potential. Their participation in community events, especially those that involve communication through writing, may be hindered.

We clearly need to do a better job teaching writing. Our instructional efforts in this area need to be informed by what is known about the factors that foster writing development and proven methods for promoting such development.

PRINCIPLE 3: WE KNOW WHAT
SKILLED WRITING LOOKS LIKE

We have a very good idea of what students need to acquire in order to become skilled writers. One way of thinking about writing development is that it is fueled (or inhibited) by students' strategic behavior, knowledge about writing, motivation, and mastery of text transcription skills (Graham, 2006; Graham & Harris, 2005).

Much of a skilled writer's time is spent planning, revising, monitoring, evaluating, and regulating the writing process. For example, college students spend almost 50% of their writing time planning and reviewing what they write (Kellogg, 1987). Business executives spend almost two thirds of their writing time planning (Gould, 1980). These strategic processes are also stressed by children who are good writers. When one study asked such children to tell what good writers do (Graham, Schwartz, & MacArthur, 1993), they emphasized these same processes. One fourth-grade child said, "Well, they take all of their brainstorming ideas and put them on a piece of paper and just write the rough draft. Then they come back and find mistakes and think of some other ideas and do it over again." The mantra of another youngster—"Plan it. Revise it. Edit it"—was echoed in one form or the other by most of the other children interviewed.

Another way to think about writing development is that it is fueled in a social and cultural way. Writers write for audiences. As Nystrand (1986) wrote, they write on the premises of the reader. They consider what effect they want to create and shape their writing to achieve that effect, anticipating what the reader will assume, learn, and infer. Even when only one person is doing the writing, it is not done in isolation because an imagined reader, an imagined objective, an imagined impact is at the core of the writing.

Knowledge also plays a critical role in skilled writing, including knowledge about the craft of writing. Skilled writers are knowledgeable about writing style, convention, genre, and rhetorical devices. Journalists, for instance, know about the "inverted pyramid," in which you present the most important information first, then tell the rest of the story in descending order of importance (Lamb, 1997).

Knowledge includes content knowledge. Skilled writers typically know a lot about their topics. When they do not have the needed information at hand, they know how to get it. Sometimes this can involve a common strategy such as consulting an authoritative source. In other instances, it may require a more innovative approach. To illustrate, Sue Hubbell, who writes children's books about bugs, employs both methods. When writing the book *Broadsides from the Other Orders*, she first obtained facts for her main characters—silverfish, katydids, daddy longlegs—by visiting the Library of Congress and reading everything that she could find. She then called the leading experts on the featured bug to gain even more interesting facts. For some bugs, such as camel crickets, there was little information and no living expert. In these cases, she raised and observed the bugs herself!

Skilled writers possess a can-do attitude. Their motivation has a positive impact on what they do when writing. For example, writers who believe in their capabilities are more likely to set challenging writing goals, plan a course of action for achieving them, exert needed effort, persevere in the face of difficulty, and believe that they will be successful (Bandura, 1995). One of our favorite stories involving a writer's sense of agency centers on the publication of the children's book *The Tale of Peter Rabbit*. It was turned down by at least seven publishing firms. One firm commented that it "smelled of rotting carrots." Despite these rejections, the author, Beatrix Potter, did not falter. She was so positive about her creation that she used her own savings to publish it. One hundred years later, it is still selling briskly.

Finally, writing is a demanding task, even for professional writers. This was illustrated in the famous quote by the sports writer Red Smith, who complained, "Writing is easy. All you have to do is sit down at a typewriter and open a vein." Skilled writers, however, make one aspect of writing look effortless. They have automatized the basic skills for transcribing words into written text, including handwriting (or typing), spelling, punctuation, and capitalization. While it is not possible to fully automatize the skills for turning ideas into well-crafted sentences, good writers have honed these skills too so that they can employ a variety of sentence types to fit their goals and purposes.

If students are to become good writers, we need to help them become strategic, knowledgeable, and motivated writers who are not hampered by inefficient or faulty transcription and sentence construction skills.

PRINCIPLE 4: WE HAVE EFFECTIVE PROCEDURES FOR TEACHING WRITING

Researchers' efforts to identify effective instructional practices in writing have involved a variety of different approaches. Traditional experimental studies involved students who received one instructional approach being compared to students who received an alternative approach or no instruction at all. In some instances, this has involved randomly assigning students to each instructional condition (Fitzgerald & Teasley, 1986). In others, it has not. Researchers' efforts have also included the application of qualitative methods. For instance, considerable insight into how best to teach writing has been obtained by studying master teachers (e.g., Pressley, Yokoi, Rankin, Wharton-McDonald, & Mistretta, 1997). Other efforts include investigations that examine the correlation between writing performance and particular teaching practices (e.g., Applebee, Langer, Nystrand, & Gamoran, 2003) as well as single-subject design studies that closely monitor the effectiveness of an intervention with a small number of students (e.g., De La Paz, 1999). Findings from these studies have produced an incredible body of knowledge about teaching writing. Cumulatively, the authors of the chapters in this book draw upon all of these research traditions and upon many different perspectives, including cognitive (Hayes, 2000) and sociocultural (Prior, 2006).

Do we know enough about effective instructional practices to help students become strategic, knowledgeable, and motivated writers who have mastered basic transcription and sentence construction skills? The answer is yes. For example, recent reviews of writing intervention studies show that a variety of effective practices enhance students' writing development (Bangert-Drowns, 1993; Goldring, Russell, & Cook, 2003; Graham, 1999, 2006; Graham & Harris, 2003; Graham & Perrin, 2006; Hillocks, 1986). These interventions include teaching students to be more strategic when planning, drafting, or revising; constructing a supportive writing environment in which such processes are valued; developing instructional arrangements where students work together to support their writing efforts; setting clear and specific goals for writing tasks; using word processing and supporting software; teaching increasingly sophisticated sentence construction via sentence combining; involving students in inquiry activities centered on the process of writing; using good models of writing to enhance students' knowledge; and teaching basic text transcription skills such as handwriting and spelling. Furthermore, the study of master teachers reveals that they employ a variety of procedures to enhance students' motivation. The authors in this volume draw upon these and other findings to develop best practices in writing instruction.

STRUCTURE OF THE BOOK

The book is divided into three parts. The first section, "Designing Writing Programs," examines writing instruction broadly. The contributing authors explore how exemplary teachers provide writing instruction (Chapter 1: Pressley, Mohan, Fingeret, Reffitt, & Raphael-Bogaert), guidelines for implementing a process writing approach (Chapter 2: Pritchard & Honeycutt), teaching writing from a developmental perspective (Chapter 3: McKeough, Palmer, Jarvey, & Bird), and developing writing across the curriculum (Chapter 4: Newell, Koukis, & Boster).

The second section, "Strategies for Teaching and Learning," focuses on how to foster the development of motivation and specific writing processes and skills. In addition, it contains a chapter on writing instruction for young children (Chapter 5: Coker) as well as one on teaching writing to adolescents (Chapter 12: Perin). Although most of the chapters in this book present best practices that can be used with younger and older students, we decided that it would be valuable to include these two chapters because they concentrate on beginning writing instruction and the culminating efforts of teachers as students move through the educational system. Four other chapters in this section concentrate on the teaching of planning (Chapter 6: Graham & Harris), revising (Chapter 7: MacArthur), sentence construction skills (Chapter 8: Saddler), and spelling and handwriting (Chapter 9: Schlagal). The other three chapters in this section examine how to foster motivation to write (Chapter 10: Boscolo & Gelati), use of the Internet to support writing (Chapter 11: Karchmer-Klein), and the assessment of writing (Chapter 13: Calfee & Greitz Miller).

The final section, "Special Populations," presents best practices for teaching writing to multilingual learners (Chapter 14: Fitzgerald & Amendum) and students with special needs (Chapter 15: De La Paz). We hope that you find the best practices presented in this book to be useful, and that they help you think about writing instruction in new ways.

REFERENCES

Applebee, A. (1984). Writing and reasoning. *Review of Educational Research, 54,* 577–596.

Applebee, A., Langer, J., Nystrand, M., & Gamoran, A. (2003). Discussion-based approaches to developing understanding: Classroom instruction and student performance in middle and high school English. *American Educational Research Journal, 40,* 685–730.

Bandura, A. (1995). Exercise of personal and collective efficacy in changing societies. In A. Bandura (Ed.), *Self-efficacy in changing societies* (pp. 1–45). Cambridge, UK: Cambridge University Press.

Bangert-Drowns, R. (1993). The word processor as an instructional tool: A meta-analysis of word processing in writing instruction. *Review of Educational Research, 63,* 69–93.

Bissex, G. (1980). *GNYS AT WRK: A child learns to write and read.* Cambridge, MA: Harvard University Press.

De La Paz, S. (1999). Self-regulated strategy instruction in regular education settings: Improving outcomes for students with and without learning disabilities. *Learning Disabilities Research and Practice, 14,* 92–106.

Diamond, J. (1999). *Guns, germs, and steel: The fates of human societies.* New York: Norton.

Fitzgerald, J., & Teasley, A. B. (1986). Effects of instruction in narrative structure on children's writing. *Journal of Educational Psychology, 78,* 424–432.

Goldring, A., Russell, M., & Cook, A. (2003). The effects of computers on student writing: A meta-analysis of studies from 1992–2002. *Journal of Technology, Learning, and Assessment, 2*, 1–51.

Gould, J. (1980). Experiments on composing letters: Some facts, some myths, and some observations. In L. Gregg & E. Steinberg (Eds.), *Cognitive processes in writing* (pp. 97–127). Hillsdale, NJ: Erlbaum.

Graham, S. (1982). Composition research and practice: A unified approach. *Focus on Exceptional Children, 14*, 1–16.

Graham, S. (1999). Handwriting and spelling instruction for students with learning disabilities. *Learning Disabilities Quarterly, 22*, 78–98.

Graham, S. (2006). Strategy instruction and the teaching of writing: A meta-analysis. In C. A. MacArthur, S. Graham, & J. Fitzgerald (Eds.), *Handbook of writing research* (pp. 187–207). New York: Guilford Press.

Graham, S. (2006). Writing. In P. Alexander & P. Wiine (Eds.), *Handbook of educational psychology* (pp. 457–478). Mahwah, NJ: Erlbaum.

Graham, S., & Harris, K. R. (2003). Students with learning disabilities and the process of writing: A meta-analysis of SRSD studies. In L. Swanson, K. R. Harris, & S. Graham (Eds.), *Handbook of research on learning disabilities* (pp. 383–402). New York: Guilford Press.

Graham, S., & Harris, K. (2005). *Writing better.* Baltimore: Brookes.

Graham, S., & Perin, D. (2006). *Writing next: Effective strategies to improve writing of adolescents in middle and high school.* Washington, DC: Alliance for Excellence in Education.

Graham, S., Schwartz, S., & MacArthur, C. (1993). Knowledge of writing and the composing process, attitude toward writing, and the self-efficacy for students with and without learning disabilities. *Journal of Learning Disabilities, 26*, 237–249.

Greenwald, E., Persky, H., Ambell, J., & Mazzeo, J. (1999). *National assessment of educational progress: 1998 report card for the nation and the states.* Washington, DC: U.S. Department of Education.

Hayes, J. R. (2000). A new framework for understanding cognition and affect in writing. In R. Indrisano & J. R. Squire (Eds.), *Perspectives on writing: Research, theory and practice* (pp. 6–44). Newark, DE: International Reading Association. Originally published in C. M. Levy & S. Ransdell (Eds.). (1996). *The science of writing: Theories, methods, individual differences, and applications.* (pp. 1–27). Mahwah, NJ: Erlbaum.

Hillocks, G. (1986). *Research on written composition: New directions for teaching.* Urbana, IL: National Council of Teachers of English.

Hines, L. (2000). *Reader's Digest,* p. 54.

Intersegmental Committee of the Academic Senates. (2002). *A statement of competencies of students entering California's public colleges and universities.* Sacramento, CA: Author.

Kellogg, R. (1987). Effects of topic knowledge on the allocation of processing time and cognitive effort to writing processes. *Memory and Cognition, 15*, 256–266.

Lamb, B. (1997). *Booknotes: America's finest authors on reading, writing, and the power of ideas.* New York: Random House.

National Commission on Writing. (2003). *The neglected "R."* New York: College Entrance Examination Board.

Nystrand, M. (1986). *The structure of written communication: Studies in reciprocity between writers and readers.* Orlando, FL: Academic Press.

Persky, H. R., Daane, M. C., & Jin, Y. (2003). *The nation's report card: Writing 2002.* (NCES 2003–529). U.S. Department of Education. Institute of Education Sciences. National Center for Education Statistics. Washington, DC: Government Printing Office.

Prior, P. (2006). A sociocultural theory of writing. In C. MacArthur, S. Graham, & J. Fitzgerald (Eds.), *Handbook of writing research* (pp. 54–66). New York: Guilford Press.

Pressley, M., Yokoi, L., Rankin, J., Wharton-McDonald, R., & Mistretta, J. (1997). A survey of the instructional practices of grade 5 teachers nominated as effective in promoting literacy. *Scientific Studies of Reading, 1,* 1–16.

Swedlow, J. (1999). The power of writing. *National Geographic, 196,* 110–132.

Part I
~

Designing
Writing Programs

1

Writing Instruction in Engaging and Effective Elementary Settings

MICHAEL PRESSLEY, LINDSEY MOHAN, LAUREN FINGERET, KELLY REFFITT, *and* LISA RAPHAEL-BOGAERT

For more than a decade, we and our colleagues have been on a quest to document the nature of effective, engaging elementary literacy instruction. It began with a search for grade-1 classrooms that were producing more impressive literacy achievement than other grade-1 classrooms (for an example, see Wharton-McDonald, Pressley, & Hampston, 1998; for reviews, see Pressley, Dolezal, et al., 2003, and Pressley, Roehrig, et al., 2003) and continues with studies of entire schools that are producing more impressive language arts achievement than otherwise comparable schools (e.g., Pressley, Gaskins, Solic, & Collins, 2006; Pressley, Mohan, Raphael-Bogaert, & Fingeret, 2005; Pressley, Raphael, Gallagher, & DiBella, 2004; Pressley & Reffitt, 2006). In general, the findings in these studies have been very consistent.

Perhaps the most salient characteristic of elementary settings that produce high language arts achievement is that students are very engaged (see Pritchard & Honeycutt, Chapter 2, this volume): That is, 90% of the time they are doing something academic, something requiring thoughtfulness, such as drafting a well-structured story or reading an appropriately challenging book, rather than something that does not require thoughtfulness, such as doing a workbook page that can be completed in less than 30 seconds, leaving many students off-task for the remaining 9½ minutes of class. A second characteristic of the most effective literacy instruction is that there is a lot of teaching occurring—in whole group, in small groups, and with individual students (e.g., reteaching as students struggle; attempting to apply an idea covered in the whole group, such as how to write an interesting first sentence for a story). Effective teachers explain much to their students about how to write and read and model writing and reading, for example, modeling revision of the first sentence of a story to make it more interesting (see Graham & Harris, Chapter 6, and MacArthur, Chapter 7, this volume). As part of such instruction, there is teaching of skills, balanced by ample opportunity to apply those skills during real writing and reading, with the teacher providing scaffolded support as students begin to use the skills they are learning.

Effective, engaging elementary literacy teachers provide just enough support so that students can make progress, with the purpose of encouraging students to accomplish as much as possible on their own—to act in a self-regulated fashion. The encouragement of such self-regulation begins on the first day of the school year and continues every day (e.g., Bohn, Roehrig, & Pressley, 2004). This encouragement is in the general context of a very positive environment, one in which students are constantly being motivated to try hard, believe that the skills and strategies they are learning will permit them to be excellent writers and readers if they use them, and attribute their successes to their efforts to use the tactics they are learning (see Graham & Harris, Chapter 6, this volume). In effective classrooms, the teacher does something every minute to motivate one or more students to complete academic tasks (e.g., Bogner, Raphael, & Pressley, 2002; Dolezal, Welsh, Pressley, & Vincent, 2003; Pressley, Dolezal, et al., 2003). We observed that effective elementary school literacy teachers employ close to 50 different motivational practices (see Boscolo & Gelati, Chapter 10, this volume) on a daily basis!

There is also something missing from these schools: punishment or the need for it. Off-task behavior and misbehavior simply do not happen very often in highly effective and engaging classrooms, so there is little need to sanction students (Bogner et al., 2002; Dolezal et al., 2003; Pressley, Dolezal, et al., 2003). Indeed, all the teaching behaviors that can undermine achievement (Brophy, 2004; Pintrich & Schunk, 2002; Stipek, 2002)—from attributing student achievement to ability or luck rather than effort to fostering competitiveness to requiring boring reading and writing tasks—simply do not occur in engaging and effective classrooms.

In addition to the teaching we observed, we were also struck by the classroom environments. The most effective and engaging teachers had classrooms that were overflowing with writing materials, books, and other tools for literacy learning and instruction (see Pritchard & Honeycutt, Chapter 2, this volume). Bulletin boards were covered with student work, and all of the furniture and areas around the room were designed for student access and learning. Classroom libraries were stocked with quality children's literature as well as student-created texts. In one third-grade classroom, the teacher and students created a post office for writing letters that expanded into all of the other classrooms in the school. Soon, each classroom had its own address and ZIP code, and the students were in charge of processing and delivering all interclassroom mail (Dolezal et al., 2003; Pressley, Dolezal, et al., 2003). The most effective and engaging teachers were mindful not only of the instruction in their classrooms, but also of the way the room environments contributed to their students' learning.

Distressingly, we would often observe in the very same building both high-quality and literacy-rich lessons in engaged and effective classrooms, and uninspiring and low-level lessons in disengaged and ineffective classrooms just down the hall. As we watched a classroom of students experience attractive and engaging instruction in grade 1, we knew it was unlikely they would receive such instruction in grade 2 and extremely unlikely that such instruction would continue throughout their elementary years. This disparity caused us to ask whether there were schools characterized by consistently engaging and effective teaching, schools in which a student might enter as a kindergartener and experience engaging instruction most years in the school. One tactic for getting an answer to this question was to study a school that specializes in providing effective literacy instruction to students who failed previously, such as the Benchmark School in Philadelphia (Pressley, Gaskins, et al., 2006). Another tactic was to spend long periods of time observing schools that produce very high language arts achievement relative to otherwise comparable schools, as documented on state and standardized tests. We have completed study of three such schools, an independent college preparatory school serving African American students in Chicago (Pressley et al., 2004), a public school serving a middle-class community (Pressley, Mohan, et al., 2005), and a public school serving an impoverished, rural community (Pressley & Reffitt, 2006).

An important first conclusion from this work is that there are schools where a student has a good chance of experiencing an effective and engaging teacher in every grade. The teaching in many of the classrooms in these schools equals or approximates the most engaging and effective elementary classrooms we studied in our previous work on effective individual classrooms. Students are mostly busy doing meaningful writing and reading and receiving both a lot of instruction about how to write and read well and a lot of support from the teacher as they attempt to apply the writing and reading skills they are learning, all in a consistently positive, encouraging environment. An important difference compared to less successful schools, however, is that in these effective schools, there is great awareness of what the students learned last year and what they will learn next year. In effective and engaging schools with high-quality language arts instruction, there is much thoughtfulness on the part of the faculty and much reflection on the development of reading and writing curricula that connect over the years, with a schoolwide vision of how students grow as writers and readers and what the school can do each year to promote positive development of literacy skills. There is also a schoolwide determination to achieve this vision, with everyone from the principal to the teachers to the classroom aides and support teachers playing his or her part every day to achieve the writing and reading goals set by the school (see Newell, Koukis, & Boster, Chapter 4, this volume).

When the editors of this book asked whether we could contribute a chapter on writing in effective educational settings, the answer was definitely yes based on our observational studies. We also cautioned that the story is pretty simple, even if it is not a story that is playing out in American classrooms and schools as often as we would like it to, and it should be noted that we do not intend to confuse the term "simple" with "easy." In fact, while the story may indeed be simple, it is not easy to execute.

THE WRITING IS ON THE WALL

Suppose that you walk into an American grade-1 classroom in May. You will see students reading a range of books, from the illustrated story and informational texts that are considered end-grade-1 level to chapter books that are more typically read in grades 3 and 4. Individual differences in reading skill are the norm at the end of grade 1 and, indeed, at every grade level. One strong impression from visiting schools around the country is that there is now a national children's literature canon as part of contemporary American reading instruction. What has been most amazing to us is that, within the same school, if there is a very engaging and effective literacy teacher who is teaching all the tricks of the reading trade to his or her students and enticing them to read often and another, less effective teacher, there will be more reading in the former compared to the latter room, but the books being read often tend to be similar. (Of course, if you listen to the discussions in the more engaging classrooms, they are often filled with more insights about what is read.)

By contrast, such similarity never characterizes the writing that occurs in the most impressive literacy classrooms we have studied compared to less impressive ones. Consider what is on the walls in Ms. Smith's grade-1 class in May compared to Ms. Jones's grade-1 class across the hall. Ms. Smith, the more effective teacher, features student writing on each classroom bulletin board and on the hallway wall outside the room. One set of papers on display is about what happened on spring break. Another is about the class trip to the minor league baseball stadium. Still another set is dedicated to "stories about spring." Immediately apparent is that most of the stories on display are long—two to five or six paragraphs—and that the mechanics are pretty good. Paragraphs are indented, sentences are capitalized and correctly punctuated, high-frequency words are spelled correctly, and lower-frequency words have credible invented spellings (i.e., the reader can figure out what the intended word is). Every student's paper is included in every set. In contrast, Ms. Jones, the less effective teacher, does not display stories in the classroom or in the hallway. By looking in some students' desks, some recent samples of writing can be found, with the best being a few lines long and with poor mechanics (i.e., little capitalization or punctuation, no real paragraphs, invented spellings that are impossible for many adults to decode). Our experience has been that such extreme contrasts are common in American schools. Thus, there are grade-1 classrooms overflowing with five-paragraph essays that are well structured and filled with interesting wording, and there are others where the best students produce a single paragraph that is made up only of high-frequency words. In the former classrooms, writing will be apparent everywhere, from classroom bulletin board displays to class-published big books of stories and essays to a collection of themed mini-books composed by students and scattered around the classroom. In the latter classrooms, an outsider will have to look hard to find examples of student writing.

Our strong impression is that the differences in writing between the classrooms and schools with the best student writers and those with the worst student writers is huge, much greater than the differences in reading among classrooms and schools. That impression is confirmed by examining information such as state testing data. For example, in even the most disadvantaged school districts in Michigan, two thirds of students typically pass the state reading test, with the state average being about 85% of students passing. It is easy to find schools with more than 95% of students passing the reading test. In contrast, the passing rate for the writing test typically is between 45 and 50%, with some schools having fewer than 25% of students passing and others having 90% passing; only a very, very few schools have 95% of students pass the writing test. That is, the range of writing performance in the state is very great relative to the range of reading performance. Having been in schools in this state with 90% or better writing passing rates and other schools with 25% writing passing rates, we know that the writing on the wall test works: Schools with high writing scores are overflowing with examples of competent student writing, with such writing being much harder to find on the walls of schools with low passing marks in writing. If there is a lot of competent student writing on the walls of the school near you, it is an excellent sign that writing at the school is good, and it says a lot about the instruction that occurs there as well. Unfortunately, there are far too many elementary classrooms with little student writing on the walls.

EFFECTIVE WRITING FOLLOWS FROM LOTS OF WRITING INSTRUCTION AND PRACTICE

If there is one generalization about writing in our work, it is that in classrooms and schools with good writing, there is a lot of writing instruction from teachers who are passionate about it. Indeed, in reviewing our field notes, we could not identify a single classroom where there was impressive writing on the wall in which there was not also daily writing instruction and practice. It was not at all unusual for 40 minutes or more of language arts instruction to be dedicated to writing in these classrooms. That instruction is complemented by writing at other times of the day, from journal writing first thing in the morning to writing as part of social studies and science instruction. Writing also occurs in the context of larger classroom projects. In one grade-3 classroom during a unit on the relationship of living things, students composed animal reports for almost 3 months that consisted of eight different sections (e.g., habitats, eating habits).

Although the exact form of writing instruction varies from classroom to classroom, effective classrooms always have some form of plan–draft–revise instruction (e.g., Flower & Hayes, 1980; Hayes & Flower, 1980; Hayes & Nash, 1996) or at least draft-and-revise, with planning less common in the primary grades than in the upper elementary and middle school grades. Students might take a day or two to draft, receive revision feedback from the teacher, redraft, receive more feedback, and then prepare a final draft, perhaps over the course of a week or more. First-and-final-draft writing simply does not occur, or not much, in effective literacy instruction classrooms (it might be relegated to a brief journaling activity on arrival at school). First-and-final-draft writing, in which students compose a first draft that serves as their final product, is much more likely to be seen in ineffective classrooms, often only in the form of a morning journal response that is drafted and never revised, perhaps never even read except by the author as he or she is composing it! In contrast, in effective classrooms, the rough drafts (or sloppy copies) get read and reflected on by the author, teacher, and classmates, who might offer peer editing suggestions. Once the writing is completed and published (i.e., a neat, final copy prepared), the author might read it in front of the class. At a minimum, it will go on the wall, with students encouraged to read and respond to others' writing and the teacher conspicuously honoring students' writing and providing genuine responses (e.g., telling the student that the spring break he or she described sounded like more fun than the spring break taken by the teacher).

In effective classrooms, teachers have high expectations of their students. We have many memories of a teacher urging a child who had been writing one-page stories to make an effort to develop a two-page story, perhaps by adding more specific details to their writing. Teachers routinely urge students to reflect with their peers to come up with more interesting words to use as synonyms or to devise an interesting ending for a story. As the final draft approaches, the pressure often is very explicit for mechanics and spelling to be as good as possible. We have certainly heard effective teachers jokingly let a student know that what he or she handed in as a final draft must really be a sloppy copy, then provide more explicit direction about what the student might do to make the paper more impressive for its presentation on the wall. Does this tactic work? The evidence this time is not just on the walls, but best depicted in the writing folders of individual students in effective classrooms. Their writing becomes much longer, more coherent, and more mechanically impressive. Review the corresponding folders in classrooms that are less effective, and there is much less evidence of growth, reflecting the fact that there is little demand for improvement in those classrooms. We have been in many classrooms where there appears to be little capable writing and where we have witnessed no incidence of students being asked to improve their writing! In such classrooms, feedback, when it occurs at all, often boils down to praise for any writing—"I just love what you have to say in your journals!" or "I'm thrilled that so many of you are summarizing the story by saying you liked it." General comments pointing to how pleased the teacher is with the writing do little to move the student along in the writing process. In contrast, when conferencing with students, the most effective teachers understand that the goal is to teach the writer, not just refine or fix the particular piece of writing.

Increasing demands on students in higher grades are also apparent from examining the scoring rubrics that teachers use to grade student writing, with students typically given these rubrics before or as they write for guidance as to what is expected (see also McKeough, Palmer, Jarvey, & Bird, Chapter 3, and Calfee & Miller, Chapter 13, this volume). The rubrics in grade 1 and early grade 2 are very simple, with students often asked to check that they indented, capitalized, punctuated, spelled high-frequency words correctly, and made credible attempts at spelling lower-frequency words. By grade 5, rubrics are quite detailed, for example, spelling out the expectations for organization, such as that there should be opening, middle, and closing paragraphs. The rubric might specify that authorial voice needs to be apparent in the piece, that there must be content reflecting research as well as the author's own ideas, that sentences must be well formed and flow from one to another, and that diverse and interesting vocabulary should be used. There would also still be a demand that the writing be mechanically sound, one reflecting higher standards (e.g., uniformly correct spelling). A grade-5 rubric in an effective classroom can include more than a page of considerations for the author as he or she plans, drafts, and revises.

One of the most interesting tactics that we have seen in effective literacy instructional classrooms is that the rubrics have stretch, meaning that students do not get rewarded for meeting an absolute standard, but rather for improving. This strategy is consistent with substantial theory and research documenting that grading for improvement is motivating (for reviews, see Brophy, 2004; Pintrich & Schunk, 2002). For example, suppose the current assignment is to write the next chapter for a book the class just completed reading. At first, it sounds like the same assignment for all students, but, with an effective teacher, it turns out to be very different, depending on the past accomplishments of each student. Thus, a student who has a history of writing long stories that are mechanically sound will be expected and encouraged to write a long next chapter. Even in this case, the teacher may find a way to encourage improvement (e.g., "Make certain you work on having a great ending, one that is a little surprising. Have the other boys at your table offer suggestions during revision conference about this"). Another student, who has never written more than a single page, may be expected and encouraged to "write a little more than a page this time." In every case, once a product that reflects substantial effort has been produced, that product is applauded, with some students reading their work during "author's chair" or all papers going into a class book or on the wall. Excellent writing is demanded from all students, with "excellent" meaning better writing than they could have done not too long ago.

We have definitely seen many kinds of writing lessons in effective classrooms. These writing lessons sometimes consist of a teacher modeling writing about a topic, perhaps developing a short essay on the overhead projector, drafting a topic sentence and then follow-up sentences.

Such modeling and explaining might go on until an entire short essay was composed, one that undoubtedly would be revisited later when the teacher explained and modeled revision. Other times, writing lessons might be more focused, perhaps dealing with mechanics (see Schlagal, Chapter 9, this volume). We have seen many, many classrooms where the day begins with students correcting a paragraph that has capitalization, punctuation, and spelling errors; the teacher then leads the students through the public correction of the paragraph either on the chalkboard or an overhead projector, reflecting with students on why corrections are being made. We have also witnessed lessons focusing on a particular skill, such as revising with more interesting words. For such a lesson, a teacher might put a student paper on the overhead projector, then go through it with the class, commenting on the words used and attempting to identify words that might make the writing more interesting. We have witnessed lessons on writing a first sentence that will grab the reader, with the teacher beginning by reading some first sentences from great stories, then providing examples of first paragraphs, some with very inviting first sentences and others without them, and reflecting with the students on how to improve those with weak first sentences.

These lessons on the higher-order writing components of planning, drafting, and revising are complemented by systematic instruction in lower-order skills. Teaching lower-order skills, such as spelling (Berninger et al., 2002; Graham, Harris, & Chorzempa, 2002), also improves student compositions. Teaching handwriting so that students can do it automatically makes sense, as students who cannot handwrite with automaticity devote much of their conscious attention to that aspect when they compose, which can undermine compositional quality (Graham, Berninger, Abbott, Abbott, & Whitaker, 1997; Graham & Harris, 2000; Graham, Harris, & Fink, 2000). All of the schools that we have studied because of their impressive language arts achievement offer systematic spelling and handwriting instruction through the elementary years.

Of course, this across-grades spelling and handwriting instruction is part of a well-thought-out across-grades writing curriculum in these effective language arts schools. Accelerating writing rubrics in part capture shifting external expectations with increasing grade. In schools in our state, grade-4 students are expected to be able to compare and contrast the positions stated in two different short passages on a topic, taking a stance as they do so (e.g., accepting the point of view in one of the passages and rejecting the point of view in the other). In the effective schools we have studied, this form of writing gets attention in grade 3, as do many other forms of informational writing. Beyond grade 3, in the Michigan schools we have studied, there is increasing emphasis on word choice and making texts interesting by varying sentence structures. As such instruction is offered, teachers are definitely aware that they are preparing their students for state expectations assessed by state tests. At the same time, they are determined that they will not teach to the test but rather offer good writing instruction, developing instruction that would make sense in an excellent elementary school even if there were no state writing assessments.

How did these schools develop their coordinated schoolwide writing curricula? They worked on it! Something that good writing teachers have impressed on us is that there is no packaged writing program that any teacher can introduce to his or her class by following scripted lessons. Each of the schools we studied seemed to have one or a few teachers who figured out some good ways for their schools to get started meeting the expectation that elementary students learn to compose well. At one school, a teacher analyzed in detail what was demanded on the state writing assessment and used those demands to design curricula for the school that met them and more. She shared her insights with other staff, with the strong support of the principal. When we studied this school, there was a very attractive and effective writing curriculum in place and the faculty were determined to learn more, with some attending professional development workshops at their own expense, bringing back what they learned to the school and their fellow teachers. On inservice days, the staff reflected on these new understandings and made decisions about what they might try next to move their composing curriculum to an even higher level. During our study, the grade-2 teachers felt that their writing curriculum could improve, and they asked us as literacy researchers for pointers about books they could consult. When we provided suggestions, they bought the books for summer study. The school also felt that kindergarten needed a stronger start in writing. The decision was made while we were there to move a teacher who was strong in teaching writing to kindergarten the next year, with this teacher immediately consulting with the kindergarten teacher considered to have the best kindergarten writing curriculum in the district. Over the summer, the new kindergarten teacher made plans for vastly improving writing in that grade. The point, of course, is that these teachers were still learning, still trying to improve. We note briefly here that in every effective school we have studied, this determination to improve, despite already teaching students well, is obvious.

Over the years, whenever we have studied effective literacy teachers, as well as not so effective ones, we have both observed and interviewed the participants. There was a striking contrast in the interview responses of the most effective teachers versus other teachers. Effective teachers, even the very experienced ones, always believe they have much more to learn and want to learn more. Ineffective teachers are much more likely to believe that they are already good teachers and have already learned how to teach. This "need to improve" attitude is especially critical with respect to the teaching of writing. First, based on the teacher education program at Michigan State University, young teachers receive very little training on how to teach writing. Second, there has been a great deal of research on how to teach students to write by using composition strategies in a self-regulated fashion, with teacher modeling and explanation of the strategies as the starting point, followed by extensive scaffolded student practice composition using the strategies. The point of emphasis here is that learning how to explain, model, and scaffold strategies takes a great deal of time and effort (see Duffy, 2003), with many composing strategies now validated as effective with elementary students (Graham & Harris, 2005), meaning there are many specific writing strategies to learn. Third, beyond the strategies approach, there are other approaches, such as Six Traits (e.g., Culham, 2003) and writing workshop (Calkins, 1994), that are particularly helpful in honing specific writing skills (e.g., developing authorial voice or interesting wording), with these approaches also requiring considerable teacher effort to learn how to use and integrate with the well-validated approach that is plan–draft–revise strategies instruction. In short, the teacher who will become broadly knowledgeable and effective in the teaching of writing has much to learn, and the starting point for every teacher who wants to be a writing teacher is to realize that there is much that can be learned.

Of course, in 2007, there is plenty of incentive for teachers across the country to want to learn more about how to teach writing. Many states have adopted more demanding writing standards than ever before (see the *www.achieve.org* website). For example, in our home state, by the end of first grade, students are expected to be able to write short narratives with a beginning, middle, and end that convey a sequence of events. They are expected to be able to write some simple poetry and informational text and to contribute to a research report as part of a class project. They are expected to do at least a little planning in advance of writing, with multiple-sentence drafts that are mechanically sound (i.e., capitalized and punctuated, with complete sentences, high-frequency words spelled correctly and lower-frequency words spelled with credible invented spellings—ones reflecting the actual sounds in the word in order of occurrence). First graders should be able to revise to improve meaning making following editing and proofreading. The first-grade writer is expected to be developing a personal style. By the end of first grade, the student is expected to be able to print legibly and be enthused about writing. Of course, with increasing grades, much more is expected with respect to all aspects of writing. Thus, by the end of fifth grade, the student is expected to set a writing purpose as part of planning and consider the audience while writing. Planning is quite elaborate, with the student using a variety of outlining strategies. Drafts are multiparagraph, with each paragraph expected to be well structured. Revision emphasizes overall organization first and foremost, with revision at the sentence and word level. Use of complex sentences is expected by the end of fifth grade. Authorial voice and perspective are expected to be clear and mechanics excellent, including correct spelling of all words. The fifth-grade student should be able to write fluently and legibly in cursive.

Recall a point made earlier, that only 45% of students in our state passed the state writing test. That test was based on the old standards, which were considerably less demanding. Teachers in our state and, we believe, across the nation are under a great deal of pressure to do much more teaching of writing and to do it well. We close this chapter by reflecting on what our studies of effective teachers and effective schools suggest for meeting the increased expectations.

WHAT SHOULD A SCHOOL DO
TO TEACH STUDENTS TO WRITE?

A school can do much to improve the composing skills of students, but much effort is required. First, a school should commit to teaching students to plan, draft, and revise (see Pritchard & Honeycutt, Chapter 2; Graham & Harris, Chapter 6; and MacArthur, Chapter 7, all this volume). This model is the one we have seen again and again in effective classrooms. It is the model explicitly at the center of many state frameworks, including the one in our state. And it is the best validated of the teaching models: When students are taught to plan, draft, and revise in a self-regulated fashion, their writing improves a great deal (see Graham, 2006).

Second, starting the process will be slow. Teachers will need an introduction to planning, drafting, and revising and lots and lots of guidance about how these activities can be explained, modeled, and scaffolded. Fortunately, there are some professional guides now available; we prefer the one by Graham and Harris (2005). There are also competing models of writing instruction that are much less explicit about teaching students to plan, draft, and revise and that compete in the professional development marketplace. In seeking out professional development for teachers, school administrators should make certain that the guidebooks and professional development they procure develop very explicit teaching of planning, drafting, and revising skills. Administrators should also recognize that it will take years for teachers to be confident teaching the full range of plan–draft–revise strategies in a source like Graham and

Harris (2005), so the only sensible model of professional development is one that occurs over years.

Third, children's writing improves through instruction and practice, occurring daily over years in an instructionally effective school. It takes a very long time for the young writer to develop all the competencies of skilled writing and that requires writing instruction to be a whole-school activity. The lone, excellent writing teacher cannot accomplish all that needs to be accomplished, with substantial growth in writing expected by the end of grade 1 and much more growth with each year of schooling. That a majority of students in our home state could not even meet the old standards makes clear that there are many reasons for educators to be thinking about how their whole schools can teach much more writing.

Fourth, as a child experiences years of instruction and practice, there must be increasing demand for improvement. Excellent writing teachers consistently demand that writing be longer and better week to week and month to month. Consistent with state standards, they also require students to write a range of narrative and informational texts as well as other genres. As they demand improvement, excellent teachers also recognize individual differences in students, with students encouraged to improve from where they are to a higher level, rather than to meet some absolute standard.

Fifth, as schools meet the demand for more writing instruction, there will be simultaneously increasing demands with respect to all other aspects of the curriculum, most conspicuously reading, but also science, social studies, and mathematics. Writing instruction must be integrated with other instruction—writing in response to reading, writing as part of social studies projects, writing as integral to scientific process instruction, and even writing about problem solving. The only way there will be time for everything in the school day is if there is integration. This also makes sense conceptually, for writing in the real world is writing across a variety of contexts, tasks, and contents.

Finally, we note that in our state students at every grade level are expected to be enthusiastic about writing. Our observation of effective classrooms and schools shows them to be very positive places where enthusiasm abounds. Elementary instruction is not just a cognitive enterprise (in this case, explicit teaching of the writing process and related skills); it is also an affective, motivational enterprise (see Boscolo & Gelati, Chapter 10, this volume). Excellent teachers create a clear sense in students that they can become writers by learning the writing strategies and skills being taught. They develop strong understanding in students that writing is a worthwhile and valuable activity, definitely worth the effort to learn how to do well. Effective teachers provide students with choices about their writing and assign interesting writing tasks. They provide consistent feedback about writing and praise for improvement, creating a context in which writing achievement is celebrated. Effective teachers also regard their student writers as purposeful authors—students in these classrooms publish products. As school administrators encourage their teachers to learn how to teach writing, they also need to encourage them to create motivating, engaging educational environments.

ACKNOWLEDGMENT

The writing of this chapter was supported by the Research Excellence Fund of Michigan State University through a grant to the College of Education, Literacy Achievement Research Center (LARC).

REFERENCES

Berninger, V. W., Vaughan, K., Abbott, R. W., Begay, K., Coleman, K. R., Curtin, G., et al. (2002). Teaching spelling and composition alone and together: Implications for the simple view of writing. *Journal of Educational Psychology, 94*, 291–304.

Bogner, K., Raphael, L. M., & Pressley, M. (2002). How grade-1 teachers motivate literate activity by their students. *Scientific Studies of Reading, 6*, 135–165.

Bohn, C. M., Roehrig, A. D., & Pressley, M. (2004). The first days of school in effective and less effective primary-grades classrooms. *Elementary School Journal, 104*, 269–278.

Brophy, J. (2004). *Motivating students to learn* (2nd ed.). Mahwah, NJ: Erlbaum.

Calkins, L. M. (1994). *The art of teaching writing*. Portsmouth, NH: Heinemann.

Culham, R. (2003). *6 + 1 traits of writing*. New York: Scholastic.

Dolezal, S. E., Welsh, L. M., Pressley, M., & Vincent, M. (2003). How do grade-3 teachers motivate their students? *Elementary School Journal, 103*, 239–267.

Duffy, G. (2003). *Explaining reading: A resource for teaching concepts, skills, and strategies*. New York: Guilford Press.

Flower, L. S., & Hayes, J. R. (1980). The dynamics of composing: Making plans and juggling constraints. In L. W. Gregg & E. R. Steinberg (Eds.), *Cognitive processes in writing* (pp. 31–50). Hillsdale, NJ: Erlbaum.

Graham, S. (2006). Strategy instruction and the teaching of writing: A meta-analysis. In C. A. MacArthur, S. Graham, & J. Fitzgerald (Eds.), *Handbook of writing research* (pp. 187–207). New York: Guilford Press.

Graham, S., Berninger, V., Abbott, R., Abbott, S., & Whitaker, D. (1997). The role of mechanics in composing of elementary school students: A new methodological approach. *Journal of Educational Psychology, 89*, 170–182.

Graham, S., & Harris, K. R. (2000). The role of self-regulation and transcription skills in writing and writing development. *Educational Psychologist, 35*, 3–12.

Graham, S., & Harris, K. R. (2005). *Writing better: Effective strategies for teaching students with learning difficulties.* Baltimore: Brookes.

Graham, S., Harris, K. R., & Chorzempa, B. F. (2002). Contribution of spelling instruction to the spelling, writing, and reading of poor spellers. *Journal of Educational Psychology, 94,* 669–686.

Graham, S., Harris, K. R., & Fink, B. (2000). Is handwriting causally related to learning to write? Treatment of handwriting problems in beginning writers. *Journal of Educational Psychology, 92,* 620–633.

Hayes, J. R., & Flower, L. S. (1980). Identifying the organization of writing processes. In L. W. Gregg & E. R. Steinberg (Eds.), *Cognitive processes in writing* (pp. 3–30). Hillsdale, NJ: Erlbaum.

Hayes, J. R., & Nash, J. G. (1996). On the nature of planning in writing. In M. Levy & S. Ransdell (Eds.), *The science of writing: Theories, methods, individual differences, and applications* (pp. 29–55). Mahwah, NJ: Erlbaum.

Pintrich, P. R., & Schunk, D. H. (2002). *Motivation in education: Theory, research, and applications* (2nd ed.). Englewood Cliffs, NJ: Prentice Hall.

Pressley, M., Dolezal, S. E., Raphael, L. M., Mohan, L., Roehrig, A. D., & Bogner, K. (2003). *Motivating primary-grade students.* New York: Guilford Press.

Pressley, M., Gaskins, I. W., Solic, K., & Collins, S. (2006). A portrait of Benchmark School: How a school produces high achievement in students who previously failed. *Journal of Educational Psychology, 98*(2), 282–306.

Pressley, M., Mohan, L., Raphael-Bogaert, L., & Fingeret, L. (2005). *How does Bennett Woods produce such high language arts achievement?* Technical Report. East Lansing MI: Michigan State University, College of Education, Literacy Achievement Research Center (LARC).

Pressley, M., Raphael, L., Gallagher, J. D., & DiBella, J. (2004). Providence-St. Mel School: How a school that works for African American students works. *Journal of Educational Psychology, 96,* 216–235.

Pressley, M., & Reffitt, K. (2006). *How does a rural school district produce such high language arts achievement?* Technical Report. East Lansing MI: Michigan State University, College of Education, Literacy Achievement Research Center (LARC).

Pressley, M., Roehrig, A., Raphael, L., Dolezal, S., Bohn, K., Mohan, L., et al. (2003). Teaching processes in elementary and secondary education. In W. M. Reynolds & G. E. Miller (Eds.), *Handbook of psychology: Vol. 7. Educational Psychology* (pp. 153–175). New York: Wiley.

Stipek, D. (2002). Good instruction is motivating. In A. Wigfield & J. Eccles (Eds.), *Development of achievement motivation* (pp. 310–330). New York: Academic Press.

Wharton-McDonald, R., Pressley, M., & Hampston, J. M. (1998). Outstanding literacy instruction in first grade: Teacher practices and student achievement. *Elementary School Journal, 99,* 101–128.

2

Best Practices in Implementing a Process Approach to Teaching Writing

RUIE J. PRITCHARD *and* RONALD L. HONEYCUTT

The teaching practices associated with the process approach to writing instruction from kindergarten to 12th grade have been delineated more in the practical applications literature than in the research literature due to the changing definitions of what the process entails and the uneven application of the approach across research studies. An overall finding of research on the process approach is that all the stages must be fully implemented if students are to build a repertoire of writing strategies. Students need structure and sequence and do not benefit from a pick-and-choose approach to teaching writing. In a smorgasbord approach, only some of the instructional components of the process approach are applied, such as when a teacher employs rubrics in grading but does not involve students in understanding and/or creating the features of the rubrics. In a piecemeal approach, process writing instruction is implemented unevenly across time or grade, as when, for example, an 11th-grade student has only literature but not writing instruction, a sixth-grade student experiences the entire writing process, a fourth-grade student only completes skills-and-drills worksheets, and a third-grade student never works in peer writing groups. Such uneven applications confound the methodological issues in studying the process approach; however, most of the research does support the use of the process approach as being more effective than other approaches in terms of improving writing attitudes and products (Pritchard & Honeycutt, 2006).

Implementation of best practices in teaching the process approach involves adopting a comprehensive, holistic instructional model, including understanding the limitations of the approach, its theoretical underpinnings, and the supporting research literature. For example, teachers of the process approach do not just have good lessons, one-shot hot topics to gain attention, and a set of how-to's. They understand the process itself, usually by having experienced it themselves as writers who share their writing with an audience, which is the premise of the professional development model designed by the National Writing Project (*www.writingproject.org*). Reading teachers recognize Sustained Silent Reading (SSR) as a way for adults to model reading. Similarly, writing teachers who use the process approach involve themselves in writing along with their students in Sustained Silent Writing (SSW). Just as reading teachers use think-alouds to model decoding, fluency, expression, and comprehension during guided reading lessons, writing teachers intentionally model all the parts of the composing process.

With a clear understanding of the research and the theoretical bases for the writing process, we can have not only good stand-alone lessons, but also ones integrated into an instructional approach. Without such bases for our decisions about lessons, we may find that we unwittingly undo one lesson in our expectations for another—as implied in the mandate "Be creative! Make no errors!" We can unintentionally present a puzzling, shifting philosophy for our students in how we teach. For example, in writing lessons, we may stress process, process, process, while in literature teaching, we emphasize right answer, right answer, right answer. Over time, and with an understanding of reader response theory, theories of composing, and principles of writing across the curriculum, teachers can integrate an overall teaching philosophy with specific methods of writing instruction and end up with a repertoire of best practices for a comprehensive writing program.

Although many theories undergird the teaching of writing, some varying by grade level, two important basic concepts need to be understood in developing lessons that are integrated, sequenced, and scaffolded: (1) Writing is a cognitive task and, as such, is also developmental; and (2) writing is a social act and, thus, moves from egocentrism to larger audiences. As a guru of writing theory, James Moffett (1981), says, "For me no discussion of language, rhetoric, and composition is meaningful except in this context, for there is no speech without a speaker in some relations to a spoken-to or spoken-about" (p. 142). If their teachers implement a process-oriented instructional model, students will participate in a community of writers intellectually and emotionally. Over the course of schooling, they will move from an audience of self to teachers, peers, authentic public audiences, and, eventually, fictional audiences. "This continuum," says Moffett, "is formed simply by increasing the distance, in all senses, between the speaker and audience. The audience is, first, the speaker himself, then another person standing before him, then someone in another time and place but having some personal relation to the speaker, then, lastly, an unknown mass extended over time and space" (pp. 142–143).

As students move along the continuum of audiences, they practice a broad range of strategies that the National Assessment of Educational Progress (Goldstein & Carr, 1996) collectively refer to as "process oriented instruction" (p. 1). These include the decisions writers make about audience and topic during prewriting, composing rough drafts, sharing their writing to gather response, and revising and editing.

In developing her theory of composing processes of 12th graders, Janet Emig (1971) noted that writing is the only literacy process that involves the hand (we use tools to write), the eye (writing leaves a public artifact), and the brain (we search prior knowledge, use both long- and short-term memory, deal with writing blocks, organize, problem-solve, etc.) We would add that composing also uses the heart. As Friere (2000) says, "All learning is both cognitive and emotional." For process-oriented teachers, this means that writing instruction must essentially deal with it all: addressing emotions surrounding writing, such as those that accompany writer's block; building confidence and motivation in writers; teaching micro-level (enabling) skills such as handwriting, desktop publishing, spelling, and sentence construction and macro-level skills such as organization, cohesion, audience, and genre. The goal in process approach instruction is for most of these cognitive and psychological skills to become automatized for writers, so that they do not have to start from scratch with each new writing event.

For purposes of this chapter, our understanding of the process approach is that it is a recursive rather than linear process of creating a text (that may be shared with an audience in oral readings or written publications) from prewriting to publication. In the process approach, not every prewriting activity will lead to a final draft, but students' understanding of the movement from first idea to finished product is an essential feature.

Other chapters in this book address in depth various aspects of composing relevant to the process approach. This chapter will describe six major lesson foci in that approach: (1) dealing with the emotions surrounding writing, (2) developing students' understanding of the writing process, (3) modeling and teaching self-regulation processes, (4) training and monitoring peer response partners and groups, (5) guiding writing development through targeted strategy instruction that addresses ideas and content, organization, voice, word choice, sentence fluency, and conventions (commonly referred to as the "Six Traits" or as the "features of writing"), and (6) developing a writing vocabulary. These components must be taught and monitored so that they become internalized by writers.

GUIDELINES AND EXAMPLES OF BEST PRACTICES USING PROCESS APPROACH INSTRUCTION

In the following sections, we describe these six foundational areas that the process approach entails, no matter at what grade level it is applied, while commenting on the key ideas that need to be addressed in instruction. We do not want to imply that best practices in teaching the process approach in elementary school be dropped in middle or high school, or that elementary students cannot accomplish some of the writing tasks usually assigned to middle or high school students. The six areas of best practices that we recommend need to be introduced and reinforced throughout the grades and adapted to particular age groups.

Address the Emotional Issues Surrounding Writing

The impact of emotions on writing has been written about extensively (Boice, 1985; Csikszentmihalyi, 1990; Maisel, 1999; Rose, 1985). Because skills and emotions are intertwined, some of the stress that fosters negative attitudes is reduced when students are provided adequate instruction and time to compose in class. Students compose more text when they are members of a positive, nonthreatening social climate in which they write frequently. Being part of a writing community means that students experience uninterrupted time for individual practice. When writing is given time and presence in the curriculum, students will improve at it.

In the elementary grades, students need to write every day, not only in various subject areas, but also in blocks of time set aside for mini-lessons that address specific features of writing and the writing process. This time provides students with the opportunity to write and practice the skills and strategies the teacher has taught, not just hear or read about them. In middle and high school, the writing community is usually based in a language arts or English class, but much of the practice of writing can occur in the disciplines. (Suggestions for writing across the curriculum are offered in Newell, Koukis, & Boster, Chapter 4, this volume.)

Tragically, many students who enjoy writing in the early elementary grades end up hating or avoiding writing by the time they enter the upper elementary grades or middle school. When individuals do not understand either the process for accomplishing a task or the end result of a specific endeavor, they can become frustrated. Lessons designed specifically to address the emotional issues and barriers surrounding writing help minimize this confusion. Across grade levels, four major factors contribute to students' unrealistic expectations and negative perceptions of themselves as writers: (1) failure to understand and apply appropriate strategies when composing text, (2) a flawed understanding of the writing process, (3) confusion about what the assignment is asking them to do (e.g., inability to deconstruct a prompt), and (4) unfamiliarity with the features of the assigned genre. All of these can be specifically addressed in targeted lessons.

When faced with a writing assignment, many students experience writer's block. Students' stress levels are greatly reduced or alleviated when teachers provide guidelines for starting and completing the assignment. With writing-on-demand tasks, such as state assessments, teachers can provide explicit instructions, practice in unlocking writing prompts, and strategies for planning. Teachers can share drafts as the students write throughout the process and showcase good images and phrases as well as whole pieces of writing. When teachers have students share best lines while students are still drafting and revising, the writers who are recognized receive an emotional boost and others often gain ideas that they can adapt to their own writing. At the end of the assignment, teachers can celebrate students' accomplishments through class publications, bulletin boards, montages, mobiles, collections, author's chair, PTA meetings, and hall displays. Moffett (1981) says that the "three things to do with final versions of writing are post, print, and perform" (p. 25). Dialogues and monologues are obvious genres to be performed, but a Readers' Theater can also be created using excerpts from the writing of many students, especially narrative or expressive writing. Moffett also advises that postwriting activities "should give writing as satisfactory a recompense as possible and at the same time provide further feedback, from a larger or different audience, about the effects of what one has written" (p. 26).

Disruptive emotions also arise when a writer has a history of fear of the blank page and recollections of how long it takes and how difficult it is to generate texts or of how bad it feels to get a failing grade on a writing assignment. Such past experiences inhibit students who define themselves as bad writers. Teachers can instruct them on how to deal with negative emotions, such as how to conquer the IC or internal critic (Boice, 1985). One creative teacher we know had his students externalize their ICs in posters. A memorable one depicted a wild-eyed monster with bleeding talons (nails punched through the poster board) that clutched essays! Teachers can also teach students what to do when they are stuck and offer strategies for how to acknowledge and control avoidance behaviors they have allowed to interfere with their focus and engagement when composing.

Best practices in teaching the process approach include assessing and attending to the positive and negative emotions surrounding writing. Validated instruments can be helpful for a writer in determining his or her feelings about writing. The Writer Self-Perception Scale (WSPS) (Bottomley, Henk, & Melnick, 1997/1998) applies to children, while the Measure of Writing Apprehension (Daly & Miller, 1975) applies to young adults and adults. A more extensive self-assessment addresses blocking in teachers and has sections that can be adapted for students (Boice, 1990). These assessments can be used by teachers to (1) identify apprehensive students; (2) aggregate scores from a class as a pre- and posttest measure to evaluate the impact of teaching; and (3) give to students for self-evaluation so they can develop their own plans for dealing with procrastination, lack of productivity, and negative emotions.

Develop Students' Understanding of the Writing Process

Equally important to fostering a climate conducive to writing and sharing is ensuring that all students understand the complexity of the writing process. Many students hold a naive view that professional authors complete their published pieces after composing one draft and doing some minor revisions. Others believe that writing is a gift from a muse that only a few special people receive. Although students report that they understand that the writing process involves generating ideas, organizing, drafting, and revising, many persist in believing that as they refine their craft, they will eventually be able to compose final drafts the first time.

Teachers must demystify the writing process for students by teaching them that, regardless of how skilled they become, all writers will perform just like professional writers: they will utilize a process, adapted to their needs, to develop their manuscripts; they will go through several stages of revision; they will seek the responses of others; they will edit for errors at the manuscript level; and they will eventually realize that writing is never perfect and always open to revision. As the French poet Valery said, "A poem is never complete; it is just abandoned." If teachers have experienced writing in their graduate classes or participated in professional development institutes such as the National Writing Project, they will have their own messy first drafts, redrafts, inserts, peer comments, mark-ups, and final drafts to share with students as examples of intentional actions to improve their writing.

Today, writers of all ages are familiar with technology. By middle school, students are adept at hand–eye coordination and can easily grasp the more advanced editing/revising capabilities of word processing programs, such as tracking revisions, strike-throughs, adding comments, changing margins and fonts, bypassing default settings, inserting graphics, etc. This is the time to make good use of desktop publishing to assemble class books and to ask students to create their own digital stories that incorporate text, music, and pictures. (See Karchmer-Klein, Chapter 11, this volume.)

Model and Teach Self-Regulation Strategies

Successful writing requires active and deliberate self-regulation of the writing process (Hayes & Flowers, 1986; Langer & Applebee, 1987). Self-regulation in writing, the counterpart of metacognition in reading, involves monitoring one's comprehension when writing as well as applying specific strategies to complete an assignment. Zimmerman and Risemberg (1997) define self-regulation as "self-initiated thoughts, feelings, and actions that writers use to attain various literary goals, including improving their writing skills as well as enhancing the quality of the text they create" (p. 76).

Students of all ages will respond to lessons that provide specific strategies for reflection and self-evaluation. For example, good readers understand the importance of activating schemas by skimming the text and thinking about what they already know concerning the reading topic. Similarly, prior to composing, good writers activate schemas by employing some form of prewriting and reflection. Students need a framework or a sequence of steps to accomplish demanding assignments. George Hillocks (1986) points out that writers require such specific instruction (he calls these "inquiry strategies" for learning "procedural knowledge") to develop content and tools for creating different kinds of discourse. Additionally, by providing guidelines, teachers can prompt self-evaluation and reward self-reflections about one's final piece on the evaluation rubric.

Train and Monitor Peer Partners and Peer Response Groups

The literature on the process approach is based on the idea that writing is a social activity and is best learned in a community. Researchers have examined the connection between the writing process and the social contexts within which writing occurs (Gere & Abbott, 1985). They attribute the effectiveness of the writing process to an essential practice—the interaction of writers with teachers and peers during conferences and small-group work. In his review of research on effective strategies for teaching writing, Hillocks (1986) determined that writing practice alone does not improve writing; rather, having writing *responded to using specific criteria for response* improves writing.

Teachers have implemented peer groups in settings across the curriculum as a way to encourage students to write and revise. Most agree that using peer groups supports the process approach by providing social benefits. These include a nonthreatening audience, immediate feedback, experience of a wide range of writing abilities, reduced writing apprehension, development of positive attitudes about writing, increased motivation to revise, increased quantity of writing, more teacher time for individual attention, and development of cooperation and interpersonal skills. The social aspects fostered in a writing community have effects extending beyond writing products. Moreover, positive effects on writing products are also pronounced when peer groups are used.

Students are highly interested in the social aspects of school, suggesting that teachers should take advantage of the benefits of peer groups and the variety of audiences that writers can reach. Issues of audience were raised in the 1980s by researchers who viewed writing as social and interactive. Developmentalists such as Barry Kroll (1978) showed us how the sense of audience for writers expands from the self to an identified "other" (often the teacher) and eventually to an audience in a situated context beyond the school. An interesting aspect of Kroll's study was how 12-year-olds attacked the problem of audience. Students were instructed to explain the rules of a game to a peer audience and then to play the game to see if the audience had understood the rules. Even when the students giving the rules learned that their audience could not play the game according to those rules, they were at a loss as to how to revise their explanations. Just as often happens when we speak to foreigners whose language we do not know, the children said the same rules louder and more slowly!

A common practice in implementing a writing workshop in the elementary grades is to introduce children to sharing their writing for response with peer partners, which are sometimes expanded by upper elementary to peer groups. By middle school, students can benefit from a sophisticated use of peer groups that can provide feedback in many areas. Some teachers prefer to distinguish between editing groups and response groups, but both need to be trained. By high school, students can be expected to share in peer groups, electronically or face to face, outside of class time.

We use a role-playing exercise to demonstrate the various personalities that arise in peer groups (the defensive author, the picky grammarian, the off-topic respondent, etc.). Then we introduce the rules for conducting an effective writing group and practice them in a modeling activity. Finally, the rules are applied to papers that students write and share with their classmates. These rules have been outlined by various experts over the years (e.g., Macrorie, 1984). The basics are: (1) the students sit facing each other with copies of one student's paper; (2) that student reads his or her piece of writing *without apology or introduction to influence response*; (3) responses begin on the writer's right and continue around the circle; (4) first responses are positive ("I like this section . . . ") or neutral ("Here, it seems like you are saying . . . "); (5) second responses can be more pointed or offer suggestions ("I need more information about . . . "); (6) throughout this process of response, the writer does not comment, explain, cheer, sigh, or groan, so as not to influence the response. Alan Glatthorn (1994) provides guidelines for how peers can respond chronologically as they read a classmate's paper ("So far I think you have said . . . "; "At this point I hope you are going to . . . "; "I'd like to hear more about . . . "; "The main feeling I am left with is . . . "). We have found his suggestions appropriate when students respond to a peer's writing using an audiotape as well as when they write their comments on peers' papers or use the comment tool in a word processing program.

By high school, with instruction, students evolve from writing for authentic audiences to writing for fictional audiences, while attending to the rhetorical choices that pertain to various types of audiences. They understand that a writer takes on a persona and that the persona can be very different from the real-life author. Literature teaching and writing are neatly coupled by high school, when readers understand that literary writers have an "implied reader" (Iser, 1974) in mind. The students get it: Writers can influence their readers, guide them to understand what they want them to understand, manipulate the direction of readers' thoughts and emotions, and perhaps transport them to the center of the writing and persuade them to experience it in the way the writer intended.

Guide Writing Development through Targeted Strategy Instruction

At every grade level, teachers must incorporate strategy instruction. Direct instruction is targeted at identified weaknesses evident in student writing in order to improve writing performance. As mentioned, research on feedback from peers and teachers shows that it improves overall writing performance (Hillocks, 1986).

The rationale behind explicit strategy instruction is that it purposely gives students the opportunity to learn to do independently what experts do when completing a task. A strategy is composed of a series of steps that, when followed, lead most learners to succeed in a given task. Good writers employ strategies for *schema activation* (thinking about personal experiences and knowledge that relate to the prompt, text features, and audience and engaging in prewriting to generate and organize ideas) and for *self-regulation* (monitoring text production, analyzing and assessing the quality of the developing text, and modifying and/or changing strategies as needed to complete the writing assignment successfully). (Planning strategies are addressed in Graham & Harris, Chapter 6, this volume.)

Strategy instruction is best introduced during group mini-lessons based on examples from students' writing and then reinforced in individual conferences. Lesson topics range from local concerns (transcription, word choice, sentence fluency, conventions) to global ones (ideas and content, organization, voice). Balanced instruction ensures that the texts students compose have sentences that are grammatically correct as well as unified around a topic (as in expository writing) or central emotion (as in expressive writing). Focus correction areas (FCAs) are a sound strategy for incrementally introducing controls and constraints in writing so that immature writers are not overwhelmed during the early stages of drafting or in the later stages of revision. Collins (1997), who developed and refined this specific form of feedback, describes FCAs as follows:

> *Focus correcting is a selective approach to correcting student writing.* When teachers focus correct, they select one, two, or three critical problem areas and correct only for those areas. Teachers can select any area for focus correction, from capitalization to the use of details. They can select areas for an individual, a group, or the whole class. (p. 1)

By limiting the number and type of FCAs, students spend more time during revision improving the content of the paper and concentrating on the substance of the writing rather than exclusively on such local concerns as punctuation and usage that might not, at that juncture, improve the quality of the text. When teaching students to assess the strengths and weaknesses of a piece of writing that they have composed, an analytic scale is more appropriate. One such common analytic scale is the primary-trait assessment rubric (also referred to as Six Traits) developed by Spandel and Stiggins (1997). This rubric focuses on six traits of writing: ideas and content, organization, voice, word choice, sentence fluency, and conventions. These writing traits are discussed in the following section.

Ideas and Content

The character Forrester in the film *Finding Forrester* (Mark, Connery, Tollefson, & Van Sant, 2000) admonished his pupil: "Write first with the heart, then rewrite with the head." For strategy instruction, this means that students must overcome their emotional blocks and focus first on fluency, rather than control, so that they learn to hone and revise from abundance. If there is not substantial text for writers to practice the strategies they learn, they are reluctant to give up anything on the page. If a teacher has assigned 100 words, students will produce 100 words and usually stop there.

It is not enough simply to have students create plans for their writing, such as the outline commonly assigned by teachers. (We have been guilty of writing the entire paper and then creating the required outline!) Mini-lessons must be presented that model how to move from the basic plan and translate the ideas to text. Teachers can offer students a variety of prewriting strategies such as perception exercises, heuristics, journaling, free writing, brainstorming, and graphic organizers that help move a plan to a document. If they have been instructed in such, by late elementary school students should know how to unlock a writing prompt or deconstruct an assignment and begin their task.

By middle school, more lessons should be inductive—that is, students are given data and asked to create generalizations from that data, rather than to locate examples of generalizations that teachers provide (deductive lessons). In Hillocks's (1986) meta-analysis of 20 years of research on teaching writing, this "inquiry approach" was found to be the most effective of six instructional foci for improving writing because it centers students' attention on strategies for transforming raw data while they examine data sets. By high school, if they have had practice in this inquiry approach, students do not need to be assigned topics. As Moffett (1981) states, "many in the profession still don't acknowledge ideas except when the writing is about books or teacher-made topics, whereas we should know that writing about books and teacher topics does not guarantee thought or hold a monopoly on thought" (p. 4). He further suggests that most students have not had enough practice in classifying experiences and creating abstractions because they "are unwittingly encouraged to borrow their generalizations from old slogans, wise saws, reference books, and teachers' essay questions, instead of having to forge them from their own experience" (p. 143). Students will respond favorably when they have choices to learn new modes and genres to expand their repertoire. Middle and high school students especially benefit from multigenre writing assignments that are less restrictive and allow for creativity (Romano, 2000).

Organization

After students have completed some of the prewriting exercises described above, they usually have an overall idea of the content they want to express. These early writings we sometimes call *zero drafts* because they precede a first draft. They are early evidence of thinking on paper. Students can then plan a general pattern of organization, a sequence of ideas, for writing their first draft. If this stage is not taught, struggling writers will generate texts that consist of listing loosely connected ideas. We call this *tickertape writing* because the ideas seem random. If the ideas are unified (all on one topic) but not coherent (related to each other), we call it the *Scotch tape approach* to organization, in which the writer summarizes this idea by someone and that idea by someone else but never takes the risk to analyze or synthesize the ideas and come up with a thesis. This happens frequently in high school writing when students are asked to write in academic formats about topics they are novices in understanding. How hard it is to write a paper on *Hamlet* for a teacher who already knows all the great interpretations! To write about books, explains Moffett (1981), is "a narrow notion of exposition. Abstracting about someone else's already high abstraction, whether it be a book or a teacher's essay question, means that certain essential issues of choice about selecting and treating material and creating classes [classifications] are never permitted to come up for the student" (p. 147). Students resort to producing writing that is what Bereiter and Scardamalia (1987) refer to as *knowledge telling* rather than meaning construction. According to these researchers, knowledge telling is when the reader can clearly see that the author has engaged in little or no planning, the text seems to have been quickly drafted, and little or no revision or reflection is evident.

Many students have found the acronym CRAFT (Strong, 2006) a useful strategy to help plan their writing. CRAFT is an acronym for: C, context for the writer, what knowledge base he or she will use, from personal experience to formal documents; R, role of the writer, the stance the writer will take when composing text (the writer may entertain, be critical, show humor, etc.); A, the audience for whom one writes (writers must know who their audience is in order to anticipate its needs); F for format; and T for topic. Strong suggests that CRAFT is also a useful guide for teachers in designing writing assignments, but it is not a straitjacket.

Voice

The term *voice* refers to an author's unique style and personality as reflected in his or her writing. Voice carries the presence of the writer to the page through choices in tone, vocabulary, syntax, and expression. Elementary students can easily grasp the extremes of voice—the formal policeman, the hip teenager, the recalcitrant child. Ken Macrorie (1984) calls moving back and forth in extremes an *alternating current*. He refers to the rhetorical shift as changing from *kitchen language* to *elevated language*. Students in the upper grades can identify and employ markers of many voices by manipulating style: What words would a shy little boy use? What words would a confident athlete use?

Students of all ages can imitate the voices of professional writers, from Dr. Seuss to Shakespeare to Biblical text. For instance, we have had high school students express an Edgar Allen Poe content—such as the eerie setting of Poe's *Masque of the Red Death* delivered by Poe in elongated, highly modified, complex sentences with many multisyllabic words—using the voice of Ernest Hemingway, with his characteristic short, staccato, matter-of-fact sentences and one-syllable words. They get it: Voice and style are intertwined.

Word Choice

Students need to know the words that suit the content and the purposes of their writing. Good readers who are poor writers are unable to report information from text using original language, suggesting that these students have a problem with vocabulary. Writing samples from good readers who are poor writers illustrate a lack of strong nouns, verbs, adjectives, and adverbs. Vocabulary is one area (as compared to spelling) that we know is best taught in context, and extensive reading can often solve this writing problem. Most of us know that vocabulary is fun to teach, especially when words are changed in a passage for effect. In teaching Theodore Roethke's poem "My Papa's Waltz," for example, changing the words *shirt* to *vest*, *Papa* to *Father*, and *Mother's countenance* to *Mama's face* completely alters the impression the reader has of the parents in the poem. We highly recommend poetry, where words are at a premium, as a good medium to teach the connotations and denotations of words, and the impact of word choice on meaning and tone. As Moffett (1968), states, "all writing expresses ideas, regardless of mode, and the higher abstractions teachers look for in familiar essay form derive in stages from lower abstractions formulated more personally and fictionally at first" (p. 4). In other words, you do not learn exposition by writing exposition all of the time. The language expertise a writer embraces in narrative, poetry, personal, and expressive writing can come to the service of composing many types of writing. Students progress by writing across genres "that allow language experiences to build on and reinforce each other in significant ways" (Moffett, 1968, p. 5).

Word choice is a fun revising activity that can be experienced in whole-class lessons with students working with their own writing. Ask students to list sense words on charts, then see if they can add one sense to their writing (touch, or texture, is often left out). If they have boring nouns, ask them to replace generics with specifics (*flowers* become *dahlias*, *friends* becomes *Bonnie and Maggie*, *book* becomes *Essays of E. B. White*). Next, ask them to use a dash after a noun group and follow it with a series of specific items in the group (*We enjoyed many fruits at the picnic—apples, oranges, black cherries, and pears*; or *I rode my bike through a maze of streets—Bellefontaine, Agnes, Benton Boulevard*). Again, students get it: The writing comes alive when you "put the reader there" (Macrorie, 1984).

Sentence Fluency

Sentence fluency refers to the use and variety of different syntax and sentence structures. Writers of all ages can become overwhelmed and sidetracked by their inability to manipulate grammar to create the effects they desire, so teachers need to address selected grammatical concepts directly and strategically. In using the process approach, the question is not *whether* to teach grammar, but *when*. We recommend that direct instruction in elementary school be based on structures that all students need to master, drawing examples from children's literature and dictated stories. In middle and high school, we suggest direct teaching of grammatical structures after a draft is produced, as part of revision. The teacher should pull out common errors from students' drafts and develop a mini-lesson around them, rather than turning to the next lesson in the grammar book. (Most grammar books we have seen are best used as references rather than lesson sequences.) We have often heard students exclaim, "But our teacher last year never taught us prepositions!" when we well know that she did! It just did not take, most likely because the need for using prepositions had not yet arisen in the students' writing.

We have excellent foundational research on how students grow syntactically (Hunt, 1977; Loban, 1976; Mellon, 1969; O'Hare, 1973). The need for understanding grammar and punctuation arises as writers take on new syntactical structures. They can then experience in their own writing how changing punctuation changes meaning. By around age 12, students' written language outstrips their spoken language, in that they use structures—such as periodic rather than cumulative sentences, introductory clauses and phrases, passive voice, appositives, etc.—in written text that are not common in their oral language. They go beyond the concept introduced in elementary school instruction (as in dictated stories) that "writing is speech written down." For example, according to Walter Loban's landmark study (1976), at around age 9, children begin to relate particular concepts to general ideas, using such connectors as *meanwhile, unless,* and *even if.* About 50% of children at this age begin to use the subordinating connector *although* correctly. They also begin to use the present participle active ("Having dieted for a week, I dove into the candy bar") and the gerund (verb turned into an *–ing* noun) as the object of a preposition ("In writing this story, I learned about myself").

As writers mature, they consolidate what they once expressed as single simple sentences (a main clause and its attachments) into embedded sentences, such as these examples provided by Kellogg Hunt (1977): A typical fourth grader writes, "Aluminum is a metal and it is abundant. It has many uses and it comes from bauxite"; while a typical eighth grader takes the predicate adjective *abundant* and turns it into a prenominative adjective in *abundant metal,* as well as coordinating three predicates, writing, "Aluminum is an abundant metal, has many uses, and comes from bauxite." The eighth grader uses more embedding, putting the main ideas from two sentences into one sentence.

It is important that teachers understand syntactic development and recognize the evidence of growth, knowing that as the student takes on the next structure, he or she will make mistakes, such as not punctuating correctly. If the attempt to use a new, more sophisticated structure is not honored by teachers, then students will write simple, correctly punctuated sentences to be safe.

Frank O'Hare's research on the effects of instruction in sentence combining was conducted with middle school children (1973). He found that, with systematic instruction based on what we know about how syntax develops, students produced in 1 year the structures that are usually expected in 4 years. We recommend that teachers use sentences taken from student writing for sentence-combining activities. Teachers can sneak in sentence-combining activities even when it is not designated writing time. For example, a good way to review events from an earlier class is to present kernel sentences that contain the main actions and events and ask students to combine them. The following were taken from a demonstration lesson on sentence combining given by a teacher in the Capital Area Writing Project, a National Writing Project professional development site at North Carolina State University: "Judy started the lesson. The lesson was complex. The research was sophisticated. Judy's sentences were complex. Sherri asked a question. The question was simple. Her sentences were simple. Judy answered her question. The answer was long. The answer was complex. The sentences were complex. Suzanne made a statement. The statement was humorous. The statement was witty. The statement was emotional." (You get the idea.)

Participants had a lot of fun summarizing the presentation while using various syntactic structures. (Saddler, Chapter 8, this volume, discusses ideas for teaching sentence construction skills.)

Many books on the market include CD-ROMs along with innovative ideas and visuals for teaching grammar, but we still believe that the best lessons are based on sentences derived from students' writing. They can practice creating structures that stretch them but are still within their reach. Instead of modeling a Herman Melville sentence, with its typical use of the present participle, they can model a Joey Smith sentence, from the boy who sits next to them in third period.

Conventions

Conventions are the mechanical aspects of writing, such as spelling, punctuation, usage, and paragraph indentation, that reveal the semantics of the writing. Demonstrating the dramatic effect that punctuation can have on meaning is the purpose of a familiar exercise where students are asked to punctuate the following sentence to illustrate two interpretations of who is "nothing," the woman or the man: "Woman without her man is nothing." Struggling writers must be shown how to read their own writing to determine coherence as well as detect errors in conventions. When asked to read aloud a piece they have composed, students commonly correct their mistakes. Therefore, teachers should not correct their students' mistakes, but rather point out the general location with a check mark in the margin and have students identify and correct the errors. After all, who needs the practice? Explaining/teaching the error and the correction to another student in the class is an effective way to solidify learning for the writer who now understands his or her error.

It is more helpful for students if they personalize the names of the different types of errors they tend to make and use these names as part of their composing vocabulary. For example, Macrorie (1984) labels beginning too many sentences with "There are . . . " and "It is . . . "—so that the subject slot is reduced to a general pronoun and the verb is a dull state-of-being verb—with the terms *There-ache* and *It-ache*. He believes (and we found this to be true in our own teaching) that students' awareness in detecting mistakes is increased when they have language that makes sense to describe the errors. A composing vocabulary develops and expands as writers need language to describe their writing.

Develop a Composing Vocabulary

Beginning in the elementary grades, students need a language to talk about their writing. An effective plan is to teach a composing vocabulary by starting with the parts of speech and the names of structures that are emerging in student writing (*simple sentence, cumulative sentence, sentences beginning with modifying phrases*, etc.). This approach is inductive, starting with the examples in students' papers and going to the label. Most textbooks are organized deductively; that is, they give the generalization (the definition of a term or the rule) and then ask students to find examples.

Beyond the basic parts of speech, the composing vocabulary includes terms used in the process approach to describe emotional issues surrounding writing (e.g., *getting stuck, writer's block*), what happens during the process (e.g., *shaping, looping, cooking*), and the features present in the products that students create (*active verbs, sense images, sentence variety, narrative examples*). For example, we use the term *prevision* for creating the rough draft so that students grasp the term *revision* as a second look at their writing, rather than as writing over in ink. The *re–* prefix also explains the word *research* as more than one look at data.

We directly teach the verb *own* in the context of writing groups. Each writer reads aloud his or her writing to gather responses and advice, but, ultimately, the writer "owns" the writing and can take the suggestions or not. Given this freedom, writers learn that they do not have to yield to every suggestion, even if the authority (often the teacher) seems to demand it. As writers review the responses they have received in their peer groups or mini-lessons, they must feel free to make their own revision decisions. Suggestions help create more options for the writer, but they do not need to dictate his or her actions. This is a learning moment for the teacher, who must realize that it is a more important lesson for students to feel like they own their writing than for them to incorporate the changes the teacher wants them to. Students participate in revising mini-lessons and in writing groups to expand their repertoire. If they choose not to incorporate into the final composition a particular revision technique—such as using a generic noun with a dash followed by specific nouns—we ask them to staple their practice sentences to the back of the assignment as "an artifact of revision," evidence that the writer can use the strategy but for this piece chose not to.

Other terms and phrases appropriate for a composing vocabulary are *fear of the blank page; focus correction area* (FCA) (Collins, 1997); *gotcha' moment* (when the writing captures the writers and they enter a *state of flow*; Csikszentmihalyi, 1990); *honoring the process* (Maisel, 1999); *hook; key concept; sloppy copy; voice; story grammar; hushing the mind* (Maisel, 1999); *I-Itis* (using the first person too much); exploding *the "Wow" moment* (in narrative, the climax of the story; Starkweather, Poole, & Horne, 2000); *tickertape writing; Scotch tape ap-*

proach; zero draft; knowledge telling (Bereiter & Scardamalia, 1987); *alternating current, kitchen language,* and *putting the reader there* (Macrorie, 1984). When students do not consider their audience, they may be creating *writer-based prose* rather than *reader-based prose* (Elbow, 1981). Our students like the term *zoom in* for when the reader needs details and the term *panoramic view* when they need to get "out of the weeds" and make a point. They use *getting off track* when a piece lacks unity. They understand the concept of *show, don't tell* as a way to use elaboration to make a point. When a student goes beyond listing and naming, the teacher can compliment him or her for *taking the opportunity to elaborate.* If the writer demonstrates accurate conventions, he or she can be praised for *providing courtesies for the reader.* When a student overcomes an internal critic, teachers can note that he or she has *conquered the IC,* and when writers tell the reader so much that the reader gets lost or bogged down, they may be reminded, "Assume your reader has a mind" (Macrorie, 1984).

By middle school, a composing vocabulary should encompass more than parts of speech or stages of the writing process, especially to make abstract terms accessible to writers. For many students, the term *coherence* may be baffling; but the phrase "words speaking to each other" (Macrorie, 1984) is not. Ask students to examine writing—their own and their classmates'—for examples of words speaking to each other. In doing this with a piece of student writing about living in the country, for example, the students in one of our classes found these words that conjured up the country: *slop, chicken fence, Betty June, Miss Effie Jean Frontaberger, Oak Ridge Road.* We also discovered that within that same text, the writer used the word *street,* which spoke to city living, not country living. He used the Latinate word *washcloth,* not the more appropriate Anglo-Saxon word *washrag.* Students had *a-ha moments* in examining these two sentences: "Every kid and widow in town congregated at our house. Even the preacher came rushing to the action." The word *preacher* conjured up a different image than would the word *minister,* and the subtle connection between the verb *congregated* and the noun *preacher* created a cohesive tie. They also noticed who was home during the day in this sleepy town: little children, widows, and the preacher. This concept of coherence in writing is highly tied to *tone* and *voice*—other terms that can be introduced.

Coherence and *unity* are difficult concepts for some students to grasp, and it is easier to recognize and honor their occurrence in writing than it is to teach them directly. We have used the visual of a jar of marbles to distinguish concepts that are commonly confused: *Unity* describes the marbles—they are all agates, for example—whereas *coherence* describes marbles glued together. When one writer declared that she had finally "glued the marbles together" in her writing, all the students shared a common understanding of what she had accomplished as a writer.

When a writer joins two senses to create an image, the teacher can use this as an example of *synesthesia*—the synthesis of senses ("loud color," "soft view of the sea," "musty feel of old crepe"). One of us (Pritchard) still remembers a seventh grader she taught in New Orleans who came rushing in declaring he had created a synesthetic image when he wrote "The blues singer had a velvet voice." A high school student was proud of the way he used *collocation* in his paper to create unity. He had been taught this composing term to refer to how words that occur in a similar linguistic environment can "speak to each other." In writing about a play, for example, one would expect such terms as *act, role,* and *scene.* If used strategically, such collocated words can bind together a paper to create unity. The most memorable composing vocabulary for students is drawn from examples in their writing. Once you have collected examples from students' writing, you have the centerpieces of your lesson. Students will get it: You learn to make choices within a repertoire at your fingertips, and you are able to describe your choices using an understandable composing vocabulary.

These six lesson foci that we have discussed for process approach teaching need to be introduced in the elementary grades and reinforced with increasing sophistication throughout middle and high school. They form the basics of writing instruction, but other aspects, such as grading, are also important. (MacArthur, Chapter 7, this volume, is devoted to evaluation of writing.) It also does not mean that the six areas of suggestions in the above list only need to be covered once. If the activities suggested above do not begin in the elementary grades, however, the task of teaching writing as a developmental and sociocultural process is much harder in the middle grades and beyond. For example, this book includes a chapter devoted to the important area of writing across the curriculum (Newell, Koukis, & Boster, Chapter 4, this volume). The foundation for using writing as a learning tool needs to be laid in the elementary grades, but in middle school, where the common philosophy is the integrated curriculum, the powers of writing to learn can be exploited. We know that most middle school students in this generation are experts at multitasking, as is evident by observing them listening to music while watching TV, talking on the phone, instant messaging, and doing their homework! Teachers need to take advantage of this predilection by tying writing to other learning activities. Further, by the middle grades, students should be writing in the modes that they are reading. Moffett (1981) advises that student productions should be examined "side by side with analogous professional writing" (p. 7). If students are reading how-to manuals, they should create how-to manuals; if they are reading poetry, essays, narratives, diaries, logs, memoirs, proverbs, auto-biographies; and so on, they also should be composing them.

CONCLUSION

A careful analysis of research studies identified throughout this chapter and this book strongly indicates that implementing best practices in writing process approach instruction results in improved student writing. This chapter summarizes some of the evidence-based practices in teaching the process approach while providing examples. Writing is such a complex task that it cannot be taught once and for all—that is, we are all apprentices in learning to write and in writing to learn. No one is consummately a good writer, for we all have the potential to change and improve. As we practice, we will make mistakes that should be acknowledged as signs of growth. When students learn more complex sentence structure, such as moving from simple subject–verb sentences to compound-complex ones, the by-product is error. When they feel they have mastered one genre, they can become novices in a new one. As teachers, we must be mindful of how writers grow and scaffold our lessons so that writers have practice in the emerging areas that are challenging them.

A significant component of sound writing process approach instruction is individual teacher-designed lessons that have powerful effects on emotions and motivation to write or on one aspect of a written product (such as grammatical correctness), even though some of these lessons cannot be directly tied to improved writing performance overall. Such innovative and enjoyable practices are an essential part of teaching writing and should not be discounted. A teacher's intuition is often a strong indicator of what works with certain populations, whether or not research has validated the instruction.

With limited time, however, a teacher must be selective in what he or she offers. We know from research that pedagogical strategies are not equal, and simply writing or enjoying writing does not in itself lead to improved writing (Hillocks, 1986). It is important for teachers to be selective and cognizant of what the purpose of the lesson is and how it builds a foundation for developing writers, rather than merely to offer gimmicks and games. Furthermore, some research suggests that it may be the absence, rather than the presence, of some practices in teaching writing that leads to improved performance. For example, allocating Fridays for spelling tests may be less valuable than presenting mini-lessons, or consider the time a student spends in identifying errors on a worksheet as time lost to holding a conference with that student about the grammatical errors in his working draft. We all must be open to letting go of some writing activities that are no more than time fillers, knowing that time is a precious commodity in the writing classroom.

REFERENCES

Bereiter, C., & Scardamalia, M. (1987). *The psychology of written composition.* Hillsdale, NJ: Erlbaum.

Boice, R. (1985). *Causes and cures of writing blocks: An annotated bibliography.* ERIC Document ED277046.

Boice, R. (1990). Blocking Questionnaire. In R. Boice, *Professors as writers: A self-help guide to productive writing* (pp. 134–153). Stillwater, OK: New Forums Press.

Bottomley, D. M., Henk, W. A., & Melnick, S. A. (1997/1998). Assessing children's view about themselves as writers using the Writer Self-Perception Scale. *The Reading Teacher, 51*(4), 286–295.

Collins, J. J. (1997). *Selecting and teaching Focus Correction Areas: A planning guide.* Rowley, MA: The Network, Inc.

Csikszentmihalyi, M. (1990). *Flow: The psychology of optimal experience.* New York: Harper & Row.

Daly, J. A., & Miller, M. D. (1975) Further studies in writing apprehension: SAT scores, success expectations, willingness to take advanced courses and sex differences. *Research in the Teaching of English, 9,* 250–256.

Elbow, P. (1981). *Writing with power: Techniques for mastering the writing process.* New York: Oxford University Press.

Emig, J. (1971).*The composing processes of twelfth graders.* (Research monograph no. 13). Urbana, IL: National Council of Teachers of English.

Friere, P. (2000). *Pedagogy of the oppressed* (30th anniversary ed.) (Myra Bergman Ramos, Trans.) New York: Continuum International Publishing Group.

Gere, A., & Abbott, R. D. (1985). Talking about writing: The language of writing groups. *Research in the Teaching of English, 19,* 362–385.

Glatthorn, A. (1994). How do I respond to someone else's writing? In P. Scanlan (Ed.), *Writing works: Finding your way with writing. Booklet no. 95* (p. 31). Christchurch, New Zealand: User Friendly Enterprises, Ltd.

Goldstein, A., & Carr, P. G. (1996). Can students benefit from process writing? *NAEPfacts, 1*(3). Washington, DC: National Center for Educational Statistics. *nces.ed.gov/pubs96/web/96845.asp*

Hayes, J. R., & Flowers, L. S. (1986). Writing research and the writer. *American Psychologist, 41*(10), 1106–1113.

Hillocks, G. (1986). *Research on written composition.* Urbana, IL: National Conference on Research in English.

Hunt, K. (1977). Early blooming and late blooming syntactic structure. In C. Cooper & L. O'Dell (Eds.), *Evaluating writing: Describing, measuring, judging* (pp. 91–104). Urbana, IL: National Council of Teachers of English.

Iser, W. (1974). *The implied reader.* Baltimore: Johns Hopkins University Press.

Kroll, B. (1978). Cognitive egocentrism and the problem of audience awareness in written discourse. *Research in the Teaching of English, 56,* 269–281.

Langer, J. A., & Applebee, A. N. (1987). *How writing shapes thinking: A study of teaching and learning.* Urbana, IL: National Council of Teachers of English.

Loban, W. (1976). *Language development: Kindergarten through grade twelve.* Urbana, IL: National Council of Teachers of English.

Macrorie, K. (1984). *Writing to be read* (3rd ed.). Portsmouth, NH: Boynton/ Cook.

Maisel, E. (1999). *Deep writing: Seven principles that bring ideas to life.* New York: Tarcher/Putnam.

Mark, L., Connery, S., & Tollefson, R. (Producers), & Van Sant, G. (Director). (2000). *Finding Forrester* [Film]. (Available from Columbia Pictures, Inc., 10202 W. Washington Blvd., Culver City, CA 90232-3195).

Mellon, J. C. (1969). *Transformational sentence-combining: A method of enhancing the development of syntactic fluency in English composition.* Urbana, IL: National Council of Teachers of English.

Moffett, J. (1968). *Teaching the universe of discourse.* Boston: Houghton Mifflin.

Moffett, J. (1981). *Active voice: A writing program across the curriculum.* Montclair, NJ: Boynton/Cook.

O'Hare, F. (1973). *Sentence combining: Improving student writing without formal grammar instruction.* Urbana, IL: National Council of Teachers of English.

Pritchard, R. J., & Honeycutt, R. L. (2006). The process approach to teaching writing: Examining its effectiveness. In C. A. MacArthur, S. Graham, & J. Fitzgerald (Eds.), *Handbook of writing research* (pp. 275–290). New York: Guilford Press.

Romano, T. (2000). *Blending genre, altering style: Writing multi-genre papers.* Portsmouth, NH: Heinemann.

Rose, M. (Ed.). (1985). *When a writer can't write: Studies in writer's block and other composing-process problems.* New York: Guilford Press.

Spandel, V., & Stiggins, R. J. (1997). *Creating writers: Linking writing assessment and instruction* (2nd ed.). New York: Longman.

Starkweather, L., Poole, M., & Horne, C. (2000). *Nailing the prompt: A teacher's guide to writing test success.* Apex, NC: Partners in Education.

Strong, W. (2006). *Write for insight: Empowering content area learning, grades 6– 12.* Boston: Pearson Education.

Zimmerman, B. J., & Risemberg, R. (1997) Becoming a self-regulated writer: A social-cognitive perspective. *Journal of Contemporary Educational Psychology, 22*(1), 70–101.

3

Best Narrative Writing Practices When Teaching from a Developmental Framework

ANNE MCKEOUGH, JAIME PALMER,
MARYA JARVEY, *and* STAN BIRD

Ms. Wilson looked at her watch and sighed. It was 4:15 and she had to pick her kids up from their afterschool program by 5:30. She had about 30 minutes to finalize the 4-week plan for her trickster tales writing unit. She had spent the last week immersing her fourth grade students in trickster tales—reading them aloud and having students read them in small groups and individually. They had discussed the character of tricksters and victims and how authors portrayed them. In order to get a sense of her students' existing understanding at the beginning of the unit, she had had them write trickster tales of their own. Her students—both girls and boys—had been interested and engaged. They had seemed to take to this genre. It had been a great beginning! But now, as she looked at their efforts, she wasn't sure how to proceed with her unit plan. There was tremendous difference between the capable writers and the more challenged ones. She focused her thinking on two particular students (see Figures 3.1 and 3.2). One had a well-organized plot that was appropriate to the trickster tale genre. The storyline was coherent and this student included a subplot in which the trickster himself was tricked. Clearly, this student had grasped what trickster tales were all about and was ready to model expert writers. But the other student faced serious spelling challenges and seemed to miss the point of trickster tales almost entirely! Ms. Wilson wondered what on earth she could do to reach both of them and all the students in between.

A DEVELOPMENTAL APPROACH
TO WRITING INSTRUCTION

Ms. Wilson's dilemma is typical of the challenges faced daily by teachers. Many articles and books have been written about how to differentiate instruction so that teaching reaches the diverse range of students present in most classrooms. What is often lacking in these accounts is a framework that allows teachers to understand how skills build on each other. In this chapter, we propose that if teachers understand how children's writing changes as their capability develops, they will have a roadmap to guide their planning and teaching. Such a roadmap lays out the route that children typically follow in their writing development. Although students move along this route at various rates, they all are attempting to master important elements of good story construction—plot structure and character development. Knowing the signposts along this route helps teachers decide on instructional goals for each student. It also offers a ready-made assessment tool when used to track students' progress

---

The trickster who got tricked

Draco the wizard was well known for the tricks he played on people though they never knew it was him till it was to late. His goal was to steal the money from a rich mans bank vault this time. He had already gotten the things he needed to go to the bank now. He went into the bank wearing a disguise to make him look the same as the rich man. Vault seventeen please he said handing the key to a banker. One of the bankers noticed that his voice was different from the usauly small nervous voice. This one was deep and booming. It was the wizards voice he realized walking over to the other banker who was attending the wizard he whispered "it's the wizard." The other banker nodded. Smiling the banker said "come with me sir" leading him to the door "we had to move the vault to a different building." He lead him to the police station saying "We moved the vault to the police station so the money wouldn't be stolen" As he walked into the station he yelled "I have got the wizard knowing his plan was foiled yanked off his disguise shrieking you will never get me but the police lunged at him anyways bringing him down to the floor he handcuffed him. Then dragging the screaming wizard threw him into a cell and the wizard never tricked another person because he had promised never to trick another person again. THE END

FIGURE 3.1. Sample of a high-functioning fourth-grade student's trickster tale. All student story samples are original and unedited.

Untitled

on one fin day Will and I were plang at my howse. the prakster Ande watid the game boy atvace so he dasifed to trek us. he made a plan to git it. so daney got a shat and daney posd as a gost and Ande side look over ther trse a gost and they lookt and they sawa a gost and Ande grab the game boy atvace and Danye came in and saw the got Ande side if tats not you they ow is it. a gost soted danye Andey and Dany ran and dropt the game boy atvanc and I pect it up and iside nice wrok will and we got it back

FIGURE 3.2. Sample of a low-functioning fourth-grade student's trickster tale.

(see also Calfee & Miller, Chapter 13, this volume). The direct pairing of instruction and assessment is a value-added component that streamlines a teacher's work.

In this chapter we

- Discuss how children's capacity to compose narratives develops from early oral stories to the complex plots created in the upper elementary grades.
- Focus on realistic fiction and trickster tales.
- Describe teaching strategies that have been found to effectively support children's story composition.
- Present teaching and learning strategies that are empirically validated through research.

The Development of Storytelling in the Preschool Years

During the preschool years, children rarely write stories. They do, however, hear and tell many stories. Family members read fairytales and realistic fiction aloud, relate events about the child and other family members, and recount daily events. The stories told by young children most often involve sharing their own real-life experiences, such as getting a new pet or having a birthday party, or retelling stories they have heard or seen in movies. During this period, children are coming to understand the nature of stories. If teachers know what most children understand about stories by the time they enter school, they will be well positioned to offer appropriate instructional activities—ones that challenge those students who have a wealth of story experience as well as ones that support students who have had fewer or different experiences. It is important for teachers to understand how storytelling develops in the preschool years as information about oral storytelling can inform their teaching of story writing.

Before children enter school, they construct an understanding of the nature of stories (Haden & Fivish, 2003; Nelson, 2003). According to

Bruner (1991), stories have certain features in common. These features are discovered gradually as children mature and gain experience in the story realm (McCabe, 1996; McKeough, Davis, Forgeron, Marini, & Fung, 2005). Early developing narrative features are:

- Sequentiality. Story events occur in a sequence, linked by connecting words such as *and, then, because,* and *but*).
- Particularity. Stories are about something in particular; extraneous events that do not relate to this particular something should not be included in the story.
- Intentional states. Story characters' actions are motivated by their intentions (i.e., goals, desires, wants, and needs).
- Canonicity and breach. In stories, the expected order of things (i.e., the canon) is breached or violated, thus situating the story character in a dilemma.

Consider the following story told by 4-year-old Ethan in response to a request to tell a story about a happy little girl and a kind old horse (McKeough, 1992).

> Once upon a time there was a girl who lived on a farm with a very good horse and she always rode to the country on the horse and they had a picnic together.

Which of Bruner's narrative features are exemplified in this story? Stories such as this can be best described as a "happily ever after" social script (Nelson, 1981)—a series of events that repeatedly occur in a set sequence focusing on a particular event. In the current example, the story centers on a typical sequence of events involving a girl and a horse. Children commonly rely on these social scripts when relating stories about events such as birthday parties, visiting relatives, or going to a restaurant (Nelson, 1981). Such stories rarely develop characters' intentions or contain a breach (the problem or goal challenge that is typical of most stories told within the Western storytelling tradition and that older children utilize).

When children are asked to retell stories, such problems or challenges do appear, largely because the child is recalling the events rather than generating them. The following retelling of a movie about a magic reindeer by a 5-year-old girl illustrates this phenomenon (Clarke-Stewart & Beck, 1999).

> Umm, the little girl is walking through the woods to find her reindeer. Then she saw tracks from him. And then she fell down and then—then

he was hurt. And then, umm, he, her dad was going to shoot him, and then he was gone.

That such problems or challenges appear in retellings indicates that 4- and 5-year-olds are capable of understanding and remembering this type of event and view it as important enough in the storyline to merit mention when many other events are omitted. Their absence in original storytelling suggests that children at this age have a limited understanding of story structure—one that includes the actions and events of social scripts but is missing the features of intentionality (i.e., characters' needs, desires, and intentions motivate the actions and events) and canonicity and breach (a violation of the norm).

The Development of Story Composition in the Elementary School Years

Intentionality and canonicity and breach move to center stage as children go from first to sixth grade. Whereas the stories of preschoolers are often characterized as social scripts and contain an action-based sequence of events, as children mature and gain more experience, their stories spontaneously begin to include references to the internal mental states and intentions of characters. This developing capacity brings children's stories more in line with the mainstream cultural norm, wherein narratives have two landscapes—the landscape of action, which pertains to states, actions, and events that occur in the physical world, and the landscape of consciousness, which involves an interpretation of these states, actions, and events that are experienced by the characters (Bruner, 1986). By about 6 years of age, children begin to include these two landscapes in their stories (McKeough, 1992).

Stories by 6-Year-Olds

Consider the following example of a typical story told by 6-year-old Jennifer in response to a request to tell a story about a happy little girl:

> There is a little girl. She was crying 'cause she had no one to play with. So a boy came. No, a little—a little, little girl came and said, "Do you want to play with me?" And she stopped crying. And they played on the swings. They went on the slide. And then they went on the teeter-totter. Then they walked along the beach. Then they—they put their bathing suits on and they played in the water and—ah—they—ah—and that's the end.

This child clearly understands that stories should contain a problem or breach of some sort—so much so that she created a problem for the little girl at the beginning of the story (i.e., she was crying) even though the task directions called for the exact opposite. The character does, of course, resolve the problem and is a happy little girl in the end. Moreover, this child's knowledge of story structure also includes an understanding that a character's intentions (in this case, her desire to have someone to play with) motivate that character's actions (i.e., first crying and then playing happily). As this story illustrates, by first grade, average-functioning children have developed a concept of story that includes the four early-emerging features of narrative outlined by Bruner (1991).

Stories by 8-Year-Olds

Throughout the subsequent years of elementary school, students elaborate on this story structure, composing increasingly complex plots with characters that have more complex intentional states. Specifically, they begin to introduce various impeding factors that delay the resolution of an initial problem. A sample of this type of story is presented in Figure 3.3. It was written by Bailey, an 8-year-old third grader, in response to a request to write a story about someone who has a problem.

As is clearly evident, Bailey creates a problem—an enormous volcano that is going to erupt is discovered by a geologist, Meaa. Meaa's efforts to warn others of the imminent danger are not successful, however, because of their refusal to believe her. This creates a second problem for Bailey's protagonist, who now must prove that the volcano really exists. Although Meaa proves the volcano's existence to one other person, in the end, they cannot convince all of the others. In structuring this more complex plot line, Bailey has also depicted characters with multiple mental states. Meaa moves from contentedly exploring to alarm to feeling hurt and finally to determination; the other story character expresses feelings of surprise/alarm and determination. Comparing Bailey's character development to Jennifer's, it becomes clear that over the 2-year period from 6 to 8 years of age, children construct increasingly complex portrayals of characters' mental and physical worlds.

In addition to plot and character development, a comparison of Jennifer's and Bailey's stories also reveals the latter's greater descriptive detail, more complex sentence structure, and appropriate use of the conjunctions *so*, which relates two events causally, and *but*, which relates two events in an opposing or adversative fashion (e.g., he ran away *but* they still chased him). Notably, the use of the conjunction *but* typically appears when a failed attempt or complication is generated. Advances from the meagerness of setting in Jennifer's story (i.e., "There is a little girl") to one that provides some context (i.e., the protagonist as a female geologist who was exploring Hawaii) can also be seen.

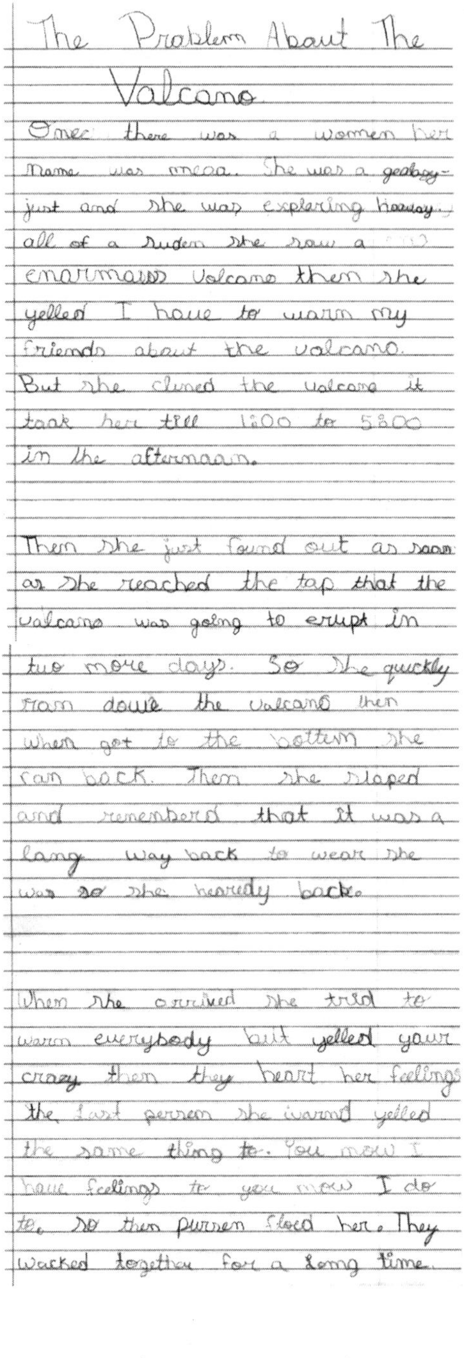

The Problem About The
Valcano

Once there was a women her
name was meaa. She was a geology-
just and she was exploring heaway.
all of a suden she saw a
enarimaios Volcano then she
yelled I have to warm my
friends about the volcano.
But she clined the volcano it
took her till 1:00 to 5:00
in the afternoon.

Then she just found out as soon
as she reached the tap that the
valcano was going to erupt in
two more days. So the quickly
from dowe the valcano then
when got to the bottem she
ran back. Then she sloped
and remenberd that it was a
long way back to wear she
was so she heariedy backe.

When she arrived she tried to
warm everybody but yelled your
crazy then they heart her feelings
the last person she warmd yelled
the same thing to. You mean I
have feelings to you mean I do
to. so then purnen sloed her. They
warked together for a long time.

FIGURE 3.3. Bailey's story. (*continued on next page*)

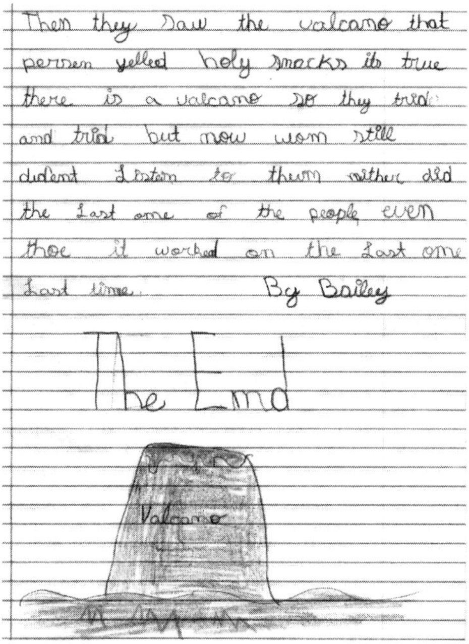
Then they saw the valcano that
persen yelled holy smacks its true
there is a valcano so they trid
and trid but now wom still
dident Listen to them nither did
the Last one of the people even
thoe it worked on the Last one
Last time. By Bailey

The End

FIGURE 3.3. Bailey's story.

Stories by 10-Year-Olds

The story composition of Emily, a 10-year-old fifth grader, illustrates the elaboration typical of students at this age and grade (see Figure 3.4). The setting is considerably elaborated in her story. The protagonist, Sally, is described as "the new girl" who is excitedly awaiting making new friends. Emily's plot is also much more complex than Bailey's in that she has constructed multiple related subplots. The first subplot focuses on the challenge Sally faces in making a new friend. The second subplot focuses on her attempts to deal with the school bully, Kacy. Her first attempt to deal with this problem—asking her new friend Mia what to do—is unsuccessful and only serves to exacerbate the problem. Within this bully subplot, another subplot is constructed, one that deals with lying to her mother about the troubles she is having at school with the bully. Righting that wrong serves to provide a resolution not only to Sally's difficulties with the bully, but also to those of her classmates.

Emily also depicts the mental states of her story characters more richly and more explicitly than Bailey does. Her protagonist goes through a wide range of emotions, from excitement to contentment to fear to guilt to greater fear (experienced during her dream) to relief and happiness. This level of plot and character complexity mirrors the classic folktale structure, where a hero must overcome multiple obstacles in reaching his or her goal, an accomplishment that makes the world a better place.

Stories by 12-Year-Olds

Whereas most 10-year-olds focus on story characters' intentions and mental states that occur in conjunction with immediate events, by age 12 a change in focus typically occurs. Immediate mental states and intentions are interpreted and, as a result, students create characters with mental states (e.g., loneliness) and traits (e.g., extroverted) that are long-term, enduring across time and situations (McKeough & Genereux, 2003). For example, a 12-year-old might describe one or more scenes in which a character is nervous when trying to make new friends and then explain the character's nervousness as being due to his or her long-term shyness or unpleasant earlier experiences.

FIGURE 3.4. Emily's story. (*continued on next page*)

The Girl Who Solved Her Problem!

There's a little Girl her name is Sally. Sally just moved from Victora to New York. Sally now has a big house. Sally went upstairs to unpack. She was so excited to go to School in two more days. Finally it was time to go to School. Sally made her lunch, fixed her hair, Ate, Brushed her teeth, Washed her face and was off to School. Sally got to School. When she got to her class She stoped and looked around. Hellow said Sally Teacher My name is Ms. Rose. My name is Sally. It's very nice to meat you Ms. Rose. Take your time and find a seat. Sally found somewhere to sit She picked a spot beside another little girl named Mia She was a pretty girl She had a nice long brown hair She was a girl who's been at the school last year. Sally had learned a lot today. She learned how to Spell, do math like three digits by one digit. The recess bell just rang. Everybody ran outside Sally thought of Mia as a nice girl So she ran up to Mia and asked her if She would like to play tag. Mia said Yes!

Two months came by. Everything was great except one thing it was another girl named Kacy She was the bully of the School but of corse the Grades only went up to Grade Six Kacy bullyed everbody in the school even Mia. It was a couple of weeks later untill Kacy Started bullying Sally Sally did'nt know what to do She asked Mia but she said just to ignore Kacy. So she did. Kacy did'nt like it So she went up to sally and toll her to meat her after school The Bell just rang. Ms. Rose said you are Dismissed Sally forgot

Everything what Kacy had said untill she saw Kacy. Sally started running as fast as she could She saw her house it was just around the corner. She ran faster but she could also her Kacys voice. She finally got to her house she stoped and turned around Kacy wasn't there Sally walk'd up the stairs and opened the door her mom was there. She asked Sally how was her day She said it was good and She ran up to her room layed on her bed and thought about what she had did to her mom. Lieing to her mom was the worst thing she did to her mom. It was time to go to sleep. Sally fell asleep really quick. She was having a dream. It was about Kacy fighting her. This dream went on untill it was time to get up. Sally got up. She could hear Kacys voice repeating and repeating. Sally could not take it anymore She had to tell her mom. Her mom got upset She went to the School and pulled the Teacher out of class and talked to her and asked her if She knew anything about Kacy bullying Sally Ms. Rose Said No! Ms. Rose said she will watch Kacy and Sally see if anything goes on Sallys mothe said OK! But I would like to talk with Kacys mom and you and me. OK said Ms. Rose I'll see if I could get a whole of her Scince that day Kacy never bullyed anyone again.

Written by: Emily Bird
★

FIGURE 3.4. Emily's story.

Narrative Composition Rubric

Based on our analysis of many children's narrative compositions, both oral and written, we developed the rubric presented in Table 3.1 (see other assessments in Calfee & Miller, Chapter 13, this volume). This rubric is unlike many in that it is based on children's developmental capacities. Each level characterizes average-functioning children's plot structure at 2-year intervals—4, 6, 8, 10, and 12 years of age. Of course, in any given classroom at any given grade, there is considerable variability in children's level of competence. Moreover, as all teachers know, even individual children show variable performance, demonstrating skills at one time but not at another. Because of this normal variability within classrooms and within individuals, the rubric should not be viewed as a grade-equivalency measure. Rather, we hope that teachers will use it as a tool to help them plan developmentally appropriate instruction for all students, whether they are above, below, or on the level of performance considered typical for their cohort.

TEACHING STORY COMPOSITION

Through our research, we have developed an instructional program for supporting the development of kindergarten and first grade students'

TABLE 3.1. Narrative Composition Rubric

Criteria	Level
The story has a sequence of temporally, causally, or referentially related actions and events that occur exclusively in the physical world.	1
The story includes explicit or implicit reference to the mental states (MS) that motivate the action. There is a problem that is immediately resolved.	2
The story has a problem and a series of failed attempts or complications, followed by a resolution, such that additional MS are mentioned or implied.	3
One impediment has more significance than the others, broadening the characters' MS and intentions. The impediment is dealt with in the outcome, resulting in a well-planned resolution.	4
The focus of the story shifts from the characters' actions/MS to *why* particular mental states are held. A constellation of MS creates a psychological profile or character trait that is represented across time and situations.	5

oral storytelling (Adams et al., 2005; McKeough et al., 1995, 2005). Our focus on oral rather than written stories was motivated by the knowledge that, because written language is new to children of this age, it demands a great deal of their attentional capacity, leaving very little capacity to use in constructing a story. By separating storytelling and story writing, we successfully improved children's understanding of plot and character—knowledge they could then apply in their written stories.

The Theory

The instructional program we developed was based on the following theoretical principles that have been validated through research.

- Stories have two landscapes—the landscape of actions that occur in the characters' outer, physical world and the landscape of mental states that occur in the characters' inner worlds (Bruner, 1990; Case & McKeough, 1990; McKeough et al., 1995).
- Children's story plots progress from simple, action-oriented plots to more complex ones that include both actions and mental states, such as intentions, feelings, and thoughts (Case & McKeough, 1990; McKeough, 1992; McKeough & Sanderson, 1996). By adolescence, students interpret why characters hold particular mental states and, as a result of this interpretation, compose stories that have characters with particular psychological profiles (McKeough & Genereux, 2003).
- Children's story cohesion increases as they learn to use conjunctions (Fox, 1993; Halliday & Hasan, 1976; McCabe & Peterson, 1988; McKeough et al., 2005).
- Teachers who present information about stories in multiple forms (e.g., pictures and text) can reach more children, helping them compose more expert-like stories (Gambrell & Jawitz, 1993; Gordon, Sheridan, & Paul, 1998; Shafrir, 1999).

The Teaching Strategies

In our program (McKeough et al., 2005), we utilized these theoretical principles to design instruction as follows.

- We built *conceptual bridges* from one level of competence to the next, supporting children's successful movement toward composing better-structured, more coherent stories.
  - First, action-oriented stories were depicted in line drawings within frames (similar to a comic strip). Next, we added

icons above the frames to depict mental states (e.g., feelings, intentions, and thoughts), including sad/happy faces, and idea lightbulbs (see Figure 3.5).

- We help students compose more coherent stories by gradually introducing them to *superglue* words (i.e., conjunctions) in the following sequence: *and, then, because/so,* and *but.*
- We simultaneously presented stories verbally, in text, and graphically, in pictures (see Table 3.2).

Although instructional procedures were organized in daily lessons, the rate of progress through the lessons was varied according to the conceptual needs of the individuals in a group. The lessons were designed so that the story topics and specific content were largely left to the child. The teacher's primary role was to offer assistance with creating coherent, well-formed plots. Finally, the program activities were intended to be fun. The teacher not only tried to help children become better storytellers, but also attempted to make storytelling an enjoyable activity that could be handled with ease.

When students' preinstruction and postinstruction oral compositions were compared, using the rubric presented in Table 3.1, we found a significant increase in plot complexity. Moreover, when we compared their stories to the stories of children taught by a master teacher who utilized a process approach to writing, we determined that our instruction approach produced significantly greater gains.

Although it is worthwhile knowing *that* children's story composi-

| Once upon a time a happy little girl was walking down the street and she saw a happy horse that she wanted to buy. | But she didn't have enough money. | So she ran home to ask her dad if he would give her some money to buy the horse. And her dad said no. | And then she asked if she could earn some money to buy the horse, and her dad said yes. | So she was living in a cottage, and she was chopping down some trees. | And on Monday she went back to that store, and she saw the horse, and she bought it, and she went home, and she went for a ride on it to the river. |

FIGURE 3.5. Story structure mnemonic with accompanying text.

TABLE 3.2. Graphic and Verbal Scaffolds Used Throughout Instruction

Graphic scaffolds	Verbal scaffolds
Story frames (as in comic strips)	Oral and written stories
Icons • Happy/sad/angry/shy face • Lightbulb to represent ideas • Thought cloud	• Individual storytelling and story writing • Joint storytelling and story writing • Story retelling
Thought cloud crowns	Choosing appropriate *superglue* words (*and, then, because, but*)
Story starter picture cards	Labeling and discussing the components of plot structure (problem, failed attempt, resolution)
Group drawing of familiar stories	Labeling and discussing story elements (setting, characters, plot)
Picture storybooks	Labeling and discussing story landscapes (actions vs. mental states)

tion improved, it is more worthwhile for teachers to know *how* and *why* it improved. To demonstrate more clearly what was involved in the instruction and how children responded to it, an outline of the sequence of instruction for both story plot and story cohesion, along with samples of students' compositions, follows.

Block 1 (Lessons 1–15)

The aim of this first block of lessons was to solidify children's action-oriented story concept and their understanding of the use of conjunctions to establish cohesion between story events. We ensured that children understood the sequence of events presented in stories by highlighting the temporal order of the events. Initially, we worked with children to model how the main events of a story we read to them might be depicted in line drawings within story frames, as depicted in the lower portion of Figure 3.5). Next, we had children tell us how other stories we read should be depicted (i.e., what we should draw in the frames to represent the story events). As the children did this, we created simple, rough line drawings. Children worked in large and small groups, retelling the stories by using the line drawings as story texts. The line drawings were also cut into separate frames for children to sequence. The aim of these activities was to help children become *explicitly* aware that stories consist of a sequence of discrete events. We also invited children to compose their own stories orally and depicted these in line drawings within story frames, which they subsequently used as texts during retellings of their own and classmates stories. To encourage children to expand their storytelling topic repertoires, we used story starter cards (depicting events such as a children's birthday party and a family swimming outing) and had children generate additional episodes of stories that we read to them. We also developed a vocabulary for talking about how stories are organized or put together. We ensured that children understood and used terms such as *event, characters, action, story frames, story starter, story topic,* and *storytelling.*

Next, in order to highlight the relationship between the story events (i.e., to develop an *explicit* understanding of story cohesion), we introduced the children to conjunctions. Instruction began with a discussion of conjunctions as superglue words, that is, words that glued the story events together. The conjunctions *and, then, because, so,* and *but* were highlighted in the stories we read to the children. Students were also explicitly encouraged to use two common conjunctions, *and* and *then,* in their own compositions. To support this occurrence, we wrote the conjunctions *and* and *then* on cards and had children insert them, as appropriate, between the story frames.

In the final two lessons in block 1, we introduced the idea that event sequences are sometimes about happy things, such as a trip to visit one's grandparents, and other times about sad things, such as losing a pet. We demonstrated to the children that they competently composed happy stories by having them reread the stories they had told in previous lessons. We also challenged them to complete stories that we started—stories that began with a problem—by having a story character think of a way to solve the problem, making the character happy again. Again, we ensured that the children knew and used labels such as *problem, idea to solve the problem,* and *solution that fixed the problem.* We depicted these elements with *mental state icons,* as is shown in the upper portion of Figure 3.5.

At the end of block 1, analysis of the students' individually composed stories revealed that they were able to construct cohesive plots that contained a problem and its resolution (with implied mental states) that were also rich in descriptive detail. The following example illustrates this type of story.

> Once there was two dogs and one of the dog's names was Amy and the other was Allie. And they were twins. They had bright blue eyes, brown shaggy fur, and they also had floppy ears. Their mom was the same as them and their dad was too. And then one day the family got lost but the dad was at work. And they were on their way to the dad's work but they didn't know where it was. And then the dad was on his way home and he saw them and he was in his car and he saw them and he got out of his car and picked up the kids and then they all went home. The End.

Block 2 (Lessons 16–30)

Instruction was aimed at helping children differentiate between action events and the mental states that motivate them. Initially, we depicted the plots of stories we read to the children in line drawings and had them add mental state icons. Children also became familiar with this structure by working in pairs, retelling first the problem portion of the story and then the resolution portion. Mental state icons, line drawings, and story starter cards also were used to help participants generate individually oral and written stories. Our aim was to provide story models (Rogoff, 1990) and to represent stories in multiple modalities (Shafrir, 1999) in order to offer attentional capacity support (Case & McKeough, 1990).

To help children link action with mental states, we highlighted the conjunctions *because* and *so* (e.g., "The boy was sad *because* he couldn't find his dog"). These two conjunctions signal a *causal* relationship, whereas the conjunction *and* signals an *adding on* relationship and the conjunction *then* signals a *temporal* relationship. In addition to drawing children's attention to the use of *because* and *so* in stories that we read to them, we helped them use those conjunctions to link actions and mental states in their own stories by writing those words on cards and having them insert the cards between the frames in the line drawings, as was done in block 1 with the conjunctions *and* and *then*.

Analysis of the stories produced at the end of block 2 revealed that typically stories contained a well-developed problem and a resolution and appropriate use of the targeted conjunctions, as the following story illustrates.

> Once upon a time there was a dragon named Polka. He had a problem because he was polka dotted but the other dragons weren't. So he tried to wipe them off but they still didn't come off. So he tried shaving cream but they still didn't come off. And then he went into the water and then all his fire got burnt out. So he had to go to a doctor to get the spots off. And then the doctor got some special cream and wiped it on his polka dots. And then they were gone. The End.

Block 3 (Lessons 31–43)

Throughout the course of these sessions, instruction focused on increasing descriptive detail of events, characters, and settings. Initially, stories that had rich setting and character descriptions were read to children, who then described the settings and characters in their own words. They generated lists of descriptive words working with the teacher and used these to elaborate on the setting and character descriptions for stories composed in block 2. Next, we read silly stories to children, in which the setting or character descriptions did not fit with the plot (e.g., a very old lady who wanted to learn how to skip rope). Children worked in pairs revising these stories by describing and drawing settings and characters that were appropriate for the plot. The list of descriptive words was expanded throughout these activities. Children also told stories using story starter cards and practiced using the descriptive words appropriately. They drew pictures of the characters in the setting, then printed the text of the story. Throughout these sessions, we continued to focus on the conjunctions *and*, *then*, *because*, and *so* to link story events—both action and mental states. Again, conjunctions were highlighted while stories were read aloud to the children and while children composed stories orally; They also inserted the correct conjunction cards between story frames while working with both types of stories.

Interestingly, as children struggled to create stories that were more elaborate, succeeding in including descriptive detail, their story coherence decreased, as the following illustrates.

> One day there was a baby Teradodon. He was flying through the air. Then a sea monster nuked his head up in the air and he bit the Teradodon. The baby Teradodon fell down then in the water. Then he had another baby. The baby flew up and then a dinosaur tried to bite him but instead he escaped. He was too small and then he grew and grew and grew into a big one. Then he squashed the T-Rex and he killed it. And then there came an Allosaur, the creature that poked him in the stomach. And then he died and then there was this other Triceratops that was running around the fields toward a baby and then a big Anklosaurus spiked his head and he died. The End.

This phenomenon, where children appear to lose competency they had already demonstrated when faced with new, higher expectations, is a familiar one for most teachers. Children's path to learning is rarely straight. Although it sometimes leads directly to the goal, more frequently it jogs backward for a while or winds around a stumbling block. Such was the case when we asked children to generate elaborative detail within a story structure that was already placing considerable demands on them. In short, in attempting to meet our expanded expectations, the children appeared to compromise the coherence of their stories.

Block 4 (Lessons 44–51)

In this sequence of sessions, we continued to focus on descriptive detail until we saw evidence that children's stories were beginning to cohere. Additionally, instruction included discussion and identification of complicating events and failed attempts in stories that were read to the children. To help children link their complicating events or failed attempts to other story events, we introduced the conjunction *but* (e.g., "The boy wanted a horse *but* his dad had no money"), using the same activities as described previously. Children also worked in pairs using *but* as a conjunction, one child generating the problem portion of a story and the second beginning the complicating event or failed attempt portion with the word *but*. Again, we depicted stories we read to children in line drawings and mental state icons (see Figure 3.5), and conjunctions were printed on cards and placed between the story frames, as appropriate. Children retold these stories and used the icons to help them organize stories of their own.

At the end of block 4, supported by these graphic and linguistic scaffolds, children successfully composed coherent stories that were rich in elaborative detail and that contained a problem, complication (or failed attempt), and resolution.

Teaching Trickster Tales to Support Students' Story Composition

We have also used developmental instruction to teach trickster tales (Jarvey, McKeough, & Pyryt, 2005) to support children's story composition. Trickster tales are considered one of the oldest and most persistent of narrative forms (Hyde, 1998). They are universal, appearing on every continent as part of the narrative heritage of many cultures (Huck, Hepler, & Hickman, 1989). The following features define trickster tales and make them ideal vehicles for teaching a more psychologically complex form of narrative composition. These features coincide with narrative abilities that are typically not yet apparent in children of age 8 and 9, but expected to develop soon.

- Generally, trickster tales have an underlying moral theme, containing lessons in how to behave in the world. The tension between fair and unfair social behavior and among individuals who attempt to override social rules is a driving force within the trickster tale.
- Through language, tricksters deliberately cover up their true intentions. This deception plays a catalytic role in the plot of a trickster tale.
- Trickster tales complicate the notion of intent in narratives by focusing attention on the interpretations (and misinterpretations) that other characters assign to a trickster's language and actions.
- Composing a trickster tale demands that students attend to the internal world of the characters and the manipulation of more than one perspective.

We developed teaching strategies with these goals in mind while considering the developmental level of our students. As the students' trickster tales at the beginning of this chapter illustrate (see Figures 3.1 and 3.2), there was considerable spread in competence levels within the class. A description of our instruction follows.

Block 1 (Lessons 1–7, 75 Minutes Each)

This block was devoted to building general understandings of the trickster tale genre, exposing students to published trickster tales and discussing the nature of tricksters and their tricks. Students discussed the relationship between tricks and pretence. Six trickster tales that represented a range of types of tricksters were read aloud, then students created a character web for each of the tricksters, including brief notes about each trickster's internal qualities (e.g., clever, selfish, funny) and motivations (e.g., likes to be admired, wants to protect his family). To build students' understanding of the nature of tricksters and trickster tales, 25–30 published children's trickster tales were made available in the classroom, and students were encouraged to select books from this collection for independent reading.

Block 2 (Lessons 8–11, 75 Minutes Each)

Block 2 involved further exploration of trickster tales and focused on developing understanding of plot and character. It began by discussing tension in the plots of trickster tales. As a metaphor for story tension, we used a toy jack-in-the-box, winding the crank until the internal spring could tolerate no more tension and released. To demonstrate the notion of tension in a narrative plot further, we had two children demonstrate a tug-of-war with a blanket. One was asked to tug a little of the blanket over to her side in a sequence of three tugs. Finally, at the third tug, the other student was instructed to yank the blanket back to the middle. This action was discussed in relation to tension in a trickster tale, as one character often tries to get more than his or her fair share until a final event restores justice. A graphic scaffold was used to sequence, along a plot line, events of two trickster tales read aloud. These events were placed either above or below a central line of equilibrium, depending on whether each was negative or positive (see Figure 3.6).

The trickster tale *The Tale of Tricky Fox* (Aylesworth, 2000) was read aloud, and each of the three trick sequences was discussed. A large sheet of paper was divided into four sections to represent the sequence of events in the first trick in the story. On this grid, one character was drawn in each box, with the negative character in the top two sections and the positive character in the bottom two sections. As each character was drawn, the students were asked what he or she said, and the dialogue was added in speech bubbles. Next, the students articulated what each character was thinking, and we recorded these words in thought bubbles. The two subsequent trick sequences in the story were also discussed, and students worked with individual copies of the drawings, adding speech and thought bubbles as they thought appropriate. This activity was meant to focus students' attention on the characters' mental states and highlight the contrast between what the trickster said and meant.

Block 3 (Lessons 12–14, 75 Minutes Each)

During this block, students worked first on creating a trickster. They decided to write about either a positive or negative trickster and constructed a character web that included their tricksters' strengths, weaknesses, desires, fears, and goals. To scaffold the interior focus further, we suggested that students select characters' names and describe their appearances in a way that reflected their personalities. Students then plotted their own story events on the tension graphic scaffold, demonstrating a rise in tension followed by a restoration of balance.

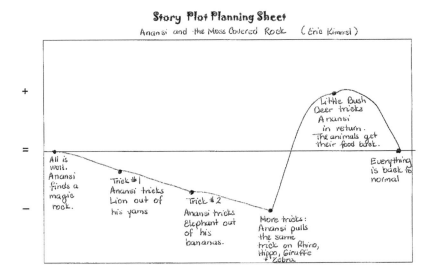

FIGURE 3.6. Trickster tales tension mnemonic.

Block 4 (Lessons 15–18, 75 Minutes Each)

Students created a story plan in which each trick sequence of their tale was illustrated. Speech and thought bubbles that showed what characters were saying and secretly thinking were included, and story action was briefly described below each illustration (see Figure 3.7). We modeled this process for students with an original trickster tale sequence. As students worked through the process of planning their own stories, they were encouraged to revise their drawings and story ideas as they wished. Opportunities were provided for students to conference with the teacher and their peers.

Block 5 (Lessons 19–22, 75 Minutes Each)

Students first discussed how to represent characters' thoughts in a narrative format and examined excerpts of text from published trickster tales that demonstrated how the authors used language to convey a character's inner thoughts. Students then used their graphic story plan to create

FIGURE 3.7. Trickster tale plot plan.

a narrative text. Finally, students participated in a final celebration of their work, which included an opportunity to share their completed trickster tales with peers.

To evaluate the success of our approach, we developed a developmental rubric that was adapted from the rubric presented in Table 3.1 but tailor-made for trickster tales. Using this rubric to assess developing writing competence, we determined that students not only improved significantly across the instruction period but also maintained their level of improvement at a 2-month follow-up assessment. Moreover, when compared to a similar group of students taught differently, our students significantly outperformed them. The two instructional approaches differed as follows: focus on plot tension versus temporal event sequence, story character versus story problem, characters' inner mental worlds versus outer physical worlds.

SUMMARY AND CONCLUSIONS

- Through the elementary years of formal schooling, children gradually increase their capacity to write descriptive and complex stories with coherent structure and plots.
- The abilities of children can be bridged in order to support them to write at a higher developmental level.
- Instruction must target children's current level of understanding initially. Only when children are aware of what they know and have a language for talking about it should instruction advance their understanding by following the typical developmental pattern.
- Teachers should focus on teaching children plot and character construction as well as the writing process.
- Teachers should provide opportunities for children to form supportive writing communities and have them share their stories (in pairs or small groups as well as in front of the entire class).
- Teachers should use developmentally appropriate scaffolding techniques to help move children's writing to a more advanced level, by:
  - Showing that stories are composed of discrete but related events by depicting story events in story frames. Events can be linked with basic conjunctions, such as *and* and *then*.
  - Showing children how to represent the emotional and mental states of characters using facial expressions and lightbulbs.
  - Encouraging children to look at other stories to see how authors have solved literary problems or developed ideas and asking them to find examples of how such authors have created feelings and messages with words.

REFERENCES

Adams, M., Bereiter, C., Campione, J., Carruthers, I., Hirshberg, J., Mckeough, A., et al. (2005). *Open court reading*. Columbus, OH: SRA/McGraw-Hill.

Aylesworth, J. (2001). *The tale of tricky fox*. New York: Dial Books for Young Readers.

Bruner, J. S. (1986). *Actual minds, possible worlds*. Cambridge, MA: Harvard University Press.

Bruner, J. S. (1990). *Acts of meaning*. Cambridge, MA: Harvard University Press.

Bruner, J. S. (1991). The narrative construction of reality. *Critical Inquiry, 18*, 1–21.

Case, R., & McKeough, A. (1990). Schooling and the development of central conceptual knowledge structures: An example from the domain of children's narrative. *International Journal of Education, 13*(8), 835–855.

Clarke-Stewart, K. A., & Beck, R. J. (1999). Maternal scaffolding and children's narrative retelling of a movie story. *Early Childhood Research Quarterly, 14*(3), 409–434.

Fox, C. (1993). *At the very edge of the forest: The influence of literature on storytelling in children*. London: Cassell.

Gambrell, L. B., & Jawitz, P. B. (1993). Mental imagery, text illustrations, and children's story comprehension and recall. *Reading Research Quarterly, 28*(3), 264–273.

Gordon, C., Sheridan, M., & Paul, J. (1998). *Content literacy for secondary teachers*. Toronto, Canada: Harcourt Brace.

Haden, C. A., & Fivish, R. (2003). *Autobiographical memory and the construction of a narrative self: Developmental and cultural perspectives*. Mahwah, NJ: Erlbaum.

Halliday, M., & Hasan, R. (1976). *Cohesion in English*. London: Longman.

Huck, C., Hepler, S., & Hickman, J. (1989). *Children's literature in the elementary school* (5th ed.). New York: Harcourt Brace.

Hyde, L. (1998). *Trickster makes this world: Mischief, myth, and art*. New York: Farrar, Straus and Giroux.

Jarvey, M., McKeough, A., & Pyryt, M. (2005). *Teaching trickster tales*. Unpublished manuscript.

McCabe, A. (1996). *Chameleon readers: Teaching children to appreciate all kinds of good stories*. New York: McGraw-Hill.

McCabe, A., & Peterson, C. (1988). A comparison of adults' versus children's spontaneous use of because and so. *Journal of Genetic Psychology, 149*(2), 257–268.

McKeough, A. (1992). The structural foundations of children's narrative and its development. In R. Case (Ed.), *The mind's staircase: Exploring the conceptual underpinnings of children's thought and knowledge* (pp. 171–188). Hillsdale, NJ: Erlbaum.

McKeough, A., Case, R., Bereiter, C., Anderson, V., Adams, M., Hirshberg, J., et al. (1995). *Story thinking*. Chicago, IL: Open Court.

McKeough, A., Davis, L., Forgeron, N., Marini, A., & Fung, T. (2005). Improving story complexity and cohesion: A developmental approach to teaching story composition. *Narrative Inquiry, 2*, 96–125.

McKeough, A., & Genereux, R. (2003). Transformation in narrative thought during adolescence: The structure and content of story compositions. *Journal of Educational Psychology, 95*(3), 537–552.

McKeough, A., & Sanderson, A. (1996). Teaching storytelling: A microgenetic analysis of developing narrative competency. *Journal of Narrative and Life History, 6*(2), 157–192.

Nelson, K. (1981). Social cognition in a script framework. In J. H. Flavell & L. Ross (Eds.), *Social cognitive development: Frontiers and possible futures* (pp. 97–118). Cambridge, UK: Cambridge University Press.

Nelson, K. (2003). Narrative and self, myth and memory: Emergence of the cultural self. In R. Fivish & C. A. Haden (Eds.), *Autobiographical memory and the construction of a narrative self: Developmental and cultural perspectives* (pp. 1–28). Mahwah, NJ: Erlbaum.

Rogoff, B. (1990). *Apprenticeship in thinking: Cognitive development in a social context.* New York: Oxford University Press.

Shafrir, U. (1999). Representational competence. In I. E. Sigel (Ed.), *The development of mental representation: Theory and applications* (pp. 371–389). Mahwah, NJ: Erlbaum.

4

Best Practices in Developing a Writing across the Curriculum Program in the Secondary School

GEORGE E. NEWELL, SUSAN KOUKIS, *and* STACY BOSTER

Teachers of English language arts have always assumed that writing can, or more emphatically, should play an important role in instruction in various content areas in the secondary school. In spite of this easy assumption, teachers' classroom experiences and a tradition of academic research suggest that the use of "writing to learn" has far-reaching implications for content-area instruction. Consider, for example, three pedagogical relationships between writing and learning: (1) to recall previously learned ideas in order to prepare for new learning activities; (2) to review, summarize, and evaluate information and experiences from multiple sources; and (3) to extend and reformulate ideas. Although each of these relationships assumes differing goals and beliefs about how students write, read, and learn, studies of school literacy have reported that, rather than a broad range of reading and writing assignments, school literacy tasks are often limited to demonstrations of previous learning (Applebee, 1981, 1984; Langer & Applebee, 1987). Why this is the case and what reforms might be necessary to change this picture have been the focus of numerous books, journal essays, and professional meetings, as well as this chapter.

In this chapter, we briefly examine recent contexts of promises to reform schooling and writing and review theoretical and empirical projects about the relationships between writing and learning. We then consider some of the elements of a successful writing-and-learning project at the secondary school level. We argue that reform is more likely to be successful when individual teachers feel assured that the changes they make are worth their and their students' time and effort. Finally, we offer several brief illustrations of effective writing-and-learning activities and written products.

THE ROLE OF WRITING
IN THE SECONDARY CURRICULUM

Over the past 20 years, as secondary school reform has included calls for writing across the curriculum, it has become a truism to say that writing develops critical reasoning skills. Higher order thinking, problem solving, and analytical thinking have, at times, all been linked directly to writing instruction. In *High School: A Report on Secondary Education in America*, Ernest Boyer (1983) argues for making clear and effective writing a "central objective of the school." In Ted Sizer's (1992) *Horace's School*, the faculty's curricular redesign includes writing across the curriculum as a key to integration and writing becomes a facultywide responsibility. More recently, the National Commission on Writing (2003) states that "American education will never realize its potential as an engine of opportunity and economic growth until a writing revolution puts language and communication in their proper place in the classroom. Writing is how students connect the dots in their knowledge" (p. 3).

Regardless of how urgently writing instructors and school reform agendas insist on the centrality of writing in the secondary school curriculum, the case needs to be made that writing activities offer something unique to specific academic subjects and not just help for English language arts teachers. Currently, the field has a strong professional base of writing teachers and a tradition of academic research to argue for such a role for writing, yet the larger social and political developments in U.S. society complicate educational reform. Statewide writing assessments, for example, can foster both effective and ineffective writing, but more often than not "formulaic writing and thinking" are privileged (Hillocks, 2002, p. 201). If states want to improve writing, thinking, and learning in all subject areas, they will have to provide teachers with the resources and time to teach writing and thinking well. This basic assumption underlies our suggestions for developing a reform effort within a writing-to-learn framework.

We argue that the nature of the writing task and the kinds of learning from text it may foster are key to understanding the importance of writing in academic learning, making writing an important tool as well as a central skill in the secondary school curriculum. Perhaps more important, we argue that when any school reform agenda asks teachers to select writing activities to promote learning, the nature of the institutional contexts that complicate a writing-to-learn agenda must be considered.

CONSTRUCTIVIST NOTIONS OF TEACHING AND LEARNING

In spite of rather convincing arguments for the value of writing in academic learning, two interrelated issues that have plagued writing-to-learn reforms must be addressed in any schoolwide writing-to-learn endeavor. First, earlier conceptions of writing to learn based on process-oriented writing instruction neglected the fundamental issue of what constitutes learning, focusing instead on the development of new activities and routines. Accordingly, *transmission* views of teaching and learning that emphasize memorization and recitation co-opted the more learner-centered underpinnings of writing for which theorists such as Janet Emig, James Britton, Donald Graves, and Nancy Martin had argued. Second, although writing-to-learn approaches have provided insights into the role of writing as a tool for learning, they have largely ignored some of the unique ways of knowing and doing in various academic disciplines. These approaches have led to two assumptions: (1) that writing should be the primary concern of the English teacher, who has the responsibility to teach generic strategies and forms for writing; and (2) that writing has no practical relevance to instruction in other content areas. Accordingly, any reform will have to consider not only how students make sense of disciplinary ways of knowing and doing, but also the realities of schooling (such as testing) that often complicate shifts toward such fundamental change. The challenge is to develop a coherent view of teaching and learning that offers a conceptually powerful way of supporting process-oriented, learner-centered approaches to writing and gives teachers an overarching framework for thinking about issues of teaching and learning in the content areas.

To offer new ways of conceptualizing models of teaching and learning, many educators and scholars are turning to *constructivist* theories of language and learning. With roots in fields as diverse as psychology, linguistics, sociology, history of science, and philosophy, constructivist approaches share a view of knowledge and mind as an active construction developed by the individual acting within a social context that shapes and constrains new understandings but not in an absolute sense.

A key principle of such a framework is that, rather than considering the content of the academic disciplines and students' experiences and knowledge as mutually exclusive concerns, constructivist views focus on learning in context—how knowledge develops within particular instructional contexts when students are engaged in activities such as transforming knowledge in textual sources using writing. This view of teaching and learning is compatible with some of the motives underlying process-oriented approaches to writing instruction and it offers, in a principled way, a description of effective teaching and learning.

What, then, are some of tenets of constructivism relevant to a reconsideration of the role of writing to learn in the secondary school? Although constructivism has been discussed and examined from a range of perspectives, the view employed in this chapter has its roots in James Britton's (1970) discussions of "language and learning" and in Douglas Barnes's (1992) notion of the "interpretation" view of learning, each of which integrates the act of communication with the process of knowing. As an example of how interpretive teaching might foster students' active construction of meaning, Barnes has described the value of "exploratory talk." Barnes's analysis of successful small-group discussions indicates that the language students use in such contexts tends to be "marked by frequent hesitations, rephrasings, false starts and change of direction. . . . That is, such exploratory talk is one means by which the assimilation and accommodation of new knowledge to old is carried out" (p. 28). Britton, in turn, has argued that uses of expressive language (e.g., free writing, journal keeping, etc.) in which the demands of formality are relaxed and the audience's judgments withheld are at once unstructured and open-ended, revelatory of the writer's thinking, and communicative only to the extent that the writer and reader have a shared context.

Although the genesis of exploratory talk and expressive uses of language are part of a longer tradition of language and learning, they have come to represent elements of a larger orientation toward literacy instruction often referred to as *process-oriented approaches*. Such a view of teaching and learning has roots in constructivist approaches to learning in that it is based on the assumption that learning is not linear and sequential but instead involves false starts and tentative explorations. Understanding will grow and change as learning progresses. Premature evaluation will short-circuit the process and stall risk taking, emphasizing correctness rather than growth and exploration (see Pritchard & Honeycutt, Chapter 2, this volume, for a discussion of process-oriented writing).

Although we believe wholeheartedly in constructivist teaching and learning, the challenges of developing and enacting such a vision should not be underestimated. Currently, U.S. schools are generally supportive of a transmission view of knowledge because they tend to follow a top-down model of authority. Administrators make decisions that teachers put into practice. Teachers are the authorities in their classroom and transmit their knowledge of facts to students. Students have the option of "doing school" in ways that lead to success or risk gaining the reputation of being bad students. A constructivist classroom, however, is structured to provide students greater control of their learning as they develop new skills and understandings. They must have room to initiate as well as respond, to explore their strengths as well as the limitations of their new understanding. The teacher must be ready to step back as well as forward, providing students with support for new skills they are still developing. In the following scenario, we present our version of the challenges of change and the demands of a constructivist vision of writing to learn. We also argue that such a change is well worth the time and effort of classroom teachers who face a range of competing demands.

RETHINKING THE ROLE OF WRITING IN THE SECONDARY CURRICULUM

Proponents of writing across the curriculum argue that writing is one of the major contexts for extended critical thinking about a particular topic. To function successfully, writing activities must be structured to support and value the role of exploration and discovery. If they are used simply as tests of memory of information presented by the teacher or textbook, the promise of writing as a tool for higher-order and critical thinking will likely be short-circuited. Accordingly, for a school or district to initiate significant change in writing instruction and in how teachers in various content areas use writing, it will need to develop:

- A broad range of writing activities for students in content-area classes that will foster content learning as well as writing development;
- A network of teachers from English language arts and other departments skilled in leadership and in developing curriculum materials based on writing;
- Expectations and tools for evaluating writing (and learning) in content-area classrooms that include the English language arts, the sciences, and the social studies; and
- A positive working relationship with school administrators who recognize the need for in-service work in the teaching of writing and provide the moral and budgetary support necessary for successful staff development.

To illustrate the above principles for school change and to explore its complexities, we offer a story of two fictitious English language art teachers, Martha and Jane. Ironically, they rely on an administrative mandate to engender change in their high school's approach to writing. Their story is an amalgamation of our collective experiences in schools where we have taught and consulted.

In this section, we address Martha and Jane's concerns. They are colleagues at Thomas Jefferson High School (TJ). Their challenge is to develop a schoolwide writing-across-the-curriculum program to strengthen the writing and thinking skills of their students while attempting to persuade their administrators and the school's faculty that the challenges of a shift toward promoting their students' more thoughtful and deeper understanding of content-area information is worth time and effort. We acknowledge that pitfalls are part of change, especially when change focuses on teachers' assumptions about what it means to teach and to learn in their classrooms. Finally, we consider some of the signs of change, including a renewed commitment to writing and to the value of thoughtfulness.

Rethinking the Role of Writing: When It's Time for Change

In recent years, Martha and Jane have noticed changes in their colleagues' discussions about what students should know before they graduate. Located in what was once a small rural community, the school has been growing exponentially, mirroring the larger community. The new population of students has brought a renewed community interest in education. More than ever, upwardly mobile middle-class parents have demanded higher standards to prepare their children to attend college after graduation.

State Standards and Achievement Tests as a Context for Change

TJ has also confronted the challenges of trying to ensure that all of its 1,500 students (grades 9–12) pass the statewide graduation test. School administration, besieged by parents' and the larger community's complaints that the school's standards are in decline, are concerned about writing, especially now that writing plays a significant role in student performances on graduation and college admission tests. When the state graduation tests were revised recently, teachers and administrators were concerned about multiple-choice items that were based on the state standards for reading, writing, science, social studies, and math, as well as new test items requiring students to compose both brief and extended written responses. The previous year's test results indicated a significant decline in the performances of the school's less successful students and a slight decline for the more successful students. There was a growing sense that all of the students struggled with test items that required some degree of composing in the response.

An Administrative Mandate

In a comprehensive high school such as TJ in which science, math, and social studies teachers have traditionally not assigned writing or used writing as a way to support their students' learning, the sudden shift to a focus on writing across the curriculum can lead to resistance and frustration. A recent mandate by the administration that teachers in all subject content areas are required to include weekly short-answer and monthly extended response writing practice to ensure higher performance on the statewide tests was received with a variety of responses. Some members of the English department complained, "We teach writing anyway. Don't give us more paperwork." Teachers in other departments worried that they didn't know how to teach writing and that "it would take away from instructional time needed to cover content." Still others were more accommodating but unsure of the implications: "I'm willing to do it, but I have no idea how to start. My instruction is lecture-based, and my assessment is objective testing. Where would writing fit?" School administrators countered the complaints of faculty by pointing out that the state graduation test includes items requiring short-answer and extended written response in all five content-area tests. They assumed that if all teachers in all subject areas required students to practice such written responses, student scores would rise. The faculty, however, was skeptical.

Seizing an Opportunity

Martha and Jane faced a dilemma. On the one hand, they reasoned that the state tests were not going away, that they wanted their students to pass the tests, and that faculty resistance to the demands of the administration was a recipe for disaster for the school and the students. On the other hand, they also realized that writing assignments and how student work is assessed send messages to students (and parents) about what is valued in their coursework. They wanted writing to become a tool for students to learn subject-area content and literacy skills. After discussing the situation with a network of teachers at TJ who were also concerned about next steps, they realized that recent changes in the state tests might offer an opportunity for rethinking the role of writing across the curriculum.

Although the tests were a burden and in many ways a distraction from Martha and Jane's valued ways of teaching, they also realized that the revised tests with items requiring short and extended written response necessitated that students learn how to synthesize and interpret concepts and ideas. Having done some coursework on writing to learn, Martha found evidence that supported incorporating test practice into the curriculum. For example, when given time to read about and discuss the issue of testing, teachers are able to shift their students' attention from practice on the surface features of tests to "the underlying knowledge and skills needed to do well in coursework and in life, as well as on the tests" (Langer, 2002, p. 17). Although one possible reaction to the administration's demands was to resent the mandate, another possibility was to welcome it as a first step toward encouraging teachers to assign more writing in science, social studies, and even English language arts classrooms. Martha and Jane realized that, ironically, the administrative fiat seemed to open the possibility for an important conversation about writing, learning, and thinking across all content areas.

Starting with "the Choir": Program Beginnings

Martha and Jane wanted to start slowly and deliberate ideas, and they knew that they would have to have the support of a core of willing and able colleagues, but they needed to know which teachers were interested in a leadership role in promoting writing. They decided to organize a low-key, afterschool meeting to take stock of teacher interest and to develop a core of committed teachers who would take action collectively.

What Counts as Good Writing across the Content Areas?

During the initial meeting with a group of interested colleagues, Martha and Jane discussed some of their concerns not only about the new state tests and the administrative mandate for test preparation, but also about teachers' perceptions of their students' writing skills. There was a general concern among the teachers that their students' writing was not all it should be and that they and many of their colleagues did not have confidence in their abilities to teach writing. Yet they were hesitant about taking time and energy to address the issues. Some of the science and social studies teachers, for example, complained that they did not have time to grade writing for English skills. This comment ignited a controversy regarding how the teachers defined writing. Some of the English teachers argued that "good" writing means errorless prose, while a social studies teacher argued for the ability to create clear and well-organized summaries, respond to essay test questions, and write research reports.

For still others, good writing was the ability to analyze ideas and persuade an audience.

At the same meeting, the teachers decided to take the time to write
down their definitions of good writing and to make a list of the types of
writing they required for their content area. Some of the conclusions
they came to after a discussion of their writing activities were helpful in
clarifying the way to approach writing in each content area. A science
lab report, a history paper, and an English literary analysis require writing in unique genres that, in turn, require differing ground rules (Sheeran
& Barnes, 1991) for what counts as a successful performance. Some of
the teachers agreed that they had not considered making these ground
rules explicit for their students. All the teachers agreed that an initial
step would be to let students know what good writing in each discipline
looked like, to make the ground rules for successful performance explicit. Students may benefit, for example, from reading the types of writing required in science not just for content, but also for how the writing
conveys different kinds of reasoning and uses of evidence (Langer,
1992).

A Second Meeting: Developing Model Writing Assignments

As a result of the first meeting, Martha and Jane discovered that the core
group of teachers was willing to continue meeting to establish a systematic way to begin using writing in their classrooms. During the second
meeting, they decided to address a practical issue—how to include writing more routinely in instruction. Some of the teachers said members of
their departments felt uncomfortable assessing students' writing because
they were not good writers themselves. The group discussed how to allay
those fears by emphasizing the differences in content and genre in various subject areas—that is, the subject-area–specific ways of gathering evidence and developing arguments. Martha commented to the group that
"proponents of writing across the curriculum are not asking social studies teachers to teach students how to write literary essays, for example,
but they are asking math teachers to assign the kind of writing that also
helps students learn the content of social studies. Asking students to
write in order to review and consolidate their understandings of concepts is a writing task that can help both teachers and students learn
why students are or are not acquiring lesson content."

The group decided that developing sample writing assignments and
examples of the writing teachers might expect from these assignments
might encourage more reluctant teachers to begin using writing. The
group, which now had at least one representative from each subject area,
felt that it was important to start to develop writing assignments right
away that they could share with their department members. Each mem-

ber decided to develop and write at least three different sample lessons: one that could be completed in a single class period, a second that might extend over several days, and a long-term project extending across a grading period. To begin this phase of the program, Martha distributed an article (Durst & Newell, 1989) that described a taxonomy of writing tasks and their benefits, giving the teachers a starting place to develop their own assignments. Besides genre-specific writing in content areas, there are some types of writing (see below) that are applicable across all areas.

- Note taking: recording information from class lectures and discussions as well as from text sources for later use
- Reporting: writing accounts of what happened, as in lab reports and descriptions of field trips
- Summarizing: looking for patterns across a range of events and ideas by generalizing, requires that the writer select and shape the information presented
- Analyzing: developing and examining the underlying reasons for why things happen and what motivates people or literary characters
- Journal writing: writing for self-discovery of ideas and personal expression; may help writers clarify their ideas and experiences
- Creative writing: literary writing such as short stories and poetry that provides personal and imaginative ways of exploring ideas and experiences

Balancing Content Coverage with Students' Learning

Another issue that a science teacher raised at this second meeting was that introducing writing to learn in a content-centered classroom tends to slow down the pace and that less content that may be included in the state tests will be covered. They discussed how the issue has been explored in writing-across-the-curriculum (WAC) research (Durst & Newell, 1989). Jane explained that the dilemma lay not only in deciding which writing task to assign but also in how to balance content coverage with students' efforts to make sense of the content. Although writing does support learning, different kinds of writing lead students to focus on different kinds of information and to think about that information in different ways (Langer & Applebee, 1987). For example, a teacher might have students listen carefully to a few minutes of lecture, then ask them to write a summary of what he or she just presented. Although such writing may slow down the lesson, it also provides students with an opportunity to formulate in their own words what they have been listening to, and it gives the teacher an immediate understanding of students' confusion. The teachers agreed to try out these writing tasks in their classrooms and report back on their efforts in a future meeting.

Evaluating Student Learning

Along with content-coverage concerns and the class time that writing consumes, a third concern emerged: how to assess writing using procedures that support learning that requires synthesis and interpretation of concepts and ideas. One of the key issues that Jane presented to the group was the need to link instructional goals, writing tasks, and assessment procedures. To illustrate this issue, she told her colleagues about a conversation she had had with her daughter, who attended a different school. Her daughter's 10th-grade biology teacher used journals in his classroom as a way to cover important biological facts. When Jane commented that this was a great idea and that she was glad to hear that science teachers were using writing, her daughter had been less enthusiastic. She felt that the journals were "just busywork" and that she had written entries just to get the journal grade. Also, she suspected that the teacher read the journal entries as if he were grading a quiz. The teacher had returned the students' entries with check marks indicating the inclusion of what he thought to be relevant information.

Jane's daughter had also reported that the science teacher's tests were often based on the chapter in the textbook and that, in order to do well on the test, students simply had to read a chapter, take notes, and then try to remember the information. On one occasion, the teacher asked Jane's daughter and her peers to create an animal based on a chapter in their textbooks on life processes and life systems. The lesson was a disaster because most of the students just copied information from the book. When some students tried to be creative, they lost evaluation points. Previous experiences with writing as a check on recall of content made it difficult for both teacher and students to shift to writing as inquiry and discovery.

The group discussed the problem of disconnect between the notion of writing as learning and assessment as information recall; simple recall seemed to devalue the process of writing to learn and thwart students' efforts to make sense of new ideas. If students use writing to reason about relevant information, then teachers need to use writing to assess such learning. One of the social studies teachers described how she had begun to focus her assignments and assessments on students' ability to add their own ideas to their reports; however, she was still trying to accept their interpretations as evidence of learning and her success as a teacher. After many years of fill-in-the-blank writing assignments and using matching and multiple-choice testing, she had become used to expecting students simply to recite information they had memorized. She said she was now "aware that my teaching is changing—I'm spending more class time asking students questions such as, 'OK. Now tell me what you mean by that?' And I now see that if I expect them to develop their own ideas and interpretations, then I will have to teach them how to do that kind of thinking." Martha and Jane looked at one another in a moment of realization "that this kind of change can be difficult and take tons of time."

Developing a Schoolwide Writing Assessment

Along with using writing as assessment within their classrooms, the teachers knew that in order to maintain support from the administration (a crucial element to making writing across the curriculum work), they would have to demonstrate that writing to learn across the content areas was improving student writing at all grade levels. A writing assessment already in place was the English department's ninth-grade writing-prompt assessment, a whole-grade assessment done at the beginning of the school year and graded holistically by the ninth-grade English teachers, who were paid to do so by the district. The assessment was used by the teachers to determine which students needed help with writing skills and to let parents know their children's level of readiness for the state test's writing component.

Martha and Jane felt that there was already administration commitment to writing assessment but that an additional goal for this core group might be the development of a new assessment tool that would be practical, valued, and reflect writing and assessment by students and teachers across the content areas, not just in the English department. If the administration was willing to pay for teachers to run a second writing assessment after a full year of implementation of a schoolwide writing program, progress could be ascertained. In the meantime, while the program was being developed, the individual teachers involved could use short-answer and extended writing activities in their classes to track writing improvement and begin to use writing as one more way to track their students' successes and monitor their struggles with content-area information (see Calfee & Miller, Chapter 13, this volume, for a discussion of writing assessment).

Expanding the School's Commitment to Writing and Learning

After the group had met twice, Martha and Jane began to realize that their goal to bring writing to the center of instruction would take more than just a small group of teachers meeting and that, even in this group, the problem was finding time to do all the work required. They knew that they had support from the administration, so they decided to put together their findings from the meetings and approach the administration with a proposal. The interested teachers were more than willing to work together to find new ways to bring writing to the forefront, but they needed common time to plan. While those most interested might be willing to work after school, if administrators could give in-school planning time by providing substitutes for teachers willing to get the plan started, more teachers might be willing to participate.

Martha and Jane then met with the principal and assistant principals to review the results of the meetings. They began by explaining their concern about the negative reaction to the mandated test practice and detailed their efforts to take a positive stance and move beyond the earlier writing initiative. They presented evidence to show that teaching with writing is supported in theory by educators, researchers, and educational organizations throughout the United States (Bangert-Drowns, Hurley, & Wilkinson, 2004; Langer & Applebee, 1987; Moje & O'Brien, 2001; Newell, 2006). They then explained that it would take more than the initial mandate and its formulas for brief and extended writing for teachers to develop writing activities that might foster learning in a range of content-area classrooms. Incorporating writing into the school would also require more than a few workshops presented by the English department or a packet of formulaic state test practice packets handed out by the administration or even a workshop presented by an outside specialist on writing across content areas (Pritchard & Marshall, 2002). Teachers would need to develop a variety of writing activities that both elicited higher-order thinking and incorporated the field-specific writing of each content area.

Martha and Jane hoped the administration would see that their teacher-initiated meetings to discuss writing were an ideal way to encourage rather than impose more writing across the curriculum. They went on to explain that their positive involvement in a summer institute sponsored by a National Writing Project (NWP) site the preceding year was an impetus for them to begin a teacher-led writing group. They hoped to combine this activity with the obvious need to incorporate more writing into each department. Teachers who have participated in the NWP are well versed in the power of writing with other teachers and of teachers writing with students. NWP participants are not always English teachers, and content-area teachers can benefit from learning about the kinds of writing that are expected in the various content areas. Another benefit of NWP style workshops is that teachers actually write. Such an informal workshop could be offered to interested teachers as a way to increase the repertoire of writing activities by sharing and practicing the ideas provided by each participant.

After the conversation, Martha and Jane then proposed that the administration release the core group of teachers for a half-day workshop to begin the process of developing a writing program for their departments. Drawing on their NWP experiences, they suggested a series of meetings where teachers could write together to establish a continuing forum to develop writing-to-learn ideas and to discuss teachers' efforts to include these ideas in the contexts of their classrooms.

Maintaining Momentum toward Becoming a "Learning Organization"

After this meeting, Martha and Jane were encouraged by the support of the administration but worried that enthusiasm would ebb if they did not figure out how to maintain momentum. One sign of hope was that the administration was receptive to their ideas; the principal even approved the half-day workshop. Martha and Jane realized that the school was slowly but surely becoming a learning organization (Easterby-Smith, 1990). With the principal and staff on board, the next step was to win over teachers and invite them to become part of the reform. To do so, Martha and Jane planned a third meeting, focused on sharing the curricular and instructional materials developed by the core group of teachers with the rest of the faculty. Martha and Jane knew they were on the right track but wondered if they had taken on more than they could handle. They counted on the enthusiasm, commitment, and ideas of the original group as they entered into a very different agenda from that of most teachers: to plan and enact professional development work with their colleagues.

The Planning Group Develops Its Own Approaches to Writing to Learn

Martha and Jane began the workshop by allowing the teachers who were part of the planning group to voice their concerns about the writing activities they had begun to experiment with in their own classes. The discussion suggested that there were three major issues that the planning group would have to work through:

1. As the teachers developed new approaches, they framed them with their own notions of teaching and learning. Consequently, the experienced teachers in the group found it quite easy to develop new activities.
2. The reforms that Martha and Jane had in mind, however, carried new notions of teaching and learning. The challenge was getting

their colleagues to consider basic changes in what it meant to teach and learn in their classrooms and subject areas.

3. As the teachers discussed new ideas about learning—for example, that students should develop their own evidence and interpretations—Martha and Jane realized that the planning group would have to develop new ways of evaluating student learning. They also realized that if assessment issues were ignored, all of their efforts to bring change would be thwarted by criteria based on memorizing and repeating what teachers had presented to students. The planning group would have to develop new assessment tools that were in line with new concepts of learning.

For example, Diane, a social studies teacher, described the difficulty she had encountered when trying to decide how to teach and assess writing that she described as "more creative or nonformulaic in nature." Diane's development of the assignment began with a strategy she had enacted a year earlier for a course titled Cultural Connections. She had her students write at the beginning of an instructional unit to assess what prior knowledge they had of five major religions—Hinduism, Buddhism, Judaism, Christianity, and Islam. Specifically, the students were asked to write down all they could in a free write. Their pre-unit responses were then held by Diane until the end of the unit, when a student was given the same assignment. Diane was then able to determine through comparison what they had learned during those weeks in class—she used this writing assignment as a tool for evaluating how much information the students had retained.

As Diane presented the project to the planning group, Jane expressed concern that the students' responses were still largely a regurgitation of facts learned about the religions rather than an analysis or synthesis of what they learned throughout the unit. She suggested that Diane assign a brief essay, written in one class period, with the following prompt:

"Now that you have learned about the five large world religions, it is time for you to analyze a particular concept or issue (such as love, war, peace, sin, a particular sin, heaven, reincarnation, etc.) from two of the religions' perspectives. What do you think their beliefs or feelings are regarding the particular concept/issue chosen? How are they be similar or different?"

Diane pointed out that she believed that the pretest–posttest free-writing assignment would suffice to assess her students' learning through writing and that the essay would take more time from class than it was worth. She believed that having the students simply list what they could recall was similar to other essay tests she had given. She checked to see if students included specific words and/or phrases in their free writing and could easily compute a score from this list. Consequently, Jane's suggestion to include a compare-and-contrast essay to evaluate students' ability to apply key concepts to a new problem raised concerns for Diane.

Jane went over the assignment more thoroughly to ease concerns. "The entire assignment only took 2 days out of class time to ensure that learning was indeed taking place," she explained. "And it has long-term payoffs too. If you take time to teach students how to do the assignment now, then you can use it for other assignments later." Jane suggested that at the end of the unit on the five religions, the assignment could be explained and then multiple examples of concepts and issues could be discussed: the afterlife, love, and war. The essay should be assigned a few days later as in-class writing, giving students time to develop their topics and even to do some research on what the five religions had to say about the selected concept. Finally, on the given essay day, students would be allowed to bring in an outline and would have one class period to write the entire essay. In spite of Jane's enthusiasm, she was sure that for Diane to remain committed to such uses of writing Jane would have to continue to work with her and encourage her.

"But Writing to Learn Doesn't Seem Very Scientific"

David, a biology teacher, also expressed problems but in a very different way. "Learning through writing," he argued, "does not seem very scientific but, rather, extremely subjective." From David's perspective, it was "difficult to teach writing in a class where students are asked to be scientists and seek out facts." Teaching his students to do extensive writing would likely take away from what he regarded as "the scientific approach," and he was unsure that they would learn the facts effectively. David became interested in trying to include more writing in his biology class when Martha reminded him that he already was teaching writing when he assigned lab reports. He was particularly concerned with their struggles with writing strong conclusions.

> "They never seem to get the point of the conclusions—they write, 'First I did this and then that.' That is not a conclusion! They also wander off in many different directions and the point of a conclusion is to pull everything together. I think I need to show them how to write conclusions. They are writing nonsense at times and yet this is a very important part of the course and the lab . . . teaching the kids some scientific skills."

Martha and Jane promised to work with David, and after the planning meeting ended, they agreed to meet after school the next day to discuss a strategy. One important point that David made was that a "good conclusion" in a lab report "should be no more than one or two sentences." They decided to begin with an assignment sheet titled "Practicing Conclusions," but they had to sort out just what David thought a conclusion was and what it contributed to a lab report. He explained, "Well, it captures the gist or the point of the whole experiment or set of observations, like when we read someone's conclusion about a political decision—what was the result?"

Jane decided that during David's first session on conclusions she would sit in on the class and see how things worked. They had decided that David would discuss conclusions with his students, review the importance of conclusions in an essay by a syndicated columnist, and then demonstrate how he would generate a conclusion based on a lab he had assigned the previous month. Below is the gist of the experiment:

> Earthworms act as nature's plows by incorporating surface plant material into the soil. They play a major role in maintaining soil fertility by recycling nutrients from the surface residues and soil structure by providing glue that holds soil particles together. Does the number of worms in the soil affect how fast surface plant material will be incorporated into the soil?

David then reviewed with the students what they had learned during the earthworm experiment. For about 30 minutes he took statements students provided, then had the students write responses to the question above as he wrote them on an overhead. He then helped the students revise them until their language was clear and their claims correctly stated. The lesson provided David and his students with a strategy for producing conclusions in future lab reports. Specifically, the sequence of activities represented a form of drafting and revising that students learned to engage in before the final form of the report was due. What seemed to be significant to David was that, as a science teacher, he was teaching his students the content and facts of biology rather than teaching the form (the job of English teachers, in his opinion). Now he had a way to teach students how to revise their conclusions before he had to review them for evaluation.

A Shared Goal: A Senior Multigenre Portfolio

As the planning group met throughout the school year, a concern developed. Many of the teachers felt dismayed by the lack of participation in the writing-to-learn activities by teachers outside of the group. Jennifer, a social studies teacher, raised the question "What's the point of spending all this time preparing material and planning writing activities if they are only used in a handful of classrooms across the school?" During Jane's student-teaching experience, she had witnessed a successful high school require a senior capstone portfolio project to be completed for graduation. Much like the multigenre project[1] (Romano, 2000) already in place in some of the senior English classrooms at TJ, the capstone project required students to write what they had learned about a topic or issue throughout their high school experience in a variety of written and expressive genres across multiple disciplines. Jennifer agreed that in order to get more teachers actively participating in the idea of writing to learn, there had to be a culminating project that would encourage teachers to get their students writing throughout the year and sharpen teachers' instructional goals in order to support their students' efforts.

Jane began developing a senior capstone project that would have students use written work from all disciplines as part of their graduation requirements. To develop a practical version of this capstone idea, Jane suggested that Deborah Meier's (1995) approach to completing a graduation portfolio would be a great starting point for TJ. Meier suggests that students submit a portfolio with fourteen different elements from various subject areas, including science and technology, second language, fine arts, mathematics, literature, and history, on topics such as autobiography, community service, ethics and social issues, mass media, and practical skills. Graduates must include written pieces for every one of the fourteen categories, and they must also complete a more extensive project in an area of particular interest, which may be one of the portfolio items explored in greater depth.

Jane argued that by introducing the senior capstone project into the school all teachers would be asked to utilize writing to learn in their classrooms as the students would need multiple pieces to choose from to aid them in the completion of their projects. The administrators supported this idea but were afraid that it might be too big a challenge to overhaul the current graduation requirements completely. The planning group members, if willing, would pilot this capstone project in their classes and work together to see what could be produced. Since most teachers in the planning group taught at least a few courses of freshmen or sophomores, the group decided to introduce the capstone project to the current freshmen

---

[1] Multigenre writing is composed of many different parts and many different genres. Each of the genres works by itself so that each is a complete piece of writing. For example, a multigenre paper could begin with a news story but include haiku, free verse, short anecdotes, dialogues, want ads, etc. The different genres in the project have the same theme or are on the same topic.

and have them complete a mini-capstone project during their sophomore year. In order to do this, more teachers of freshmen and sophomore would need to be taught how to do the project, but it would not be as difficult with administrative support. If the pilot proved to be successful, a full 4-year senior capstone project could then be put in place as a graduation requirement, with the core group offering their colleagues workshops on how better to use writing to learn in their classrooms.

Developing Writing-to-Learn Unit Plans to Support the Senior Capstone Project

The members of the planning group agreed that the easiest way to get more teachers involved in the senior capstone project would be to give them doable ideas for incorporating writing to learn in their classrooms. This became the focus of the pilot. Each of the three departments represented at the workshop came up with lists of possible writing-to-learn assignments with the help of written resources (Meier, 1995). The lists of writing assignment topics were then fleshed out into full lessons and unit plans with overarching questions so that teachers would have information to get started and could easily move into the idea of writing to learn.

Writing to Learn in English

The English teachers generated writing assignments that could be used in English courses or that could be modified for use in other disciplines. For example, Jane suggested that freshmen psychoanalyze a main character from *We All Fall Down* by Robert Cormier (1991); the assignment was phrased, "Pretend you are a psychologist and write up a case study of the character you picked to analyze." Martha included an assignment for seniors in which they had to use a modern-day character to create a parody of the Prologue to the *Canterbury Tales*. After writing the detailed parody with their modern-day characters, the students then had to post it to an online discussion board and respond to at least three other parodies online. Adrienne stated that because her ninth graders often complained about the peculiar worldview of characters in *Romeo and Juliet*, she had the idea of asking her students to consider the social world of sixteenth-century Verona, Italy. She did so by developing an assignment that asked her students to define the roles, beliefs, norms, and values constituting the characters' actions based on the students' knowledge of the historical and cultural forces shaping the Renaissance world. Using the idea of fate shaped by the alignment of the stars, a dominant theme in *Romeo and Juliet*, she was able to connect this seemingly outdated notion to modern-day astrology and horoscopes. Specifically, students were assigned to work in groups according to a sign (water, earth, air, or fire), research their signs, and then write a collaborative paper in which the personality of a main character from *Romeo and Juliet* could be understood according to the sign. In this way, the ninth graders not only studied the cultural and social setting for Shakespeare's play, but also examined the motives and purposes of key characters.

Social Studies Asks Students to Think for Themselves

In the social studies group, Jennifer came up with several questions: Does history truly repeat itself? Is terrorism always wrong? Do revolutionaries differ from terrorists or common criminals? Were the founders of the United States terrorists? Why or why not? Using one well-known historical event, students were asked to show that a similar event had occurred at some other point in history according to their research. With the question "What constitutes a terrorist versus a revolutionary?" students had to compare and contrast, then apply what they had learned by considering the actions of American revolutionaries. Sarah, also a social studies teacher, said that she had been trying to move into teaching more recent historical events whenever possible. One idea regarding the Cold War was to have students pretend to be a student in the 1960s or 1980s and write a personal essay considering whether they were confident in the president's ability to win the Cold War against the Soviet Union.

Science Connects It All

David believed that it was possible to work in a research paper on HIV when discussing how viruses evolve and become immune to certain vaccines. By asking students to research the virus, they would need to explain in writing how HIV might be spread differently within certain cultures due to social practices and interactions. Rachel, a fellow biology teacher, pointed out that, in the sciences, writing is instrumental to the development of new discoveries. One way to foster student interest prior to lab experiments was to have students leave the confines of the classroom to observe something interesting in the field. Later, their field notes could be synthesized when they were asked to summarize and analyze what they had observed. To help improve interest in a dry topic such as the components of an animal cell, Rachel used the idea of analogies and metaphors. After comparing of the workings of a cell to the functions of a high school, Rachel asked her students to create, in writing, their own metaphors for the biology of animal and plant cells.

As the group members returned to their respective departments with the activities they had shared, they hoped that the initiative would grow to include all members of each department. Each committee member scheduled a time to introduce his or her ideas at an already planned department meeting, and writing to learn in all curriculums was off to a start.

How Will Martha and Jane Know When Instruction Has Improved?

Building an effective writing program is a slow process. There is no quick cure for "the writing problem." Still, Martha, Jane, and school administrators can watch for a variety of signs of progress. As they walk the halls of their school and visit some of their colleagues' classrooms, writing will be more in evidence in all subject areas. Teachers will be talking with their classes about how to gather information or how to use what is already known in writing about a particular topic; students will be working on their own writing or discussing it with their classmates; completed writing will be evident in a variety of places, from teachers' bulletin boards to school and department websites.

At the same time, the danger signals will begin to disappear. Passing rates on statewide proficiency tests and students' performance on the writing sections should stabilize and then rise. Essay items should be in greater evidence in school examinations. Students who struggle with writing should have a writing center to go to or some other clearly established way of obtaining support. The informal comments of students and teachers should begin to shift from how bad things are to how well students seem to be writing and how comfortable it is to write in all classrooms rather than just in English language arts.

To provide a more systematic test of a school's progress toward a strong writing across the curriculum program, below is a checklist to guide the development of a schoolwide writing policy. The items are taken from the National Council of Teachers of English website Planning a Secondary Schoolwide Writing Policy Meeting the Writing Challenge to the Nation.

What Are the Characteristics of a Secondary Schoolwide Writing Policy?

____ Administrators are committed to writing and lead by example.
____ All teachers in a school are committed to teaching writing.
____ Teaching writing is an integral part of all subjects and classes.
____ Writing practices are based on current and effective research about writing.

___ Students are given time and multiple opportunities to write.
___ Teachers consistently evaluate their writing instruction.
___ Student writing is assessed in multiple ways.

What Practices Do Schools with Effective Writing Policies Follow?

Research suggests that schools that consistently develop fluent, highly competent writers follow established practices. They:

- Allocate adequate time and resources to advance student learning by having students write every day, in every subject
- Help administrators and teachers understand how to assess writing to enrich student learning
- Support teachers in gaining a sophisticated understanding of writing processes and in selecting appropriate strategies to advance every student as a writer
- Provide insights and strategies to administrators, families, and community members to help them work together to advance student writing
- Commit to building a culture of writing over time that will sustain growth and achievement through a student's academic career and beyond

How Can Teachers Start a Schoolwide Writing Program?

A writing policy will be most effective if it develops and builds on the knowledge that teachers, administrators, and other key members of the instructional teams possess. Representatives of each of these groups must be involved from the outset. Here are some key steps:

1. Provide training for all staff.
2. Audit instructional practices, support structures, and assessment procedures.
3. Evaluate the basis of writing practices. Align them with research best practices.
4. Allow time and opportunities for writing and responding to what is written.

Changing Schools/Changing Practice

Our scenario of Martha and Jane's well-orchestrated efforts to bring change to their high school suggests many of the institutional and professional constraints that they encountered and in some instances were able to overcome.

Institutional Constraints and Support

- Almost immediately, Martha and Jane had to ground their efforts in preparation for statewide proficiency tests that required students to write both brief and more extended responses to items test makers assumed high school students should be able to answer. In our scenario, they had little choice in this matter, but rather than ignoring their school administrators' demands, they leveraged test preparation into a schoolwide writing movement.
- Administrative support for Martha and Jane's efforts was critical. Without it they would not have had the opportunity to continue their writing program, and their colleagues might not have been so willing to persevere when discouraged.
- The fact that their colleagues in social studies and the sciences were concerned by content coverage made change difficult. Martha and Jane realized that a critically important step toward constructivist teaching and learning occurred only when their colleagues began to focus their attention on students' interpretations of and reasoning with subject-area content.
- Teachers were more successful when they moved away from worries of evaluation and considered their students' writing as work in progress or assignments that did not require grades.
- The portfolio evaluation of student writing will be a significant change for a large segment of the school population in that it was coupled with a senior capstone project. Although it will require more planning and instructional support, an opportunity will be created to focus on the quality of student thinking and on students' demonstration of their increasing mastery of valued ways of knowing and doing in a range of content areas.

Professional Constraints and Change

- Although the teachers were able to describe their students' writing as incoherent and recognize that their information was incorrect, they had difficulty articulating the rules of evidence and ways of arguing that they wanted their students to understand. This caused Martha and Jane a great deal of concern. They helped their colleagues shift to more constructivist ways of thinking about teaching and learning by focusing the teachers' concerns on the quality of students' thinking rather than on their reciting of correct information.

- In many cases, their colleagues seemed quite surprised that higher-level thinking skills can be taught and learned and that such instruction will look quite different from the teacher-centered transmission approaches they had developed. Put another way, Martha and Jane had to become teacher educators by applying what they had learned from their experiences as participants in a NWP site.

FINAL THOUGHTS

We began this chapter by arguing that the effective teaching of writing is an essential component of schools with programs that will help all students develop the interrelated writing, reading, and reasoning skills that are the cornerstones of thoughtful and disciplined thinking. Our hope is that practitioners will use this chapter as a means for reflecting not only on their own beliefs and assumptions, but also on the actions necessary to contribute to a professional learning community that supports both teachers and students in moving toward such a vision.

Within the student-centered, constructivist framework necessary to accomplish school reform with a writing-to-learn agenda, the teacher plays a central role, choosing the appropriate materials, providing the structures that ensure learning will take place, and helping students complete the tasks they undertake. In doing so, the teacher encourages students to take a more central role in their own learning by advancing their interpretations and opinions and checking them against their experiences and the logic of the texts from which they are expected to acquire new ideas and experiences. Such constructivist-oriented classrooms will be more complicated and less predictable than the transmission-oriented classrooms that assume an easy transfer of basic skills and knowledge. Such a change is complex—it is individual as well as social, personal as well as collective, historical as well as experimental—but we argue that it is necessary for students' personal and intellectual development and for the kind of schools that will prepare them for success in our complex technological and information-based culture.

REFERENCES

Applebee, A. N. (1981). *Writing in the secondary schools: English and the content areas.* NCTE Research Report 21. Urbana, IL: National Council of Teachers of English.

Applebee, A. N. (1984). *Contexts for learning to write.* Norwood, NJ: Ablex.

Bangert-Drowns, R. L., Hurley, M. M., & Wilkinson, B. (2004). The effects of school-based writing-to-learn interventions on academic achievement: A meta-analysis. *Review of Educational Research*. 74 (1), 29-58.

Barnes, D. (1992). *From communication to curriculum* (2nd ed.). Portsmouth, NH: Heinemann.

Boyer, E. (1983) *High school: A report on secondary education in America*. New York: Harper & Row.

Britton, J. (1970). *Language and learning*. Coral Gables, FL: University of Miami Press.

Cormier, R. (1991). *We all fall down*. New York: Delacorte Press.

Durst, R. K., & Newell, G. E. (1989). The uses of function: James Britton's category system and research on writing. *Review of Educational Research*, *59*(4), 375–394.

Easterby-Smith, M. (1990). Creating a learning organization. *Personnel Review*, *19*(5), 24–28.

Hillocks, G. (2002). *The testing trap: How state writing assessments control learning*. New York: Teachers College Press.

Langer, J. (2002). *Effective literacy instruction*. Urbana, IL: National Council of Teachers of English.

Langer, J., & Applebee, A. N. (1987). *How writing shapes thinking*. NCTE Research Report 22. Urbana, IL: National Council of Teachers of English.

Meier, D. (1995). *The power of their ideas: Lessons for America from a small school in Harlem*. Boston: Beacon Press.

Moje, E. B., & O'Brien, D. G. (Eds.). (2001). *Constructions of literacy: Studies of teaching and learning in and out of secondary school*. Mahwah, NJ: Erlbaum.

National Commission on Writing. (2003). *The neglected "R": The need for a writing revolution*. Princeton, NJ: College Entrance Examination Board.

National Council of Teachers of English. *Planning a secondary school-wide writing policy: Meeting the writing challenge to the nation. www.ncte.org/prog/writing/policy/110594.htm*

Newell, G. E. (2006). Writing to learn: How alternative theories of school writing account for student performance. In C. A. MacArthur, S. Graham, & J. Fitzgerald (Eds.), *Handbook of writing research* (pp. 235–247). New York: Guilford Press.

Pritchard, R. J., & Marshall, J. C. (2002). Do NWP teachers make a difference? Findings from research on district-led staff development. *The Quarterly. www.writingproject.org/cs/nwpp/lpt/nwpr/407*

Romano, T. (2000). *Blending genre, blending style: Writing multigenre papers*. Portsmouth, NH: Boynton/Cook Heinemann.

Sheeran, Y., & Barnes, D. (1991). *School writing: Discovering the ground rules*. Philadelphia: Open University Press.

Sizer, T. R. (1992). *Horace's school: Redesigning the American high school*. Boston: Houghton Mifflin.

Part II

~

Strategies for
Teaching and Learning

5

Writing Instruction for Young Children

Methods Targeting the Multiple Demands That Writers Face

DAVID COKER

When teachers examine the writing of a young child, they frequently focus on a single quality, such as organization, attention to genre conventions, handwriting, degree of elaboration, or spelling. A child learning to write does not have the luxury of being selective. The writing process requires that children integrate many different kinds of information from many sources.

Imagine the task for a first grader who has been asked to write about one thing she learned during a class field trip to the science museum. To make sense of the assignment, she should be aware that writing serves as a tool for communicating ideas. Even in the highly regulated context of a classroom assignment, she needs to appreciate how people use writing to share information, and she must recognize that her teacher expects her to describe the experience well enough so that someone who did not join the class would understand.

The child sorts through her memory of the event, which could include everything from the demonstration of static electricity given by the guide to the argument she had with a friend on the bus to the miraculous water faucets in the bathroom that turn on when you put your hands in the sink. From the collection of memories of the field trip, she must decide which events are relevant to the task and which ones are not. To make the decision, she might be thinking about the expectations of her reader, who is probably her teacher, who created the assignment. She also needs to choose how to frame her writing. Will she follow the generic conventions of fairytales and begin with the line "once upon a time"? Perhaps she will select the style of a newspaper and adopt a more dispassionate perspective. The decision will draw on her knowledge about how writers package and present their text.

Once she has decided how to organize the piece, she must select the right words to represent her memories. The ideas are then connected to each other and planned at the sentence level. In order to write the words, she draws on her spelling knowledge. If she has difficulty spelling any of the words, which is highly likely, she might use a common spelling strategy such as segmenting the word into its individual sounds. When the sounds are isolated, she relies on her knowledge of the alphabetic principle to select the right letter or letters to represent each sound.

Even if she has quick access to a word's spelling, she needs to be able to write the letters. If her recall of the letter shapes or the motor plans for forming letters do not operate swiftly, she may labor just inscribing the words on the page. If her handwriting demands close attention, she runs the risk of forgetting her plans for words and sentence structure. As she writes, she must follow the conventions that dictate that she print in a row from right to left and use spaces to separate words. During the entire process, she also works to maintain her attention on the writing task and to try to ignore her best friend who has just slipped her a drawing on the way to the pencil sharpener.

The previous description was intended to demonstrate that writing is an immensely complex language task. The challenges that children face as they develop into writers are substantial; however, thoughtful, responsive writing instruction can support young students and speed their growth as writers.

This chapter focuses on the writing development of children from preschool through the early elementary school years. In the first part of the chapter, I describe some of the major challenges that children face as they learn to write. These challenges include:

- Understanding how we use writing to communicate
- Unlocking the conventions or concepts of print
- Discovering that the alphabet is used to represent speech sounds
- Developing knowledge of the world and of text genres
- Writing or typing well enough to express ideas fluently

I also present instructional approaches designed to address each of these challenges. The instructional methods were selected because they are appropriate for preschool and early elementary classrooms, and they have been demonstrated to be effective. At the end of the chapter, I describe a writing lesson taught by Mrs. Nelson in her kindergarten classroom. In the context of a single lesson, Mrs. Nelson demonstrates how teachers can provide engaging instruction that addresses many of the writing challenges that students face.

There are two principle goals for this chapter. First, I hope that readers will come to appreciate the substantial challenges involved in young children's writing, particularly the confluence of skills and knowledge necessary to write well. I also hope that the instructional examples provide teachers with an understanding of some effective teaching methods to help young students develop into skillful writers. The description of the writing challenges students face as well as the instructional suggestions reflect the theoretical position that writing development is complex and can be attributed to the interplay of cognitive, social, cultural and instructional forces (Coker, 2006).

CHALLENGE 1: UNDERSTANDING HOW
WE USE WRITING TO COMMUNICATE

One essential lesson for young students is that writing is a way to share ideas and communicate. This fundamental insight about writing must be learned through experience with writing and print (Tolchinsky, 2001). Very young children learn that oral language is a symbolic system used for communication. A crucial difference between speaking and writing is that young children have considerably more experience with oral forms than they do with written forms.

By the time children enter preschool or kindergarten, they understand an enormous amount about how we use oral language to communicate. Even though nearly every preschooler knows that spoken words can serve a range of communicative functions, there are stark differences in children's language skills based on their experiences at home. One startling example of this was provided by Hart and Risley (1995), who have shown that children have vastly different early language experiences and that those experiences at home are closely related to the development of vocabulary knowledge.

Similarly, children's exposure to the uses and practices of writing and reading varies widely (Purcell-Gates, 1996). The amount and nature of exposure children have to writing and text-related practices may be related to how well they understand the way writing functions (Purcell-Gates, 1996). In one study of low-SES (socioeconomic status) students, Purcell-Gates and Dahl (1991) found that children entering first grade differed in how well they understood the uses and communicative nature of print. The differences in print understanding were related to the students' success in literacy instruction. Children who see the adults in their lives using writing in a variety of ways to express their ideas and to communicate may come to appreciate the utility of writing faster and better.

Children need to be introduced to the various ways in which we use writing to communicate in society and to gain practice using writing as a form of communication. As Wong and Berninger (2004) noted, an important instructional goal for developing writers is to learn that writing is similar to speaking because both offer ways to communicate with others. Children benefit from opportunities to see how adults use writing and to practice those forms.

In the classroom, teachers can create opportunities for students to observe and participate in authentic literacy activities through the use of thematic play areas. For example, by setting up a classroom post office where students can mail notes to each other and to others outside the classroom, teachers can create opportunities for students to use writing in a meaningful way. Other literacy-rich play areas might include a restaurant with menus and notebooks for servers to record patrons' orders. In a study of preschool literacy environments, Morrow (1990) created a veterinarian's office with a waiting room supplied with magazines and books. Students could take the roles of doctors and nurses to record the condition of the imaginary animals who were treated. In this study, teachers modeled the writing and reading behaviors commonly found in the setting, and over time children incorporated the literacy behaviors into their play.

Another effective way to increase students' participation and exposure to writing activities is to supply classrooms with a range of writing materials. Morrow (1990) found that simply adding books, bookmaking materials, and various types of paper and pens resulted in children engaging in more writing behaviors in their classroom play. In another study, students in first-grade classrooms with access to writing materials were found to write longer descriptions in first through third grades (Coker, 2006).

The understanding that writing serves a communicative function is essential for young students to grasp. Teachers who create opportunities in their classrooms for students to write may be enhancing students' awareness of the instrumental use that writing plays in society.

CHALLENGE 2: UNLOCKING THE CONVENTIONS OF PRINT

Experienced writers take their understanding of the rules of print for granted. As I drafted this chapter, I did not have to remind myself that English is written in a horizontal line, that one writes along that line from left to right, and that words are bounded by spaces; however, children are not born knowing these conventions of print. Very early in the developmental process, children benefit from specific activities designed to expose them to print and to familiarize them with the rules of text. By interacting with text, children can learn the conventions of print. In this way, reading experience can benefit children's writing knowledge. One effective approach for young children who are learning about print is to fill classrooms with books and to engage students in interactive book reading.

One crucial practice for classroom teachers is making sure that children are surrounded by many different kinds of books. Neuman (1999) demonstrated that flooding child care centers with books and training providers to engage in literacy activities can support children's engagement with print. The children who received the intervention developed their understanding of the concepts of print faster than the children who did not. Teachers also must engage in literacy activities to encourage students to interact with print.

One particularly effective practice is interactive book reading. During an interactive, or shared, book-reading lesson, the adult acts as a guide for the child. In one-on-one situations, the child and adult look at the text together, and the adult engages in a number of practices to draw attention to the content of the book and to the way that print operates. The book-reading practices involve drawing the child's attention to salient features of the text, including the print. As adults read, pointing with a finger helps illustrate the directionality of print and the way words are represented as isolated units. Good book-reading sessions involve discussion about how the illustrations contribute to the text's meaning and draw attention to new vocabulary or unusual syntax. Parent–child book reading has been identified as a powerful contributor to a range of skills, including emergent literacy skills such as name writing, letter identification, and sound blending and language skills such as vocabulary knowledge (Bus, van IJzendoorn, & Pellegrini, 1995).

Although book reading has been associated with a wide variety of literacy-related skills, not all book-reading practices are linked to student gains. Bus (2001) points out that the best book-reading practices involve drawing students into the text by making connections between the story and the children's experiences and interests.

One successful classroom adaptation of book-reading practices is dialogic reading (Whitehurst, Crone, Schultz, Velting, & Fischel, 1999). The dialogic reading intervention aims to engage students in the reading process by having them assume the role of the storyteller. Teachers using dialogic reading follow the child's storytelling efforts closely and prompt the child with questions. For very young children, questions that teachers pose relate directly to the story, such as asking them to describe what a character is doing or to identify something in an illustration. For preschoolers, the questions are designed to be more complex, to encourage students to think about the overall story. The more challenging questions encourage children to make connections between the text and their lives. For example, a teacher might ask if a child has ever experienced something that happened in the book. Dialogic reading has been found to have a positive impact on language skills such as vocabulary as well as a range of emergent literacy skills. In particular, the intervention was related to positive effects in children's knowledge of several print conventions including identification of the print, directionality of print, and the mechanics of writing (Whitehurst et al., 1999).

Another way that teachers modify the book-reading practice for the classroom is through the use of big books. These oversized books are typically propped on an easel or stand where all students can see them. During the session, the teacher models the reading practice by pointing to highlight the features of print such as directionality, spaces between words, and the relationship between words and the story. Big books have also been found to be effective when students can follow along in their own copies of the text. When teachers model reading behaviors with a big book as students follow along in their own copies, students have the opportunity to handle the book and track print themselves.

Modeling the writing process with young students also provides teachers with the opportunity to highlight important print conventions. As teachers compose on a large flip chart or chalkboard, children observe how writers do things like separate words with spaces and write from left to right. Wong and Berninger (2004) recommend daily teacher modeling of writing to underscore the relationship between sounds and letter patterns, to demonstrate how writing is used for communicative purposes, and to practice spelling. By engaging students in print and modeling writing behaviors, teachers can facilitate students' understanding of the conventions of written language.

CHALLENGE 3: DISCOVERING THAT THE ALPHABET IS USED TO REPRESENT SPEECH SOUNDS

An important insight that children make as their understanding of the writing system expands is that print represents the sounds of language.

In their work with Argentinean preschoolers, Ferreiro and Teberosky (1979) found that children frequently believed the length of a word was related to the size of the object it named. For example, they interviewed children who reported that the word for *bear* must be bigger than the word for *duck* because a bear is so much larger than a duck. As children's experience with print grows and they begin to understand that letters represent the sounds in words, they gradually abandon theories that do not successfully account for the way print operates.

In English, knowing the names of letters may provide children with an important source of knowledge about the relationship between oral language and the alphabet. Since many 4- and 5-year-olds can recite the alphabet and can match letters with their names, Treiman, Tincoff, and Richmond-Welty (1996) examined whether children use their letter knowledge in their spelling attempts. The relevance of letter names to children's spelling was assessed in a study that compared the spellings of words that begin with the same letter. Students spelled a series of word pairs. One word in each pair began with the sound that matched the letter name, and the other member of each pair began with a sound that did not match the letter name. For the letter *b* the words *beaver* and *bone* were contrasted. *Beaver* begins with a sound that matches the name of the letter, but *bone* does not. Words that began with sounds matching the letter were spelled more accurately. The results suggested that letter-name knowledge may offer children insight into the way the alphabet works. There are a variety of effective methods that teachers can use to enhance young children's letter knowledge.

Frequently, children learn their first letters through their own names. For many young children, their name is the earliest word they recognize, primarily because it is familiar and meaningful (Bloodgood, 1999; Clay, 1975). The importance of names to children often results in their learning to write their names before other words and learning the letters in their names before other letters. As children practice writing and spelling their names, they gain experience matching letters to sounds. Having a stable relationship between the graphic and phonological form of a name provides children with key insight into how writing works.

Writing instruction can capitalize on children's interest in their names by providing opportunities for children to print their names. Once children can write and spell their names fairly well, teachers can make connections between the initial sounds in the name and other words. For example, a teacher might ask 3-year-old Tobias how to spell *table*. If he were unsure, she could make the connection to his name explicit and encourage him to compare the initial sounds of *table* and *Tobias*. Knowing that his name begins with a *t*, he may listen to *table* and realize that it begins with the same sound.

Drawing on children's interest in and knowledge about their names offers one instructional approach to the challenge of linking sounds to letters, which is known as the alphabetic principle. Many children learn some letters through the spontaneous analysis of their own names supported by their parents or teachers, but explicit instruction is also important to ensure that young children know all the letters in the alphabet.

In many preschool classes, teachers engage in a wide range of activities to teach children the alphabet, such as the alphabet song. Teachers also post the letters in the classroom and refer to them at meaningful moments. During book reading, teachers may draw students' attention to specific letters that are prominent in the text.

Another successful way to teach children the alphabet is through the use of mnemonic clues. Ehri and Roberts (2006) reviewed several approaches and concluded that pairing an illustrated mnemonic with letter sounds was effective. The technique involves having a character for each letter, such as Polly Parrot for the letter p. When the letter is taught, children are shown an illustration that integrates the shape of the letter with the character. This pairing is designed to boost children's memory of the letters and the sounds connected to the letters. Although teachers can create their own characters for each letter, there are commercial programs on the market that utilize this approach (Ehri & Roberts, 2006).

Another effective approach to learning the relationships between sounds and letters involves drawing students' attention to individual sounds in words (phonemes) and practicing writing letters (Berninger et al., 1998). One goal of this intervention is to teach students that sound-to-letter relationships often involve more than one letter. Berninger and her colleagues (2002) have pointed out that when children receive phonics instruction in the context of learning to read, the lessons often target the relationship between single letters and sounds. Little attention is usually devoted to the role played by multiletter spelling units. When children attempt to spell words by applying phonics knowledge in the reverse direction, they tend to look for single letters to represent single sounds. For students operating with this assumption, spelling words with vowel teams or digraphs can be frustrating. In order to avoid this confusion, Wong and Berninger (2004) recommend explicit instruction on the relationship between phonemes and functional spelling units. As children learn how these functional spelling units represent sounds in words, their spelling skill has been shown to improve (Berninger et al., 1998). In addition, phonics instruction is recommended that proceeds from the phoneme to the grapheme so that it is directly transferable to the spelling process.

The explicit instructional programs described above use a coordinated, systematic plan to introduce students to the alphabetic principle.

Students also benefit from the opportunity to practice with the spelling system as they write on their own (Tolchinsky, 2001). Students' attempts at conventional spelling have been called *invented spelling*. Practice with invented spelling has been shown to promote spelling development because it allows children to test and refine their theories of how the writing system represents sounds (Tolchinsky, 2001).

Encouraging invented spelling can play an important role in fostering spelling knowledge. In fact, the linguist Charles Read, who first wrote about the importance of children's invented spelling, encouraged teachers and parents to foster a positive attitude toward invented spelling and writing in general (Read, 1986). In addition to remaining open to children's experiments with spelling, teachers also can use students' writing to gauge their level of spelling knowledge and to tailor instruction to fit their needs. Before teachers can do either of these things successfully, they must understand the underlying logic behind invented spellings.

As Read (1986) has pointed out, "children's beginning spelling is essentially phonetic" (p. 1). When children know enough about the writing system to map letters onto sounds, they frequently make spelling mistakes based on the sounds of words. This can be seen when kindergartner Michelle spells *wrecking* as RIKING. The silent *w* is absent and the short *e* is spelled with an *i*. Since the vowel sound in *wrecking* sounds more like *i* than it does *e*, Michelle's error is understandable.

Teachers will profit from an understanding that unconventional spelling patterns often reflect students' burgeoning knowledge of the alphabetic principle. One example of this is Michelle using an *i* to spell the short-*e* sound in *wrecking*. Once teachers can analyze spelling mistakes, they can design instruction that addresses the particular point of confusion. Spelling development for many students follows a sequence that begins with initial consonant sounds and moves through vowel sounds, consonant and vowel letter combinations, and spelling patterns based on word derivations (Bear, Invernizzi, Templeton, & Johnston, 2003). Spelling instruction, such as word study, that is sensitive to students' developmental level and provides opportunities for students to work with orthographic patterns has been found to be effective (Bear et al., 2003; see Schlagal, Chapter 9, this volume, for a discussion of spelling).

CHALLENGE 4: WRITING OR TYPING WELL ENOUGH TO EXPRESS IDEAS FLUENTLY

In many kindergarten and first-grade classrooms, handwriting instruction is nonexistent. Based on their experiences as students, many teachers believe that the sole function of handwriting lessons is to improve the appearance of printing or cursive. Furthermore, with personal computers widely available, very few important documents are handwritten any more. In some schools, primary-grade children receive instruction in keyboarding; however, these lessons are not widely offered.

Despite the assumption that handwriting does not affect writing quality, research on handwriting and composition quality suggests it may be very important. In one study of handwriting, Graham, Berninger, Abbott, Abbott, and Whitaker (1997) examined the impact of handwriting on both the quality and the production of text. For students in the primary grades, handwriting measures were related to both the quality and the compositional fluency of their writing. As children write, they must manage several tasks at once. During the composition process, a number of things need to be considered, including the topic, the structure of the piece, and the words to be selected as well as other concerns such as spelling. If handwriting is difficult and requires considerable effort, the child may not have enough resources to develop the ideas well, write in complete sentences, or determine the correct spelling of words. Children whose handwriting is fluid and automatic are able to transfer their ideas onto paper without experiencing an information bottleneck. From this perspective, handwriting is a low-level process that must be accomplished quickly and efficiently so that higher-level tasks can receive attention.

Based on their research, Berninger and Richards (2002) made several recommendations for successful handwriting instruction. First, teachers should adopt explicit methods and limit lessons and practice to brief periods of only 5–10 minutes. They also recommended that opportunities to write connected text follow handwriting instruction. Opportunities to write after handwriting instruction are designed to help children transfer their handwriting to the authentic writing task. The sequence of instruction should begin with attention to the formation of the letters. Once letters can be produced with reasonable accuracy, instruction should target automatic production of letters (see Schalagal, Chapter 9, this volume, for a discussion of spelling).

Berninger's (1998) instructional method begins with attention to manuscript letters. The intervention combines attention to the physical formation of the letters with the higher-order task of writing. Although cursive letters were traditionally taught sometime around third grade, Berninger and Richards (2002) suggest that instruction in keyboarding skills may be of greater value and should begin by first grade. (It is not clear whether keyboarding instruction should be initiated *before* first grade.)

CHALLENGE 5: DEVELOPING KNOWLEDGE
OF THE WORLD AND OF TEXT GENRES

In order for writing to be a meaningful activity for children, they must have something to say. Children come to school with personal experiences that can vary widely, from participating at a county fair to watching cartoons and talk shows on television to attending a ballet production. As teachers search for writing lessons that tap this vast range of experiences, they learn that few activities are equally engaging for all students. One solution to the problem of uneven background knowledge is the personal story. One reason many teachers focus on the personal narrative (sometimes called the *bed-to-bed story*) is that all children have relevant background knowledge. Teachers know that most children can write about some event or sequence of events in their lives, even is it is just the morning classroom routine. While the personal narrative offers many opportunities to practice a wide range of important writing skills, students also need practice with other kinds of writing.

Given opportunities and exposure to print and texts, children will explore their ideas and produce a broad range of texts spontaneously (Bissex, 1980). When children come to school without having experienced a wide range of ideas or kinds of writing, teachers can enhance their background knowledge by exposing them to different ideas and texts. Even students like Bissex's son Paul, whose home offered many opportunities to engage with print, depend on teachers to broaden their understanding of the world and the world of text.

A time-honored method of introducing children to the ideas and language used in books is reading aloud. As discussed earlier, read-alouds can be instrumental in highlighting the conventions of print, although typically children are more attracted to the stories than to the instructional possibilities. The primary draw of hearing books is the delight experienced through a new and possibly unimagined world. As children delight in the text, they may experience contexts, learn new words, and expand their understanding of the world.

Although children's fiction has been the mainstay of preschool and elementary school classrooms, children also need to hear other kinds of books. By choosing text that addresses topics related to classroom lessons, teachers can develop students' background knowledge in ways that will support their engagement in lessons as well as their ability to write about specific topics.

Children's genre knowledge can benefit from exposure to a wide variety of books. Early understandings of the conventions of stories and various informational texts draw heavily on oral language experiences. As early as kindergarten, children demonstrate an awareness that texts differ depending on their purpose (Donovan & Smolkin, 2006). For most students in kindergarten or the early primary grades, genre knowledge is nascent. In order to apply genre conventions to their own writing, students need more exposure to the varieties of texts that will be important later in their lives. Although the research on the impact of genre instruction is thin, there is support for surrounding students with a variety of different types of books. One study found a positive relationship between the range of text genres in the first-grade classroom library and students' writing growth through third grade (Coker, 2006).

Providing students with ready exposure to all types of print is important for their developing genre knowledge. Principals and teachers should work to stock classroom libraries with books of all types. It is important to integrate all these types of books into the curriculum. Teachers who discuss the classroom books in their lessons may find that students are more motivated to explore new kinds of books.

The practice of reading a variety of books to children has been shown to support their acquisition of genre knowledge (Donovan & Smolkin, 2006). As genre knowledge grows, so does children's ability to apply that knowledge to their own writing.

AN ILLUSTRATION OF INSTRUCTION

When writing instruction is most productive, it addresses a range of skills and practices relevant for good writing. Of course, not all lessons can target every important aspect of writing, but in many lessons teachers can address more than one facet of it. The following lesson from Mrs. Nelson's kindergarten classroom illustrates how instruction can provide direction and practice in many of the important challenges that young writers face.

In her kindergarten classroom, Mrs. Nelson devotes 45 minutes to writing workshop nearly every day. Often the writing lessons and activities build on topics from other parts of the curriculum. Mrs. Nelson planned this lesson around the class's science unit that focused on endangered animals. She leveraged the students' interest in the material to engage her kindergarteners in multiple aspects of writing.

Mrs. Nelson began the lesson by calling the children to the carpet. When they were seated and quiet, she began the lesson.

MRS. NELSON: Today I want you to do something good writers do. Sometimes good writers use lots of detail, but sometimes it's done to make a quick point. Who's seen lots of advertisements for McDonald's, or Coke? How many of you have seen them with a million words?

(*Many students raise their hands.*)

MRS. NELSON: I haven't seen one. Could you read a Junie B. Jones book on a sign as you're going down the road?

STUDENT: Too quick.

MRS. NELSON: So you need something quick [for an advertisement]. You see "Drink Coke." The author's not saying it's a sweet brown liquid, it bubbles, and all those details. They want you to know "Drink Coke." How many of you have seen the commercials for milk with famous people? They say, "Got Milk?" What did the author want you to know?

STUDENTS: [Multiple responses.]

MRS. NELSON: All they needed to say was "Do you have milk?" Today, you're going to have some fun making a simple sign that's going to get to the point about saving the Earth. Think about what bothers you with the Earth. Who wants to give me an example of what bothers them?

STUDENT: [En]dangered animals.

MRS. NELSON: Give me an example.

STUDENT: Stop making animals endangered.

MRS. NELSON: Others?

STUDENT: Let animals cross the street?

MRS. NELSON: How about "Leave trees alone"? I'll give you a big piece of posterboard. First, write your message, and not in teeny-weeny letters. When you're going down the road and you see a sign (*writes in small letters on board*), is that going to catch your attention?

STUDENTS: No.

MRS. NELSON: You're going to write it to grab the attention of the kids in the hall. Watch this (*writes something very small*). Can you read that? Anyone having trouble reading that?

STUDENTS: [Various responses.]

MRS. NELSON: You're going to put big words on your poster, like is. (*Writes "Save animals" very large on the board.*)

STUDENT: As big as a school?

MRS. NELSON: Well, if it's as big as a school, it won't fit on the posterboard. Usually someone doing a commercial also uses an illustration to grab your eyes, or sometimes a fancy border. I want you to make a sign that makes kids stop and think. Today, you're going to work on the floor because the poster is big. I want to see lots of detail in your drawing (not your writing), colors, and I want to see you make your point. I'm going to take the really good ones and hang them all over the school. If you're wearing red, get a coffee can and pick a spot. [Mrs. Nelson uses metal coffee cans to store pencils, pens, markers, and other writing materials for students.]

In the course of her brief lesson, Mrs. Nelson was able to highlight multiple characteristics of the writing system that are important to young writers. Her lesson referenced the communicative function of written language, the conventional arrangement of print, the relationship between speech sounds and written words, and the importance of background knowledge as well as genre knowledge. Even though she spent relatively little time on each point, her lesson was designed to draw students' attention to these challenges.

At the beginning of her discussion, Mrs. Nelson reminded students of their experience with the form of writing that was the focus of the lesson—signs. She knew the students were familiar with advertising signs, so she led a discussion about the communicative function of signs. A unique feature of signs is that they are designed to communicate a single idea. As she explained to the class, "Sometimes good writers use a lot of detail, but sometimes it's done to make a quick point."

The discussion of signs also underscored the understanding that people write to communicate. Mrs. Nelson made this point particularly salient by referencing a written form that children have experienced outside of the classroom. For the students who have read and thought about roadside signs, Mrs. Nelson may be subtly signaling that writing has an important communicative function in their lives outside of school just as it does in school.

After a discussion of the conventions of signs, she encouraged students to create their own signs. The activity was designed to allow students to express their views about the importance of protecting the environment. From their science unit, the children understood that the natural world was threatened by humans, and they were making signs that would function like billboards. Messages such as "Save the animals" or "Stop wrecking habitats" were designed to change people's behavior. Mrs. Nelson explained that she would post the signs around the school so that other students could read them. One implicit message in this lesson was that students could use written signs as a way to express their ideas. Furthermore, the ideas that students expressed would be displayed, just like signs are along the road. Not only will the kindergartners share their ideas through the signs, but they may also be able to change people's behavior. In this lesson, students experienced writing as a tool to share ideas and potentially influence behavior.

During her mini-lesson, Mrs. Nelson discussed the conventions of signs and modeled how to make one. After explaining that signs need to be brief so they can be read quickly, she also added that the letters should be big. She then wrote her message on the board in big letters, modeling for students the process of forming the letters and arranging the words. In this example, Mrs. Nelson did not discuss how she wrote from left to right and left spaces between words; she might have done so if she thought it would benefit the students. Instead she modeled the way to write words on a sign, giving students an opportunity to see how a writer composes text.

After her mini-lesson on signs, Mrs. Nelson walked around the room monitoring the children's progress and having brief conferences with them. When she asked Michelle what she was planning to write, the following exchange occurred:

MICHELLE: Stop wrecking.

MRS. NELSON: That's a good one. Maybe you can start right here. (*Points to a spot on the paper for Michelle to begin writing. Michelle writes* Stop *and then pauses.*)

MRS. NELSON: What vowel is it?

MICHELLE: *a?*

MRS. NELSON: Wr-e-cking (*Stretches the word out for Michelle*). Stop wr-e-cking, wr-e-cking. (*Says the word several more times, stretching out the vowel sound.*)

MICHELLE: (*Writes* riking.) Stop wrecking habitats.

MRS. NELSON: Habitats, that's even better.

In this exchange, Mrs. Nelson helped Michelle with a difficult vowel sound by stretching the word out. After Michelle produced a word that reflected the sounds in *wrecking*, Mrs. Nelson complimented her and moved on. The goal of the lesson had been met even though Michelle still has a lot to learn about conventional spelling.

In Mrs. Nelson's writing lesson, students composed signs based on their study of endangered animals. During that unit, Mrs. Nelson had used a wide range of books that provided scientific information about animals, their habitats, and the wider ecological system. By including nonfiction books in her unit, Mrs. Nelson helped enrich students' background knowledge about endangered animals and the reasons for their declining numbers. It seems unlikely that children would acquire this kind of scientific information without access to nonfiction books.

The lesson on writing signs about endangered animals also made many of the characteristics of the sign genre explicit. At the beginning of the discussion, Mrs. Nelson asked the class how many students had "seen a sign with a million words." She used the question and the students' responses to describe one of the defining features of signs: their brevity. An example she introduced was the "Got Milk?" campaign because the message is distilled into only two words. Mrs. Nelson's point was that good writers understand the structure of signs, and, as a result, the message must be expressed as succinctly as possible.

Another benefit of the sign-writing activity is the development of students' understanding about the kinds of information that writers need. First, writers need to have knowledge about the topic (in this case, endangered animals). Through their science lessons and read-alouds, the students had learned about the topics surrounding this issue. Now as sign writers they could draw on that knowledge. For their signs to be persuasive, students also were taught that they need to know how signs work. This understanding of the features of the sign genre coupled with background knowledge about the issues made it possible for them to write something that could change people's ideas about saving the Earth.

CONCLUSION

For young children to develop into accomplished writers, they must learn to manage the substantial challenges of writing. By supporting their acquisition of writing processes and knowledge, teachers can guide students to deepen their understanding of writing. Many of the instructional methods described in this chapter detail ways to expose children to specific aspects of the writing system or process. Some of the recommendations made in this chapter have the potential to enhance more than one area of students' writing knowledge. For example, the use of book-reading interventions can enhance background knowledge, conventions of print, and the understanding that writing is a communicative act.

It is also important to note that by themselves these approaches will only have a limited effect on children's writing development. Children also need to write on a daily basis. As Tolchinsky (2001) asserted, "it is by being exposed to writing and by using writing that children will learn to master it" (p. 95). The tasks of writing about a field trip to the science museum or of creating a sign about endangered animals have real value for young children. These challenges offer opportunities for children to experiment with the writing system and to generate and refine their notions of how writing works.

REFERENCES

Bear, D. R., Invernizzi, M., Templeton, S., & Johnston, F. (2003). *Words their way: Word study for phonics, vocabulary and spelling instruction.* Upper Saddle River, NJ: Prentice Hall.

Berninger, V. W. (1998). *Process assessment of the learner: Guides for reading and writing interventions.* San Antonio, TX: The Psychological Corporation.

Berninger, V. W., & Richards, T. L. (2002). *Brain literacy for educators and psychologists.* London: Academic Press.

Berninger, V. W., Vaughan, K., Abbott, R. D., Begay, K., Coleman, K. B., Curtin, G., et al. (2002). Teaching spelling and composition alone and together: Implications for the simple view of writing. *Journal of Educational Psychology,* 94(2), 291–304.

Berninger, V. W., Vaughan, K., Abbott, R. D., Brooks, A., Abbott, S. P., Rogan, L., et al. (1998). Early intervention for spelling problems: Teaching functional spelling units of varying size with a multiple-connections framework. *Journal of Educational Psychology,* 90(4), 587–605.

Bissex, G. L. (1980). *Gnys at wrk: A child learns to write and read.* Cambridge, MA: Harvard University Press.

Bloodgood, J. W. (1999). What's in a name? Children's name writing and literacy acquisition. *Reading Research Quarterly,* 34(3), 342–367.

Bus, A. G. (2001). Joint caregiver–child storybook reading: A route to literacy development. In S. B. Neuman & D. K. Dickinson (Eds.), *Handbook of early literacy research, Volume 1* (pp. 179–191). New York: Guilford Press.

Bus, A. G., van IJzendoorn, M. H., & Pellegrini, A. D. (1995). Joint book reading makes for success in learning to read: A meta-analysis on intergenerational transmission of literacy. *Review of Educational Research,* 65(1), 1–21.

Clay, M. M. (1975). *What did I write?* Auckland, New Zealand: Heinemann.

Coker, D. (2006). The impact of first-grade factors on the growth and outcomes of urban schoolchildren's primary-grade writing. *Journal of Educational Psychology,* 98, 471–488.

Donovan, C. A., & Smolkin, L. B. (2006). Children's understanding of genre and writing development. In C. A. MacArthur, S. Graham, & J. Fitzgerald (Eds.), *Handbook of writing research* (pp. 131–143). New York: Guilford Press.

Ehri, L. C., & Roberts, T. (2006). The roots of learning to read and write: Acquisition of letters and phonemic awareness. In D. K. Dickinson & S. B. Neuman (Eds.), *Handbook of early literacy research, Volume 2* (pp. 113–131). New York: Guilford Press.

Ferreiro, E., & Teberosky, A. (1979). *Literacy before schooling* (K. G. Castro, Trans.). Portsmouth, NH: Heinemann.

Graham, S., Berninger, V. W., Abbott, R. D., Abbott, S. P., & Whitaker, D. (1997). Role of mechanics in composing of elementary school students: A new methodological approach. *Journal of Educational Psychology,* 89(1), 170–182.

Hart, B., & Risley, T. (1995). *Meaningful differences in the everyday experience of young American children*. Baltimore: Brookes.

Morrow, L. M. (1990). Preparing the classroom environment to promote literacy during play. *Early Childhood Research Quarterly, 5*, 537–554.

Neuman, S. B. (1999). Books make a difference: A study of access to literacy. *Reading Research Quarterly, 34*(3), 286–311.

Purcell-Gates, V. (1996). Stories, coupons, and the TV: Relationships between home literacy experiences and emergent literacy knowledge. *Reading Research Quarterly, 31*, 406–428.

Purcell-Gates, V., & Dahl, K. L. (1991). Low-SES children's success and failure at early literacy learning in a skills-based classroom. *Journal of Reading Behavior, 23*(1), 1–34.

Read, C. (1986). *Children's creative spelling*. London: Routledge & Kegan Paul.

Tolchinsky, L. (2001). *The cradle of culture and what children know about writing and numbers before being taught*. Mahwah, NJ: Erlbaum.

Treiman, R., Tincoff, R., & Richmond-Welty, E. D. (1996). Letter names help children to connect print and speech. *Developmental Psychology, 32*(3), 505–514.

Whitehurst, G. J., Zevenbergen, A. A., Crone, D. A., Schultz, M. D., Velting, O. N., & Fischel, J. E. (1999). Outcomes of an emergent literacy intervention from Head Start through second grade. *Journal of Educational Psychology, 91*, 261–272.

Wong, B. Y. L., & Berninger, V. W. (2004). Cognitive processes of teachers in implementing composition research in elementary, middle, and high school classrooms. In C. A. Stone, E. R. Silliman, B. J. Ehren, & K. Apel (Eds.), *Handbook of language and literacy: Development and disorders* (pp. 600–624). New York: Guilford Press.

6

Best Practices in
Teaching Planning

STEVE GRAHAM *and*
KAREN R. HARRIS

Good writing is demanding for novices and for professional writers. The writer Stephen Lealock captured the challenging nature of this task, noting, "Writing is no trouble, just jot down ideas as they occur to you. The jotting is simplicity itself—it is the occurring which is difficult" (Phillips, 1993, p. 338). Even a book as seemingly simple as *Cat in the Hat* took over a year to write, with Dr. Seuss complaining that every sentence was "like pangs of birth" (Brodie, 1997, p. 78).

Children also recognize the challenging nature of writing, and their explanations of why writing is difficult range from amusing to insightful. One youngster told us that children have difficulty writing because "they don't know where the pencil sharpener is." Another blamed such difficulties on "having a fake hand." The responses of other children focused on the problems of getting language on to paper: "They don't know how to spell words" or "they can't write straight." Still others identified planning and generating content as the culprits: "They don't think before they write" or "they can only think of a teeny-tiny story or just one sentence." Other children blamed poor teaching: "Some kids don't know how to write because they have never been taught how to write."

Even though writing is a demanding task, it is not an impossible one. Many youngsters become excellent writers, with some pursuing careers as professional writers. Too many children, however, experience difficulty learning to write. The most recent data from nationwide evaluations of students' literacy progress shows that three out of every four children achieve only partial mastery of the writing skills they need at their respective grade levels (Persky, Danne, & Jin, 2003). These students would likely empathize with Charlie Brown, the popular character in the *Peanuts* comic strip, who tells his pen pal, "Some days I feel like I'm writing uphill."

In this chapter, we tackle one part of the learning-to-write puzzle: how to enhance the process of planning in writing. The basic assumptions underlying this goal are that planning is an important part of skilled writing, developing writers plan infrequently or ineffectively, and efforts to enhance planning behavior can have a positive impact.

PLANNING IS IMPORTANT

Although there is much variety in how skilled writers go about the process of composing text, planning plays a central role in the writing of many successful authors. For example, while riding a train through the English countryside, the basic idea for a boy and the wizard school he attended popped into the mind of J. K. Rowling, creator of the *Harry Potter* series. Over the next several months, she invested every free moment planning the first book, jotting down ideas and stories about this magical boy. She plotted out other books in the series, too, "figuring out the story lines, the specific elements of each adventure, and the important message that readers young and old would take away from each book" (Shapiro, 2000, p. 87).

Planning is not just the domain of professional writers. College students spend about one fourth of their writing time planning, whereas business executives may devote two thirds of their writing time to this process (see Graham & Harris, 2000). Creating a written plan in advance of writing can be especially advantageous because it provides an external memory, where ideas can be stored without the risk of losing them and are readily available for inspection, reflection, and reconceptualization. Planning in advance can reduce the need to plan while writing, freeing needed resources to engage in other processes that demand attention, such as turning ideas into well-crafted sentences.

MANY DEVELOPING WRITERS MINIMIZE
THE ROLE OF PLANNING IN THEIR WRITING

Some of the youngsters that we have interviewed over the years made it clear that they recognize that planning is a critical element of good writing. When asked what good writers do, one third grader told us, "They take their time to think about it." Another student indicated, "They think first, then write a little down, then they think again, then write a little more, then they finally get the whole idea." Other students, however, appeared to be confused about the concept of planning, defining it as "writing with a pencil," "writing my neatest," or "trying your best and doing it." Finally, some students described creative but generally ineffective ways of planning. One young man told us, "Write big so that it takes up more space."

Many developing writers employ an approach to composing that minimizes the role of planning (Scardamalia & Bereiter, 1986). They start writing with little or no forethought (less than 1 minute, even when prompted to plan in advance), generating ideas on the fly as they write. This approach is illustrated in one of our favorite *Peanuts* cartoons, where a disheveled Peppermint Patty shares her paper with the class: "Wind blows your hair around when you're walking to school, and after you get there you don't have a comb. It also gives you something to write about when you can't think of anything else, and you can't see what you're reading."

Although this approach to writing (knowledge telling) is used at times by everyone (e.g., when you write a note to another person letting him or her know where you are going), it is not an effective strategy for many types of writing, such as reports, essays, or stories. These tasks typically require more than just generating or retrieving ideas as you go. A good story includes a plot, is organized in a logical manner, and must capture the interest of the intended audience. These elements are more likely to be realized when forethought, planning, and reflection are part of the process (Graham & Harris, 2005).

ENHANCING DEVELOPING WRITERS' PLANNING
BEHAVIORS IMPROVES STUDENTS' WRITING

Louis L'Amour, a prolific writer of western novels, advised that "A writer's brain is like a magician's hat. If you're going to get anything out of it, you have to put something in first" (L'Amour, 1990, p. 62). While there are many things the developing writer's brain needs, knowing how to plan is one of the most important. This was demonstrated in a recent review Dolores Perin and I (Steve Graham) completed (Graham & Perin, 2006; also see Perin, Chapter 12, this volume). We examined the effectiveness of a variety of procedures for teaching writing to students in grades 4–12. Three of the interventions specifically involved instruction designed to facilitate or enhance students' planning when writing. For each of these interventions, we calculated an average weighted effect size (averaged across studies and weighted for the number of students in each study) that provided an indication of the strength of each method. An effect size of 0.2 is considered small, 0.5 moderate, and 0.8 large.

Two of the interventions involved providing students with some form of support in carrying out one or more aspects of planning. One of these, *prewriting*, involved engaging students in activities designed to help them generate and/or organize ideas for writing. These activities took place before students composed their first draft. They included procedures such as brainstorming ideas, organizing ideas using a semantic web, reading to locate ideas, and briefly demonstrating how to plan in advance. The second method, *inquiry*, involved engaging students in activities that helped them develop ideas and content for a particular writing task through the processes of question formulation, observation, and analysis. For example, students might generate some questions and hypotheses about peer interactions, observe how their peers interact, draw inferences about these interactions in light of their questions, and share what they learned in a written report. Both of these approaches had a small but positive effect (effect size = 0.32 for both interventions) on the quality of students' writing.

The third intervention, *strategy instruction*, involved explicitly teaching students strategies for planning, revising, or both. To illustrate, in a study by De La Paz and Graham (1997), students in grades 5–7 were taught how to plan a persuasive essay by analyzing both sides of a controversy as well as generating, evaluating, and organizing possible writing ideas in advance of writing. These planning strategies were described, the rationale of each was discussed, the teacher modeled their use, and students practiced until they could apply them on their own. Providing such instruction had a powerful effect on the quality of students' writing. When we looked only at studies that focused on strategy instruction for planning, the average effect size was large (1.03).

We would like to draw one important but subtle distinction between strategy instruction and the other two approaches, prewriting and inquiry. With strategy instruction, the goal is student mastery or independent use of the planning processes targeted. It is assumed that once students have mastered these processes through explicit instruction, they will value them and continue to use them. Mastery of the processes involved in planning is more indirect with the other two approaches. It is assumed, for example, that students will acquire important knowledge about planning as a result of repeatedly using a prewriting graphic organizer or through the structure the teacher provides in an inquiry activity. It is further assumed that students will come to value this knowledge and apply it on their own. Each of these approaches (strategy instruction versus prewriting and inquiry) has the same goal, but they employ somewhat different methods for achieving them.

SO WHAT ARE BEST PRACTICES
FOR PLANNING INSTRUCTION?

In the following sections, we lay out some general guidelines for increasing the likelihood that students will engage in planning when writing. We then examine the use of prewriting activities, inquiry, and strategy instruction as means for facilitating and enhancing students' planning for writing. We devote most of our attention to planning strategy instruction, since it is a more powerful approach to improving the quality of students' writing (Graham & Perin, 2006).

Create an Atmosphere That Supports Students' Planning

Value, Expect, and Encourage Planning

A basic goal in helping developing writers become good planners is to create a writing environment in which planning is valued. Students need to know why planning is important, how it helps the writer, and when to use it. These points can be introduced through whole-class discussion and reiterated frequently, with students being asked to explain each point, including that planning should occur both before and during writing.

It is important that planning become a predictable part of students' writing. One obvious means for promoting this goal is to establish a predictable classroom writing routine, where students plan as well as draft, revise, edit, and publish their work. Planning can be further reinforced during writing conferences by asking students to describe how they intend to plan an upcoming paper or what planning has already occurred for a work in progress.

Planning is also more likely to flourish if it is given proper encouragement. One way to encourage students to plan is by praising noteworthy planning behavior. Such praise should specifically identify the noteworthy behavior (e.g., "What a great idea; you plan to tell your story from the point of view of the rats in the story of the Pied Piper") and why it is praiseworthy (e.g., "This will certainly make your story different and interesting."). Another means for encouraging planning behavior is to ask students to keep notes on how they planned a series of papers, with the goal of identifying which planning strategies were most useful and why.

Authentic and Engaging Writing Tasks

When students do not value writing or a specific writing task, they may exert as little effort as possible to complete it (Graham & Harris, 1997). This lack of effort is illustrated in the letter below, written to a sick classmate (Cosby, 1998, p. 15):

> Dear Erika:
>   I hope you get well soon.
>   Mrs. Dickey forced us to write this letter.
>   So I am not writing it because I like you.
>   Your friend,
>   Leon

This child's tactic was simply to get the job done as quickly and easily as possible. He did little planning because he had little investment in or regard for the task.

One way to avoid such apathy (and increase the likelihood that students will engage in planning) is to involve students in writing activities that are authentic and aimed at a real audience. They are much more likely to plan if they value the writing task. This was evident in a classroom we observed a couple of years ago. The class had taken on the task of cleaning up a local stream. As a part of this effort, they wrote letters to the mayor, city council members, other influential citizens, and local newspapers. They further wrote a proposal for and obtained a grant from the city government to help them clean up the stream. The youngsters were highly committed to this project, and it showed in how they acted and wrote. They were self-directed, doing most of the work with little teacher direction. They spent a considerable amount of time planning each written product, considering what they wanted to accomplish, what they needed to say, and how it needed to be pitched to the intended audience.

Supportive Writing Environment

Another way to increase the likelihood that students will plan their writing is to create a classroom environment that is supportive, pleasant, and nonthreatening. Children are less likely to exert the effort needed to plan if they view the classroom as an unfriendly, chaotic, or punitive place (Graham & Harris, 1997). Although some students are able to overcome such barriers, others evidence a mental withdrawal or evasion of productive work in these situations. Listed below are some things that can be done to create a supportive classroom environment:

Create a setting in which students feel free to take risks when writing.

Establish an exciting mood during the writing period.

Provide opportunities for students to arrange their own writing space.

Allow students to modify assigned writing topics and select their own topics.

Encourage students to help each other with specific aspects of their writing.

Ask students to share works in progress and completed papers with each other.

Conference with students about current writing projects.

Praise students for their accomplishments and effort.

Reinforce students' writing by displaying their best work in prominent places.

Promote a can-do attitude.

Prewriting Planning Activities

Prewriting planning activities include students learning more about a writing topic by gathering information from a book, discussing the topic with peers, viewing a film, listening to a tape, interviewing an expert, or participating in a relevant experience. Prewriting activities can also involve students generating what they already know about a topic or want to know through the process of brainstorming or free writing (i.e., students write down whatever occurs to them without worrying about mechanics, structure, and so forth). Students can be further asked to generate and organize ideas in advance of writing by completing an outline or a graphic organizer, such as a semantic web.

To make prewriting activities maximally effective, it is important that teachers explain their purpose, describe what students are to do, and even model one or more aspects of the activity. This process will help ensure that students can carry out the prewriting activity correctly. For some prewriting activities, such as watching a film or participating in a relevant experience, it may help to devise a set of questions that help focus students' attention on the most important information (these questions can be generated by students, too). Finally, teachers can judiciously combine prewriting activities to facilitate the planning process. For example, in a study by Vinson (1980), ninth-grade students brainstormed ideas for their papers as a class. They then split into pairs and discussed which ideas to use in their individual papers. This was followed by students organizing their ideas before writing their paper.

Inquiry

Inquiry involves engaging students in activities that help them develop ideas and content for a particular writing task by analyzing relevant data (real or imagined). As defined by the National Writing Project (Nagin, 2003), inquiry activities "include comparing and contrasting cases to develop inferences about similarities and differences, explaining how evidence supports or does not support a claim, collecting and evaluating evidence, imagining a situation from a perspective other than one's own" (p. 27).

Inquiry can involve observing objects to draw inferences. For example, students could examine objects that presumably belong to a person in order to draw inferences about that individual's personal qualities before writing about him or her (Hillocks, 1982). Likewise, students could perform various exercises and observe and record in brief written descriptions the sensations they experienced, identifying similarities and differences in bodily sensations (Hillocks, 1979). Students could also be asked to create a hypothetical example to clarify an idea. For instance, to explore the concept of disability, with the goal of writing a story about a real or fictional person with a disability, students could imagine and discuss a day in the life of someone in a wheelchair. This activity could be extended by spending a day wheelchair bound and comparing imagined observations with lived experiences.

Strategy Instruction in Planning

Another way of helping students to plan better is to tackle the problem head-on by directly teaching them how to plan (this can include teaching them independently how to use prewriting and inquiry strategies; see the compare/contrast strategy at the end of this chapter for example). This tenet underlies strategy instruction. Students are explicitly and systematically taught specific strategies for planning their compositions, with the goal that they will learn to use these procedures independently and flexibly.

What is a strategy? It is a course of action for accomplishing a specific objective (Graham & Harris, 2005). First and foremost, strategic behavior is purposeful. It involves a conscious decision to undertake a series of actions (mental, physical, or both) to meet a desired goal. This is humorously illustrated by a young girl who planned to use her mother as the subject of her paper on the "person I most admire" (desired goal) and then asked her mom, "tell me some of the things that I most admire about you" (course of action) (Ponder, 1995, p. 146).

Strategies contain "how to" or procedural knowledge. This knowledge can vary in terms of its specificity. For example, a strategy used by novice reporters to include who, what, when, where, why, and how when describing an event is less directive than this legendary algorithm for setting type: "Set type for as long as you can hold your breath without getting blue in the face, then put in a comma, when you yawn put in a semicolon, and when you want to sneeze, that's time for a paragraph" (Graham & Harris, 2005, p. 41). Strategies can also vary in their general applicability. A strategy such as brainstorming can be applied to a wide variety of writing tasks, whereas the five W's (i.e., Who, What, . . .) and H strategy just presented is best used to describe an event involving one or more persons.

Strategies involve more than just procedural knowledge for accomplishing a goal, as is illustrated in a *Calvin and Hobbes* cartoon in which Calvin has been given the assignment to read a chapter in a book. He describes a strategy for accomplishing this task, indicating that the secret is to break the chapter down into manageable chunks and deal with each chunk one step at a time. Although he clearly has a workable strategy, he tosses the book aside, saying, "I first ask myself, do I even care?" As this cartoon demonstrates, strategies involve a goal and a plan, but they also require the will to embark on the designated course of action and the effort to see it through. Intentions and know-how have to be paired with will and effort for writing strategies to be effective.

In the next section, we present eight principles for teaching planning strategies. Collectively, they promote effective, independent, flexible, and motivated strategy use. We then illustrate how two teachers working together applied these principles to teach a strategy for planning and writing an informative report.

Principles for Teaching Planning Strategies

Although the effectiveness of the principles described below has not been tested for each one, their combined impact has been assessed. Each of these principles is incorporated in the Self-Regulated Strategy Development model (SRSD; Harris & Graham, 1996), which has been used to teach writing strategies to school-age students in more than 25 studies (Graham & Harris, 2003). When compared to other approaches to strategy instruction that include some but not all of these features, the SRSD model is more effective—average effect size for SRSD studies was 1.14 versus 0.62 for other approaches to strategy instruction (Graham

& Perin, 2006). As we noted earlier in this chapter, an effect size of 0.80 is large, whereas an effect size of 0.50 is moderate. It is also important to note that these principles are not completely separate, as there is some overlap among specific principles and instructional procedures for actualizing them.

- *Principle 1. Teach the planning strategy explicitly by modeling its use and scaffolding student learning until students can apply the strategy effectively and independently.* This process of explicitly teaching a strategy moves from the teacher showing students how to apply it to scaffolding students' use of the strategy until they can do it correctly on their own. Thus, responsibility for applying the strategy increasingly shifts from the teacher, who first models the strategy and the thinking involved in its application, to students. The teacher can facilitate this transition by applying the strategy with students (collaborative modeling), having students apply the strategy together (shared responsibility), and providing students with needed but faded assistance as they apply it individually.

- *Principle 2. Make the learning of the planning strategy an interactive process between teachers and students.* While it is important to scaffold learning so that responsibility for applying a planning strategy moves from teacher to students, this strategy should not be taken to imply that students should be viewed as passive recipients of the teacher's knowledge. Instead, they should be viewed as active collaborators. This view includes discussing with them the purpose for learning the planning strategy, asking them for feedback on how to improve it (or how to improve instruction), and encouraging them to help each other as they learn to apply it. If strategy instruction is to be effective, students must come to own the strategy they are learning. This is more likely to happen if they view themselves as partners in the learning process.

- *Principle 3. Help students develop the knowledge, skills, or processes needed to use the planning strategy effectively.* It is easier for students to learn a specific planning strategy if they have already mastered any of the skills, processes, or knowledge needed to apply it. For example, a very successful strategy for planning a story is to have students generate possible ideas for their paper by answering a series of questions based on basic story elements, such as who the main characters are, when and where the story takes place, what the main character wants to do, what happens, and so forth (Graham & Harris, 1989). A good starting point for teaching this strategy is to make sure that students are familiar with these basic story elements and can identify them in stories.

- *Principle 4. Tailor strategy instruction in planning to meet each student's needs.* The late comedian Milton Berle recognized that instruction in many classrooms follows a one-size-fits-all approach when he responded to "Son, I'm worried about you being at the bottom of the class" with "Pop, they teach the same stuff at both ends." If we are to avoid this situation, instruction must be tailored so that it is effective with both stronger and weaker students. For example, students with learning difficulties typically require more intense and explicit instruction to master strategies that other children acquire more easily (Graham & Harris, 2005). Thus, instruction for these students might be adjusted by:

Supplying additional explanations of why the strategy is being learned and how it works

Re-modeling how to apply the strategy

Developing mnemonic devices to help students remember the steps of the strategy

Providing extended feedback and support as students practice using the strategy

Addressing roadblocks that interfere with learning the strategy

• *Principle 5. Make the learning of the planning strategy criterion-rather than time-based.* It should not be expected that all students will master a planning strategy at the same pace. For example, some students may need additional time to learn prerequisite skills, processes, or knowledge (see principle 3), and others may take longer to make the transition from teacher help in applying the strategy to independent use (see principle 1). While differences in learning pace complicate the teaching process, instructional efforts can be minimized and even wasted when instruction is terminated prematurely.

• *Principle 6. Help students develop the motivation to learn the planning strategy and to continue to use it once instruction has ended.* An ancient Chinese proverb captures one fundamental truth about learning: "Teachers open the door, but you must enter yourself." This is especially true when students are being encouraged to do something new that requires a lot of effort. Many students typically approach planning as knowledge telling, planning as they go. This approach works quite well for some types of writing assignments, such as composing a personal narrative. Since it works some of the time (reinforcing its use) and requires little effort, some students may not readily apply a new and more demanding planning strategy. Students may also fail to use a new planning strategy because they do not value it, either because they do not believe it is effective or they had little voice or investment in learning it. Procedures for enhancing students' motivation to learn and use a new planning strategy include:

Enthusiastic teaching

Establishing the importance of effort in learning and using the planning strategy

Promoting a can-do attitude

Providing opportunities for students to establish how the strategy improves their writing

Praising and reinforcing students' effort and use of the strategy

Fostering students' ownership of the strategy

• *Principle 7. Teach students procedures that will help them regulate their use of the planning strategy.* An essential part of mastering a planning strategy is learning how to regulate its use, fostered in part through teachers modeling the planning strategy and the scaffolded assistance provided as students move toward independent use of the strategy (see principle 1). Mastery can also be promoted by directly teaching students self-regulation procedures such as goal setting, self-monitoring, self-instruction, and self-reinforcement (Graham & Harris, 2003). For instance, a student who is impulsive could be taught to remind himself "slow down and take my time" while using the strategy. Likewise, monitoring strategy use and its effectiveness can increase the likelihood that students will value and continue to use a new planning strategy.

• *Principle 8. Ensure that students will be able to apply the planning strategy flexibly.* The application of a new planning strategy is not just dependent on mastering how to do it and being motivated to use it; it also requires knowing when and where to apply it as well as how to adapt it to new situations. Procedures that promote flexible and continued use of a strategy include:

Having students identify when and where the planning strategy can be used

Having students identify if and how the strategy needs to be modified for new situations

Assigning homework that requires students to apply the strategy in new situations

Discussing students' successes and challenges in applying the strategy in new situations

Periodically revisiting the strategy to be sure that students are using it successfully

An Example: Teaching a Planning Strategy for Writing an Informative Report

Background

Our example of best practices in planning strategy instruction is drawn from a school in the Washington, DC, area. It is situated in a mostly middle-class, blue-collar neighborhood but includes children from a nearby federally subsidized apartment complex as well as students from a more affluent white-collar neighborhood. Almost 40% of the students in the school qualify for a free or reduced-price lunch, and the school's population is culturally diverse, with no ethnic group populous enough to form a majority.

The primary approach to writing instruction in the school is writers' workshop (Calkins, 1986). The basic characteristics of this approach, at least in this school, include: extended opportunities for writing; writing for real audiences, engaging in cycles of planning (e.g., prewriting activities or free writing), translating (e.g., putting plans into action), and reviewing (e.g., evaluating, revising, and editing); personal responsibility and ownership of writing projects; high levels of student interactions with each other; a supportive writing environment (including positive feedback from peers); self-reflection and -evaluation (through writing portfolios and rubrics); and personalized assistance and instruction (through activities such as conferencing and mini-lessons). Thus, the general guidelines for creating an atmosphere that supports students' planning were in place, including a supportive classroom environment, engaging writing tasks, and valuing and encouraging of planning.

During the fall, two teachers at the school, Ms. Johnson (a regular fourth-grade teacher) and Ms. Danoff (the special education teacher), decided to work together to teach students more explicitly how to plan a story. With this strategy, students generated ideas for each of the basic parts of a story (see Graham, Harris, & Mason, 2005); these notes provided an initial writing plan that students embellished and upgraded as they wrote. The strategy had five steps:

- *Step 1.* Students think of a story idea to share with others.
- *Step 2.* They prompt themselves to "Let My Mind Be Free" as they brainstorm ideas for each part of their story. This self-statement reminds them to generate as many ideas and keep the brainstorming process open as long as possible.
- *Step 3.* They write down the reminder for each story part and record ideas they brainstorm for each part below it. The reminder is: **W–W–W; WHAT = 2; HOW = 2.** These letters stood for:

Who is the main character; who else is in the story?
When does the story take place?
Where does the story take place?
What does the main character want to do; what do other characters want to do?

What happens when the main character tries to do it; what happens
   with the other characters?
How does the story end?
How does the main character feel; how do other characters feel?

- *Step 4.* Students write their stories, using their notes as a guide.
- *Step 5.* As students write, the emphasis is on creating a good
story. Students are encouraged to add new ideas as well as elaborate and
modify their initial thoughts in order to write a story that makes sense
and that others will find enjoyable.

They taught this strategy through a series of mini-lessons embedded in
the classroom writing program, using the eight principles described (via
the SRSD model; Harris & Graham, 1996). Learning this strategy had a
positive impact on students' story-writing skills, and the two teachers
were eager to apply this same kind of approach to report writing.

Report-Writing Strategy

The strategy for planning a report (MacArthur, Schwartz, Graham, Molloy,
& Harris, 1996) taught by the two teachers also involved five steps and
also was taught via the SRSD model (the eight principles are highlighted
in parentheses in the description of how the strategy was taught). The
five steps are:

- *Step 1.* Students brainstorm what they already know about the
topic of their report and identify other areas or concepts where information is needed. For instance, a student working on a report on lemurs
started by listing that they were monkeys with large eyes and ringed
tails, active at night, lived in trees, and found in jungles and zoos. Although the student's knowledge about lemurs was limited and not completely accurate, it provided a starting point for thinking about what else
he needed to know. With this knowledge in mind, he listed five things he
wanted to learn more about: what they look like, where they live, what
they eat, whether they can be pets, and what their habits are.
- *Step 2.* Students take their lists of what they know and want to
learn and organize this information on a map or chart that shows the relationships among ideas. Students are encouraged to place items on their
map as either main ideas or details.
- *Step 3.* Students gather additional information about their topic.
Pertinent information is added to the map, inaccuracies deleted or corrected (e.g., lemurs are only *related* to monkeys), and categories revised
or rearranged. Information can be taken from a variety of sources, in-

cluding books, encyclopedias, magazines, the Internet, and interviews. As students gather new information, they ask themselves three questions:

> What do I want to know?
> What is the main point of this section (or speaker)?
> Is this information on my map?

• *Step 4.* Once students are ready to write, the map provides a resource that summarizes what they know about the topic. Before writing, they organize this information for writing by numbering which main idea will come first, second, third, and so forth.

• *Step 5.* Students are encouraged to continue the process of planning as they write. This may include stopping to locate additional information, confirming the accuracy of a particular piece of information, or reorganizing their organizational format.

Teaching the Strategy

Before teaching the report-writing strategy, Ms. Johnson and Ms. Danoff considered what they knew about the students, the demands of the strategy, and the classroom writing program. They concluded that they could not teach the strategy through a series of mini-lessons, as was done with the story-planning strategy, because it was much too complicated and time consuming. As a result, they decided to suspend writers' workshop while they introduced and modeled how to use the strategy. They further decided that Ms. Danoff would take the lead in introducing and modeling the use of the strategy (principle 1), as she had more experience with this kind of teaching. Both teachers played an active role in every phase of instruction, however, allowing them to address individual students' needs (principle 4). Ms. Danoff focused her attention on a group of four struggling writers (all with learning disabilities) by scheduling additional time to work with these children separately. She did the same for several other students who also needed extra help.

To apply the report-writing strategy effectively, students must be able to generate and organize information from multiple sources. Although the two teachers thought that most of the students in the class were reasonably skilled at using brainstorming to generate what they knew, they were less certain that all the students were able to effectively use semantic webs to organize their ideas (principles 3 and 4). Based on reports written by students in the fall, it was evident that many students did not have a clear conception of what constituted a good report. The teachers further thought that some of the students, including the struggling writers, might experience difficulty managing a task of this complexity. For these students, they decided that it was important to include instructional procedures in the teaching routine to ensure students mastered the strategy and developed a can-do attitude (principles 4, 5, and 6).

Before introducing the report-writing strategy to the whole class, Ms. Danoff held a conference with each of the four struggling writers who would receive extra help (principle 4). At this time, they discussed how the child had gone about planning the report written in the fall, and Ms. Danoff emphasized that the student would profit from learning a new approach for planning a report (principle 6). She stressed that this approach would help the student write a more complete and informative report, "one that was more fun to share with other people." She then described the strategy, and they talked about how it would be taught. Ms. Danoff emphasized that the student could master the strategy by making a commitment to learning it, emphasizing the importance of effort in this endeavor. Each student indicated that he or she would work hard to learn the strategy.

In a session with the full class, the two teachers next worked on helping students develop the background knowledge and skills needed to write good reports and apply the planning strategy (principle 3). First, the class brainstormed good ideas about how people work together (principle 2). Next, they were split into groups of four or five children and asked to discuss what makes a good report and why it is important to write good reports. Then the groups shared their ideas with the whole class as Ms. Johnson recorded them on a chart.

The following day, students worked in groups of three (consisting of a manager, reader, and writer) to identify the characteristics evident in an example of a good report they were given (principles 2 and 3). As the groups shared their ideas, Ms. Danoff recorded them on a second chart. Next, they referred to the ideas they had placed on the chart the previous day to see how their prior and current knowledge matched. Each group made a web combining the most important information from the two charts. At the end of the session, students started a log in their writing journal, where they recorded what they learned each day and how it would help them (principles 7 and 8).

The activities in these first two whole-class sessions required that students carry out two processes, brainstorming and semantic webbing, that are essential to successful use of the report-planning strategy (principle 2). These activities helped make sure students understood the purpose of report writing and the characteristics of a good report but also allowed the teachers to assess students' facility with these two processes. For several of the students, Ms. Danoff arranged a teaching session later in the day to work on semantic webbing, as these children had not yet mastered the process (principles 4 and 5).

During the next whole-class session, each student received a chart listing the steps of the report-writing strategy, and Ms. Danoff described in detail how the strategy worked. The class discussed the reasons for each step as well as how and when to use the strategy (principles 2, 7, and 8). Their ideas were recorded on a chart that remained on the wall for the rest of the school year. As a homework assignment, students were asked to memorize the steps of the strategy, using the following words as reminders: choose, brainstorm, organize, read, and write and say more (principle 1). The teachers explained that students were memorizing the steps, "so that you won't have to keep looking them up." They also encouraged students to make up a silly sentence (mnemonic) to help them remember the reminding words (e.g., "Choose, Brainstorm, Organize—they will help you read, write and say more"). Most of the students in the class memorized the steps easily, but the four struggling writers with learning disabilities required some additional practice with Ms. Danoff (principles 4 and 5).

In two subsequent sessions, Ms. Danoff modeled how to use the planning strategy to write a report while thinking out loud (principle 1), providing students with a visible and concrete model of how to apply it. Students participated in this activity by helping her as she planned and wrote a report, giving suggestions for content, where to place items on the web, how to turn an idea into a sentence, and so forth (principle 2).

As she modeled how to use the strategy, Ms. Danoff held a running dialogue with herself designed to demonstrate the types of things writers say to themselves to help them focus their attention ("What do I need to do?"), stay on task ("Keep going"), monitor performance ("Does this make part make sense?"), reinforce themselves ("What a great idea"), and cope with frustration ("I can do this"). Once the report was finished, the class discussed the importance of what we say to ourselves as we work and write (principles 2, 7, and 8). Students volunteered examples of positive and negative things they said to themselves when writing. The class then identified the types of things Ms. Danoff said that helped her do a good job when planning and writing the report. Students developed and recorded on a card one or more personal statements they would use while writing (principle 8).

Writers' workshop was resumed at this point, as students began to use the strategy to plan and write their own reports. For the struggling writers, this phase of instruction began with them collaboratively planning a report with Ms. Danoff (principle 4) to make sure these students understood how to use the strategy correctly. Ms. Danoff did a second collaborative report with two of these children, as they were not yet ready to apply the strategy without her directing the process (principles

1, 4, and 5). The other students in the class began this phase of instruction by collaboratively writing a story with a peer, assisted by Ms. Johnson as needed (principles 1 and 2).

As students used the strategy to plan and write reports, they continued to reflect on what they were learning in a daily entry in their journals (principle 8). The teachers also reminded them to use their personal statements to help them manage the writing process. As students became increasingly proficient in applying the strategy, the teachers increasingly encouraged them to be more independent, relying as little as possible on the teachers or their peers for help (principle 1). At this point, the students were encouraged to use their personal statements covertly ("in your head"). Although most of the children in the classroom were able to use the strategy independently after writing three reports, the four struggling writers with a learning disability required more time to master it (they needed to write between four and five reports).

To help students more fully personalize the report-planning strategy, they were asked to share how they thought they could make it better (principles 6 and 8). Suggestions for improving it included: "Do brainstorming and webbing together"; "Do not brainstorm for unfamiliar topics"; and "Number on the web what will appear first, second, third, and so on in the report." Because some of them were forgetting to check to see if they used all of the ideas generated in their plan, the students decided to add a sixth step to the strategy:

- *Step 6.* Students consult their map to make sure that they included all of the information they planned to use. A check is placed next to each item included in the report.

The Effects of Teaching the Strategy

It took 6 weeks for children in this class to master the planning strategy for writing a report. The teachers thought that it was time well spent, commenting their students will "have to write reports every year from now on" and "now they know how to do so." The overall quality of students' reports improved, even for the struggling writers. To illustrate the positive benefits of this instruction, we share a report written by one of these children after instruction. The previous report written by this student, in the fall, included just a couple of disjointed sentences.

Germs

Germs are tiny cells that get into people's body and make you look sick. Who get germs? People like us get germs on your hands, from cats and dogs, and lots of other places like which fight germs. White blood that your blood has works very hard to kill germs.

How do you feel? You feel like throwing up; you feel sick; stomach aches come to you; you get fever, pain, breaks, aches, and rashes. You feel all these things when you have germs inside your body.

From where do they come? They come from old metal and dirt. There is even germs in food, in the air, from the hands. There is even germs in water, and everything that you touch that is not clean.

What happens when you have germs? You cough, you get allergies, you get a cold, you have a feeling to throw-up. That all happens when you have germs in your body. All things that you read here comes from germs in your body. The skin is your protection against germs.

OTHER PLANNING STRATEGIES

In addition to the two planning strategies presented already, there are many other planning strategies that have been effective in improving the quality of students' writing (see Graham & Harris, 2005; Graham & Perin, 2006; Harris & Graham, 1996). In closing, we present several of these evidence-based planning strategies.

Planning a Compare/Contrast Paper

The strategy described below provides a structural framework for carrying out the thinking and organizational processes involved in planning a compare/contrast paper (Englert et al., 1991).

- *Step 1.* The student identifies what is to be compared and contrasted ("Joe and I"), who will read the paper ("Joe"), and the purpose for writing it ("so Joe and I will know how we are the same and different"). These answers are recorded at the top of a sheet of paper. Next, the student brainstorms ideas about the two items to be compared, writing them below the material he or she has already placed on the planning sheet. The student then decides how the items will be grouped (e.g., by physical features, how they act, what they like to do, and so forth), recording this information at the bottom of the planning sheet.
- *Step 2.* The student develops a text structure map on a second sheet of paper. On this piece of paper, the student lists each of the categories identified during step 1 (e.g., physical features) and records how the items are alike and different on each of these dimensions.
- *Step 3.* The student uses the map generated in step 2 as a guide for writing the paper. The student continues to plan as he or she writes, including fleshing out initial ideas by adding an introduction, conclusion, details, key words, examples, and so forth.

Planning a Persuasive Paper

When writing a persuasive paper, the writer should carefully consider both sides of an argument, decide which side to support, and build an argument that is both compelling and fair. The *STOP & DARE* strategy is designed to help students do this (De La Paz & Graham, 1997). The word STOP serves as a general reminder to stop, reflect, and plan before writing, and each letter acts as a prompt to carry out the following activities.

- Suspend judgment—Students record their thoughts about each side of the topic on a sheet of paper. They write their ideas for one side of the argument on the left side of the paper and their ideas for the other side on the right side of the paper. To help them generate as many ideas as possible, students consult the following three cue cards: (1) Did I list ideas for each side? (2) Can I think of anything else? Try to write more. (3) Another point I haven't considered yet is . . .
- Take a side—On their planning sheet, students write "For" above the list of ideas that shows the side they will defend and "Against" above the list of ideas on the other side.
- Organize ideas—Students place a star next to ideas they plan to use and those they plan to refute and number them in the order they plan to use.
- Plan more as you write—This step reminds students to use the plan they developed and to continue the process of planning while writing.

To make sure that they write a complete persuasive essay, the mnemonic DARE reminds them to check to see if they included these four parts: Develop a topic sentence; Add supporting ideas; Reject arguments for the other side; End with a conclusion.

A More General Planning Strategy

All of the planning strategies examined so far have been designed for specific writing tasks. The final strategy presented is more general and can be used with most writing tasks. This strategy involves setting goals for what the paper will accomplish, generating possible ideas for the paper, and sequencing them before writing. The mnemonic STOP and LIST serves to remind students what they need to do with this strategy (Troia, Graham, & Harris, 1999).

- *Step 1.* The mnemonic *STOP* reminds students to set goals or establish their purpose for writing. Each letter stands for a word to direct student behavior: *Stop* and *Think* Of *Purposes*. Examples of purposes, or goals, include "write a funny story to share during writing time" or "tell my younger brother how to play checkers." Students record their purposes for writing at the top of a piece of paper.

• *Step 2*. The second word, *LIST*, reminds students to generate and organize ideas for their paper. Again, each letter stands for a word that directs student behavior: *List Ideas* and *Sequence Them*. When listing ideas, students brainstorm possible content for their paper. Keeping their writing topic and goals in mind, they generate as many ideas as they can, recording them below the goals from step 1. Next, they examine these ideas, select the ones they plan to use, and number them. Ideas they decide not to include are crossed out.

• *Step 3*. Students use their plan to guide their writing efforts. They are encouraged to continue the planning process while writing, adding new ideas to the plan, expanding existing points, culling redundant or unimportant details, and modifying the organizational structure.

CONCLUDING COMMENTS

The procedures emphasized in this chapter enhance students' planning behavior by teaching students how to plan or by putting into place procedures that support planning (such as prewriting and inquiry methods). This emphasis does not exclude students developing plans of their own volition. In fact, an important part of becoming a self-regulated writer is learning how to develop novel plans for familiar and unfamiliar writing tasks.

REFERENCES

Brodie, D. (1997). *Writing changes everything*. New York: St. Martin's Press.

Calkins, L. (1986). *The art of teaching writing*. Portsmouth, NH: Heinemann.

Cosby, B. (1998). *Kids say the darndest things*. New York: Bantam.

De La Paz, S., & Graham, S. (1997). Effects of dictation and advanced planning instruction on the composing of students with writing and learning problems. *Journal of Educational Psychology, 89*, 203–222.

Englert, C., Raphael, T., Anderson, L., Anthony, H., Steven, D., & Fear, K. (1991). Making writing and self-talk visible: Cognitive strategy instruction in writing in regular and special education classrooms. *American Educational Research Journal, 28*, 337–373.

Graham, S., & Harris, K. R. (1989). A component analysis of cognitive strategy instruction: Effects on learning disabled students' compositions and self-efficacy. *Journal of Educational Psychology, 81*, 353–361.

Graham, S., & Harris, K. R. (1997). Self-regulation and writing: Where do we go from here? *Contemporary Educational Psychology, 22,* 102–114.

Graham, S., & Harris, K. R. (2000). The role of self-regulation and transcription skills in writing and writing development. *Educational Psychologist, 35,* 3–12.

Graham, S., & Harris, K. R. (2003). Students with learning disabilities and the process of writing: A meta-analysis of SRSD studies. In L. Swanson, K. R. Harris, & S. Graham (Eds.), *Handbook of learning disabilities* (pp. 383–402). New York: Guilford Press.

Graham, S., & Harris, K. R. (2005). *Writing better.* Baltimore: Brookes.

Graham, S., Harris, K. R., & Mason, L. H. (2005). Improving the writing performance, knowledge, and self-efficacy of struggling young writers: The effects of Self-Regulated Strategy Development. *Contemporary Educational Psychology, 30,* 207–241.

Graham, S., & Perin, D. (2006). *Writing next: Effective strategies to improve writing of adolescents in middle and high school.* Washington, DC: Alliance for Excellence in Education.

Harris, K., & Graham, S. (1996). *Making the writing process work: Strategies for composition and self-regulation* (2nd ed.). Cambridge, MA: Brookline.

Hillocks, G., Jr. (1979). The effects of observational activities on student writing. *Research in the Teaching of English, 13,* 23–35.

Hillocks, G., Jr. (1982). The interaction of instruction, teacher comment, and revision in teaching the composing process. *Research in the Teaching of English, 16,* 261–278.

L'Amour, L. (1990). *The education of a wandering man.* New York: Bantam.

MacArthur, C., Schwarz, S., Graham, S., Molloy, D., & Harris, K. R. (1996). Integration of strategy instruction into a whole language classroom: A case study. *Learning Disability Research and Practice, 11,* 168–176.

Nagin, C. (2003). *Because writing matters: Improving student writing in our schools.* San Francisco: Jossey-Bass.

Persky H., Daane, M., & Jin, Y. (2003). *The nation's report card: Writing.* Washington, DC: U.S. Department of Education.

Phillips, B. (1993). *Phillip's book of great thoughts and funny sayings.* Wheaton, IL: Tyndazl House.

Ponder, J. (1995). *Readers' Digest,* p. 146.

Scardamalia, M., & Bereiter, C. (1986). Written composition. In M. Wittrock (Ed.), *Handbook of research on teaching* (3rd ed., pp. 778–803). New York: MacMillan.

Shapiro, M. (2000). *J. K. Rowling: The wizard behind Harry Potter.* New York: St. Martin Griffin.

Troia, G., Graham, S., & Harris, K. R. (1999). The effects of teaching students with LD to plan mindfully when writing. *Exceptional Children, 65,* 235–252.

Vinson, L. L. N. (1980). *The effects of two prewriting activities upon the overall quality of ninth graders' descriptive paragraphs.* Unpublished doctoral dissertation, University of South Carolina, Columbia, SC.

7

Best Practices in Teaching Evaluation and Revision

CHARLES A. MACARTHUR

Teachers of writing generally view revision as an important aspect of the composing process, and it is included in some form in most approaches to writing instruction. Revision is important for two reasons. First, revision is an important aspect of the composing process that is used extensively by proficient writers (Fitzgerald, 1987; Hayes, 2004). As Donald Murray (1991) famously declared, "Writing *is* revising, and the writer's craft is largely a matter of knowing how to discover what you have to say, develop, and clarify it, each requiring the craft of revision" (p. 2). When writers revise, they have opportunities to think about whether their text communicates effectively to an audience, to improve the quality of their prose, and even to reconsider their content and perspective and potentially transform their own understanding. To become proficient writers, students must learn to revise effectively.

Second, in an instructional context, revision provides an opportunity for teachers to guide students in learning about the characteristics of effective writing in ways that will not only improve the current piece, but also carry over to future writing. In learning to revise, students get feedback from readers on their work, learn to evaluate their writing, and discover new ways to solve common writing problems. Thus, revising is a way to learn about the craft of writing.

Despite the importance accorded revising by teachers, students at the elementary and secondary school levels generally do little substantive revising (McCutchen, Francis, & Kerr, 1997; Rijlaarsdam, Couzijn, & van den Bergh, 2004). Proficient adult writers revise frequently both during writing and after completing a draft. They evaluate their writing in terms of their goals and audience and make changes in overall organization and content as well as smaller changes in language and conventions. In contrast, school-age writers, especially struggling writers but also average writers, usually confine their revisions to relatively minor changes in wording or corrections of errors. Teachers often find it difficult to get students to engage in more extensive and meaningful revision.

The purpose of this chapter is to provide guidance to teachers on ways to help their students develop revising skills and to teach revising in a way that improves overall writing ability. The information in the chapter is based on research into revising processes and instructional methods. First, I describe cognitive models of revising to provide a framework for understanding what students need to develop. Second, I review research on instructional methods for revising. Finally, I provide classroom examples of revising instruction that incorporates approaches to teaching and supporting revision based on the research.

COGNITIVE MODELS OF REVISING

What do proficient writers do when they revise? Answers to this question can help us understand what less proficient writers need to learn and can inform the design of instruction. The most prominent models of the cognitive processes involved in writing have been developed (and revised) by Hayes and his colleagues (Hayes, Flower, Schriver, Stratman, & Carey, 1987; Hayes, 2004) and by Bereiter and Scardamalia (1987). The discussion here is based on those models with an emphasis on the most instructionally relevant aspects. I would like to make several points about revising processes.

First, theoretical models of revising use a broad definition of revising that includes "changes made at any point in the writing process" (Fitzgerald, 1987, p. 484). Thus, revision includes mental evaluation and revision of sentences before writing them, changes in text during writing, changes in plans, and evaluation and revision of completed drafts. In contrast, in practice, teachers and researchers view revision more narrowly, as changes to text already written. Teachers have the greatest opportunity to teach students about good writing when students evaluate and change what they have already written; however, it is worthwhile keeping in mind that what students learn while revising can be applied during writing in ways that are not visible to the teacher.

Second, proficient writers have relatively sophisticated conceptions of and goals for revising. They see revising as a matter of evaluating all aspects of their writing that affect whether they have achieved their purposes. They keep their overall purposes and audience in mind as they evaluate the organization and content of their papers as well as the language and errors. Cognitive models of writing processes describe revision as a process of detecting differences between the intended meaning and the actual meaning. That is, writers have goals and purposes for writing and evaluate what they have written to see whether they have achieved their goals. Some writers see revising even more expansively, as a "re-seeing" of their ideas and a chance to transform their own knowledge (Murray, 1991).

In contrast, struggling writers have limited conceptions of revising and unclear goals and purposes for writing. They have a narrow understanding of revising as correcting errors and making a neat copy (MacArthur, Graham, & Schwartz, 1991). In addition, they may not have clear goals and purposes for their writing as a whole. It is possible to get students to make more substantive revisions simply by giving them specific goals for revising. For example, in one study, students made more substantive revisions and improved their papers when given simple directions to add ideas to make their papers more interesting (Graham, MacArthur, & Schwartz, 1995). It is also possible to affect revising by asking students to consider their audience and goals. In another study, students produced better persuasive essays when given a goal (and minimal procedural support) to revise with a specific audience in mind who would disagree with their position (Midgette, Haria, & MacArthur, in press).

Third, revising requires all the skills involved in good reading comprehension (Hayes, 1996). Writers must distance themselves from the writing and critically evaluate the text. To make changes in the text as a whole, writers must construct the gist of the text by attending to the main ideas and organization. To identify problems of clarity, they must read as readers and evaluate whether the content is clear with reasonable inferences. Without good reading skills, writers may read their intended meanings into the text and fail to see problems with the text as it actually exists. Reading comprehension skills parallel revision skills at all levels of text from overall organization to the sentence level. The difference is the purpose for reading—to understand versus to identify problems and improve the text.

Fourth, proficient writers have extensive knowledge about criteria for good writing and about typical writing problems. Like English teachers, they know to look for an interesting lead, clear thesis, and good

paragraph structure. They may automatically detect some kinds of problems in grammar and clarity. This knowledge includes general criteria
and criteria specific to particular kinds of texts. For example, in revising
a persuasive essay, they know that a good essay should consider opposing positions in a respectful way and marshal arguments against them.
This knowledge of criteria and typical problems helps them detect and
diagnose specific problems in their texts. In contrast, younger and less
proficient writers know little about evaluating writing. Typical upper elementary students, when asked why they like one paper more than another, cite length and conventions, topic, and general characteristics,
such as "it's funny" (Graham, Schwartz, & MacArthur, 1993). When
they do detect a problem, they often decide to rewrite the sentence rather
than diagnose and fix the problem.

Finally, proficient writers have solid metacognitive self-regulation
skills. They can switch flexibly to evaluation and revision during writing
when they notice problems or have a new idea. When revising a draft,
they can manage the multiple processes involved—keeping audience and
purpose in mind while critically reading the text and considering possible revisions. In contrast, less proficient writers have difficulty managing
the complexity of the writing process. Thus, they may restrict their revising to problems at the sentence level. De La Paz, Swanson, and Graham
(1998) found that struggling writers could make revisions at the overall
organizational level as well as the sentence level if they were provided
with procedural support in the form of prompts to consider the text as a
whole before evaluating sentences.

These cognitive aspects of revising—goals and conceptions of revising,
critical reading skills, knowledge of evaluation criteria, and self-regulation—
are connected to the types of revising instruction that research has found
to be effective.

RESEARCH ON REVISING INSTRUCTION

In this section, I review research on several approaches or methods to
teaching revision. Further research is needed, but the findings are generally consistent across instructional studies and with research on revising
processes.

Evaluation Criteria and Self-Evaluation

One approach to improving revising skills is to teach students to evaluate their writing or that of their peers using specific criteria and then to
revise their papers based on the evaluation. Hillocks, in his meta-analysis

of writing instruction studies (1986), reported that six studies using this approach found moderately strong effects on revision and writing quality. In addition, teaching self-evaluation is a key part of strategy instruction methods described below.

Two factors seem to be important in designing instruction in evaluation and revision. First, specific evaluation criteria seem more effective than general criteria such as content and organization. One way to make criteria specific is to teach them within a particular genre. For example, in teaching about narratives, one might make content and organization more specific by using evaluation criteria such as "Are all the story elements included?"; "Are the characters clearly described?"; and "Does it show how characters feel?" Specific criteria are easier for students to learn and use in making revisions. Then, as students learn about various genres, they will come to understand that organization and content are always important criteria, but that they are applied differently depending on the type of writing. Specific evaluation criteria are not always genre-related. For example, criteria of clarity ("Is there anything difficult to understand?") and detail ("Where could I add more information to make it more interesting?") are also specific enough to teach.

Second, it is important not only to teach students to evaluate their papers but also to give them support and practice in applying the criteria in making specific revisions. One way to practice such application is to display papers with particular kinds of problems on a chart or overhead and then model and discuss how to apply a particular evaluation criterion and revise the paper to improve it. For example, in teaching the criteria of clarity, the teacher might display papers with missing information or unclear referents and guide students to find the problems by asking questions about the content. Then the teacher and students could collaboratively generate sentences that would clarify the content. Students may need extensive practice to learn to apply the criteria and to make revisions to solve problems.

Critical Reading

A few studies have improved revising skills by asking students to read texts critically and identify comprehension problems. For example, Holliway and McCutchen (2004) had students write descriptions of tangram figures (shapes of people, animals, etc. made from geometric blocks). Then one group received feedback on the accuracy of their descriptions while a second group read other students' descriptions and tried to use them to identify one tangram figure from a group of four similar ones. Students who had the reading experience were better able to revise their own descriptions and to write better first draft descriptions. This study and similar ones demonstrate the importance of critical reading and understanding the perspective of readers.

These studies do not provide direct examples of how to teach revising—all of them used somewhat artificial writing tasks like describing tangrams rather than more natural topics—but they demonstrate two important principles. First, as the cognitive models suggest, revising is closely related to critical reading. Thus, it makes sense to integrate instruction in critical reading and writing, especially revising. Second, the importance of reading in revising is part of the reason peer revision methods can be effective. The experience of reading papers written by peers that may have a variety of problems can be a valuable way to improve one's own writing.

Peer Revising

Peer revising is a common feature of writing-process classrooms, and it is often recommended as a way of providing student writers with an audience of readers who can respond to their writing, identify strengths and problems, and recommend improvements. Students may learn from serving in roles of both author and editor. The critical reading required as an editor can contribute to learning how to evaluate writing. Peer revising is most effective when it is combined with instruction based on evaluation criteria or revising strategies. At the elementary and secondary levels, when students are given general instructions about response and revision or asked to engage in peer evaluation without specific guidance, they often are reluctant to criticize each other or are unable to provide significant help because their evaluation and revision skills are limited (Dipardo & Freedman, 1988).

When peer revising is integrated with instruction in evaluation and revision, it can be very effective. Boscolo and Ascorti (2004), in a study of elementary and middle school students, focused on the issue of clarity or comprehensibility—that is, understanding what readers might find difficult to understand. Students wrote personal narratives and worked in pairs to evaluate and revise them using the following procedure: The student serving as editor read until she found an unclear point, asked the author for clarification, and then discussed with the author how to fix the text until a change was agreed on and made. The students improved their ability to identify comprehension problems in text and to write text without such problems.

Strategy Instruction

One of the most extensively studied and effective approaches to teaching revising is cognitive strategy instruction. Graham (2006) reviewed six studies that taught revising strategies and another five that taught a combination of planning and revising (see Graham & Harris, Chapter 6, this volume, on planning). He reported large and consistent positive effects on the amount of revision and the quality of writing. In these strategy instruction studies, teachers explained the revising process explicitly, modeled the strategy with think-alouds, provided guided practice with feedback, and gradually worked toward independent mastery by students. Many of the studies also included support for metacognitive, self-regulation strategies.

Most of the studies included teaching students to evaluate their own writing using specific criteria often related to genre or text structure. For example, in one study (Graham & MacArthur, 1988), fifth- and sixth-grade students with learning disabilities (LD) learned a strategy for revising persuasive essays. The steps in the strategy guided them to (1) read your essay; (2) find the sentence that tells what you believe and ask whether it is clear; (3) add two reasons why you believe it; (4) *SCAN* each sentence (Does it make *Sense*? Is it *Connected* to my opinion? Can I *Add* more? *Note* errors); (5) make changes; and (6) reread and make final changes. The strategy included evaluation criteria related to persuasive writing as well as non-genre-related criteria for comprehensibility, elaboration, and errors. Tutors explained the parts of a simple persuasive essay and then explained and modeled the strategy. Students memorized the steps and practiced applying the strategy with support until they could do it independently. Students increased the number of substantive revisions and improved the quality of their papers following instruction.

Many strategy instruction studies include peer revising or classroom interaction and integrate planning and revising strategies. Such studies are described below.

Word Processing

Computers are powerful and flexible writing tools that can support writing in many ways, particularly for struggling writers (for a review, see MacArthur, 2006). They can ease the physical process of writing, enable students to produce error-free final copies, support publication, and make revision possible without tedious recopying. Using a word processor by itself, however, has not been shown to result in more or better revision. Word processing in combination with writing instruction appears to have modest positive effects on writing quality, especially for struggling writers. Furthermore, research that has focused specifically on teaching revising strategies in combination with use of a word processor has found improvements in revising and writing quality. In my experience, it is considerably easier to teach revising strategies if students can do the revisions on a word processor, as it makes them less reluctant to apply revising strategies they have learned.

Strategy Instruction Combined with Other Elements

Most studies of instruction in strategies for revision include multiple components. Most revising strategies incorporate specific evaluation criteria, often based on genre or text structure. Many of them involve interaction with peers or teachers in peer-response groups, classroom formats like author's chair, or teacher conferencing. Some involve word processing. Some involve teaching strategies for both planning and revising. Programs that have been implemented for a full year are especially likely to include multiple components. In this section, I will describe two intervention studies that illustrate strategy instruction in combination with other elements.

The cognitive strategy instruction in writing (CSIW) program (Englert, Raphael, Anderson, Anthony, & Stevens, 1991) was designed to teach expository writing to upper elementary school students, including high-achieving (HA), low-achieving (LA), and learning-disabled (LD) groups. Students learned planning and revising strategies for writing different types of expository texts (e.g., explanation and compare/contrast). An overall writing strategy was represented by the mnemonic POWER (Plan, Organize, Write, Edit, and Revise). In the planning strategy, students identified the topic, audience, and purpose; brainstormed content; and organized the content using a graphic organizer appropriate for the particular text structure. In the editing and revising steps, students evaluated their text alone and with a peer using a set of evaluation questions that included general criteria like clarity as well as criteria related to the specific text structure. For example, for compare/contrast writing, evaluation questions asked whether the paper told how the two things were the same and how they were different. "Think sheets" were used to scaffold the planning and revising strategies until students internalized them. The strategies were taught over the course of a year in classroom settings that emphasized peer collaboration, teacher scaffolding, and extensive dialogue between teachers and students about writing processes. Teachers modeled the strategies, and peers discussed their writing and applied the revising strategy in peer-response groups. All three groups of students (HA, LA, and LD) made gains in the quality of their expository writing. No separate analyses were done specifically for revising.

Along with some colleagues, I studied a reciprocal peer-revising strategy that included strategy instruction, peer interaction, instruction in specific evaluation criteria, and word processing (MacArthur, Schwartz, & Graham, 1991; Stoddard & MacArthur, 1993). Students used word processors to write and revise their papers. A pair of students who had each completed a draft worked together, taking turns as author and editor. The strategy included five steps, given as directions to the student serving as editor: listen as the author reads the paper; tell what you liked best; read the paper and ask the evaluation questions; discuss questions and suggestions; author makes changes. The evaluation questions could vary depending on the students and the type of text.

In preparation for engaging in peer revising, students learned specific evaluation criteria and how to apply them to make revisions. For example, teachers presented the criterion of clarity as a question: "Is there anything difficult to understand?" They used the overhead projector to display examples of papers that were clear and papers that had various kinds of obstacles to comprehension, such as missing information or unclear referents. Using think-aloud modeling, teachers read a paper, had difficulty understanding it, thought of possible solutions, actually made changes, and read the improved version. Students practiced as a whole class and then in groups applying the evaluation question to papers not written by anyone in the class and revising them. Using papers written by students they did not know made it easier for them to be critical. They repeated the process for each evaluation criterion. Finally, they engaged in the peer-revising strategy using the criteria they had practiced and applying them to their own writing. Both studies demonstrated that the instruction led to more substantive revision and improved quality of writing.

Summary of the Instructional Research

In planning methods for teaching revision, teachers can choose from several approaches that are supported by research on revising processes and by instructional studies. Research on cognitive processes describes revising as a complex set of processes that depends on a writer's goals and purposes for writing, critical reading ability, knowledge of evaluation criteria and typical writing problems, and self-regulation ability. The instructional approaches discussed make sense in terms of these underlying cognitive and social processes. Teaching evaluation criteria and self-evaluation processes makes sense because proficient writers use their knowledge of criteria for good writing. Teaching critical reading makes sense because rereading to revise involves all the same skills as reading comprehension, from comprehending complex sentences to getting the gist to making inferences. Peer collaboration makes sense because a major consideration in revising is whether the writing communicates effectively to an audience. In addition, peer revising gives students opportunities to practice critical reading to detect problems as editors. Strategy instruction makes sense because revising, like planning, is a complex process requiring writers to coordinate multiple skills and attend to multiple considerations.

Teachers should not adopt specific instructional plans directly from research studies. Rather, they need to integrate instruction in revising with the rest of their writing and reading instruction, selecting elements of evidence-based practices that work and using them in ways that maintain their effectiveness. In the next section, I describe examples of teaching revision as part of an integrated writing curriculum.

INSTRUCTIONAL EXAMPLES

In this section, I give two examples of how revision can be taught as part of instruction. The first example describes instruction in a fourth-grade class that is learning to write narratives. The second example focuses on a unit on persuasive writing in a middle school classroom. Both examples are composites of instruction from research projects and other examples of instruction that my colleagues and I have worked on, and both illustrate instruction that is organized around a particular genre of writing. Knowledge about common genres is an important part of students' developing understanding of writing, and genre helps organize writing around purposes as well as making both planning and revising instruction more specific. As students learn about basic genres, they develop the ability to generalize their knowledge to new purposes and forms for writing.

Revision in a Fourth-Grade Unit on Narrative Writing

It is early November in Ms. A's fourth-grade classroom; the students are accustomed to the schedule of writing workshop three times a week. The class includes a range of abilities, from a few students who are fluent and imaginative writers to a couple of students with LD who struggle with reading and writing. The writing routine includes mini-lessons, time for independent writing, sharing with peers in small groups and in whole-class readings, and teacher conferences. Students engage in prewriting and revising activities. They display their work in the classroom and publish selected pieces in a classroom magazine that is sent home to parents. They write on a wide range of self-selected and teacher-assigned topics, including personal narratives and reports on issues and content they are learning. Ms. A believes that arranging for students to share and publish their work enhances motivation and helps them see writing as a meaningful activity.

Mindful of the curriculum, which includes narrative, informative, and persuasive writing, Ms. A decides to initiate a unit on narrative writing. She teaches the class a strategy for planning and writing stories. Students learn the elements of stories—character, setting, problem or goal, actions, and resolution—and use that knowledge to plan stories before writing them (see Graham & Harris, Chapter 6, this volume). She differentiates instruction by expecting all students to plan and write papers that include all the story elements, while expecting her better writers to produce more elaborate plans and stories.

As students develop mastery in planning and writing complete stories, she introduces instruction in evaluation and revision. She sees this instruction as a way for students to focus on the quality of their stories and to learn how to write stories that are more interesting and effective.

Ms. A decides to teach a peer-revising strategy that combines use of evaluation criteria with the peer revising that fits with her workshop approach. Students will work in pairs, taking turns as editor and author to discuss both their papers. Pairs work better than small groups because it takes too long to focus on more than two papers; in addition, in pairs, each student has a clear responsibility. The steps in the strategy, written as directions to the editor, are as follows:

1. Listen while the author reads the paper.
2. Tell what the paper was about and what you liked best about it.
3. Read the story (or listen to it again) and ask the evaluation questions: [Evaluation questions go here.]
4. Discuss the evaluation and ways to make the paper better.
5. Author makes changes.

First, Ms. A has to select evaluation criteria that are worth teaching. She decides to begin with characters because characters' personalities and the way they approach problems are central to narratives. In particular, she wants students to describe characters' personalities, feelings, and motivations. She translates these ideas into the following evaluation questions: Are the characters described clearly? Does the author show how the characters feel? Can you tell why the characters act the way they do?

She begins her instruction by integrating reading and writing. She explains to her students that they can learn how to write better stories by paying attention to how other authors write. She discusses how important characters are in stories—that stories are all about characters and their problems and that we enjoy stories because we get to know the characters and see how they deal with problems. She reads the first chapter of Louis Sachar's *Dogs Don't Tell Jokes* (1991), which begins with an engaging description of Gary, the class clown. She discusses what the author tells us about the character and what the reader can predict about the problems he will have. Then she introduces the evaluation questions and asks students to discuss how the author achieved these things.

Discussion of characters in stories is presented here as an introduction to teaching students to evaluate and revise their own stories, but note that this focus on characters also makes sense as reading comprehension instruction. Thinking about the personalities and motivations of characters is an important aspect of reading comprehension. Talking about characters is a good way to begin teaching students to make inferences when they read. As noted at the beginning of this chapter, critical reading and reading to revise have much in common. In this case, the teacher chose books that used fairly direct ways of conveying character so that students would be more likely to be able to use the techniques in their own stories.

The next part of instruction is one of the key elements: teaching students to evaluate writing and to revise based on the evaluation. Ms. A explains to the students that they can use these evaluation questions to revise their stories and those of other students. She posts the evaluation questions on a bulletin board for easy reference. Then she models the process. She begins by using stories from students in other classes so that students in her class will feel free to criticize and revise the stories. Later, students will practice evaluating and revising their own papers with peer support. She chooses stories that have all the basic story elements but are lacking in character development. Here is a sample story and modeling script:

> One Christmas, two brothers Jim and Thomas went up to New Hampshire with their family. When they got there there was a lot of snow on the ground and it was really cold out. The very next day they both went skiing. They raced each other down the hill. Jim went over a small jump and went flying in the air. He crash landed. When Thomas skied over to him, he found he had broken a leg. There was no one around because they had skied off the course. Thomas didn't know whether to stay with Jim or go for help. Finally, he skied down the hill and found the ski patrol. The ski patrol came and rescued Jim. The ambulance took him to the hospital. Luckily he was okay after his leg healed.

Ms. A: (*Reads the story and then thinks aloud.*) Okay, this story has characters, setting, a problem, and a resolution. The problem is that one of the brothers breaks a leg, and the solution is that the other one finds the ski patrol, who rescue him.

Now, I want to use the evaluation questions to see if I can revise the story to make it more interesting. The questions are all about characters. I'll ask all the questions and then try to revise the story.

The first question is "Are the characters described clearly?" Well, it tells me their names and that they are brothers. And they can ski. That's about all. I'd like to know more about them. I'd like to know how old they were and whether they were good skiers.

The second question is "Does the author show how the characters feel?" It's important to know how the characters feel in a story, and it's better if the author shows us through their actions instead of just saying it. This story doesn't say anything about their feelings. How do you think they felt when Jim broke his leg?

STUDENT: Scared!

MS. A: I bet they were scared, especially because there was no one around.

The third question is "Can you tell why the characters act the way they do?" Let's see. What did the characters do? They had a skiing accident. Is there some reason these boys had an accident? It sounds like they went off the regular ski trails, which wasn't very smart. Why did they do that? Do you have any ideas?

STUDENT: Maybe one of them dared the other to do it.

MS. A: That's a good idea. That would explain why they did it and make the story more interesting.

Okay. Now let's see if I can revise it. I'll add information about the characters. I think I'll make them very competitive with each other, which would explain why they were racing and got into trouble. Okay. "One Christmas, two brothers Jim and Thomas went up to New Hampshire with their family." I'll add some information here. "They were 12 years old and they were looking forward to skiing, which was their favorite sport." There. That tells us that they knew how to ski. "They were twins and were always trying to beat each other." Okay, that gives them a reason to be racing.

(Reading) "When they got there there was a lot of snow on the ground and it was really cold out. The very next day they both went skiing. They raced each other down the hill." Okay, I'm going to add something here about the dare. Let's see. "They both wanted to be the first one down the hill. Jim yelled to Thomas, 'I'm taking a shortcut through the woods. Bet you can't follow me.' Jim turned into the woods and Thomas raced after him."

Ms. A continues the revising, adding information about Jim's pain from the broken leg and how scared they both were. When she is done, she reads the story over and discusses how much better it is now because you can tell more about the characters and why they acted like they did.

After this initial modeling, Ms. A provides ample practice with the whole class and in collaborative groups. She displays stories of varying quality on the overhead projector and engages students in applying the evaluation questions and, when they identify weaknesses, in revising the story. She begins with whole-class practice, which gives students a chance to see each other applying the strategy and gives her a chance to prompt and guide them; however, whole-class practice does not engage enough students actively. Therefore, she also has students work on papers in small groups. Working together, each group evaluates a paper and makes revisions. Ms. A visits with the groups and gives feedback on their use of the evaluation and revising process. All groups work on the same papers so that they can discuss their evaluations and revisions with the whole class.

When Ms. A thinks the students have some understanding of the evaluation criteria, she introduces the full peer-revising strategy. She posts the strategy with the evaluation questions on the board. Then she models the strategy with the help of her teaching aide. The aide reads a paper she has written, and the Ms. A thinks aloud to model how she applies the evaluation questions. Then the two have a discussion about how to revise the paper to improve on those criteria.

Students then begin using the strategy in pairs to evaluate and revise their own papers. Ms. A requires the students to take notes on the evaluations and suggestions made by the editor to compare them to the actual revisions. She conducts conferences with the pairs, asking them to show her how they applied the strategy. These conferences give her an opportunity to see whether students are using the strategy successfully and to give appropriate support. If she sees that a number of students are having trouble with one of the evaluation criteria, she can provide more modeling and practice for the whole class.

One of the challenges of strategy instruction in general is to get students to see the value of the strategy so they will be motivated to continue to use and improve it. Ms. A does several things to promote this sense of the value of the strategy. First, when she conferences with pairs of students, she gives them feedback both on how well they used the strategy and on the quality of their papers. This combined feedback encourages the students to see how the strategy helps their writing. Second, when students share their papers in the class, they acknowledge the assistance of their editor. Ms. A often asks them to describe some way the editor helped them. Third, she emphasizes that expert writers have editors, too. She asks students to help edit her papers and talks about how her colleagues read and edit her papers before she turns them in for her college classes.

Finally, when Ms. A collects the final drafts and grades them, she uses the evaluation criteria as an important part of her grading. This alignment between students' self-evaluations and the teacher's grading encourages students to see the self-evaluations as important.

As the students master these particular evaluation questions, Ms. A goes on to teach new criteria. More likely than not, the class will by then be involved in learning a new type of writing with a new planning strategy and evaluation criteria appropriate to that form of writing.

Revision in an Eighth-Grade Unit on Persuasive Writing

Mr. B takes a somewhat different approach to teaching evaluation and revising in a unit on persuasive writing in his middle school English class. He works closely with the rest of his teaching team, and they have planned together to work on persuasive writing across the curriculum. Mr. B will take the lead to introduce persuasive writing in his English class, and other teachers will build on what his students learn. For example, the social studies teacher plans to engage the students in debates about immigration in American history followed by persuasive writing on various aspects of this broad issue.

Like Ms. A, Mr. B plans to teach both a planning and revising strategy, but he plans to connect the elements of the two strategies more closely and teach them together. The connection between the planning and revising strategies will be text structure, the elements of a type of text. Students will learn a strategy for planning persuasive essays that is based on an argumentative text structure. An argumentative essay includes a thesis or position, reasons, elaborations on those reasons (including supportive examples and evidence), and a conclusion. In addition, by eighth grade, students are expected to consider opposing positions and reasons and refute them. Although even elementary school students have a basic understanding of persuasion, persuasive writing is quite difficult for middle and high school students. It requires careful analytical thinking to generate reasons, connect reasons and evidence, and refute opposing positions.

Because of the difficulty of the task, Mr. B plans to use the evaluation strategy directly to support students in using the elements of argument that are in the planning strategy. Thus, the evaluation criteria will focus on the elements of an argument—position, reasons, elaborations, opposing positions, and refutations. He develops a self-evaluation scale for the students to use in evaluating their own papers and when working in peer revising (see Figure 7.1). He will use this same rating scale in grading and commenting on students' papers.

Before any instruction in persuasive writing, Mr. B has the students write two persuasive essays, one on an assigned topic and one on an is-

Score each question: 1   Needs revision
                       2   Okay
                       3   Excellent

Did I state my position clearly?	1	2	3
Are my reasons clear and well supported?			
First reason?	1	2	3
Second reason?	1	2	3
Did I consider the opposing position?	1	2	3
Did I refute the opposing position?	1	2	3
Did I use good transition words?	1	2	3
Did I conclude by summarizing my reasons?	1	2	3
Is the tone appropriate?	1	2	3
Is my essay persuasive?	1	2	3

Total points _____
What could I change to make my argument more persuasive?

FIGURE 7.1. Evaluation of a persuasive essay.

sue of their choice. He will ask students to revise these essays later so they can see how much they have learned about persuasive writing. They also provide a pool of writing samples that he can use in other classes to teach the evaluation and revision strategy.

Instruction begins with critical reading and analysis of persuasive texts. Critical reading is an important aspect of Mr. B's instruction for three reasons. First, his ultimate goal is for students to be able to read and listen to other people's perspectives and to respond by explaining and supporting their own views, not just to give their own opinions. He believes that his students will be engaged by a discussion of controversial issues and that such discussion will help them understand the purpose of persuasive writing and something about what it takes to be persuasive. Second, reading and analyzing texts is a way to show students the essential elements of persuasive writing that are used in the planning and revising strategies. Third, critical reading is very similar to the kind of rereading and evaluation required to revise their own writing. In both cases, students must read to identify reasons, evidence, and other elements and think about whether the reasons are convincing.

For one critical reading activity, Mr. B brings in copies of a newspaper editorial and several letters to the editor on a locally important issue, prohibiting smoking in restaurants and other public places. He is careful to choose an editorial that includes several reasons and directly addresses opposing positions. After a brief discussion of what one has to do to support an argument, he models analyzing the argument in the editorial. As he thinks aloud, he highlights, in different colors, the position, reasons, and refutations of opposing arguments. As he highlights the reasons, he thinks aloud about whether the reasons are really separate or all part of the same reason. He also thinks aloud about whether the evidence is good and whether he agrees. As he highlights the refutations, he thinks aloud about who might have those opposing positions and whether the author has answered them effectively. The process of highlighting the elements gets students to focus on the structure of the argument and consider each reason and its evidence. Then Mr. B asks students, working in small groups, to analyze the letters to the editor in the same way. Students then write brief letters to the editor of their own.

Next, Mr. B introduces the evaluation scale and models using it to evaluate and revise essays written by students unknown to his class. Middle school students are particularly reluctant to criticize their peers on any task assigned and graded by a teacher. Using papers from unknown students makes it easier for students to evaluate and criticize the work. Mr. B focuses attention, first, on the criteria about a clear position and reasons. As he models, he uses think-alouds to show his reasoning, but he also involves the students in the discussion. This sort of collaborative modeling allows the teacher to direct the overall process of applying the criteria but encourages student participation. Here is an example of collaborative modeling:

Student text displayed on overhead projector:

> I think smoking should be banned in some public places.
>   Some people can't handle other people smoking around them. They could either get sick or really choked up. Secondhand smoke can also be a problem. A child could be around someone smoking and inhel smoke and can become very sick.
>   Smoking can also be very rude. It can be very disgusting when your eating something and someone's cigarette smoke blows into your food. Lots of pollutants can get into the air.
>   People might disapprove because it is free country and they can smoke if they want to. But they probably don't know how much it is harmful to other people and the earth.

MR. B: (*Reads whole essay.*) Okay. Now I need to use the evaluation questions to help me figure out how to improve this essay. Let's see. Is the position clear? It says smoking should be banned in some public places. So I know which side the author is on, but I'm not sure about *some* public places. Does it mean *all* public places? Does anyone have an idea about how to fix that?

STUDENT A: We could just say *all* public places.

STUDENT B: We could say restaurants. It mentions them later.

MR. B: How could we say that?

STUDENT B: "I think smoking should be banned in all public places including restaurants and stores."

MR. B: (*Crosses out and inserts the needed words.*) Okay. That's better. I think I'm going to rate this a 2 now. It's okay but not great because it isn't elaborated on at all. The next evaluation question is whether the reasons are clear and supported. Let's find the reasons and underline them. There are two paragraphs here, so each should have a separate reason. This one starts "Some people can't handle other people smoking around them." Do you think that is clear?

STUDENT C: I don't think so. *Handle* could mean a lot of things. I think the author is talking about people getting sick. That's what the rest of the paragraph is about.

MR. B: I agree. How can we revise that first sentence to make it clearer?

STUDENT C: "Secondhand smoke can make other people sick."

STUDENT D: "If people smoke in public places, other people can get sick from the smoke."

MR. B: Both of those are good ideas. I like using the term "secondhand smoke." And I also like referring back to the idea about public places. Let's try, "If people smoke in public places, other people can get sick from the secondhand smoke." (*Writes.*) That's better. The rest of the paragraph still needs some work, but let's get the rest of the reasons fixed before we do that.

MR. B: Let's look at the next paragraph. "Smoking can also be very rude." Again, I'm not sure what that really means. Why is it rude? The next sentence says it's disgusting when you are eating. I think the author means that the smoke is unpleasant. Is that a different reason from the first paragraph?

STUDENT A: I think so. The first paragraph was about the smoke making people sick. Disgusting is something else. They just don't like the smoke.

MR. B: I think you're right. So this paragraph should be about other people not liking the smoke. Let me think how to say that. "When other people are eating, smoke can be very disgusting." I'm not sure I like that word, *disgusting*. Any other ideas?

STUDENT: "When other people are eating, smoke can be very unpleasant."

STUDENT: "When people are eating, they shouldn't have to smell cigarette smoke."

MR. B: Both of those ideas are good. (*Writes.*)

The discussion continues a while longer. Mr. B considers how the support for the two reasons could be improved and evaluates how the author considered the opposing position. In the end, he reads the revised paper and comments that it is much better, although it could be even better with more content.

Over the next few days, Mr. B has students work in pairs to evaluate and revise more essays written by students unknown to them. They use the evaluation scale to support their evaluations. Mr. B also continues to evaluate and revise papers as a whole-class activity. The papers range widely in quality and include some essays that are well written and need little revision. Mr. B, however, always manages to find some way to improve the paper by strengthening the support for its reasons or the way the paper responds to the opposing position. As part of the discussion, students talk about whether they agree with the positions taken and whether they think the evidence is convincing. Persuasive writing is not just about whether writers follow the form; the content of the reasons and evidence is critical, and it is part of what they evaluate.

When students are consistently able to evaluate essays and revise them, Mr. B introduces a planning strategy for persuasive essays. Students already have a clear idea of what is required for an effective essay. The planning strategy helps students generate and organize their ideas before writing. It asks them to list reasons and evidence on both sides of the issue so that they are prepared to defend their position and respond to potential opposing positions.

Students then begin writing persuasive essays and applying the evaluation scale to revise them. Mr. B has them work in pairs to evaluate and revise their papers. Students now are able to help each other because they have learned how to analyze and evaluate persuasive essays. Their natural reluctance to criticize each other is tempered somewhat by the knowledge that the teacher will be grading their papers on the same criteria that they are using. He also asks them to evaluate and revise the essays they wrote before instruction to show them how much they have learned.

The students write on a range of persuasive topics. They write on policy issues that are meaningful to middle school students, such as whether students should have after-school jobs. They also write about the literature they are reading; Mr. B raises challenging questions about whether characters should have taken the actions they did, and the students respond, drawing evidence from the book as well as from their experience. Students also start to use the planning and revising strategies for assignments in other classes. Mr. B has worked together with the team of teachers so that they are all familiar with the strategy. Using the strategies in multiple classes addresses the common problem of maintenance and generalization.

Mr. B's instruction included several of the components that research has shown are important to learning to revise. He provided meaningful writing tasks with a clear goal to persuade an audience. Sometimes the audience was peers; other times it was an imagined audience but one within students' experience. He taught critical reading of persuasive essays as well as evaluation criteria and how to use those criteria to revise papers. He engaged students in whole-class and peer dialogue about evaluation and revision. Finally, he arranged with his colleagues to use the strategies across content areas.

CONCLUDING REMARKS

In closing, I would like to summarize a few principles for teaching revision in ways that help students develop their overall writing skills. First, it is important to provide a classroom context in which writing has meaningful goals. One of most common and best ways to make writing meaningful is to arrange authentic writing tasks that are read by peers and other audiences, but authentic audiences are not the only way to provide meaningful goals. Students can also be engaged in writing tasks with clear goals based on learning specific objectives, such as the task of describing tangrams mentioned above (Holliway & McCutchen, 2004). Revision is a process of comparing the actual text to the intended text; thus, it depends on the goals for the writing task.

Second, peer interaction and teacher–student dialogue are essential to learning to evaluate texts. Peers and teachers are first readers for students' writing, and students learn from serving as editors as well as from hearing the responses of others to their writing. Peer collaboration is also highly motivating, and it reflects the reality that most writing tasks outside of school are surrounded by rich oral communication.

Third, revision begins with evaluation, and the primary reason students have difficulty revising is that they do not know how to evaluate their writing. Thus, it is important to teach students specific criteria for evaluation and how to revise based on those criteria. Most effective approaches to teaching revising involve instruction in evaluation.

Fourth, it is valuable to integrate reading comprehension instruction with instruction in evaluation and revision. Critical reading is similar in many ways to reading for revision; the main difference is in the purpose—reading to understand versus reading to identify problems and revise.

Fifth, word processing is a helpful tool in learning to revise. It simplifies the physical processes of revising and removes an important disincentive to revision—recopying. It also encourages students to produce final copies for publication, which is one of the main motivations for revising.

Finally, strategy instruction is a highly effective way to improve students' revising skills and the overall quality of their writing. Most strategy instruction in revision pulls together elements of evaluation criteria, peer interaction, and self-regulation. Much of the research combines instruction in strategies for planning and revising.

REFERENCES

Bereiter, C., & Scardamalia, M. (1987). *The psychology of written composition.* Hillsdale, NJ: Erlbaum.

Boscolo, P., & Ascorti, K. (2004). Effects of collaborative revision on children's ability to write understandable narrative texts. In L. Allal, L. Chanqouy, & P. Largy (Eds.), *Revision: Cognitive and instructional processes* (Vol. 13, pp. 157–170). Boston: Kluwer.

De La Paz, S., Swanson, P. N., & Graham, S. (1998). The contribution of executive control to the revising of students with writing and learning difficulties. *Journal of Educational Psychology, 90,* 448–460.

DiPardo, A., & Freedman, S. W. (1988). Peer response groups in the writing classroom: Theoretic foundations and new directions. *Review of Educational Research, 58,* 119–149.

Englert, C. S., Raphael, T. E., Anderson, L. M., Anthony, H. M., & Stevens, D. D. (1991). Making writing strategies and self-talk visible: Cognitive strategy instruction in writing in regular and special education classrooms. *American Educational Research Journal, 28,* 337–372.

Fitzgerald, J. (1987). Research on revision in writing. *Review of Educational Research, 57,* 481–506.

Graham, S. (2006). Strategy instruction and the teaching of writing: A meta-analysis. In C. A. MacArthur, S. Graham, & J. Fitzgerald (Eds.), *Handbook of writing research* (pp. 187–207). New York: Guilford Press.

Graham, S., & MacArthur, C. A. (1988). Improving learning disabled students' skills at revising essays produced on a word processor: Self-instructional strategy training. *Journal of Special Education, 22,* 133–152.

Graham, S., MacArthur, C. A., & Schwartz, S. S. (1995). The effects of goal setting and procedural facilitation on the revising behavior and writing performance of students with writing and learning problems. *Journal of Educational Psychology, 87,* 230–240.

Graham, S., Schwartz, S. S., & MacArthur, C. A. (1993). Knowledge of writing and the composing process, attitude towards writing, and self-efficacy for students with and without learning disabilities. *Journal of Learning Disabilities, 26,* 237–249.

Hayes, J. R. (1996). A new framework for understanding cognition and affect in writing. In C. M. Levy & S. Ransdell (Eds.), *The science of writing* (pp. 1–27). Mahwah, NJ: Erlbaum.

Hayes, J. R. (2004). What triggers revision? In L. Allal, L. Chanqouy, & P. Largy (Eds.), *Revision: Cognitive and instructional processes* (Vol. 13, pp. 9–20). Boston: Kluwer.

Hayes, J. R., Flower, L., Schriver, K. A., Stratman, J. F., & Carey, L. (1987). Cognitive processes in revision. In S. Rosenberg (Ed.), *Advances in applied psycholinguistics*. Vol. 2. *Reading, writing, and language learning* (pp. 176–240). New York: Cambridge University Press.

Hillocks, G. (1986). *Research on written composition: New directions for teaching*. Urbana, IL: ERIC Clearinghouse on Reading and Communication Skills.

Holliway, D. R., & McCutchen, D. (2004). Audience perspective in young writers' composing and revising. In L. Allal, L. Chanqouy, & P. Largy (Eds.), *Revision: Cognitive and instructional processes* (Vol. 13, pp. 87–101). Boston: Kluwer.

MacArthur, C. A. (2006). The effects of new technologies on writing and writing processes. In C. A. MacArthur, S. Graham, & J. Fitzgerald (Eds.), *Handbook of writing research* (pp. 248–262). New York: Guilford Press.

MacArthur, C. A., Graham, S., & Schwartz, S. (1991). Knowledge of revision and revising behavior among learning disabled students. *Learning Disability Quarterly, 14*, 61–73.

MacArthur, C. A., Midgette, E., & Haria, P. (in press). *The effects of content and audience awareness goals for revision on the persuasive essays of fifth- and eighth-grade students*. Reading & Writing: An Interdisciplinary Journal.

MacArthur, C. A., Schwartz, S. S., & Graham, S. (1991). Effects of a reciprocal peer revision strategy in special education classrooms. *Learning Disabilities Research and Practice, 6*, 201–210.

McCutchen, D., Francis, M., & Kerr, S. (1997). Revising for meaning: Effects of knowledge and strategy. *Journal of Educational Psychology, 89*, 667–676.

Midgette, E., Haria, P., & MacArthur, C. A. (in press). The effects of content and audience awareness goals for revision on the persuasive essays of fifth- and eighth-grade students. *Reading and Writing: An International Journal*.

Murray, D. (1991). *The craft of revision*. Austin, TX: Holt, Rinehart, & Winston.

Rijlaarsdam, G., Couzijn, M., & van den Bergh, H. (2004). The study of revision as a writing process and as a learning-to-write process: Two prospective research agendas. In L. Allal, L. Chanquoy, & P. Largy (Eds.), *Revision: Cognitive and instructional processes* (Vol. 13, pp. 189–208). Norwell, MA: Kluwer.

Stoddard, B., & MacArthur, C. A. (1993). A peer editor strategy: Guiding learning disabled students in response and revision. *Research in the Teaching of English, 27*, 76–103.

8

Improving Sentence Construction Skills through Sentence-Combining Practice

BRUCE SADDLER

In many societies, writing is an essential tool for communication and an important tool for learning. In school settings, writing is often the primary way students demonstrate their knowledge and academic competence both in class and on high-stakes educational assessments.

Researchers and teachers have recognized that writing is a very intricate process and a very complex facet of the language arts, representing the pinnacle of the language hierarchy (Graham, 1997; Hillocks, 1986). While engaged in the writing process, a writer must work through four structural levels: overall text structure, paragraph structure, sentence structure (syntax), and word structure (Bereiter & Scardamalia, 1987; Hayes & Flower, 1986; Rohr, 1994). It is important for a writer to be comfortable with all these levels because difficulties on any level may cause the overall composition to suffer.

Of the many difficulties writers encounter when engaged in the complex act of writing, crafting sentences that accurately convey the intended meaning is particularly challenging (Isaacson, 1985). Although all writers need to manipulate sentences creatively, at times each sentence can be a test of their abilities. Manipulating sentences is both effortful and critical. One well-written sentence may make the reader want to read the next one; conversely, the flow of a story can be compromised by a faulty rhythm in a sentence.

Because of the importance of this skill in the overall writing process, direct, systematic instruction in it may be necessary for many students. In this chapter, an instructional method that provides direct practice with sentence construction skills, called *sentence combining*, is presented.

First, I provide the reasons sentence construction skills need to be taught directly; next, I explain why sentence-combining instruction is effective in teaching these skills; then, I suggest how sentence combining can be included within the overall writing curriculum; finally, I provide two classroom examples to illustrate how sentence combining could be taught within a second-grade and a 10th-grade class.

RATIONALE FOR DIRECT INSTRUCTION OF SENTENCE CONSTRUCTION SKILLS

Young writers usually begin writing individual words or phrases on paper, then sentences, then paragraphs. They learn to create sentences expressing what their teachers term "complete thoughts." Then they move on to sentences that declare, question, or exclaim. Finally, they string together enough sentences to make a paragraph and, eventually a short story. However, our language is so flexible that this process can be derailed at many points along the way as young writers become entangled while trying to express their thoughts within the structure of a sentence. Therefore, writers can benefit from direct practice in constructing sentences (Saddler & Graham, 2005).

Constructing effective sentences is important to young writers for several reasons. First, knowledge of effective writing formats at the sentence level allows writers to translate their thoughts into text. Second, constructing well-designed, grammatically correct sentences may make the material students write easier for others to read. A story crafted with one simple sentence after another without variety quickly becomes boring. Likewise, a story replete with excessively long, complex sentences becomes difficult to follow. In either case, if grammatical issues are present due to malformed sentences, the reader's mind is distracted from the writer's intent (Saddler & Graham, 2005).

SENTENCE COMBINING

Only one approach to teaching sentence construction skills has received the sustained attention of researchers. This approach, called sentence combining, was developed in the 1960s, when researchers and teachers were looking for alternatives to teaching formal grammar (parts of speech, sentence diagramming).

Since then, more than 80 studies conducted during the last 40 years have demonstrated with few exceptions that sentence combining is an effective method for helping students produce more syntactically mature sentences (e.g., Cooper, 1973; Crowhurst & Piche, 1979; Hunt, 1965; O'Hare, 1973; Saddler & Graham, 2005). (Syntactical maturity is the ability to write a variety of complex and compound sentences within a story.) Researchers have documented the positive effects of sentence-combining practice with writers from elementary school through college. Various aspects of sentence-combining instruction have been researched, including which genre of writing (persuasive, narrative, expository) is most affected by such instruction, how oral training in sentence combining may improve written text, and if sentence-combining instruction might improve reading rate and comprehension.

Three underlying questions have driven this research. First, what effect does sentence combining have on a writer's syntactical maturity? Second, can sentence combining improve the overall quality of writing? Third, will sentence combining improve reading comprehension?

Sentence-combining practice improves the syntactical maturity of children at nearly all grade levels. Hillocks (1986) reported that more than 60% of the sentence-combining studies performed between 1973 and 1985 produced significant results on measures of syntactical maturity, 30% reported improvements at a nonsignificant level, and only 10% showed no improvement or mixed results.

A recent literature review of the effect of grammar teaching on writing development by Andrews and colleagues (2006) provided further support for the effectiveness of sentence combining as a means of improving the syntactical maturity of students between the ages of 5 and 16 in English. In this review, Andrews and colleagues cited two studies as particularly important: one by O'Hare (1973) and the other by Saddler and Graham (2005).

O'Hare (1973) found that the sentence-combining activities he taught led to highly significant growth in syntactical maturity. In fact, by the end of the study, eighth graders were displaying the same level of complexity in their writing as might be expected of 12th graders. Sentence-combining practice also led to gains in writing quality. Because of these results, O'Hare (1973) concluded that "teachers of writing surely ought to spend more time teaching students to be better manipulators of syntax. Intensive experience with sentence combining should help enlarge a young writer's repertoire of syntactic alternatives while supplying him with practical options during the writing process" (p. 76).

Saddler and Graham's study (2005) was designed to examine the effectiveness of sentence-combining instruction coupled with peer instruction on the sentence-construction abilities of skilled and less skilled writers (including writers with learning disabilities). The 44 fourth-grade writers in the sample received either sentence-combining or grammar-based instruction. In both groups, the writers worked in pairs to support and encourage each others' acquisition of the writing skills being taught. The researchers found that sentence-combining instruction was more effective than grammar-based instruction in improving sentence-combining skills and had a positive impact on writing quality.

BENEFITS OF SENTENCE COMBINING

As a curriculum supplement, sentence combining provides direct, mindful practice in manipulating and rewriting basic phrases or clauses into more syntactically mature or varied forms. For example, if a student characteristically composes simple kernel sentences such as "My dog is fat. My dog is black," he or she can learn through sentence-combining practice to combine or embed these kernel sentences into more syntactically complex and mature sentences, such as "My dog is fat and black" or "The fat black dog is mine," depending on what idea in the sentence he or she wishes to emphasize. Likewise, if a student produces sentences that are overly complex or ambiguous, he or she can learn to decombine the sentences back into their basic kernels and then recombine them into a more cohesive and understandable whole.

The benefits of sentence combining rest on three principles. First, students need instruction in formulating a concept of what a written sentence is and the syntactical options that are available to them when producing a sentence. Sentence combining can help some students understand choices available to them at the sentence level. Second, once the process of sentence formation and reformation becomes automatized, the overall cognitive strain of writing is reduced, and the student can free up cognitive space to attend to higher-level functions such as awareness of audience needs, what constitutes good writing, or how to navigate the process of writing. Third, gains in syntactical fluency lead to quality writing (Strong, 1986).

Sentence-combining exercises can prompt students to use syntactical options in their writing by providing them practice in consciously controlling and manipulating syntax (Saddler, 2005). Through the process of decombining and recombining sentences, students can learn to untangle, tighten, and rewrite sentences that may be too complex for a reader to easily understand. Instead of longer sentences, the value of sentence combining may reside in making sentences and whole discourse better through employing a variety of syntactical forms—the goal being clarity of thought instead of complexity. Therefore, sentences can be shorter if they are more effective in getting the writer's message across to the reader.

INSTRUCTIONAL RECOMMENDATIONS

In the next section, I present two classroom vignettes of sentence-combining instruction at different grade levels. The first example illustrates how sentence combining can be included with a second-grade class, while the second depicts sentence-combining instruction with a 10th-grade class.

Example 1: Second-Grade Class

This class included three children with learning disabilities and writing disabilities and several other children who struggled with various aspects of writing. The teacher, Ms. Asaro, instituted sentence-combining practice to help these children construct better sentences and better stories.

Many of the students in Ms. Asaro's classroom tended to create very short sentences that sounded similar. Not only were many of the students writing sentences that were short, simply constructed, and lacking in descriptive words, but many also used a very repetitive subject–verb–object pattern that gave the reader the impression of immature writing and made their stories choppy and difficult to read. Others produced massive run-on sentences connected by a long series of ands, while still others scattered sentence fragments throughout their compositions.

These difficulties on the sentence level affected the overall quality of their stories. Although Ms. Asaro used a variety of writing prompts and always allowed the children a choice in what they wrote about, their stories were typically short and rather boring. She believed that many of her students could say more in their stories, but because they lacked the skill to write well-constructed, interesting sentences, they could not accurately translate their ideas and emotions into text. Based on her analysis of her students' writing strengths and needs, she decided to supplement her writing workshop time with sentence-combining instruction.

Ms. Asaro began by introducing the exercises as an activity that could help writers create more interesting sentences that sound better to readers. She suggested that skilled writers frequently rework their sentences to help convey their message better and explained that even in her own writing she would often change her sentences around to decide if she could write her ideas in a better way.

She started with a whole-class discussion by projecting a pair of simple kernel sentences on the overhead projector and modeling how to combine them. To help everyone understand the basic process of combining sentences, she chose two sentences that were as similar as possible, except for the words to be combined: "The dog is little. The dog jumped high." She suggested that, for these exercises, there is usually more than one combination possible and not to worry about making mistakes because mistakes were opportunities for learning. Then she read both sentences out loud and said, "Hmmm . . . Well, one way to put these two sentences together would be to say 'The little dog jumped high.' " She wrote the new sentence on the overhead transparency and explained her reasoning in combining the sentences in the way she chose and why she believed the new combination sounded better. She showed that, when she combined the sentences, she moved words or parts around, deleted or changed words or parts, and/or added words or parts to the sentences to make them sound better and convey her ideas more clearly.

Ms. Asaro then performed several additional combinations while increasing the amount of discussion and quality judgments the students provided and decreasing her own input. Her goal was to prompt the students to rely on the knowledge of English they had developed from years of listening and reading to decide on the correctness and sound quality of a combination, which is exactly what she wanted them to do when they wrote stories. The discussion that commenced led to some interesting opinions about why a certain combination sounded better and why adding a word here or there made the thought clearer. Even students who seldom participated in class discussions added their ideas to the mix.

After this introductory session, Ms. Asaro began all of the subsequent sessions with oral practice. First, she reasoned that when combining sentences the ear must hear alternatives to be able to choose the sentence that sounds best (Strong, 1986). She realized that in her own writing she often reread a passage of text out loud to hear the sound. Second, her students' handwriting and spelling skills were still developing, and, as a result, the physical act of writing impeded the speed with which they could write sentences. Practicing orally circumvented this difficulty, saved precious class time, and allowed for additional practice opportunities with the skill being learned.

Oral practice was included by arranging her class in pairs, presenting kernel sentence clusters on the overhead, and asking the pairs to discuss the kernels and provide examples of combinations orally. She randomly called on pairs to give their combinations and wrote several different examples on the overhead. These were then read aloud to determine which sounded best.

Although writing is sometimes viewed as a solitary activity, Ms. Asaro believed that much of the potential power of sentence-combining exercises resided in playing with language within a group environment of idea exchanges. She felt that when many students approached an identical writing task at once, they became aware of the solutions available from other writers close to their level of maturity and experience, so, during these oral exercises, she always encouraged group discussions, feedback, evaluation, reflection, and praise.

Following oral practice, Ms. Asaro would have a brief partner practice session where students worked together to write out combinations for several additional kernel sentence clusters. The students frequently wrote their responses on a transparency and then presented their versions on the overhead. Ms. Asaro always asked for several possible solutions for each problem and discussed each thoroughly, praising success and supporting improvement as needed.

Sources for Material

Although Ms. Asaro's district did not possess a curriculum for sentence combining, finding sources for exercise content was actually fairly simple. Initially, she created kernel sentences from a collection of short stories the class was reading by reducing a passage into very simple short sentences. Then the kernels were rewritten by students working in pairs. The new versions were read by each pair to the class and followed by group discussions of each version.

Ms. Asaro also found that classroom activities or school happenings could be sources of inspiration, along with the lives and interests of her students. Newspapers and magazines also furnished interesting content for her to develop sentence-combining exercises. Many of these sources offered a bonus by providing her students with information on a new concept or reinforcing a lesson from a science or social studies unit.

Types of Exercises

When developing exercises from these sources, Ms. Asaro followed two guidelines (Strong, 1976, 1986). First, she set up the exercises so that the base clause came first, followed by one or more modifying sentences. For example:

Base sentence:	The bird flew.
Modifying sentence:	The bird was blue.
Combination:	The blue bird flew.

Second, she used two types of clues to prompt the children on the important information they needed to keep from the second sentence. The first clue was an underlined word:

The professor had written many books.
The professor was <u>wise</u>.

This problem resulted in the combination:

The wise professor had written many books.

The second type of clue was a connecting word enclosed in parentheses at the end of the sentence to be combined:

Kristie fell over the laundry basket.
She lost her balance. (because)

This problem resulted in a combination such as:

Kristie fell over the laundry basket because she lost her balance.

After the students were comfortable with these exercises, Ms. Asaro eliminated the clues. Without the clues, the students had to decide what important material in the second sentence to include within the first when the two were combined.

Once she realized that her students were comfortable with combining two sentences, she began to ask them to combine longer sequences of sentences (without clues) that could be combined in multiple ways. For example:

The dog barked.
The dog was brown.
It was in a cage.
It was angry.

This group of sentences elicited many interesting combinations and provided a fun conversation concerning which of the versions sounded best. For example:

The brown dog barked because it was in a cage.
The angry brown dog was barking in its cage.

When combining multiple sentences, Ms. Asaro prompted her students to add additional descriptive words to the completed sentence. For example:

Barking angrily, the huge brown dog walked around his cage.

Skill Sequence

Initially, Ms. Asaro relied on skill sequence suggestions created by Cooper (1973; see Table 8.1) as a guide and adjusted the topics to coincide closely with the needs of her students within their own compositions. Ms. Asaro believed that a writer's own work is the best arena to learn any writing skill. Although the contrived exercises were effective in increasing the variety and overall quality of the sentences her students wrote, she wanted to move away from this format as rapidly as possible. As soon as her students understood and were comfortable with combining sentences, she began asking them to work and rework the sentences within a current piece of their writing. Such tailoring of the skills she taught made her teaching time more effective and the skills themselves more relevant to her students at their individual stages of understanding and need.

To provide group practice that focused on a specific skill, Ms. Asaro projected a paragraph from one of her students on the overhead and asked the class to suggest ways the sentences could be improved. She paired up her students and provided a paper copy of the paragraph to each pair. She challenged them to talk together to discover how the paragraph could be changed. After they had written down their ideas, the class read various versions out loud and discussed how each was different from the original text.

Ms. Asaro believed that using her students' own work was the most natural way to engage them at their level of need and provide direct resolution of problems associated with a current piece of writing. In addition, since in any written work sentences build on one another to create a unified whole, her students could explore the effect a change in rhythm of one sentence might have on others. Also, because the answer to what makes a good sentence depends mostly upon the purpose of that sentence within the context of a composition, allowing them to practice selecting options within their own writing made sense.

Judging Correctness

During the practice sessions, the concern Ms. Asaro most often faced was gauging "correctness." Her students wanted to establish objective

TABLE 8.1. Possible Sequence of Sentence-Combining Exercises

1. Inserting adjectives and adverbs
   Examples: The man ate the veggie burger.
   The man was <u>starving</u>.
   The starving man ate the veggie burger.

   The man ate the veggie burger.
   He ate <u>hungrily</u>.
   The man ate the veggie burger hungrily.

2. Producing compound subjects and objects
   Examples: Bruce wanted to read.
   <u>Mary</u> wanted to read.
   Bruce and Mary wanted to read.

   Kristie wanted pasta.
   Kristie wanted <u>broccoli</u>.
   Kristie wanted pasta and broccoli.

3. Producing compound sentences with *and* and *but*
   Examples: Maren wanted to play outside.
   Sarah wanted to play inside. (but)
   Maren wanted to play outside, but Sarah wanted to play inside.

4. Producing possessive nouns
   Examples: I like the kitten.
   It is <u>Kevin's</u>.
   I like Kevin's kitten.

5. Producing sentences with adverbial clauses using connecting words (*because*, *after*, *until*, and *when*)
   Example: We went to school.
   We wanted to learn to read. (because)
   We went to school because we wanted to learn to read.

6. Producing sentences with relative clauses.
   Example: The student will be first.
   The student <u>is the closest to the door</u>. (who)
   The student who is the closest to the door will be first.

7. Inserting appositives.
   Example: Steve spoke to the class.
   Steve is <u>a great storyteller</u>.
   Steve, a great storyteller, spoke to the class.

Note. For a more detailed discussion on sequencing sentence combining exercises, see Cooper (1973).

criteria to help them test the correctness of different sentence combinations, perhaps because they were more familiar with being told something was right or wrong rather than being told, "That's good, but there might be a better way to say it."

Although our language does have rules that govern syntax, Ms. Asaro believed that using complex grammatical terminology to judge correctness would have been counterproductive. She stressed effectiveness as a much better indicator of merit than correctness. She felt that gauging effectiveness encouraged risk taking by welcoming mistakes as opportunities for discussion and problem solving. Within this context, mistakes became sentences that could be formed in better ways. This view was especially beneficial for her less skilled writers, who were often unwilling to take risks with their writing. In addition, emphasizing effectiveness helped her students understand that there is often not one right answer in writing; rather, there may be multiple solutions that require introspection to decide on the best option.

Ms. Asaro found three standards (Nemans, 1995) helpful in aiding her students to gauge the effectiveness of responses: clarity and directness of meaning, rhythmic appeal, and intended audience. Initially, she modeled and discussed the standards, then directed student pairs to use the standards to rate each other's writing.

Measuring Improvement

Although Ms. Asaro felt that her students were improving, she began to look for evidence that sentence combining was making a difference and exactly what difference it was making. In what ways was her students' writing changing? Was the time she was investing in sentence combining justified?

After analyzing her class's stories from before and after sentence-combining instruction, there were two areas in which Ms. Asaro noticed improvement. The first was a reduction of punctuation errors. As she had often taught, punctuation helps organize sentence elements. What she did not anticipate was that through the combining–decombining–recombining process her students would have hands-on practice using punctuation elements. As they increased the complexity of their sentences, they learned, for example, that commas were needed to set off elements from one another and that they could create rhythmic appeal within a sentence. They talked about when and where punctuation was needed and where it was not. Overall, their compositions became much cleaner in terms of punctuation and more appropriate usage, which led to a marked decrease in both fragments and run-on sentences.

The second benefit was in the overall quality of the stories they wrote. Her students' writing became more enjoyable for her to read. They had far fewer repetitive subject–verb–object sentences and run-ons, leading to a more satisfying rhythm to their writing and pieces that simply sounded better.

These improvements did not occur overnight. Sentence combining was not a quick fix; it took time and effort. Ms. Asaro had to dedicate instructional time to teaching sentence combining, but she did not allow the practice to detract from her other writing tasks. She kept the sessions short—no more than 10–15 minutes, several times per week—and the practice lively, believing that if the sessions became drudgery to teach, they would be even more so to learn.

Example 2: 10th-Grade Class

The second example involves teaching sentence combining to a 10th-grade social studies class. In this class, four students had identified disabilities, but many more struggled with various aspects of writing. The teacher, Mr. Thomas, wanted to improve his students' ability to write essays about historical figures and to help them remember more about the period of history they were studying.

Mr. Thomas realized that his students' writing needed assistance in several areas. Many of his students produced papers filled with run-on sentences and fragments. They frequently used the connectors *and*, *but*, and *or* to create long sentences or failed to include punctuation where it was needed. Few of his students invested effort in revising their papers.

Run-On Sentences and Sentence Fragments

Mr. Thomas realized that his students' run-ons and fragments might be occurring because they had difficulty understanding when and where to use punctuation. He analyzed their writing to determine the kinds of errors being made and found that the run-on sentence mistakes fell into one of two categories: failing to use periods to separate thoughts that could stand alone and using too many conjunctions to connect ideas within a single sentence.

He believed that his students often failed to add needed punctuation because they were trying to create sentence variety. As they did not understand or had not specifically practiced how to create grammatical complexity in stories, they ended up with run-ons. In order to provide support for this need, he first explained to his class that a sentence is like an island that can stand alone (Saddler & Preschern, in press). Then he provided the students with two sentences to combine and explained how each sentence could stand alone because it had a subject, predicate, and modifiers. Next, he asked the students for examples of ways to combine the sentences without using a connecting word such as *and*, *but*, or *so*. This process was repeated during mini-lessons at least three times per week. In addition to his students' papers, he found that his social studies textbook provided great content for the creation of exercises.

Mr. Thomas used a similar activity to help eliminate run-on sentences that used conjunctions to connect too many ideas. When introducing the activity, he wrote the overused conjunction on a picture of a bridge (Saddler & Preschern, in press). Then he explained to students that conjunctions, specifically *and*, *but*, and *so*, work as bridges to link ideas. When there are too many bridges in a sentence, it becomes difficult for the reader to cross and understand. He then wrote a run-on sentence (e.g., "George Washington went to the river and then he got into the boat and then he sailed across the wide river with his troops") on the board and replaced all the *ands* with pictures of bridges to help students visualize this. Once his students saw how run-ons could be confusing, they began to understand the purpose and function of these conjunctions. Mr. Thomas noticed that this realization caused a decrease in the number of run-on sentences his students wrote.

Revising

Mr. Thomas believed it was important to integrate the sentence-combining exercises with other components of the writing process as soon as possible because the quicker any learned skill taught during a mini-lesson was integrated into actual writing, the greater the likelihood that the skill would actually be adapted into his students' writing toolbox. One way he found to incorporate sentence-combining skills directly into the writing process in a meaningful way was during revising (see MacArthur, Chapter 7, this volume, on revising).

Before Mr. Thomas began sentence-combining practice, he believed that his students mainly saw the revision process as one of editing. They seemed to operate under a least-effort strategy, meaning they changed what was easiest to change. He noticed that they would conduct "housekeeping" by fixing spelling, capitalization, formatting, and perhaps punctuation rather than engaging in real revising—namely, molding the sound of text to make a message clearer or providing an audience with what they need to know.

He began to include lessons on revising using the sentence-combining skill being practiced. For example, he would place a student's writing sample on the overhead and look for specific places in the essay where a conjunction could be used to connect two shorter sentences or where a phrase could be embedded to create a better sounding sentence or to add variety.

While conducting these lessons, Mr. Thomas would think out loud and model the thought process involved in choosing to make a certain combination. He used a variety of self-statements to help his students "see" what he was thinking. For example, he would say, "What do I have to do here?" to define the problem. He also used "Does that make sense?"; "Is that the best way that part can sound?"; and "Can I say that better?" as self-evaluations and "I really like the sound of that part" for self-reinforcement.

After modeling the revision process, Mr. Thomas began to have the students edit their own pieces of writing using the sentence-combining skills being practiced. The goal was for them to find two or three places to add sentence variety. For example, if a lesson had been taught on writing more sophisticated paragraphs through the use of participial phrases, he had the students either choose a sentence that could be embellished using a participial phrase or identify two sentences that could be combined to create one sentence with a participial phrase. If necessary, he would help them find places to make changes.

After his students had proofread a previous paper, he had them write a new one. In this new piece, he required students to include at least two sentences that targeted the writing goal. For example, if they were working on cause-and-effect subordinate clauses, he required them to include two sentences that correctly used either *because, since, so,* or *even though* for transition words.

Another great way Mr. Thomas found to have students increase their sentence-combining and revising skills was to have them proofread each others' work. He arranged students in pairs and had them search for one sentence they thought was well written in their partners' work and one place where there could be a revision using the sentence-combining skill being practiced. He then allowed the students about 10–15 minutes to work as he circulated and provided assistance as needed. He then prompted the students to provide one positive comment and one suggestion to their partners.

After several weeks of brief sentence-combining practice sessions, Mr. Thomas noticed that the amount of revisions climbed in his students' work. Because he kept the rough drafts his students produced, he was able to notice that they were changing words, adding phrases and clauses, and reworking entire sentences far more frequently and effectively.

CONCLUSIONS

Although sentence-combining exercises have proven effective in increasing the syntactical fluency of writers, they represent only one component within a writing program. These exercises cannot replace other validated writing instruction practices, nor are they a quick fix, as changes in writing behavior take time and much practice. They cannot meet every challenge skilled or less skilled writers will face during the composing process. Teachers should not rely on them exclusively; however, when sentence-combining exercises are used as one component of a well-rounded writing program that includes ample time for writing, conferencing between peers and teachers, mini-lessons to increase skills, ample teacher modeling, and choice in writing assignments, they can fill a void for many writers. Through meaningful discussions, they can provide every writer with controlled, disciplined practice in constructing a variety of interesting and meaningful sentences.

REFERENCES

Andrews, R., Torgerson, C., Beverton, S., Freeman, A., Locke, T., Low, G., et al. (2006). The effect of grammar teaching on writing development. *British Educational Research Journal, 32,* 39–55.

Bereiter, C., & Scardamalia, M. (1987). *The psychology of written composition.* Hillsdale, NJ: Erlbaum.

Cooper, C. R. (1973). An outline for writing sentence combining problems. *English Journal, 62,* 96–102.

Crowhurst, M., & Piche, G. L. (1979). Audience and mode of discourse effects on syntactic complexity in writing at two grade levels. *Research in the Teaching of English, 13,* 101–109.

Graham, S. (1997). Executive control in the revising of students with learning and writing difficulties. *Journal of Educational Psychology, 89,* 223–234.

Hayes, J. R., & Flower, L. S. (1986) Writing research and the writer. *American Psychologist, 41,* 106–113.

Hillocks, G. (1986). *Research on written composition.* Urbana, IL: ERIC Clearinghouse on Reading and Communication Skills.

Hunt, K. W. (1965). *Grammatical structures written at three grade levels* (Research Rep. No. 3). Champaign, IL: National Council of Teachers of English.

Isaacson, S. L. (1985). *Assessing the potential syntax development of third- and fourth-grade writers* (Doctoral dissertation, Arizona State University, 1985). Digital Dissertations, AAT 8513591.

Nemans, B. S. (1995). *Teaching students to write.* New York: Oxford University Press.

O'Hare, F. (1973). *Sentence combining.* Champaign, IL: National Council of Teachers of English.

Rohr, H. M. (1994). *Writing: Its evolution and relation to speech.* Brockmeyer, Germany: Universitatsverlag Dr. Norbert.

Saddler, B. (2005). Sentence combining: A sentence-level writing intervention. *Reading Teacher, 58,* 468–471.

Saddler, B., & Graham, S. (2005). The effects of peer-assisted sentence combining instruction on the writing of more and less skilled young writers. *Journal of Educational Psychology, 97*(1), 43–54.

Saddler, B., & Preschern, J. (in press). Improving sentence writing ability through sentence combining practice. *Teaching Exceptional Children.*

Strong, W. (1976). Close-up: Sentence combining. *English Journal, 24,* 56–65.

Strong, W. (1986). *Creative approaches to sentence combining.* Urbana, IL: ERIC Clearinghouse on Reading and Communication Skills and the National Council of Teachers of English.

9

Best Practices in Spelling and Handwriting

BOB SCHLAGAL

Spelling and handwriting are among the least glamorous topics in today's language arts. By contrast, in the 19th and a portion of the 20th century, schooling in literacy involved heavy emphasis on penmanship and spelling along with a great deal of drill and practice.

Broadly speaking, two forces have helped push spelling and handwriting to the margins of the curriculum. The first was a shift in instructional priorities in the late 20th century that emphasized personal communication while de-emphasizing grammar, spelling, punctuation, and handwriting in composition. (These latter are sometimes regarded as unimportant surface features that have little to do with written communication itself.) The second force is a contemporary emphasis on electronic forms of communication. Word processing programs and the spell-check function have led some to believe that teaching children how to spell or write legibly is no longer necessary. This is not the case. There will continue to be many settings in which fluid, legible handwriting and correct spelling are essential.

The curricular swing that pushed handwriting and spelling to the sidelines of the language arts is no different from other such trend-driven shifts. As is always the case, heavy emphasis on one aspect of the curriculum leads to neglect of others, but recognition of that fact does not mean a return to historic concepts and practices is in order. Any renewed emphasis on spelling and handwriting must take into account what we now know about the significance of these skills and the role they play in the overall picture of reading and writing. What contemporary research reveals is that although these aspects of literacy are not ends in themselves, they are nonetheless foundational. Serious deficits in one or both of these skills can undercut success in writing and reading. Indeed, these skills play a deeper role than is popularly thought, though a very different one than our ancestors conceived.

SPELLING

Throughout much of U.S. educational history, spelling was a core element of literacy instruction. In fact, early American reading instruction involved spelling out loud, letter by letter, any word to be learned. In other words, spelling was used to facilitate reading. Given the refinements of modern phonics programs, this approach seems strange, but there was some merit to it: Reading and spelling are both rooted in knowledge of the spelling system and its patterns. This relationship between reading and spelling is seen in the fact that most poor spellers are poor readers (there are notable exceptions), but virtually all good spellers are good readers.

Currently, there is a good deal of confusion among teachers about the English spelling system and methods for teaching it. Many continue to believe that learning to spell is a rote memory process. If memorization is the key to spelling, the particular sorts of words students study are not important. For this reason, many teachers choose to "enhance" the time spent on spelling by fusing it with curricular vocabulary. The spelling words for a week might be drawn from new words introduced in a social studies unit, a science chapter, or a novel being read. Students are then responsible for both the spelling and the definitions of the words.

One of the problems with this approach is that it offers little information about the spelling system. Although curricular words may at times be thematically related, they seldom have any relationship to one another by spelling pattern. They are lists of isolated words to be memorized one at a time. Students may study and retain some of these words, but they will get very little information about the workings of the spelling system. Further, these words present a high degree of challenge. Students not only must learn to spell them, but also to pronounce, read, and define them. Readers might recall the familiar high school practice of assigning students lists of obscure vocabulary words to learn and put in sentences. How many of these words do most students recall and use a year later?

An example of this vocabulary approach can be seen a third-grade class I visited several years ago. The weekly spelling test for the class had been drawn from a social studies unit on Native Americans. Five of the 10 words that I wrote down after leaving the class were:

education
native
shaman
culture
environment

The teacher admitted in later conversation that many students struggled with spelling in her class and that their retention was generally not good.

Interestingly, this vocabulary approach to spelling is an unconscious recreation of a method commonly used in 19th-century U.S. schoolhouses. A book that was used in the New York City grammar schools is a good example. It is partially titled *Henderson's Test Words in English Orthography with Full Definitions* (Henderson, 1865), and, as the city superintendent states in the introduction, it "comprises nearly all the work in spelling required" for learners in the upper elementary grades. The book consists of approximately 1,300 random polysyllabic words. Teachers picked a number of words to assign each week, depending on how much they wished to "stretch" their students. The following sample consists of five words drawn from the first 20 in Henderson's 1865 speller:

Vi-*cis*-si-tude
In-*dict*-a-ble
Con-va-*les*-cent
Ir-re-*triev*-a-ble
Mil-lin-e-ry

When comparing these five words to the five sample words from the third-grade class, one can see that two approaches have much in common. In each case, the words to be learned are challenging, low-frequency words to be added to memory one at a time.

Early Spelling Research

Based on research undertaken in the 20th century (Schlagal, 2001), two very practical kinds of modifications were made to spelling books. The first was based on a widespread recognition that despite heavy emphasis on spelling in U.S. schools, they were not producing a nation of effective spellers (Hanna, Hodges, & Hanna, 1971). The second was based on the demonstration that English spelling is more orderly and predictable than many had claimed.

Word Frequency

Several major changes were made to spelling books in the 1930s. The most important of these was the creation of word lists drawn from recently completed counts of the most commonly used words (Hanna et al., 1971). Words were selected based on the frequency of their appearance in speech, print, and writing and were presented in groups of slowly increasing difficulty. That is, spelling lists were created so that younger children learned shorter, higher-frequency words, while older children learned longer, lower-frequency words. Thus second graders might be assigned words like *mask*, *first*, or *queen*, while fifth graders might be assigned words like *address*, *imitate*, or *apartment*. Organizing words this way provided a general control of difficulty, and it guaranteed that the words students studied for spelling were words they used and needed for their writing (Hanna et al., 1971).

The new approach made spelling easier and more practical—a clear advantage over vocabulary approaches. Nonetheless, the learning strategy remained essentially the same. Words presented in spelling books were still unrelated by pattern; therefore, each word was a separate item to be approached through memorization.

Generalization

The memorization position was often dominant in U.S. education, although there were some notable exceptions. The second innovation came from a demonstration that English spelling possessed a far higher degree of order than many had thought. In the 1960s—assisted by newly available computer technology—a group of researchers examined a large body of words not just in terms of strict letter–sound correspondences, but looking at these correspondences in relation to position in words (*kick* but not *ckik*), their relation to stress patterns (consonants double, as in *omitting*, if the stress is on the syllable before the affix), and meaning elements (past tense is spelled *-ed* regardless of sound, e.g., /walkt/, /fannd/, /started/). (Only a very small group of words was found to have any truly unpredictable letters.) When rules such as these are factored into the study of English, then it appears to be a system that can be learned by and large through pattern generalization rather than strict memorization.

Based on this demonstration that English spelling is largely systematic, many spelling books began to offer lists of words that were organized to highlight patterns within the system. Control of difficulty was still maintained by word frequency and length, but the words were no longer structurally random. Instead of a list of second-grade words, for example, having many different spelling patterns, the new lists might have between one and four patterns, with sets of words illustrating a select spelling feature. Thus the words served to show the working of parts of the system and could be generalized to other words not being taught. Additionally, explanations were included in the text to make explicit the principle or pattern being taught. This presentation of graded and organized lists had an advantage over older lists in that instead of memorizing 20 individual words the student learned small groups of structurally related words.

Current spelling books remain organized around spelling patterns and generalizations and for the most part resemble their later-20th-century predecessors. Despite offering a clear advantage over the rote memory approach, they do contain an inherent weakness: Spelling books are organized strictly by grade level. Although this organization may meet the needs of average learners, it is less likely to meet the needs of children at the top and bottom of their classes—that is, some may experience far too little challenge to promote learning, while some will experience far too much. These latter students have long been observed to experience minimal gain from their efforts (Schlagal, 2002). A further difficulty with modern spelling books is that they are typically filled with activities and motivational games that have no research base and that do not contribute to students' understanding of spelling patterns (Schlagal, 2002).

Developmental Spelling Research

Since the late 1970s, educational researchers have shifted their focus away from spelling materials and instructional plans and toward learners (Schlagal, 2001). Working from linguistic insights provided by Charles Read (1975), Henderson and Beers (1980; see also Templeton & Morris, 2000) demonstrated that young children's misspellings were not the result of faulty memory. Instead, they were shown to be ingenuous and predictable. Errors like FEH (*fish*) could be explained by the fact that there is no single alphabet letter that represents the /sh/ sound, but the letter *h*, if pronounced slowly, contains it. Further, the short-*i* sound is closer by position in the mouth and by sound to the letter name *e* than the letter name *i*. These errors, therefore, were not based on imperfect memorization but on accurate analysis of sounds and shrewd use of alphabet letters to represent them.

Here are a few compositions by kindergarteners. Each is a little more sophisticated in spelling development than the previous one.

T D ES MI DLS BR DAY.
[Today is my doll's birthday.]

DER MAMA I DO NOT LIK THE WA U AR AKDN TO ME. LOVE ALICE
[Dear Mama, I do not like the way you are acting to me. Love, Alice.]

POLR BERS DIW NOT HIBRNAT IN WINTIR.
[Polar bears do not hibernate in winter.]

Henderson and others (see Templeton & Morris, 2000) have provided a description of spelling development as it changes over time. These changes initially reflect a growing control of sound or phoneme analysis (see also Fitzgerald & Amendum, Chapter 14, this volume). For example, the first child in the examples above shows only partial phoneme awareness in her spellings of *to* (T), *day* (D), and *dolls* (DLS). By contrast, the third child is showing very complete awareness of the phonemic structure of even complex words like *hibernate* (HIBRNAT) and *winter* (WINTIR). Despite the completeness of the child's analyses, the words are not spelled conventionally. Notice that the second child's spelling of *acting* (AKDN) is also phonemically complete (given her Southern accent) as are her spellings of *way* (WA) and *you* (U), but both show an undeveloped sense of the appearance of English words.

As children's ability to map sounds to letters grows through practice and by exposure to print, many of their direct letter–sound associations grow more conventional (Henderson & Beers, 1980; Read, 1975; Templeton & Morris, 2000). This growing ability to map sounds to letters becomes a kind of glue that helps hold words in memory. As their knowledge of words increases, and as they are taught reading and spelling in school, children have more information from which to develop more sophisticated theories about the system. Invented spellings gradually become more conventional in appearance as children begin attending to how sounds are spelled, not just to single letters, but also to patterns of letters. Here is an example. (The student's inventions are capitalized.)

Let me stay up to MIDNITE PLEES, PLEES, PLEES! I won't make NOYSE.
I just want to jump on the bed down STARES like Bobbys TRAMPA-
    LEEN.

In this composition, the student shows a high degree of accuracy in basic letter–sound mapping. Consonant blends, short vowels, and basic high-frequency vocabulary are under control. Errors occur, however, as the child tries to spell vowel patterns, as in the words *midnight, please, stairs, trampoline,* and *noise.* (Earlier phonetically driven efforts at these words might have looked like these: MEDNIT, PLEZ, STARS, etc.)

As students gain control of basic long-vowel and vowel-blend patterns, they face problems caused by operations like e-drop and consonant doubling (Schlagal, 1992), and as these more dynamic ways of representing sound by pattern come under control, students struggle to sense how meaning is also represented by spelling patterns (Templeton & Morris, 2000). That is, students must learn to recognize that meaning relations take precedent over sound in upper-level vocabulary. These relations can be seen in word pairs like the ones below. (Note that one word in each pair has a challenging element for which sound provides no reliable cue. These elements are indicated by brackets and clarified in the partner word indicated with **bold** print.)

> regul[a]r–regularity
> norm[a]l–normality
> colum[n]–columnist
> compete–comp[e]tition
> si[g]n–signature

To summarize, studies of spelling development have provided helpful descriptions of learning as it changes over time. These changes reflect a movement from early, partial analyses of speech sounds to conventional sound-to-letter matching to sound-pattern representation and finally to meaning-pattern representation. While there is debate about whether to describe this progress in terms like *stages, accumulative phases,* or *overlapping waves,* there is general agreement that spelling development unfolds in predictable ways across time. From a practitioner's point of view, this area of research opens up instructionally useful possibilities.

Developmental Spelling Instruction

Based on research and clinical work with poor readers and poor spellers, the late Edmund H. Henderson (Henderson, 1990; Henderson & Beers, 1980) developed a systematic approach for teaching spelling without the use of traditional materials. The popular *Words Their Way* (Bear, Invernizzi, Templeton, & Johnston, 2004) is a classroom adaptation of this approach. Because Henderson found that there was a strong connection between spelling and reading ability, he did not separate teaching spelling from teaching word analysis and word recognition. Based on a systematic assessment of children's current word knowledge (Henderson, 1990; Schlagal, 1992; see Appendix 9.1), Henderson sought to improve students' word recognition and spelling ability in very precise ways. He elaborated a system of categorization or word-sorting tasks in which children compare and contrast spelling patterns within groups of words highlighting the features they may be using but confusing. In other words, word-study activities are created to connect to and extend children's current grasp of the spelling system.

A group of first graders, for instance, might be having difficulty spelling short vowels correctly. Therefore, they would be directed toward categorization activities involving the sorting of known single-syllable words using strongly contrastive short vowels. A sort might be constructed using the following words as *headers*. That is, the words below in italics establish the categories under which children will name and sort words into the short-*a*, -*i*, and -*o* columns.

mat   sit   cop

A completed sort might look like this:

mat	*sit*	*cop*
nap	big	not
rag	dip	dog
mad	lid	rob

In this activity, a child is given a word card. The child (1) names the word, (2) places it in the proper category, and (3) reads down the list of words in that category. Reading down the list gives the student a chance to catch any mistakes and provides repeated experience reading the individual words. Children take turns naming and sorting words until all words have been placed. At that time, the teacher guides the students as a group to read down a single list and tell "how all the words are the same." The children might say "They all have *a*." The teacher then asks, "What sound do you hear *a* making in these words?" and so on. This process is repeated for each list. Note that varied words with the same pattern and pronunciation can be added or substituted for challenge across a period of study. These could involve not only different words but other features like consonant blends (beginning and/or ending), consonant digraphs, and the like.

Reading research indicates that basic print skills must be learned accurately but also learned to the point of being automatic (Perfetti, 1985). That is, all facets of letter–sound recognition, word analysis, word recognition, and text reading must be done quickly, accurately, and effortlessly. For this reason this word-sort activity (and its variants) is intended to be practiced over the course of a number of days until children can quickly name and accurately sort each word. As this activity becomes automatic, students should be checked on their ability to spell the words correctly. The purpose of this short-vowel word study is to assist with automatic word recognition, enhance sensitivity to letter–sound relationships, and promote accurate spelling of the basic short-vowel word patterns. In other words, word sorting done in this way is at once a word recognition, phonics, and spelling activity.

When students catch on to a short-vowel sort, an additional strategy can be helpful. In this activity, the teacher makes words for students to read, changing the elements to highlight the particular letter–sound structure with which they are working (Morris, 2005). (Pocket charts and letter cards or a magnetic surface and magnetic letters can be helpful here.) To begin, the teacher creates a short-vowel word and begins to manipulate beginning, middle, and final elements. For example, she might make and ask children to read the following word:

f-a-t

She might start by changing beginning sounds (the easiest),

f-a-t—b-a-t—r-a-t—m-a-t

move to final sounds (more difficult),

m-a-t—m-a-p—m-a-n—m-a-d

and finally to the medial vowel (the hardest)

m-a-d—m-i-d—m-o-d.

The teacher changes one letter sound at a time at first. If children can handle each of these manipulations, she can begin to change more than one, as follows:

r-a-t—f-i-t—b-a-g—d-o-g.

Blends and digraphs can be added for additional challenge.

In a reversal of this task, the teacher provides sets of letters to children, asking them to make words that she names. By dictating predictable short-*a*, -*i*, and -*o* words to students, the teacher can see more closely who is able to make and transform the words quickly and easily and who requires more time and practice. When students make words themselves in this way, they are forced into greater attention to details of sound and letter choice than is needed for the recognition of words. (Notice that the words represent only patterns that are currently being studied and never ones that have not yet been taught.)

When students have mastered short-vowel words and can handle most consonant blends and digraphs (like the writer of the trampoline story described earlier), they are prepared to move into the study of basic vowel patterns. Here, the student is introduced to the way a single vowel can represent different sounds based on the spelling pattern of the word. A completed sort of this kind might look like this:

back	*came*	*card*
flat	tape	sharp
fast	flame	farm
slap	cake	hard

By comparing, contrasting, and sorting the above words, students can see that the letter *a* may take on different sounds based on the spelling pattern—*cac*, *cace*, or *carc*—in which it occurs. It is important that students note both the sound that *a* makes in a correctly sorted column of words and the structure that cues it. The decision-making process in word sorts helps emphasize order within and across words and can assist with pattern generalization (Morris, 2005; Templeton & Morris, 2000).

Note that the *a*-pattern sort (above) contains the now well-known short *a*. It is important that students be able to contrast what is new with what is already understood. If too much new material is presented at once, confusion is often the result (Henderson, 1990; Morris, Nelson, & Perney, 1986). That is why only one long-vowel pattern at a time is typically introduced. Once the above patterns have been mastered, another form of long *a* (e.g., *-ai-* or *-ay*) can be added.

Again, as a sort moves toward mastery, using the make-a-word activity provides another important form of practice. To illustrate how this might work with vowel patterns, the teacher makes the following word:

f-a-d

After the children have read the word *fad*, she might change it by adding a silent *e* (f-a-d-e) and asking what the word has become. She might continue manipulating the target structures like this:

f-a-d-e—b-a-n-e—b-a-n—b-a-r-n—b-l-a-m
b-l-a-m-e—a-r-m—a-r-k—b-a-r-k—b-a-k-e
b-a-c-k—f-l-a-c-k—f-l-a-k-e—s-n-a-k-e—s-n-a-g

As before, reading the words should be followed by students making the words themselves. The teacher can also make the operation more explicit by asking students to explain the transformations: "Why did the *a* change its sound here? What did the silent *e* do to the vowel? Can you hear the *a* when it's combined with an *r*?" (Although learning terminology is not essential for grasping these spelling patterns, this can be a useful place to introduce terms like *short a*, *long a*, and *r control*.)

The basic *a* patterns are typically easiest for most children. Once these are mastered, one can move through other vowel patterns. The following sequence is representative. (Items in parentheses can be substituted or included one by one after the previous patterns have been mastered.)

e-pattern:	*get*	*need*	*he*	(*mean, deaf*)
i-pattern:	*swim*	*drive*	*girl*	(*right, my, wild*)
o-pattern:	*stop*	*rope*	*corn*	(*boat, soon, sold, hook*)
u-pattern:	*mud*	*huge*	*burn*	(*few, blue, juice*)

Students who have gained control of basic short- and long-vowel patterns are developmentally ready to examine the operations involved in the addition of *-ed* and *-ing* endings. In this case, students are directed to become aware of the structure of the base word in order to determine whether modifications in spelling are needed. In other words, if you add *-ed* or *-ing* to one-syllable short-vowel words ending in two or more consonants (*back*, *blast*), then you do nothing to the base word (*backing*, *blasted*). If, however, the word ends in a single consonant, then you must double that consonant before the ending (*trap–trapping*). If you add *-ed* or *-ing* to a long-vowel word with a vowel pair (*sleep*, *boat*), then you do nothing to the base word (*sleeping*, *boating*). If, however, the word ends in a silent *e*, then the *e* is dropped (*scrape–scraping*).

Errors involving the joining of syllables may continue across grades if the correct strategies are not carefully taught (Schlagal, 1992). Many spelling series present the doubling/*e*-drop principle by listing words in their completed form; although the text will give an explanation of it, there is likely to be no specific study of the principle in action. A word-sort approach engages children in the manipulation of the words both in their base and inflected forms.

In order to highlight the doubling/*e*-drop operation, the teacher might begin with a single vowel, as follows.

tape	*taping*	*tap*	*tapping*
	shaping		grabbing
	shaved		batted
	taming		clapping
	trading		fanned

Headers for the base words are included so that students have a point of reference. Each time a word is handed to a student, the student says the word, places the word in the correct column, indicates if the vowel is long or short, and spells the base word. For example, the child might read *shaping*, place it under *taping*, then say, "long *a*; it comes from *shape*: s-h-a-p-e." In this way, the child has to remove the *-ing* and restore the *-e*. As students grasp the operation, the task can be reversed so that they sort the base word (e.g., *clap*), indicate whether it is short or long, then spell the inflected form (*clapping*). These kinds of manipulations can lead to a practical realization of what is happening in these operations.

Once the doubling/*e*-drop sort has been mastered, the teacher can guide students through the same operation with other vowels. As the principle is grasped in these single-vowel conditions, students can move to sorting with multiple vowels.

For older students, word sorts take on additional interest as meaning comes into play. This initially involves the use of simple prefixes (*un-*, *re-*, *ex-*) and suffixes (*-ful*, *-less*, and *-ness*) and moves on to roots like *-tract-*, *-spect-* and *-port-*. After a group like the one below has been sorted, students should examine the words, say what is the same in a column, and try to guess the meaning of the common root.

tractor	*spectator*	*portable*
subtract	inspector	report
attract	spectacular	transport
distraction	respect	supportable
traction	spectacles	import

This method parallels the follow-up activities above in which students are directed to discover the common spelling pattern and say how it functions in the target words. In this case, by trying to think through to the common root meaning, students begin to sensitize themselves to spelling pattern–meaning connections in upper-level vocabulary. This kind of word sorting can assist both in spelling and in extending vocabulary knowledge (Bear et al., 2004).

In sum, developmental spelling instruction has several advantages. First, it is tailored precisely to the instructional needs of individual students through ongoing individual assessment. Second, it builds skill through specific word and general pattern recognition. Third, it develops spelling ability through the manipulation of patterns that may be generalized to other words of the same kind. Additionally, word sorts can be adapted to any number of interesting games and activities (Bear et al., 2004; Ganske, 2000; Morris, 2005).

Not all students, however, are at the same developmental level in a given classroom. Therefore, it is a challenge for the teacher using this approach to individualize instruction across several groups. This requires appropriate assessment and placement and the use or development of instructionally relevant word-sort activities. In addition, this approach requires teachers to learn about children's spelling development, the spelling system itself, and word-study routines. Clearly, such knowledge is of value to both the teacher and the student, but not all teachers have this knowledge or are willing to invest the time to acquire it. Developmental spelling instruction is designed to aid students in mastering the spelling system and its patterns. Although this mastery is essential to becoming a skillful speller, this approach does not generally include explicit instruction on high-frequency irregular words. These kinds of words must be taught separately, although they can be examined by their contrast with predictable spelling patterns.

Many teachers wish to maximize student learning through appropriate instructional placement, but they may not have the time or experience to design a developmental spelling sequence. As an alternative, teachers can adapt well-organized basal spellers for that purpose. This approach (described below) draws on strengths of spelling books, while addressing their primary weakness: the implication that one speller meets the needs of all students in a grade.

Current Instructional Research

Spelling experts have long argued that a single-grade-level spelling book does not meet the needs of every child in a class (Hanna et al., 1971; Schlagal, 2002; Templeton & Morris, 2000). Although many students will gain meaningfully from its use, some (working at an independent level) will find little new to learn, while others (working at a frustration level) will find far too much that is unfamiliar to benefit from instruction. Of particular concern in this setting is the latter group of students.

Morris and his colleagues (Morris et al., 1986) demonstrated that students working at a frustration level (scoring below 40% accuracy on a curricular spelling assessment) made errors in spelling that were far poorer in quality than students working above that level. Morris further studied the gains of low-spellers after a year's worth of grade-level spelling book instruction in their classrooms (Morris, Blanton, Blanton, Nowacek, & Perney, 1995). Although the poor spellers did well on end-of-week tests, their long-term retention and mastery of spelling concepts was poor in comparison with their instructional-level peers, who made significant strides in both areas. Yet when poor spellers were placed in lower-grade-level books, where they had a better foundation of word knowledge, they performed just like their higher-functioning peers. That is, when studying words at an appropriate level of difficulty, they retained the majority of the words they studied across the year, and they developed concepts that allowed them to spell accurately words they had not studied, something their frustration-level peers were unable to do (Morris, Blanton, Blanton, & Perney, 1995). Further, these results were uniform despite marked differences in the amount of time different teachers gave to spelling or the varied methods (including word sorts) they used for teaching.

Adapting Spelling Books to Meet Every Child's Needs

Contemporary spelling books provide a useful resource for teachers and, if used in innovative ways, can be an important and useful component of instruction. Due to their use of word frequency, organized lists, and a clear progression of difficulty, spelling books can be adapted in several ways to make spelling instruction more interesting and more effective.

Accurate placement is a key to success in spelling instruction. Instructional groups may be created by using a curriculum-based assessment. If one is not available with the current spelling series, one can be made from a random selection of about 30 words from the master list taught across the year. A diagnostic developmental inventory like the Qualitative Inventory of Word Knowledge (Schlagal, 1992) may also be used. (See Morris et al., 1986, and Palmer, 2004, for validity and reliability data.) Students who score well below 40% in accuracy on such assessments should be placed in spelling books for the previous grade or in lists drawn from those books. The errors of those who score between 30 and 40% should be examined carefully for quality. If their words are off by only one or two letters, then they may be considered instructional at grade level. If the errors reveal a greater loss of quality, then they should be considered frustrational. Students who score 85% or above may be asked to search out their own lists of more challenging words with the same patterns as those in the grade-level list.

Although the most important feature of this approach is appropriate placement, sorting activities can be used with the book's lists to help students grasp patterns that are being taught in a given week of instruction (Brown & Morris, 2005; Graham, Harris, & Fink-Chorzempa, 2002; Schlagal, 2002). The following kinds of activities spread across the week can be lively, engaging, and instructionally powerful. (Although there might be two or three groups studying different words, each would be doing the same activities.)

- Monday: First, a pretest is given on words for the week. Second, children score and correct any errors, copying the correct spelling over twice. (This process calls attention not only to what words the children need to pay special attention to, but also to what feature(s) of the words they need to learn.) Third, the teacher leads the children through a word sort to highlight the patterns being emphasized in that week's words.
- Tuesday: First, children receive enlarged copies of the words for the week on a sheet of paper. These are cut up and sorted by the same categories as on Monday. When these have been checked, students may form pairs and play Concentration (sometimes called Memory) or any other game in which words are matched by pattern.
- Wednesday: Students may do word hunts in printed material for words using the same patterns as those in the week's words. Speed sorts using a stopwatch or some other game emphasizing speed and accuracy are also helpful at this point in the week.
- Thursday: Students can check each others' spellings with partners, with one student calling out the words and the other spelling them out loud (an example for each category may be given for reference) or writing them in appropriate columns on a dry-erase board or something similar.
- Friday: The weekly spelling test is given. Teachers may combine all the words into one list that each child tries (children are only graded on the words they studied that week). Other ways of giving separate tests can involve assistants, parent volunteers, or the use of tape recorders. A similar program to this one was subjected to careful research and found effective with struggling second-grade spellers (Graham et al., 2002).

An advantage to adapting spelling books for instructional-level work is that they provide a ready resource of graded and organized word lists from which to engage in developmentally appropriate spelling instruction. Because basal spellers have patterned lists, they can also be adapted for word-sorting activities (although this may not be as important as placing children at the right level of difficulty). Spelling books can save a teacher considerable effort, eliminating the time needed to create or extract appropriate lists of words from some other source. Adjusting spelling instruction along students' instructional levels ensures that spelling instruction is developmentally appropriate, but any adaptation of this kind requires greater planning and organization on the part of teachers.

BEST PRACTICES IN HANDWRITING

Well-developed penmanship was once a requirement for all business and professional work. Students worked hard to develop an elegant and legible hand, and penmanship was a major focus in business colleges. Beginning in the 1930s, handwriting instruction ceased being a separate school subject and was folded into spelling and writing instruction. Recent emphasis on meaning in writing (at times to the exclusion of other skills), the availability of computer-based writing technology, and an all-too-crowded school curriculum have made handwriting seem an area of little importance. Perhaps nothing speaks so directly to the reduced status of handwriting at this time than the current edition of *The Handbook of Research on Teaching the English Language Arts* (Flood, Lapp, Squire, & Jensen, 2003). Of its more than 1,000 pages of text, less than one is given to handwriting.

Despite the diminished place of handwriting in the curriculum and the broad availability of word processing programs, fluent and legible writing remains a necessary practical skill. In the academic world alone, it is needed for adequate note taking, state proficiency tests, and standardized tests requiring handwritten essays. Although elegant, well-crafted penmanship is no longer a strict requirement for academic or business success, there are consequences for sloppy and illegible work. Poor handwriting influences judgments about the quality of written work (Briggs, 1980) and even about the education or intelligence of writers. Students' perceptions of their own handwriting also affect their judgments about themselves as writers (Graham, 1992; Graham & Weintraub, 1996).

Poorly developed handwriting can affect more than judgments about written content and writing ability. In combination with poor spelling and by itself, it can contribute to disability in written expression (Graham, Harris, & Fink, 2000). Just as a failure to develop accurate and automatic decoding can impair comprehension in readers (Perfetti, 1985), failure to develop legible and automatic letter and word formation may interfere with content in writing (Jones & Christensen, 1999). Students who struggle to retrieve letters from memory, to reproduce them on the page, and to scale them to other letters have less attention available to spend on spelling, planning, and effectively expressing intended meanings. In contrast, when the component skills of writing are automatic, writers are free to devote their energy to the composition itself—although attention alone is not enough to guarantee improved content. Because of the excessive labor and unattractive results involved in such writing, students are more likely to avoid or minimize the process when possible (Graham & Weintraub, 1996).

There is evidence that direct instruction and sufficient practice in handwriting can play a significant role in preventing the development of writing disabilities among younger students (Graham et al., 2000). This important fact should be considered both from the point of view of regularly planned instruction in the primary grades and from the point of view of intervention among students who struggle with handwriting.

Issues in Handwriting

There is a long-standing controversy over the best way to teach the formation of letters. Should children be introduced to writing through a traditional manuscript alphabet and later bridged into cursive, as was common throughout most of the 20th century? Should students begin with cursive to prevent the difficulties of learning a new way to write in later grades? Or should they be taught a slanted or italic version of print that is designed to connect with cursive and so ease the difficulty of transition?

Those who favor introducing writing through manuscript argue that vertical, lower-case letters are close to what children encounter in print and that printed letters in writing are easier for them to read (Sheffield, 1996). In addition, they argue that children who come to school with letter knowledge will have learned and been exposed to basic manuscript forms. By making explicit instructional connections with what children already know, teachers avoid the problem of having to revise or correct what their students may have already learned. Further, advocates argue that forming manuscript letters involves far fewer fine-motor movements than does forming cursive or slanted letters and is therefore easier for young children.

Those who advocate beginning with cursive state that writing is more a kinesthetic than a visual act (Sheffield, 1996). Because an element of word knowledge is motor memory (Hanna et al., 1971), it is said that developing memory for spellings is easier when words are written in a continuous flow rather than when composed of physically separated letters. Although teaching cursive may make greater demands on students in the beginning, it is also said that there are immediate benefits to this approach, even for beginners. For example, because *b* and *d* are formed differently in cursive and are not mirror images of one another, reversal problems can be avoided from the outset. Also, because letters within words are connected, children are said to be able to manage the problem of spacing *between* words more easily, and, as mentioned above, children do not have to make the time-consuming and often imperfect transition from manuscript to cursive in second and/or third grade.

Most advocates of the cursive-only approach are concerned primarily with disabled readers and writers (Sheffield, 1996). Teaching these students cursive is often part of the instructional retraining process. Tutors or therapists seek to undo the fixed, imperfect, partial learning that characterizes disabled reading and writing and to rebuild them on a firmer foundation. Training students in cursive is often an integral part of this process. Whether the experience of clinicians working with disabled writers provides the best insights for general education is unclear. Despite the logic of the cursive-only claims, there is too little research at this point to verify them, especially for normal populations (Graham & Weintraub, 1996).

Because of the difficulty that many children experience in making the transition from manuscript to cursive, some advocate the use of a slanted initial teaching alphabet that is more like cursive than vertical manuscript. It is claimed that this promotes easier and more complete adaptation to cursive. Many schools choose to use slanted or italic letter forms in their handwriting instruction precisely because of these transitional problems.

A distinct shortcoming of a slanted or italic alphabet involves the increased number and complexity of strokes that young children must perform in order to make the letters (Graham, 1992). As a result, students are less able to produce consistently well-shaped and proportioned letters. In addition, evidence does not support the claim that slanted alphabets assist in the transition to cursive or result in quicker, more fluid, or more legible writing (Graham & Weintraub, 1996).

Due to its relative simplicity and comparative legibility, the evidence appears to support the use of the traditional manuscript form with a transition to cursive later in the primary grades. The question remains: What practices best assist students in developing good handwriting?

Handwriting Instruction

Because careful teaching and practice of handwriting can facilitate fluency in writing and may prevent writing disabilities (Graham et al., 2000), it is important to provide explicit instruction and sufficient opportunity to practice correct letter formation. Short daily practice sessions are likely to be more effective (and more interesting) than longer, less regular sessions. Although there should be time to practice handwriting as a separate skill, should not replace time for regular writing. There should be abundant opportunity in the classroom for students to write meaningfully and purposefully so that they can apply and extend the skills they acquire through separate practice (Graham & Weintraub, 1996; Henderson, 1990).

How the alphabet is best introduced is not a settled matter nor is the order in which letters are best taught. ABC order is not necessarily the most effective way to introduce letters, in part because the reversible letters *b* and *d* come so close to each other. (Thoroughly teaching one before teaching the other is likely to reduce confusion.) Further, if letter sounds are taught with letter names, the sounds for the vowels *a* and *e*— short sounds as in s*a*d and b*e*d—are initially confusing to young children (Read, 1975). Therefore, a teaching order in which confusable letters and sounds are carefully separated seems preferable to a strict ABC order.

Teacher modeling of correct letter formation is an important component of instruction. For beginners, both visual and verbal modeling (i.e., the teacher demonstrates how a letter is made correctly while describing how it is formed) appears to be the most effective means of introducing a letter prior to practice (Graham & Weintraub, 1996). Teacher explanations appear to be less effective for students in higher grades than modeling alone (Graham & Weintraub, 1996). Perhaps, already knowing the letters, older students find teacher explanations unneeded and distracting. Nonetheless, clear and correct models are an important ingredient in guiding students to effective practice.

Copying a letter from a correct model is helpful to students' practice, and it can be made more effective by adding several components. The teacher can provide a model in which numbered arrows indicate how the strokes are to be made (Berninger et al., 1997). After examining the model carefully, the student should cover it and write the letter from memory. Incorporating numbered arrows and adding a simple visual memory technique appears to be more effective than other forms of copying. This method has an interesting parallel in the helpful "look, say, cover, write, check" tradition in spelling practice (Henderson, 1990). Students can also benefit from learning to verbalize a set of rules for forming a letter so that they can guide themselves through the process, but the verbal guide should be one easily committed to memory (Graham & Weintraub, 1996).

Implementing research-based handwriting instruction need not be dull or routine. Some programs combine story- and song-based instruction with research-based methods in ways that are memorable, engaging, and pleasurable. An example of this is the British Letterland program (Wendon & Freese, 2003). In Letterland, an imaginary land where letters come to life, a letter is first introduced as a pictogram. That is, the outline of each letter is used to create a character. For example, the letter *c* is introduced as Clever Cat. Her face is drawn within the arc of the *c* and her ears above it. Once Clever Cat has been examined, students are shown the plain letter *c* and told that much of the time she cannot be seen because she likes to keep it a secret that she is there. Students are then given a sheet of paper with a large letter *c* and invited to draw their own picture of Clever Cat's face like the one on the pictogram card.

Prior to learning to write the letter *c*, children are told that Clever Cat likes to be stroked "smoothly and carefully," then introduced to a poem that may be sung or chanted and that explains how she likes to be stroked: "Curve round Clever Cat's face to begin. Then gently tickle her under her chin" (p. 35). The teacher then models slowly tracing the pictogram as students recite the verse. This is then repeated as the teacher traces over a letter C without the pictogram. Next, the teacher draws a large *c* on the board while the children trace it in the air, imagining that Clever Cat is still visible within her letter. Students then practice stroking Clever Cat on their own, working from arrow-guided models. Children may also animate the letters they have written by drawing in the characters they know.

Children are also taught sounds in this program. In an effort to reduce confusion, letters are introduced in a way and order designed to aid correct orientation and to distinguish confusable sounds clearly one from another. When a minimum number of letters and sounds has been learned, students begin using the pictograms (and props) to act out the sounds of simple consonant–vowel–consonant words in *live spelling*. Thus, letter formation, letter sounds, and phonemic analysis are carefully introduced and regularly exercised from the beginning of the program. Children are engaged in these potentially difficult and dull activities not as drill but as forms of dramatic, artistic, and imaginative expression.

CONCLUSION

More than anything else, contemporary research on spelling and handwriting tells us that these skills are not unimportant. They are not merely decorative elements of the writing process, but building blocks. Neglecting them can lead to social, educational, and personal consequences. Further, poorly developed spelling or handwriting can affect the higher-level literacy processes in which they are embedded. Although there is no reason to return the practice of these skills to the place they held in the 19th century, there is every reason to give them a more important role in the curriculum. Much that we know now can improve the quality and efficiency of spelling and handwriting instruction. By carefully considering the research, classroom teachers can find or create thoughtful programs to advance learning and increase engagement and interest in these core aspects of literacy.

REFERENCES

Bear, D. R., Invernizzi, M., Templeton, S., & Johnston, F. (2004). *Words their way: Word study for phonics, vocabulary, and spelling instruction*. Columbus, OH: Merrill.

Berninger, V., Vaughn, K., Abbott, R., Abbott, S., Rogan, L., Brooks, A., et al. (1997). Treatment of handwriting problems in beginning writers: Transfer from handwriting to composition. *Journal of Educational Psychology, 89*, 652–666.

Briggs, D. (1980). A study of the influence of handwriting upon grades using examination scripts. *Educational Review, 32*, 185–193.

Brown, J., & Morris, D. (2005). Meeting the needs of low spellers in a second-grade classroom. *Reading and Writing Quarterly, 21*, 165–184.

Flood, J., Lapp, D., Squire, J. R., & Jensen, J. M. (Eds.). (2003). *Handbook of research on teaching the language arts*. Mahwah, NJ: Erlbaum.

Ganske, K. (2000). *Word journeys: Assessment-guided phonics, spelling, and vocabulary instruction*. New York: Guilford Press.

Graham, S. (1992). Issues in handwriting instruction. *Focus on Exceptional Children, 25*, 1–14.

Graham, S., Harris, K. R., & Fink, B. (2000). Is handwriting causally related to learning to write? Treatment of handwriting problems in beginning writers. *Journal of Educational Psychology, 92*, 620–633.

Graham, S., Harris, K. R., & Fink-Chorzempa, B. (2002). Contribution of spelling instruction to the spelling, writing, and reading of poor spellers. *Journal of Educational Psychology, 94*, 669–686.

Graham, S., & Weintraub, N. (1996). A review of handwriting research: Progress and prospects from 1980 to 1994. *Educational Psychology Review, 8*, 7–87.

Hanna, P. R., Hodges, R. E., & Hanna, J. S. (1971). *Spelling: Structure and strategies*. Boston: Houghton Mifflin.

Henderson, E. H. (1990). *Teaching spelling* (2nd ed.). Boston: Houghton Mifflin.

Henderson, E. H., & Beers, J. W. (Eds.). (1980). *Developmental and cognitive aspects of learning to spell: A reflection of word knowledge*. Newark, DE: International Reading Association.

Henderson, N. P. (1865). *Henderson's test words in English orthography with full definitions; also, a list of modern geographical names with their pronunciations for the use of grammar schools and academies*. New York: Clark & Maynard.

Jones, D., & Christensen, C. A. (1999). Relationship between automaticity in handwriting and students' ability to generate written text. *Journal of Educational Psychology, 91*, 44–49.

Morris, D. (2005). *The Howard Street tutoring manual: Teaching at-risk readers in the primary grades* (2nd ed.). New York: Guilford Press.

Morris, D., Blanton, L., Blanton, W. E., Nowacek, J., & Perney, J. (1995). Teaching low-achieving spellers at their "instructional level." *Elementary School Journal, 96*, 163–177.

Morris, D., Blanton, L., Blanton, W. E., & Perney, J. (1995). Spelling instruction and achievement in six classrooms. *Elementary School Journal, 96*, 145–162.

Morris, D., Nelson, L., & Perney, J. (1986). Exploring the concept of "spelling instructional level" through the analysis of error-types. *Elementary School Journal, 87*, 181–200.

Palmer, L. F. (2004). Acquisition of English orthography by ESL students and its relationship to their reading performance. Unpublished doctoral dissertation, Appalachian State University, Boone, North Carolina.

Perfetti, C. A. (1985). *Reading ability.* New York: Oxford University Press.

Read, C. (1975). *Children's categorization of speech sounds in English.* Urbana, IL: National Council of Teachers of English.

Schlagal, R. (1992). Patterns of orthographic development into the intermediate grades. In S. Templeton & D. Bear (Eds.), *Development of orthographic knowledge and the foundations of literacy: A memorial Festschrift for Edmund H. Henderson* (pp. 32–52). Hillsdale, NJ: Erlbaum.

Schlagal, B. (2001). Traditional, developmental, and structured language approaches to spelling. *Annals of Dyslexia, 51*, 147–176.

Schlagal, B. (2002). Classroom spelling instruction: History, research, and practice. *Reading Research and Instruction, 42*, 44–57.

Sheffield, B. (1996). Handwriting: A neglected cornerstone of literacy. *Annals of Dyslexia, 46*, 21–35.

Templeton, S., & Morris, D. (2000). Spelling. In M. L. Kamil, P. B. Mosenthal, D. P. Pearson, & R. Barr (eds.), *Handbook of reading research*, Vol. 3 (pp. 525–543). Mahwah, NJ: Erlbaum.

Wendon, L., & Freese, G. (2003). *Letterland: Teacher's guide.* Cambridge, UK: Letterland.

APPENDIX 9.1. QUALITATIVE INVENTORY
OF WORD KNOWLEDGE, SHORT FORM

Level 1	Level 2	Level 3	Level 4
trap	train	scream	popped
bed	thick	noise	plastic
when	chase	stepping	cable
wish	trapped	count	gazed
sister	dress	careful	cozy
girl	queen	chasing	scurry
drop	cloud	batter	preparing
bump	short	caught	stared
drive	year	thirsty	slammed
plane	shopping	trust	cabbage
ship	cool	knock	gravel
bike	stuff	send	sudden

Level 5	Level 6
explosion	mental
justice	commotion
compare	declaration
settlement	musician
measure	dredge
suffering	violence
needle	wreckage
preserve	decision
honorable	impolite
lunar	acknowledge
offered	conceive
normal	introduction

10

Best Practices in Promoting Motivation for Writing

PIETRO BOSCOLO *and* CARMEN GELATI

One of the best-known educational guides for teachers of writing in elementary school, *Writing: Teachers and Children at Work* (Graves, 1983, p. 3), opened with the statement "Children want to write." The introductory sentence was the same in the 20th anniversary edition of the book (Graves, 2003), where the author wrote in the preface that he would only add the words "if we let them." Graves's faith in children's natural will to write raises the question: Do students really want to write? On the one hand, in Graves's statement there is implicit criticism of traditional writing instruction that privileges the production of texts according to literary models and on topics often detached from students' personal interests and experiences. This criticism underlies the perspective of the so-called writing-process movement, an approach to writing instruction born in the early 1960s and developed over the following two decades, of which Graves is a major exponent. A great merit of the process approach has been to put emphasis on classroom conditions that can make writing attractive to students: student freedom to select topics on which to write, attention on the writing process rather than its products, student collaboration, and teacher–student conference. The approach also seems to have influenced the concept of motivation to write in school. According to many teachers, a motivated student is one who is willing to express feelings and ideas in written form, writes fluently, and is never in the situation experienced by many students of not knowing what to write. On the other hand, over the past two and a half decades, psychological and educational research has shown that writing is a cognitively demanding activity and that students may sometimes be unable to write, even if they want to. Thus, from a psychological perspective, the assertiveness of Graves's statement has been questioned. Moreover, the various components of that "want" (e.g., learning goals, interest, self-concept, and self-regulation) have been investigated empirically by motivational research, and from these studies a more complex meaning of motivation to write has emerged.

This chapter has two objectives. The first is to analyze, in the light of recent research findings, the meaning of motivation and lack of motivation to write in school and of some constructs and terms frequently used in relation to this topic. The second is to outline and illustrate with examples some guidelines for instructional practice aimed at fostering student motivation to write.

MOTIVATION—AND LACK OF MOTIVATION— TO WRITE AS AN ATTITUDE TOWARD WRITING

School writing is a complex activity that requires a long apprenticeship, from preschool children's scribbles to writing words and simple sentences in early primary school to high school compositions in which students are expected to elaborate on concepts and ideas in an appropriate form. During this apprenticeship, students not only acquire the cognitive and linguistic knowledge and abilities that are the equipment of a competent writer, such as how to use genre structures and morphological and syntactic rules, but also learn a lot of things *about* writing. For instance, they come to construe writing as an engaging or, alternatively, a repetitive and boring activity and as a more or less important subject in the curriculum and a more or less relevant one for their future study and life. In sum, students develop a set of beliefs, many of which are implicit, about the functions and role of writing in school instruction (Bruning & Horn, 2000).

Recent conceptualization on motivation has argued that student engagement in a discipline includes two components (Brophy, 1999). One is a sense of competence, the extent to which a student feels able to engage in a task. The other is the meaningfulness of the activities in which a student is engaged—that is, the extent to which a learning task is perceived by the student as relevant to personal objectives. Consistent with this conceptualization, in this chapter we argue that motivation to write (rather than a will or drive) is an attitude to, or view of, writing. It is based on the set of beliefs that students develop through writing activities, through the various situations and tasks in which they are asked to write and use their written productions. In turn, students' attitude toward writing influences their approach to specific writing tasks and the degree to which they are willing to engage in those tasks.

Lack of motivation to write can also be conceptualized in terms of attitudes and beliefs that develop through school years as the result of repeated writing experiences. We may agree with Graves (1983) that at the beginning of elementary school children really want to write. Studies in emergent literacy have shown that children are involved in various forms of preconventional writing before schooling (Tolchinsky, 2006). Unfortunately, during their school years, the will to write in many cases decreases and even disappears, and the child's discovery of writing as a way of expressing and communicating is often a promise that subsequent writing instruction cannot maintain. There may be several explanations of students' loss of motivation to write. First, writing is often taught in a rigid way, with the teacher emphasizing conformity to text types and writing conventions. Unlike reading, which children are able to use in any subject quite early in elementary school, writing is usually not perceived by students as a flexible tool for acquiring, elaborating, and communicating knowledge, but as a discipline in itself. Second, students are often given writing tasks as exercises detached from other classroom activities, according to teachers' instructional goals that students cannot share or understand. Third, writing tasks are often boring. Students are regularly asked to narrate, describe, expose, and argue in written form, but these are not always enjoyable tasks, especially when there is no audience except the teacher, and writing often turns into routine practice.

Lack of motivation may not be due only to unattractive writing tasks. Together with beliefs about writing, students also develop self-perceptions and beliefs about themselves as writers, their writing competence, and their ability to manage writing tasks. Being motivated to write is closely related to a student's self-perception of writing competence. Many studies over the past two decades have analyzed the role of student self-perception of competence and self-efficacy in writing.[1] As Pajares and Valiante (2006) have persuasively pointed out, the degree to

---

[1] The phrases "self-perception of writing competence" and "self-efficacy for writing" are often used as synonyms, although they refer to two different motivational variables: self-perception of writing is an individual's evaluation of his or her writing ability (e.g., "I am able to express my ideas clearly in written form"), whereas self-efficacy regards an individual's belief about his or her future performance in a specific writing task (e.g., "I think that I will write a good report").

which an individual perceives him- or herself able to perform a task influences his or her performance; in turn, an improved performance makes that individual feel more competent. From a motivational point of view, self-perception of competence is closely connected to an individual's involvement in writing as well as to the quality of his or her self-regulation. The relationship between these aspects is a bidirectional one: a student is unlikely to be involved in writing if he or she is not self-efficacious; in the same way, feeling competent about writing makes a student more willing to write. Availability of cognitive and metacognitive tools, such as strategies for generating ideas from memory or for self-monitoring while writing, helps a student feel competent and, therefore, more willing to write.

In sum, motivated students can be defined as those who value and are willing to use writing as a worthwhile activity or means of expression, communication, and elaboration. Motivated students are realistically self-confident about their ability to use writing successfully, and this sense of competence is a condition and a source for feeling satisfied and engaged when writing. The concept of motivation to write as defined here is different from the concept of intrinsic motivation to write adopted implicitly by the process approach and explicitly by some scholars (e.g., Oldfather, 2002; Oldfather & Dahl, 1994). In general, intrinsically motivated behavior is when an individual is gratified for his or her own sake, not for external reward, and basic psychological needs for competence, autonomy, and relatedness can be satisfied (Deci & Ryan, 1985). A behavior is extrinsically motivated if it is carried out under the promise of a reward or the threat of punishment. According to the self-determination theory within which intrinsic motivation is conceptualized, intrinsic and extrinsic motivation are opposite poles but should be viewed as lying along a continuum including different degrees of external regulation from extrinsic motivation ("I wrote this composition to avoid the teacher's punishment or to demonstrate that I am good at writing") to identification ("Writing is an important and worthwhile activity for me") to intrinsic motivation ("I enjoy writing"). A child is often intrinsically motivated to write in early schooling, but unsuccessful writing experiences due to the increasing complexity of writing with school grade may transform his or her original will to write into extrinsic motivation, concerned with teacher evaluation rather than with the process of writing. This attitude may be difficult to change, as shown by some recent intervention studies in which writing activities were extensively used in learning different subjects in different grades, history and science in elementary school (Boscolo & Mason, 2001) and literature in high school (Boscolo & Carotti, 2003). The results of these studies confirmed the positive effects of writing on learning already emerging from re-

search on writing to learn. In general, after the interventions, participants reported that they felt more competent in writing and considered it
more useful, but they did not report liking it more.

Therefore, a student's intrinsic motivation often leaves room for a more
complex view of writing that implies his or her realistic self-perception
of competence as well as an awareness of the difficulty of writing. This
attitude should not be considered negative, as the student is willing to
engage in writing; however, it can hardly be called strictly intrinsic motivation. Therefore, we think that a motivated student is not always eager
to write but, with differing degrees of awareness, wants to write because
he or she thinks that writing is a worthwhile activity (although not always an enjoyable one).

ABOUT AUTHENTIC AND
INTERESTING WRITING TASKS

In defining motivation to write as basically a student's attitude, we have
pointed out that this attitude influences involvement in a writing task.
Of course, a student's involvement in a task is not only a consequence of
positive beliefs, but also of the attractiveness of the writing task. What
does "attractive" mean when related to a writing task? In recent years,
two adjectives in particular have been used to qualify the writing tasks
and activities that students feel most involved in: "authentic" and "interesting."

"Authentic" has been used in relation to writing with two different
meanings. The first meaning is related to a student's expression of a personal point of view or feeling, the so-called writer's "voice." One of the
prominent aspects of the process approach has been emphasis on the importance of expressing one's thoughts and feelings through writing. According to Elbow (e.g., 1981), a well-known exponent of this position,
writing instruction should enable students to discover their voice, which
results in "authentic" writing. The second meaning has recently been underlined in relation to the need to involve students in authentic writing
tasks (Bromley, 1999; Bruning & Horn, 2000). According to Hiebert
(1994), authentic literacy tasks are those that involve children in immediate uses of literacy for enjoyment and communication. An example is
fifth graders writing to the city council seeking more traffic lights near
their school and including a report they compiled. Hiebert (1994) also
gave examples of inauthentic tasks, in which literacy exercises such as
the use of compound words or sentence combining are practiced for
some undefined future use (p. 391). While agreeing with Hiebert (1994)
on the need to underline the authentic dimension of school writing, we
wish to add some comments on the meaning of this adjective. The exam-

ple of a fifth-grade petition may lead to believing that authenticity is synonymous with practical relevance. Writing in a classroom may be relevant to the degree to which students are faced with a real problem that can be solved using writing, such as a petition or a letter to a newspaper. Authentic writing, however, is not only aimed at achieving a practical goal. Stressing the communicative function of writing too much might lead to quite inauthentic writing activities, such as communicating in written form with friends (it is much easier to talk in person or on the phone) or writing a journal that will be read by nobody. Studies in writing mostly conducted from a social constructivist perspective have emphasized the social dimension of writing and the importance of making students aware that writing is a fundamental tool of communication. We think that stressing the social dimension of writing does not mean only emphasizing communication; writing is also a social activity because we can share, discuss, and comment on it with others.

What children should realize is that writing is a flexible tool through which many functions can be realized and goals achieved. Any writing task can be authentic: for example, an email message is authentic as a quick way of communicating; a formal letter is also authentic but in another context. Both literary and everyday writing can be used fruitfully to make students aware of the different ways in which thoughts and feelings can be authentically expressed. A useful practice may consist of a class discussion about the similarities and differences among various texts: an e-mail written by one of them, a formal letter written to or by the teacher, a graffito by which an anonymous young man declares his love to his girlfriend. All these messages, though different from one another, have a communicative function. In the discussion, students can be invited to express their comments on these messages and discover something new about tone, use of words, and voice—in sum, about writing as a way of communicating.

Unlike "authentic," the meaning of "interesting" has been analyzed in depth in psychological and educational studies over the past two and a half decades. From these studies, a basic distinction between situational and individual (or personal) interest (Hidi, 1990) has emerged. Situational interest is generated by particular conditions and/or objects in the environment because of their novelty. This type of interest is usually transitory, as is the situation from which it arises. Individual or personal interest is a relatively enduring disposition to attend to objects and events and to re-engage in certain activities over time. Both types of interest are related to writing in school.

Many teachers think that giving students interesting topics for compositions or letting them choose their own topics, as suggested by the process approach, is a useful way to promote motivation to write. Interesting topics are those related to students' personal experiences and interests (e.g., sports, games, TV, problems of adolescence), on which they are supposed to have a lot to write. This instructional practice is based on the unwarranted assumption that if a topic is interesting it is also interesting to write about. In fact, being interested in baseball does not necessarily mean being interested in writing about baseball. The problem is not finding an interesting topic, but making writing interesting. An interesting topic is a good starting point, but what can motivate students to write is the awareness that writing on that topic is worthwhile. For instance, writing an account of an event (an interesting topic) may be aimed at collecting and comparing the different ways in which the students in a class perceived and construed that event. Then, writing may be followed by students' analysis of their own and classmates' narratives and a discussion of differences and similarities in narrating compared with an narration external to the class (e.g., a newspaper). Writing on the event may be an occasion for students to express their voices and become aware of a new and authentic function of writing. These written narratives might be used a few weeks later to allow students to elaborate on their previous thoughts and feelings after rereading their work. This practice may contribute to creating a literate community in the classroom (Nolen, 2007), an idea we will return to later. From this community, we would expect students' positive attitudes to writing to develop; that is, their willingness to view and use writing as a real communicative, elaborative, and expressive tool. In other words, students develop a personal meaning of writing through classroom activities.

DEVELOPING MOTIVATION TO WRITE

We have argued that a basic source of students' lack of motivation is the writing tasks themselves, which may be perceived by students as boring, difficult, and/or detached from their personal experience in and out of the classroom. Now, we outline a frame for instructional practices aimed at avoiding these shortcomings and leading students at different school levels to perceive writing as a worthwhile and attractive activity. The frame consists of three guidelines, based on the conceptualization and findings of recent research on motivation and writing (Bruning & Horn, 2000; Hidi & Boscolo, 2006, 2007).

Making Students Experience Writing as a Useful Activity

The adjective "useful" may not appear to be very appropriate to writing, the instrumental value of which does not need to be underlined. In fact, "useful" has two meanings related to writing activities in the classroom.

The first is that what is written, individually or in collaboration, should have a value or relevance for the students. Later, we present an example of useful writing in the form of devising rules for group formation in a fourth-grade class. Such a project, which does not belong to a specific discipline, is aimed at producing a text as the result of collaborative work. Another example is related to students' attempts to play with genres, to which we also return later, under the heading "challenging tasks." In some cases, creative texts can be obtained from this play by modifying and renewing old texts. Over the past two and half decades, writing researchers have emphasized processes rather than products, also as a reaction against traditional writing instruction aimed at making students write "good" texts, and students' planning and revisions have often been considered more important than their written products. While recognizing the theoretical and educational relevance of the process approach to writing, we argue that one motivating aspect of writing is related to a student's production of a useful text, where "useful" means having an informative, practical, or aesthetic value. Students should be taught to value writing not only as an activity, but also for its products, particularly when they are the result of collaborative work.

The usefulness of writing does not only regard the production of a text that can be used in the classroom. There is another, less obvious form of usefulness that regards writing as a tool for learning. Several types of writing, such as notes, schemas, and outlines, facilitate students' elaboration and retention of knowledge, thus improving learning (see Tynjälä, Mason, & Lonka, 2001, for reviews). Although in recent years this function of writing has been investigated, there are very few studies on the motivational aspects of writing to learn. We present now an example of a writing activity in which writing is closely connected to the study of literature in a grade-9 class (Boscolo & Carotti, 2003). The literature teacher assigns the reading of a literary text as individual homework. Then a classroom conversation focuses on students' responses to the reading. The reactions are usually expressed orally, but some students prefer to write theirs down. The homework reading is commented on by the students and the teacher. The students take notes on the comments and organize them as a homework exercise. Regarding the literary text, students also identify with the teacher's guidance some keywords to describe characters and events of the literary text they have been given. For instance, one of the themes identified by the students in Henry James's *Washington Square* was the generational conflict between Catherine and her father. This theme is then used to interpret the text. Students' interpretations, some related to their personal experiences, are written in individual notebooks, then developed in a final report, which is discussed in the classroom. This activity helps students understand that there are various types of writing—some more informal, such as

notes, and others more structured, such as a report or composition—
that may accompany an activity and give or take meaning to or from
each moment of it. There is also a second consequence, more directly
concerned with motivation: The shift from interest in a topic or task
(formulating rules for the whole class) to the discovery that writing does
not necessarily lower that interest, since it is through writing that the
project achieves its objective. Obviously, the role of the teacher is crucial
because the discovery should not be compromised prematurely by severe
evaluation of the written product.

Fostering the Communicative Function of Writing

Traditional school writing is usually a solitary behavior through which a
student can demonstrate what he or she has learned and be subsequently
evaluated by the teacher. In recent years, the social dimension of writing
has been greatly stressed by the social constructivist approach to literacy
and literacy learning. This approach has argued that writing is a social
activity not only because what one writes can be read by someone else
(in the classroom, usually the teacher), but also because writing can be
performed in an interactive context. Spivey (1996) has analyzed thoroughly the various aspects of the social dimension of writing: the collaborative construction of a text, the revision through which a text is
amended and improved, and intertextuality, through which a writer uses
what others have written. The social dimension of writing is clearly related to reading; in co-constructing a text, as in classroom collaboration,
as well as in sharing written ideas and thoughts with schoolmates, the
two literate practices are closely related. When the production of a text
is aimed at achieving a common objective (for instance, preparing a bro-
chure for an exhibition organized by the school or a playbill for a school
performance), the planning, writing, and revising of this text can be
done collaboratively. Not only is the final text communicated, but so are
the salient phases of its production.

Communication may happen during the production of a common
document and, less obviously, during individual writing, such as when students take notes during a classroom discussion or lecture to prepare a report or just record some concepts emerging from the discussion that they
have been impressed by. These forms of writing may turn out to be useful
in subsequent classroom discussions as elements for giving students a first
idea of community of discourse. Showing them that individual writing,
such as note taking, also has an interactive component may help them understand the close connections between writing and classroom activities.

Nolen (2007) uses the notion of a literate community to describe
those classrooms in which literacy activities establish and maintain rela-

tionships among individuals. Literate communities have social norms that facilitate the development of interest in literacy by establishing the group's shared identity as readers and writers. In these classrooms, reading and writing provide opportunities to experience writing as a tool for self-expression and communication, whereas in traditional classrooms writing is basically an individual activity. Writers and readers switch roles frequently, and the resulting communication of feedback and ideas provides multiple opportunities for interest development. In contrast, traditional writing instruction focuses more on teaching the skills of writing, and the main purpose for becoming literate is that it is an important school subject. In literate communities, students develop their identities as writers through activities in which they are involved with teachers in producing worthwhile material or expressing and sharing their own ideas with schoolmates.

Giving Students Novel and Challenging Tasks

Miller and Meece (1999) conducted an interesting study with third graders of different achievement levels and from classes with different levels of exposure to high-challenge tasks. High-challenge academic tasks were considered those that required writing multiple paragraphs, involved student collaboration, and lasted more than a single lesson. It emerged that high achievers preferred high-challenge academic tasks, whereas low and average achievers not familiar with challenging tasks felt less confident in dealing with these tasks. Regardless of exposure, all students generally disliked low-challenge tasks. Of the two criteria adopted by Miller and Meece (1999) to distinguish levels of challenge of writing tasks—complexity (length of writing and duration) and the individual/collaborative dimension—complexity seems to have particularly influenced average and low achievers' uncertainty about their ability to complete high-level tasks.

Challenge is not the same as complexity. A challenging task is one that not only presents some difficult aspect, but also stimulates a student's will to engage in it. The cognitive approach has conceptualized writing as a problem-solving process where the solution is the production of a text that fulfills the writer's communicative goal. This problem-solving dimension is emphasized in particular in two writing activities: when students' writing is aimed at achieving a goal such as communicating to an audience and when students have the opportunity to play with genres.

Through various reading and writing experiences, students get to know genres. A possible challenging task is rewriting a text (e.g., a poem, a story, a fairytale), changing some elements (for instance, the protagonist, the setting, or the goal of a story). Rewriting is seldom an enjoyable task, but in this case it may be if the challenging objective is to invent a new story or a new poem. Two conditions have to be satisfied: first, the structure of the original text must be respected; second, any change in the original text (e.g., changing the setting or introducing a complicating event) must be consistently included in the composition. If, for instance, the story was originally set in winter, a change from winter to summer requires other changes—in the characters' behavior and/or in specific episodes—to keep the story coherent. In the classroom, this work can be carried out in small groups, each involved in producing the best new text. In elementary school, playing with writing is an activity students are willing to engage in (Boscolo, 2002). Playing means, for instance, manipulating stories by changing characters, motives, or the sequence of episodes to obtain new, more amusing, or curious endings within the constraints of text coherence. It may mean rewriting a short text avoiding certain word categories or composing a meaningful short text (a "cento") using words taken from titles of newspaper articles and reading passages or creating images and metaphors with colors to describe the seasons. This writing is called "creative" because it is aimed at creating new meanings, making children discover novel and challenging uses of language, and it is also children's first contact with intertextuality, in which they realize that new meanings are usually constructed by means of old words and phrases. Children not only enjoy themselves practicing it, but also test and increase their linguistic competence (under the teacher's guidance). Moreover, their efforts may produce texts that merit being collected in a classroom portfolio. The use of challenging tasks may contribute to motivation to write if children are able to manage them, as recent studies on interest have shown. Later, in high school, this type of play may become a fruitful tool for analyzing (no longer for fun!) literary texts in greater depth. For older students, literary competence also implies being able to work and play with texts.

WRITING DIFFERENT TEXT TYPES IN ELEMENTARY SCHOOL: SOME EXAMPLES OF MOTIVATING LESSONS

So far, we have analyzed the concept of motivation to write and the meanings of related words and concepts. In the following pages, some examples of writing instruction aimed at promoting motivation to write are presented. They are parts of an instructional intervention designed to encourage children to experience writing as a useful and enjoyable collaborative classroom activity (Boscolo & Cisotto, 1997).

The intervention was based on the view of writing as a flexible tool and a collaborative activity. It had three major features. First, writing took place throughout learning activities from beginning to end. In elementary school, children are often asked to write a report on a scientific activity or a classroom discussion as a means of concluding the activity and producing final material for a teacher to evaluate. In the intervention, writing was used extensively in relation to the moments or phases of an activity, not only at the end of it; for instance, a science experiment conducted in class provided an opportunity for students to experience various types of writing, such as comments, notes, and impressions as well as the final report. Thus, the teacher's focus was on presenting writing as a flexible, multipurpose tool, not on making the children conform to "good" text types.

Second, writing was proposed as an activity connected to crucial classroom situations. The different functions of writing in meaningful classroom activities, such as science experiments and classroom discussions, were stressed, in contrast with more typical instruction in which writing is taught as an ability related to other language skills but separate from other subjects.

Third, writing was performed as a collaborative activity. Students worked in groups during the various phases of the learning activities and produced collaborative texts. Even the writing they did individually, such as taking notes, was used for participation in group activities. Collaborative writing had important implications for the teacher's evaluation of children's texts. The written work of the experimental group was revised by the teacher and classmates. Revision by classmates was carried out in a collaborative activity in which each writer was also a reviser. The relationship between writer and reader/reviser was therefore symmetrical, and revision was not perceived as risky or threatening. The teacher did not emphasize and correct children's mistakes but facilitated self-correction and helped them improve. It should be underlined that the extensive use of collaborative writing did not exclude individual writing in situation-oriented classes. Individual writing was aimed at consolidating children's writing ability by having them practice writing on topics closely connected to the classroom activities they were engaged in, such as organizing notes taken during a discussion, exposing the phases of a common project, or highlighting the positive and negative aspects of discussing. Individual writing was an occasion for practice through which the children could also reflect on classroom collaborative activities.

The intervention was articulated into three segments, focusing first on argumentative, then narrative, and finally expository discourse. The activities of each segment had a common sequence:

- *Problem presentation:* The starting point for classroom activities was a stimulating problem children had to solve. The problem might involve some aspect of classroom life (how to form groups), text production for a real audience (writing the plot for a play to be performed), or a science experiment.
- *Idea generation:* The children contributed to solving the problem by expressing their ideas in classroom discussion. The generation of ideas was facilitated by a set of writing activities aimed at allowing the children to regulate their participation (e.g., note taking, recording impressions, regulating speaking turns).
- *Discussion and evaluation:* The ideas recorded were discussed, compared, and evaluated. Writing was still used as a regulation tool, but children's activities also focused on text production.
- *Synthesis and production:* The children's ideas became a product, used to compose a collaborative text (in the case of argument and narrative) or to check understanding (in the case of exposition).

We illustrate this sequence in relation to three text types: argumentative, narrative, and expository.

Argumentative Text: Writing the Rules for Group Formation in the Classroom

Problem Presentation

The teacher proposed some stimulating and involving questions. The most popular of these was "What should the criteria for group formation in your class be?" The teacher explained that the criteria adopted would actually be used for group formation in the class. Other questions that were considered included whether home tasks are useful to learning and whether a recent and very popular series of stories for children including horror and sex elements should be considered appropriate material for young readers.

Idea Generation

Collective discussion followed the question, combined with writing to serve the following functions: (1) as a tool for regulating turn taking ("While waiting, write your idea on a sheet of paper, so you will not forget it"), (2) as an informal tool for recording ideas expressed by other students as well as oneself, (3) as a tool for determining the most important points during the discussion, and (4) as a tool for synthesizing the results of the discussion. The children were encouraged to formulate their first conclusions and use their informally written ideas to dictate the points of agreement on the criteria of group formation to the teacher, who wrote them on the blackboard.

Discussion and Evaluation

Children discussed in small groups one of the conclusions they had reached during idea generation (i.e., a criterion proposed for group formation). They used their notes to recall the previous points and to guide the discussion. They also took new notes on colored paper, according to a strategy suggested by the teacher, with one color for a positive contribution, another for a negative suggestion, and another for a "stroke of genius." For example, for the argument that "groups should be formed with children of different competence levels," a positive contribution was "if a child is in a trouble, he or she can be helped by the other group members"; a negative suggestion was "if a child isn't specialized in anything, he or she can do nothing in the group"; and a stroke of genius was "all children have to learn." This phase ended with the construction of the first draft of texts in the small groups.

Text Production

The group works were read to the whole class, and a composition was written collectively: (1) for each group, a child read the draft aloud, soliciting comments and requests for clarification, while other members of the group took notes on suggestions for how to improve the text as well as on informal comments and reflections; (2) the drafts of each group were used for the collective composition, which was carried out through self-dictation (that is, the children discussed and selected the best criteria, formulated them orally with the teacher's help, then wrote them in their notebooks); (3) a small group of students wrote the formulated criteria on a poster in the classroom.

Narrative text: Creating a Narrative

Problem Presentation

The children had to find interesting topics with concrete objectives on which to write for a real audience; in this case, they were to prepare a booklet of stories as a Christmas gift for their parents. Other possibilities were to write a funny story for a pen pal or the plot for a play to be performed at the end of the school year.

Idea Generation

In collecting ideas for a tale, the children freely expressed their ideas, which the teacher wrote on the blackboard. The children also wrote their own and their classmates' ideas on cards.

Discussion and Evaluation

These ideas were analyzed and evaluated in a collective discussion. For example, the class agreed on a narrative core, "a girl who can express five wishes for Christmas." Children recorded comments, doubts, and suggestions. The ideas about characters, place, episodes, and sequence were organized, and several alternatives in sequence were explored in collective or small-group discussions. The children used their idea generation notes to propose changes and/or to plan story development.

Text Production

The collaborative construction of the plot and first sketch of the narrative were performed as a writing workshop:

- The material generated in the planning phase was used to construct the text.
- When in doubt, the children used a dictionary and asked the teacher and other children for advice.
- The children showed their written materials to classmates to check clarity and coherence. Classmates' advice stimulated the writer to revise and try a new, more satisfactory elaboration.
- Children read their own stories, and others were invited to make comments and criticism. Sometimes it was the writer who expressed his or her doubts.
- The stories of several children and/or groups were integrated and connected: for instance, children who wrote stories with a similar character or narrating a similar event were invited to integrate them into a more complex one.

At the end, the best stories were selected by the students and included in the booklet.

Expository Text: Checking a Hypothesis

Problem Presentation

Some scientific topics (e.g., the transformation of kernels into popcorn; what happens to sugar in water) suggested by meaningful situations (e.g., a school party) were proposed to the children.

Idea Generation

The teacher invited the children to write some questions (e.g., What inside an ear of corn becomes popcorn?) in order to:

- Explore children's previous knowledge of the phenomena.
- Guide their first discussion and observation during the experiment.

Discussion and Evaluation

What children had written about their knowledge was read aloud and discussed. During the discussion, a child could change his or her hypothesis by correcting with a different color of ink. During the experiment, writing was used:

- To describe the procedure, materials, conditions.
- To collect data (e.g., about weight and water level) to be represented in a table (numbers and drawings were used as well as words).
- To record comments about what was happening. Since the children paid great attention to the experiment, systematic recording was difficult (and probably boring) for them.

Text Production

Children used all their written comments concerning previous knowledge and setting up the experiment. They modified what they had written by adding or replacing information, commented on what they had understood about the observed phenomenon, and corrected their initial hypotheses. In this phase, writing was used by the children to check their understanding.

In the intervention, the teacher had several roles, which included having children "discover" a problem, stimulating idea generation, and regulating discussion, and two main functions regarding writing in particular. The first was to introduce children to the uses of writing in new and meaningful situations. The teacher suggested how to use writing (for instance, showing how to use note taking to remember or record salient ideas in a discussion), modeled the writing behavior, and helped children solve problems in collaborative composition. The second function was to help children become self-regulated writers. The teacher discussed writing difficulties with them both individually and in small groups, suggested solutions and strategies, and gave feedback on ongoing and final productions. At the end of the school year, the children were evaluated by the teacher, who took into account the collaborative texts as well as other texts written individually during school, but outside the experimental intervention.

THE ROLE OF THE TEACHER IN
PROMOTING MOTIVATION TO WRITE

The role of the teacher is crucial in promoting motivation to write for two reasons. The first reason is that a teacher's beliefs about writing influence the ways in which he or she organizes the writing setting and instructional practices. For instance, the way a task is organized reflects both the role of writing in the curriculum and the teacher's view of writing and writing instruction. A view of writing as mainly focusing on reproducing text types or, alternatively, on students' personal elaboration of knowledge and experiences has implications for how specific writing tasks are organized in the classroom and how writing is related to other disciplines. Making students aware of the multiple functions of writing in a literate community, which we have considered a necessary step in promoting a positive attitude toward writing, requires the teacher to believe that writing is not only a relevant subject or ability in the curriculum, but an important experience through which students should be helped to find a personal meaning in literate practices. Moreover, the teacher's view of writing also influences students' motivation to write. If a teacher views writing as a basically individual ability, he or she will tend to promote motivation mainly through assigning interesting topics when possible. If, instead, motivation is viewed and valued as an attitude to be developed and improved through meaningful activities, the setting of writing tasks will be clearly different.

The second reason is that writing instruction is a complex matter that requires the teacher to choose tasks, activities, and strategies carefully and focuses in particular on the following aspects related to motivation to write: interest, collaboration, and evaluation. Writing tasks cannot be always interesting, novel, or aimed at successfully achieving tangible results. Becoming a competent writer requires a student's involvement as well as exercise—that is, a balance of more involving moments, in which writing appears novel and interesting, and less involving ones, in which a student organizes his or her learning experiences through writing. We think that while students view writing in the classroom as consisting of meaningful experiences, they may also view less challenging tasks as important, not necessarily boring aspects of their becoming writers.

This balance should also characterize the use of group versus individual writing in the classroom. The examples of good practices in this chapter are all of collaborative writing. We view collaborative writing as an essential element for leading students to appreciate and enjoy writing as a process and product, but collaborative and individual writing should be viewed and adopted in a dynamic relationship. Opportunities for collaborative writing may be those in which ideas are generated, written texts are compared and revised, and a common product is obtained and evaluated. Individual writing, on the other hand, may be the moment at which students express their thoughts and voices, being aware that what one writes individually may be the source of other collaborative experiences with classmates, or in which they elaborate a meaningful experience, for instance by practicing a genre discovered through a classroom activity.

The teacher's evaluation of student writing is also related to the individual–collaborative dimension of writing in the classroom. We do not ignore that poor evaluation may be unavoidable in a class and may lower students' self-efficacy beliefs and self-perception of competence and, subsequently, their interest in writing. A writing portfolio, through which a student may become aware of his or her advancement in writing, is now a self-evaluation method adopted in schools as a tool that documents the development not only of writing competence, but also of motivation to write, through a student's narration and description of his or her involvement, satisfaction, and frustration in various writing experiences (Calfee, 2000; Calfee & Perfumo, 1996). We think that, when learning to view writing as a meaningful activity, students should also be helped to recognize and face its complexity. Being motivated to write also means being able to manage the challenges and difficulties of writing: giving students the necessary tools to face these challenges requires the teacher to analyze carefully the task difficulty and students' levels as well as self-perceptions of competence.

A CONCLUDING REMARK

This chapter was based on two main assumptions. The first assumption was that young children may be intrinsically motivated to write, but through various writing activities over their school years they often develop a negative attitude toward writing and toward themselves as writers. The second assumption was that instructional practices may influence a student's attitude either positively or negatively. Promoting motivation to write means reconstructing students' attitudes toward writing through activities from which a view of writing as a meaningful activity can emerge. In other words, motivating students to write means helping them construct positive beliefs about writing and replace negative ones. It should also be clear that this construction is neither quick nor easy, and during the long apprenticeship of learning to write students and teachers may find occasions for disappointment. Teachers, in particular, should be aware that the development of beliefs may not be linear and that students should be supported in their efforts to become not only competent but motivated writers. We conclude this chapter by applying the concept of motivational scaffolding (Renninger, 1992) to writing. Interest in writing should be supported as well as interest in learning. The meaningful writing activities that a teacher organizes to stimulate and sustain students' motivation to write may be isolated moments of classroom life for students, interesting and enjoyable but not sufficient to create an enduring attitude toward writing. It is up to the teacher to create continuity among these moments, such as by pointing out the contributions of individual students, outlining the value of the results attained, and inviting students to find new and challenging writing tasks.

REFERENCES

Boscolo, P. (2002). *La scrittura nella scuola dell'obbligo. Insegnare e motivare a scrivere.* [*Writing in compulsory school. Teaching and motivating to write*]. Rome, Italy: Laterza.

Boscolo, P., & Carotti, L. (2003). Does writing contribute to improving high school students' approach to literature? *L1—Educational Studies in Language and Literature, 3,* 197–224.

Boscolo, P., & Cisotto, L. (1997, August). *Making writing interesting in elementary school.* Paper presented at the seventh biannual meeting of the European Association for Research on Learning and Instruction, Athens, Greece.

Boscolo, P., & Mason, L. (2001). Writing to learn, writing to transfer. In P. Tynjälä, L. Mason, & K. Lonka (Eds.), *Writing as a learning tool: Integrating theory and practice* (pp. 83–104). Dordrecht, The Netherlands: Kluwer.

Bromley, K. (1999). Key components of sound writing instruction. In L. B. Gambrell, L. M. Morrow, S. B. Neuman, & M. Pressley (Eds.), *Best practices in literacy instruction* (pp. 152–174). New York: Guilford Press.

Brophy, G. (1999). Toward a model of the value aspects of motivation in education: Developing appreciation for particular learning domains and activities. *Educational Psychologist, 34,* 75–85.

Bruning, R., & Horn, C. (2000). Developing motivation to write. *Educational Psychologist, 35,* 25–37.

Calfee, R. C. (2000). Writing portfolios: Activity, assessment, authenticity. In R. Indrisano & J. R. Squire (Eds.), *Perspectives on writing* (pp. 278–304). Newark, DE: International Reading Association.

Calfee, R., & Perfumo, P. (Eds.). (1996). *Writing portfolios in the classroom.* Mahwah, NJ: Erlbaum.

Deci, E. L., & Ryan, R. M. (1985). *Intrinsic motivation and self-determination in human behavior.* New York: Plenum Press.

Elbow, P. (1981). *Writing with power: Techniques for mastering the writing process.* New York: Oxford University Press.

Graves, D. H. (1983). *Writing: Teachers and children at work.* Portsmouth, NH: Heinemann.

Graves, D. H. (2003). *Writing: Teachers and children at work* (20th anniversary ed.). Portsmouth, NH: Heinemann.

Hidi, S. (1990). Interest and its contribution as a mental resource for learning. *Review of Educational Research, 60,* 549–571.

Hidi, S., & Boscolo, P. (2006). Motivation and writing. In C. A. MacArthur, S. Graham, & J. Fitzgerald (Eds.), *Handbook of writing research* (pp. 144–157). New York: Guilford Press.

Hidi, S., & Boscolo, P. (Eds.). (2007). *Writing and motivation.* Oxford, UK: Elsevier.

Hiebert, E. H. (1994). Becoming literate through authentic tasks: Evidence and adaptations. In R. B. Ruddell, M. R. Ruddell, & H. Singer (Eds.), *Theoretical models and processes of reading* (pp. 391–413). Newark, DE: International Reading Association.

Miller, S. D., & Meece, J. L. (1999). Third graders' motivational preferences for reading and writing tasks. *Elementary School Journal, 100,* 19–35.

Nolen, S. (2007). The role of literate communities in the development of children's interest in Writing. In S. Hidi & P. Boscolo (Eds.), *Writing and motivation* (pp. 241–255). Oxford, UK: Elsevier.

Oldfather, P. (2002). Students' experiences when not initially motivated for literacy learning. *Reading and Writing Quarterly, 18,* 231–256.

Oldfather, P., & Dahl, K. (1994). Toward a social constructivist reconceptualization of intrinsic motivation for literacy learning. *Journal of Reading Behavior, 26,* 139–158.

Pajares, F., & Valiante, G. (2006). Self-efficacy beliefs and motivation in writing development. In C. A. MacArthur, S. Graham, & J. Fitzgerald (Eds.), *Handbook of writing research* (pp. 158–170). New York: Guilford Press.

Renninger, A. (1992). Individual interest and development: Implications for theory and practice. In K. A. Renninger, S. Hidi, & A. Krapp (Eds.), *The role of interest in learning and development* (pp. 361–395). Hillsdale, NJ: Erlbaum.

Spivey, N. (1996). *The constructivist metaphor.* San Diego, CA: Academic Press.

Tolchinsky, L. (2006). The emergence of writing. In C. A. MacArthur, S. Graham, & J. Fitzgerald (Eds.), *Handbook of writing research* (pp. 83–95). New York: Guilford Press.

Tynjälä, P., Mason, L., & Lonka, K. (Eds.). (2001). *Writing as a learning tool.* Dordrecht, The Netherlands: Kluwer.

11

Best Practices in Using the Internet to Support Writing

RACHEL KARCHMER-KLEIN

Recently, Karen, a fourth-grade teacher, told me she was interested in using the Internet to support her writing instruction. While she was not completely comfortable with technology, she recognized the Internet's potential and wanted to explore how it could enhance her teaching and her students' learning. Like many teachers, Karen had good intentions to incorporate the Internet into her classroom, and her school clearly supported technology use. There was a cart of wireless laptop computers available for teachers to sign out, a computer lab, two Internet-connected desktop computers per classroom, and an instructional technology support teacher whose primary responsibility was to help teachers use technology effectively. Karen's knowledge of the Internet had developed from her participation in several school-sponsored activities, including the completion of technology inservice workshops, distance learning education courses, and daily e-mail use for approximately 7 years. However, the pressures associated with state testing, the adoption of new report card procedures, and the daily focus on mandated curriculum standards made it difficult for Karen to find time to research and practice effective ways of using the Internet to support writing. She explained:

"I think the Internet is a fantastic resource for both kids and teachers. I see other people using it in their teaching and I get jealous. But I don't know where to start and I don't know how to make it a part of my classroom so that I can expose students to the technology while also teaching them how to write."

Karen's uneasiness about making the Internet an integral part of the curriculum is not unique (Karchmer, Mallette, Kara-Soteriou & Leu, 2005). In the National Education Technology Plan (2005), the U.S. Department of Education documented the lack of teacher technology proficiency across the country and the need to provide much greater support at the school level. The report states:

> Teachers have more resources available through technology than ever before, but some have not received sufficient training in the effective use of technology to enhance learning. Teachers need access to research, examples and innovations as well as staff development to learn best practices. (pp. 42–43)

Interestingly, while many teachers are unsure of how to use the Internet in the classroom, there are also many who are knowledgeable about and comfortable with it. In fact, most of what we know about best practices in using the Internet to support reading and writing comes from the good work of classroom teachers who use technology on a regular basis (Karchmer et al., 2005). Their daily interactions with students along with their interest in technology puts them in an exceptional position to share critical insight into how the Internet can support the language arts as well as other disciplines. For instance, look at the creative work of Susan Silverman (*www.kids-learn.org*), Dale Hubert (*www.flatstanleyproject.com*), and Marci McGowan (*www.mrsmcgowan. com*). Each of these teachers has developed highly successful collaborative Internet projects, practices in which two or more classrooms study similar topics and share their findings through writing and visual arts over the Internet (Leu, Leu, & Coiro, 2004). Likewise, Janice Smith (*home.earthlink.net/~jesmith*) and Rennebohm Franz (*www.psd267.wednet.edu/ ~kfranz/index.htm*) have developed classroom websites where they created space to publish their students' writing, an opportunity for students' work to be shared with a much greater audience than what the teacher alone can provide.

The purpose of this chapter is to stimulate teachers' interest in using the Internet to help students develop their writing skills. To this end, the chapter is divided into three sections. First, I examine the unique attributes of the Internet and how they influence the process of writing. Second, I share classroom examples framed by how they may match teachers' time, interest, and expertise levels. Third, I conclude with a series of principles to consider when planning to make the Internet an integral component of the classroom.

RESEARCH ON THE INTERNET AND WRITING

Technology is increasingly being recognized for its potential to support K–12 writing instruction. Research has shown the positive effects of word processing (e.g., Goldberg, Russell, & Cook, 2003; Russell & Plati, 2001), spell-check (e.g., MacArthur, Graham, Hayes, & De La Paz, 1996), speech recognition (e.g., Quinlan, 2004), and multimedia software (e.g., Daiute & Morse, 1994) on different stages of the writing process. Moreover, this research examined technology use by a variety of users, including average-achieving writers (Reece & Cummings, 1996), at-risk learners (Howell, Erickson, Stanger, & Wheaton, 2000), and students with identified learning disabilities (MacArthur et al., 1996).

Unfortunately, while one of the most powerful technologies of our time, the Internet has yet to be systematically studied for its effects on students' writing achievement (MacArthur, 2006). What we do know is that the Internet is characterized by a set of unique attributes, each of which influences the act of writing (Reinking, Labbo, & McKenna, 1997). First, electronic text, the medium by which information is communicated over the Internet, encompasses several features that set it apart from the printed text found in traditional books (Reinking, 1998). Electronic text allows for the seamless incorporation of audiovisual features. Graphics, audio, and video can be inserted to add depth to text or to act as the text itself. The inclusion of these features can make the text interactive. For example, the author can add digitized speech to support reading comprehension or video clips to refer to particular content (Reinking & Rickman, 1990). Electronic text is also easily manipulated. Writers can change background colors, font styles, and the placement of graphics to determine the best format for their writing. Moreover, they can continuously change the text because it is so easily adaptable. What one person reads on Monday may be different than what another reads on Tuesday. Additionally, electronic text structure tends to be nonlinear. While traditionally printed text typically includes a progression of events, electronic text is not fixed. Rather, writers are able to use hyperlinks to direct their readers from one page to another. This notably changes the role of the writer "because the author is not only the creator of new texts (and meanings) but also the facilitator of meanings by providing an index of specific WWW texts and images available in cyber-space" (Mitra & Cohen, 1999, p. 189).

A second unique attribute of the Internet that influences writing is the outlet it provides to authentic audiences. Work published on the Internet can be accessed by anyone with a connected computer and the web address. This attribute is beneficial to writers who want to project their message to a large audience or for those whose work is rarely shared with outside readers. In fact, teachers report an increase in students' motivation to write well when they know their work will be published on the Internet (Karchmer, 2001). It also seems that Internet publishing encourages students to pay more attention to spelling conventions and the overall appearance of their final products. Along with the opportunity to communicate with this larger audience comes the responsibility of recognizing the culturally and linguistically diverse nature of the Internet (The New London Group, 2000). Calkins (1994) argues the importance of identifying audience prior to writing so that writers can target their work to meet their readers' skills and expectations. This is a great challenge, as the Internet has no boundaries. Instead, writers must think critically about how they will use the features of electronic text to help them effectively communicate intended meaning and must acknowledge that some readers could misconstrue their work.

The third unique attribute of the Internet is the opportunity for writers to interact with their audience. Research on students' writing has shown that teachers' comments focus mostly on proofreading concerns. Students then tend to make peripheral revisions to their work concentrating on mechanics rather than substantive changes (Matsumura, Patthey-Chavez, & Valdes, 2002). By inviting critique from outside audiences via the Internet, writers may recognize the social context of their work, leading them to consider different perspectives on their ideas and to think more deeply about how best to approach revision (Beach & Friedrich, 2006). Furthermore, the opportunity to interact with an Internet audience reaffirms the readership that might otherwise be too abstract for some students to grasp. Young children in particular have difficulty understanding the vastness of the Internet community. Responses from real people validate the far-reaching effects of the Internet's capabilities.

These unique attributes of the Internet require new ways of thinking about writing and writing instruction. Specifically, how do we prepare K–12 students to use the Internet to communicate effectively with others? We can only speculate about the best approaches, yet it is clear that teachers around the world are taking advantage of the Internet by engaging their students in technology-based writing practices, by providing them opportunities to develop electronic texts, and by publishing their work online for others to read and critique.

INTERNET PRACTICES THAT SUPPORT WRITING

My interest in technology over the past 10 years has led me to examine several hundred educational websites. I keep a log of noteworthy sites that I refer to when needed. Noteworthy websites, in my opinion, are those that document their development over time, communicate to a variety of audiences, are organized and reader-friendly, and/or include innovative ways of using technology to teach. When I was asked to write this chapter, I reviewed the log and spent time focusing on if and how the websites supported students' writing. It was clear that there were numerous types of Internet practices and, more important, that each required different levels of teacher time, interest, and expertise. I found this to be most interesting in light of my earlier conversation with Karen. I wondered which practices would be best for teachers just getting started? Which practices were challenging but doable with some technology support? And which practices would be most appropriate for more experienced Internet users? This section is framed around these questions with the hope that teachers will find practices that match the time, interest, and expertise they have to put toward incorporating the Internet into their curriculum.

Just Getting Started: WebQuests

Brian, Renee, and Lois are working diligently on campaign posters while Trish and Sam write the speech for the class debate. They are campaigning for Bill Gates, hoping to convince their sixth-grade classmates to vote for him at the schoolwide presidential election next week.

"We really need a slogan," says Renee.

Brian agrees, "Yeah, something that catches people's attention. All presidents have slogans."

Lois reminds her group that their teacher, Ms. Randall, gave them websites to refer to for examples of presidential slogans. They huddle in front of one of the classroom computers, and Sam types in the first web address.

"The slogans are all short—maybe three words. How can we capture Bill Gates in three or four words?" asks Brian.

Trish responds, "Let me read you our speech. See if the words inspire you to vote for him and maybe you'll be able to come up with a motto."

These sixth graders have been studying the presidential election process. To make the concept concrete, Ms. Randall engaged them in a WebQuest titled "Meet Your New President," by Sherita Love (*slove.myweb. uga.edu/Courses/EDIT6150/index.htm*). This WebQuest, developed for third through eighth grade, examines the importance of informed voting and persuasive writing. Students work in groups and choose candidates from a list of current business, political, and social leaders such as Hillary Clinton, Bill Gates, and Oprah Winfrey. Their task is to create a presidential campaign and persuade the student body to vote for their candidate. They learn about the election, the campaigning process, and their candidate's background through Internet research and then share their findings through the power of persuasive writing. The project concludes with a schoolwide vote.

This classroom scenario is an example of a WebQuest, an Internet-based inquiry practice. Bernie Dodge and Tom March of San Diego State University developed WebQuests in 1995 with the idea of creating an Internet practice that focused students' attention on the examination and analysis of information rather than the act of searching for it (Dodge, 1997). Framed by curriculum standards, these projects are designed and submitted by educators to The WebQuest Page (*webquest.sdsu.edu/*). While WebQuests can focus on any discipline, writing is an integral part of many of them.

Every project found on the WebQuest database includes the same components, organized around student and teacher pages. The student page begins with a rationale for participating in the project and an overview of the associated tasks that sets the goals and objectives. Next, step-by-step directions of the process are listed, explaining how to complete each task and directing students to teacher-approved websites, necessary handouts, and other materials. The next section includes evaluation methods suggested by the project's author. Most utilize assessment rubrics with detailed descriptions of grade expectations. The final section summarizes what should be learned during the project. Some summaries are long and elaborate, pinpointing all areas of learning, but many include just a brief description. The teacher page incorporates the same content but also lists state standards supported by the project and the National Educational Technology Standards (NETS) for teachers and students. These additions are critical, as they emphasize the direct connection between the WebQuests and curriculum content (Karchmer-Klein & Layton, 2006).

To search for WebQuests, go to The WebQuest Page (*webquest. sdsu.edu/*) and click on the Find WebQuests link to connect to the WebQuest Search page. From here, teachers can take one of two approaches to locating appropriate writing projects. One approach is to focus on a specific writing genre. For example, type in the word *poetry.* This search identifies 20 WebQuests targeted at all grade levels. Most of the projects introduce students to different types of poems by directing them to read and analyze particular poetry books or websites with examples. Students then create their own poems using what they learned from the models. A second approach is to consider writing as part of content-area teaching and search by curriculum topic. For example, suppose your third-grade class is studying sharks. Type the keyword *shark* into the WebQuest Search page and several projects will come up. One is "Shocking Sharks," by Pat Dobson and Laura Carlson (*projects.edtech. sandi.net/sessions/sharks/index.html*). This project requires students to work in pairs to research different species of sharks. Students first read and analyze information found on teacher-selected websites. Next, they identify two types of sharks to study in depth and chart the similarities and differences between them on a graphic organizer created in the software program Inspiration. Using the organizer and their lessons on persuasive writing, students write a commercial for Sea World, inviting tourists to visit the sharks in person. Although this WebQuest focuses on the science topic of sharks, it also hones writing skills. A list of other noteworthy WebQuests that incorporate writing can be found in Table 11.1.

Even though WebQuests are relatively easy to locate and participate in, they still require time to implement effectively. Teachers must prepare students with basic Internet skills like typing in URLs, manipulating the mouse, and following hyperlinks. If more complex technologies will be used, teachers must model them and provide time for students to practice before starting the WebQuest. Most important, teachers must take time to identify WebQuests that match their learning goals. While the focus of the WebQuest may be writing, reading is an integral component. Therefore, it is critical to keep in mind the appropriateness of the WebQuest for the particular population of students with whom it will be used. Many of the projects span four or five grade levels. Teachers must carefully examine both the content and readability of the websites to be sure their students can effectively interact with the text. If teachers find a WebQuest that they really like but are afraid is too challenging for students, they can modify the project in several ways. One option is to pair better readers with ones who struggle. This way the stronger reader can help navigate the text, but both students can collaborate on the writing activity. Another option is to conduct the WebQuest with the whole class. Using a projector and computer, the teacher can facilitate analysis of the Internet resources by conducting shared reading of the websites.

WebQuests are a good place for novice Internet educators to start incorporating technology into their writing curriculum. They are struc-

TABLE 11.1 Noteworthy WebQuests Found on The WebQuest Page (*webquest.sdsu.edu/*)

Genre	Title, description, URL	Grade
Poetry	"Kidd's Rime Time Circus" Designed to introduce and familiarize fourth-grade students with five different types of poetry. Students are encouraged to create one of each of the types of poetry. Students will also be asked to go on an Internet scavenger hunt to gain a greater knowledge of these types of poetry. *www2.franciscan.edu/webquests/kiddsrime/*	4
Poetry	"Poetry Quest" By discovering the types of poetry and breaking poetry and its elements down into manageable and understandable areas, students will be able to identify multiple forms of poetry and express themselves in some of those forms. Students then write a reflective essay about the process.\ *www.rccsd.org/RKeim/index.htm*	6–9
Persuasive argument	"Island Colonization" Groups of four to five students work together to create a persuasive argument for or against colonization of a newly discovered island. *teacherweb.com/TW/TaipeiAmericanSchool/BrendaHuff/index.html*	3–5
Persuasive argument	"Fat Facts" Trends in our country indicate an obesity epidemic. With this epidemic comes the danger of chronic illnesses such as type-2 diabetes, heart disease, and cancer. In this WebQuest, students research the topic and design informative and persuasive projects using technology. *teacherweb.com/MD/OxonHillMS/FatFacts/index.html*	6–8
Personal narrative	"All About Me" This WebQuest will guide students through each step of writing a personal narrative. Students visit the schoolhouse where they will read and research on the Internet to discover each step in the writing process. *imet.csus.edu/imet7/damos/webquest/281_group_project/group_project/schoolhouse.htm*	3–5
Personal narrative	"Wanted: Wild West Outlaws" After reading *Holes* by Louis Sachar, students will take a look at other outlaws similar to Kissin' Kate Barlow. They will create a wanted poster of the most wanted outlaw in the Wild West and write that outlaw's story using first-person narrative. *members.cox.net/nanstevenson/default.htm*	5–6
Informational text	"Ark Helpers Society" Members of the Ark Helpers Society are zookeepers who must design an informational brochure about an endangered or threatened animal of their choice. *www.ufrsd.net/staffwww/stefanl/Webquest/animals/index.htm*	6–12
Informational text	"Please Help Our Ocean Animals!" The aquarium workers are sick and need the expertise of a class of students learning about ocean animals. The children can choose to become experts on one of four animals. Students research the animal they have chosen, draw a habitat for it in KidPix, and make a sign for their animal's aquarium home with four important facts about it. *www.bedford.k12.ny.us/wpes/webquest/*	K–2

tured activities, which enable students to complete them independently. They do not follow a specified timeline, so teachers can decide their own beginning and ending dates, and they tend to require only basic technology skills like Internet searching and word processing. Furthermore, there are hundreds of WebQuests shared on the Internet, so teachers can start by using other educators' projects, and, if they become hooked, they can develop their own.

More Challenging but Doable: Collaborative Internet Projects

In an effort to prepare preservice teachers to use technology in their own practice, I engage my undergraduate teacher education students in a collaborative Internet project (CIP) titled "Unfortunate Collaborations" (*comsewogue.org/~ssilverman/snicket/*). A CIP is a practice in which two or more classrooms study similar topics and share their findings through writing and visual arts over the Internet (Leu, Leu et al., 2004). This CIP, developed by Susan Silverman and me, is based on Lemony Snicket's *The Bad Beginning* (1999). Along with the preservice teachers, fifth- and sixth-grade students from New York are participating. They have all read the book and participated in class and online discussions about each chapter. The preservice teachers are working in small groups to develop writing response activities representing a combination of genres (e.g., poetry, letter writing, informational writing). The grade students will choose from these activities and respond to at least one; their work will be posted on the website to share with the Internet audience.

Preservice teachers Lila, Sean, and Thomas work diligently on their activities, regularly referring to their class notes on writing and the Lemony Snicket text.

"I think the activities need to be interesting to the students or they won't pick them," states Sean.

Lila agrees. "One way to do that might be to include some neat technology. Maybe they could create some illustrations in a graphics program to go along with their writing."

Thomas interjects, "I think it might also help to include models. Like for the poetry, we could include a link to a kid-friendly website so they can see what haikus look like."

After 45 minutes of brainstorming, their list was complete:

- Informational text: Write a short biography of Lemony Snicket. Research information about him on the Internet. Include as much information as you can find, including where he finds his motivation.
- Persuasive writing: Devise a plan to rescue Sunny from the tower

and write a persuasive argument convincing Violet to use your plan. You can write it as a letter. Include a map of the escape route using a graphics program.

- Letter writing: Using a graphics program, create a postcard from the Baudelaire children to their friends describing what their life is like since moving in with Count Olaf.
- Poetry: Write a haiku about Sunny's thoughts as she was trapped in the cage. A haiku is a type of poem that is three lines long and follows a 5–7–5 syllable pattern. Look at the following website for examples by kids: *www.kidzone.ws/poetry/haiku.htm*.

I will post the entire class list of writing activities on the project website along with a due date for the work to be submitted to the project coordinators. An advantage of CIP is that participating teachers do not need the technical know-how to publish on the Internet. Their focus, instead, is to allocate time for student response. Once the work is done and posted online, my preservice teachers and I will compare and contrast the work, analyzing how fifth and sixth graders respond differently to the same writing activities.

Teachers have utilized CIPs for years (Leu, Leu, & Coiro, 2004). I found that those who regularly participate in CIP do so for three reasons. First, most projects focus on connections between content and students' background knowledge, something teachers believe is important for making learning concrete. For instance, "Stellaluna's Friends," one of Susan Silverman's first CIPs, was based on the book *Stellaluna* by Janell Cannon (1993). The participants were required to read the story and study a species of bat indigenous to their geographical location. After completing their research, students shared their findings through writing genres such as poetry, letters, and narrative text (*www.kids-learn.org/stellaluna/index.htm*). This project was particularly useful because the participants were located all over the world, including the United States, Australia, and New Zealand, providing an insightful look at the relationship between bats and geography. Students were able to compare what they knew about bats living in their own area to information shared by students across the country and around the world.

Second, teachers value CIPs because they allow students to participate actively in their own learning. Reflecting again on "Stellaluna's Friends," project, students were given a choice of which genre to use to share their research findings. This choice is typical of most CIPs. Students feel invested in their work because they make decisions about how they participate. Also, most CIPs require the use of some technology, such as basic word processing and scanners or more sophisticated software like graphics programs or databases. After time to practice with the technology, students actively participate by creating responses that reflect their ideas.

A third reason teachers value CIPs is that they help students recognize and appreciate differences among their peers, as is poignantly illustrated in the creative writing posted on the "iEARN A Vision" CIP website (*www.iearn.org/avision/*). iEARN, the International Education and Resource Network, is a nonprofit organization that connects 20,000 schools in more than 109 countries for the purpose of creating a safe place for young people to communicate. The latest project is an international online publication that captures teenagers' perspectives of "the things around them and even across borders regardless of cultural and racial diversity." The compilation of work posted there can precipitate rich discussion about geography and current events. For instance, several students wrote about the December 2004 tsunami that made worldwide headlines. Figure 11.1 is a poem written by an Indian teenager. Analysis of these writings can teach students an important lesson about how tragedy, for example, can affect people in similar and differ-

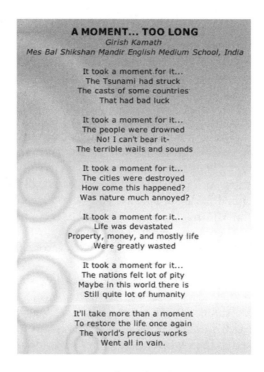

A MOMENT... TOO LONG
Girish Kamath
Mes Bal Shikshan Mandir English Medium School, India

It took a moment for it...
The Tsunami had struck
The casts of some countries
That had bad luck

It took a moment for it...
The people were drowned
No! I can't bear it-
The terrible wails and sounds

It took a moment for it...
The cities were destroyed
How come this happened?
Was nature much annoyed?

It took a moment for it...
Life was devastated
Property, money, and mostly life
Were greatly wasted

It took a moment for it...
The nations felt lot of pity
Maybe in this world there is
Still quite lot of humanity

It'll take more than a moment
To restore the life once again
The world's precious works
Went all in vain.

FIGURE 11.1. Poem from the "A Vision" project.

ent ways. Furthermore, although work on this site is posted in English, it is not the first language of most of the participants. Therefore, the authors must have learned to consider their words carefully so their thoughts would be clearly conveyed to people of differing backgrounds and locations. This type of opportunity is priceless because it confronts students with the multicultural community found on the Internet (see Karchmer-Klein & Layton, 2006, for a more thorough description of CIP).

There is no specific set of guidelines that all CIPs follow; however, from my experience participating in and developing CIPs, there are certain ones teachers should look for in the project description. A targeted audience should be stated, along with an explanation of the project's appropriateness for the grades. A good CIP will make a strong case for participation based on its ability to interest students and the match between the project and curriculum standards. In fact, teachers should only participate in a CIP that supports required content so that it becomes an integral component of instruction rather than a supplementary activity.

The project coordinator should have experience designing and implementing CIPs. Many times, coordinators will link new projects to existing ones so participants can see models of their previous work. Working with a veteran coordinator is helpful, particularly for first-time participants. He or she can provide technical assistance if needed and/or suggestions on ways to modify the project best to meet different expectations. His or her experience may also give teachers peace of mind knowing that the project will be completed as planned.

It is important that CIP include tasks with specific submission deadlines. This component manages teachers' expectations and allows them to schedule a realistic amount of time to work on the project. Some projects, such as "Unfortunate Collaborations," require reading a specific text prior to working on the writing activities. Other activities, like "Stellaluna's Friends," require students to conduct research. These activities must be factored into the time allocated for CIP work in the classroom.

Finally, one of the most important guidelines that should be included in a CIP description is how students' work will be submitted to the project coordinator and posted on the project website. When CIPs first became popular, some project coordinators allowed teachers to mail students' work to them through the postal service. It was the coordinator's responsibility to scan it into the computer and post it on the website. Times have changed, and many coordinators assume teachers have basic technology skills. They require all student work to be electronically submitted.

Like WebQuests, CIPs are easy to find. A Google search of the term identifies more than 2 million projects designed for K–12 education. To focus the results, it is best to search a project registry such as Global SchoolNet Internet PROJECT Registry (*www.globalschoolnet.org/GSH/pr/index.cfm*), a portal where you can search for appropriate CIPs by subject or grade level. An additional strategy is to remain in contact with project coordinators who implemented well-run CIPs. These coordinators, such as Susan Silverman, Marci McGowan, and Patti Knox, are usually happy to let you know about their next CIP. A list of noteworthy CIPs can be found in Table 11.2.

CIPs are good practice for teachers who want their students to write for a much larger audience than they can provide. If chosen well, they fit

TABLE 11.2. Noteworthy Collaborative Internet Projects

Title	Description and URL
Susan Silverman's Webfolio	At this site you will find projects developed by Susan Silverman, an educational leader in the area of CIPs. *www.kids-learn.org*
Unfortunate Collaborations	At this site you will find an Internet project completed by middle school students and preservice teachers. The project is based on Lemony Snicket's *The Bad Beginning*. *comsewogue.org/~ssilverman/snicket/*
Homepage of Patti Knox	At this site you will find projects developed by Patti Knox, an instructional technology coordinator for a school district in Ohio. *www.northcanton.sparcc.org/~ptk1nc/index.html*
My Town Is Important	At this site you will find a K–4 Internet project focused on geography and history. Participating classes study their town and share findings through poetry posted on the website. *www.mrsmcgowan.com/town/index.html*
Global SchoolNet Internet PROJECTS Registry	At this site you will find hundreds of CIPs developed for K–12 classrooms. You can join an existing project or post your own for others to participate in. *www.globalschoolnet.org/GSH/pr/index.cfm*
iEARN A Vision Project	At this site you will find the results of the A Vision creative writing project, a crosscultural examination of current topics written by teenagers all around the world. *www.iearn.org/avision/*

seamlessly within the classroom curriculum, which is especially important given the emphasis on standards-based learning across the country
(Karchmer-Klein & Layton, 2006). They are a little more challenging
than WebQuests because they require classrooms to finish by a specified
date and work needs to be submitted electronically, but they are easily
modified. They can be as simple or as complex as the teacher chooses.
For instance, teachers can decide the types of technology to be used for
the writing activities based on its availability in their school, their com-
fort level, and students' knowledge of the software. Novices tend to stick
with word-processing and basic graphics programs, whereas teachers
with more experience may use slide shows, spreadsheets, or electronic
graphic organizers. Technical support is available from the project coordinator if necessary, and many schools have instructional technology
support teachers who can help.

For the More Experienced: Classroom Websites

Mrs. Sharp projects the classroom website on the screen in the front of
the classroom. Her fourth graders have posted their latest work, an animal research report, and they received several comments from readers in
the electronic guestbook. Mrs. Sharp reads each of the comments aloud
to the class as the students listen intently.

> We are a first-grade class in Texas and we were excited to read your ani-
> mal reports. We have foxes and rabbits and catfish near us. We do not
> have any cougars or bears. Thanks for sharing your work.—Mr. Lambardi's
> first graders

> Dear Mrs. Sharp and Students:
> We enjoyed reading the work on your website. We found it when we
> did a search for animals in Pennsylvania. We live in Pennsylvania too.
> We are in Wilkes-Barre. We see the same kinds of animals where we
> live.—Ms. Tobey's second-grade class

"This next comment is very interesting to me," says Mrs. Sharp. "The
reader has some important comments about our work. I want you to
think about what he says carefully and then we'll discuss it." Mrs. Sharp
reads the comment to the class:

> Hi there, Class! I just spent time reading the animal research reports. I'd
> have to say that I was most impressed by Sean's report on the grouse. It
> was informative, yet concise, and it had a couple of nice pictures. I also
> found Taylor's explanation of ruminants very interesting. A couple of
> you guys should go back and do some fact checking, though. I'd buy an

eagle making it to 40 years old, but to 400 or more years?!?!! Even giant tortoises don't live THAT long! And if I run into one of Pennsylvania's 20 POUND squirrels I'm going to run for my LIFE! But, those are minor things that are easily corrected. Anyway, keep up the good work!—Mr. Finn from Minnesota

"I wrote the report on the eagle and I'm pretty sure I read on the nature website they live up to 400 years old," explains Chelsea.

"Maybe we can check the website again to make sure?" suggests Carrie.

"Good idea! Chelsea, do you know the website address?" asks Mrs. Sharp.

Chelsea types the URL into the computer and the eNature site comes up. It is a reliable source developed by a nonprofit organization and now run by the National Wildlife Federation, the nation's largest conservation organization. Chelsea searches for the section on eagles. Once finding it, Mrs. Sharp reads it to the class, "Eagles in captivity live approximately 40 years and eagles in the wild live between 10 and 12 years."

"I guess my information was wrong. I must have added an extra zero to the 40," admits Chelsea.

Bryan raises his hand and says, "That's okay, Chelsea. It's on the website, so it won't be hard to fix. You can just make the changes and we can update the site."

This scenario reflects the recursive relationship developed by the Internet between the author and her audience. That is, not only does the author share thoughts and ideas through writing, but the audience has an opportunity to reflect and respond. It is then the author's decision to revise the original work in light of audience feedback. What is unique about this relationship is that the Internet audience is unknown. It is virtually impossible to please all readers given the spectrum of ideologies represented, but this relationship can be perceived as a critical opportunity for students to consider the social context of their work in a way not typically supported in the K–12 classroom.

Classroom websites are used by teachers all over the world. The purpose behind them varies from teacher to teacher, yet most sites seem to have similar components. There is usually a teacher biography, which provides a useful context for understanding the website and what is included. Some teachers post classroom rules, expectations, and assignments if they plan to use the site as a tool to communicate with parents. Many sites have a section devoted to classroom news, a good place to involve students by having them write updates on the latest content learned in class. Additionally, as online publishing becomes an integral component of classrooms, most websites include a link to student work.

Teachers report that students are more motivated to write when their work is read by an Internet audience (Karchmer et al., 2005). Therefore, online publishing is becoming a much more widely used practice. Patty Taverna's Second Grade Website is a fantastic example devoted to students' online publications (*www2.lhric.org/pocantico/ taverna/taverna.htm*). Each link connects the reader to a variety of Internet writing projects. For example, in math, students learned to use words and pictures to pose mathematical equations. Using a graphics program, they wrote and illustrated a variety of word problems. In language arts, her students learned about how powerful word choices could depict clear images for readers. After visiting a local farm, students wrote short essays using their senses to describe the experience and drew an accompanying picture in a graphics program (see Figure 11.2 for an example). Again, this work was posted on the Internet for others to read.

Ms. Taverna has documented her writing assignments by maintaining links to past students' work from 1997 through 2006. This record is

On a chilly and sunny morning I took a nature walk along the paths at the Stone Barns. I looked closely at the black dappled ponies bucking in the field next to the pond. In the distance I could hear the wind blowing against the leaves in the trees. I rubbed my fingers across a bright, orange-skinned pumpkin sitting on top of a bale of hay as I dashed into the hay barn courtyard. I enjoyed the smell of the red, orange, and yellow chrysanthemums near the outdoor café then it was time to go back to school. I said, "That was fun!"

FIGURE 11.2. Example of a student's descriptive essay on Ms. Taverna's classroom website.

a wonderful way of illustrating her growth as a teacher. It also provides her current students with models of how to use technology to enhance their writing.

If student work is included on the classroom website, a guestbook, where readers can post comments like the one shared earlier in this section, is strongly recommended. Guestbooks can be designed in different web-authoring programs like Dreamweaver or downloaded for free from websites such as Bravenet (*www.bravenet.com*). Keep in mind that advertisements may be downloaded as well and become part of the website. If you are unable to include a guestbook, include the teacher's email address or an email address specifically designated for the project.

Perhaps the best way to begin publishing student work is to examine other teachers' classroom websites. There are several ways to locate exemplary sites. The Miss Rumphius Award recognizes excellent classroom websites. Members of the RTEACHER listserv, a literacy- and technology-focused discussion group managed by the International Reading Association, give the award (*www.reading.org/resources/community/ links_rumphius_info.html*) to twice-nominated sites with exceptional resources for teachers. TeacherNet.com maintains a long list of noteworthy classroom websites from pre-K through high school (*www.teachernet. com/htm/classroomsites.htm*). Classroom websites can also be found by searching school district websites. If you start at your own school district, you may find your colleagues are already publishing student work on the web. Table 11.3 lists noteworthy classroom websites.

Developing and maintaining a classroom website is the most challenging Internet-based practice described in this chapter for two reasons. First, the teacher must have the skills and time to create the website. While improved web-authoring programs are making the process much easier, it can still be an arduous task as you learn the technology. Second, once the website is developed, it is important to maintain it by updating regularly, which can be time consuming, especially for elementary-level teachers, who shoulder the responsibility of posting student work.

There are ways to alleviate some of the pressures of keeping a classroom website. First, keep the website simple. Since you are the designer, you can make it as basic or complex as you choose. Second, make good use of any technology support available in your school. Most instructional technology support teachers I work with feel they are underutilized. Third, tap into your students' knowledge of technology. Mary Kreul, a fourth-grade teacher, has her students update their classroom blog each month. It is their responsibility to report the latest news and activities taking place in the classroom. Many students maintain their own websites. Ask them for ideas and technical help if you run into a problem.

TABLE 11.3. Noteworthy Classroom Websites

Title	Description and URL
Ms. Smith's English Page	This classroom website showcases writing projects created by Ms. Smith's eighth-grade students. *home.earthlink.net/~jesmith/*
A Kindergarten Class— Mr. Fontanella's Welcome	This classroom website showcases writing projects created by Mr. Fontanella's kindergarten students. *www.jsd.k12.ak.us/hbv/classrooms/Fontanella/ fontanejhbvHome.html*
Ms. Taverna's Second Grade	This classroom website showcases writing projects created by Ms. Taverna's second-grade students. *www2.lhric.org/pocantico/taverna/taverna.htm*
Ms. Kreul's Class Blog	This classroom blog is a space for Ms. Kreul's fourth graders to write about what takes place in their classroom. There is also a link to the class home page, where students' writing projects are showcased. *marykreul.teacherhosting.com/blog/*
Sunnyside School Primary Multiage Class	This classroom website showcases writing projects created by Ms. Franz's first- and second-grade students. *www.psd267.wednet.edu/~kfranz/index.htm*

In addition to thinking about the design of the website, teachers must also consider the types of electronic text their students will write, which depends upon the technology available in school. It is advised initially to keep the text basic, using word-processing and graphics programs, digital cameras, or scanners to insert pictures. Students can gradually move up to including video, audio, and hyperlinks as they become more familiar with the technology. Most important, students need to be taught how to construct effective electronic text. They need to understand how these unique features add meaning to the written word. Therefore, teachers must emphasize the importance of creating integrated text where the multimedia components support the meaning of the presentation, rather than creating flashy text that lacks content and cohesiveness.

CONCLUSION

Different levels of time, effort, and technology proficiency are needed to implement each of the Internet writing practices described in this chapter. When looking at all three, however, several guiding principles emerge that should be considered when planning to make the Internet an integral component of your writing curriculum.

- Internet writing practices can be as simple or as complex as the teacher chooses.
- Internet writing practices should be modified to meet the needs of a particular group of students.
- Internet writing practices support required curriculum standards.
- Internet writing practices encourage students to think about the social implications of their work.
- Internet writing practices promote deeper understandings of the multicultural community through technology-based social interactions.
- Internet writing practices help students learn the literacy skills necessary to be successful in the 21st century.

This chapter is about making the Internet a part of writing instruction. Perhaps more important, it is about classroom teachers' willingness to take risks. Using the Internet practices and principles described here as a guide, I hope teachers are able to create new visions for learning in their classrooms.

REFERENCES

Beach, R., & Friedrich, T. (2006). Response to writing. In C. A. MacArthur, S. Graham, & J. Fitzgerald (Eds.), *Handbook of writing research* (pp. 222–234). New York: Guilford Press.

Calkins, L. M. (1994). *The art of teaching writing*. Portsmouth, NH: Heinemann.

Cannon, J. (1993). *Stellaluna*. New York: Harcourt.

Daiute, C., & Morse, F. (1994). Access to knowledge and expression: Multimedia writing tools for students with diverse needs and strengths. *Journal of Special Education Technology, 12*(3), 221–256.

Dodge, B. (1997). *Some thoughts about WebQuests*. Retrieved January 17, 2006, from *webquest.sdsu.edu/about_webquests.html*

Goldberg, A., Russell, M., & Cook, A. (2003). The effect of computers on student writing: A meta-analysis of studies from 1992–2002. *Journal of Technology, Learning, and Assessment, 2*(1), 1–51.

Howell, R. D., Erickson, K., Stanger, C., & Wheaton, J. E. (2000). Evaluation of a computer-based program on the reading performance of first grade students with potential for reading failure. *Journal of Special Education Technology, 15*, 5–14.

Karchmer, R. A. (2001). The journey ahead: Thirteen teachers report how the Internet influences literacy and literacy instruction in their K–12 classrooms. *Reading Research Quarterly, 36*, 442–466.

Karchmer-Klein, R. A., & Layton, V. (2006). Literature-based collaborative Internet projects. *Reading Research and Instruction, 45,* 261–294.

Karchmer, R. A., Mallette, M. H., Kara-Soteriou, J., & Leu, D. J. (2005). *Innovative approaches to literacy education: Using the Internet to support new literacies.* Newark, DE: International Reading Association.

Leu, D. J., Leu, D. D., & Coiro, J. (2004). *teaching with the Internet K–12* (4th ed.). Norwood, MA: Christopher-Gordon.

MacArthur, C. A. (2006). The effects of new technologies on writing and writing processes. In C. A. MacArthur, S. Graham, & J. Fitzgerald (Eds.), *Handbook of writing research* (pp. 248–262). New York: Guilford Press.

MacArthur, C. A., Graham, S., Hayes, J. B., & De La Paz, S. (1996). Spelling checkers and students with learning disabilities: Performance comparisons and impact on spelling. *Journal of Special Education, 30,* 35–57.

Matsumura, L. C., Patthey-Chavez, G. G., & Valdes, R. (2002). Teacher feedback, writing assignment quality, and third-grade students' revision in lower- and higher-achieving urban schools. *Elementary School Journal, 103*(1), 3–22.

Mitra, A., & Cohen, E. (1999). Analyzing the web: Directions and challenges. In S. Jones (Ed.), *Doing Internet research: Critical issues and methods for examining the net* (pp. 179–202). London: Sage.

The New London Group. (2000). A pedagogy of multiliteracies: Designing social futures. In B. Cope & M. Kalantzis (Eds.), *Multiliteracies: Literacy learning and the design of social futures* (pp. 9–37). London: Routledge.

Quinlan, T. (2004). Speech recognition technology and students with writing difficulties: Improving fluency. *Journal of Educational Psychology, 96,* 337–346.

Reece, J. E., & Cummings, G. (1996). Evaluating speech-based composition methods: Planning, dictation, and the listening word processor. In C. M. Levy & S. Ransdell (Eds.), *The science of writing: Theories, methods, individual differences, and applications* (pp. 361–380). Mahwah, NJ: Erlbaum.

Reinking, D. (1998). Synthesizing technological transformations of literacy in a post-typographical world. In D. Reinking, M. McKenna, L. D. Labbo, & R. Kieffer (Eds.), *Handbook of literacy and technology: Transformations in a post-typographic world* (pp. xi–xxx). Mahwah, NJ: Erlbaum.

Reinking, D., Labbo, L., & McKenna, M. (1997). Navigating the changing landscape of literacy: Current theory and research in computer-based reading and writing. In J. Flood, S. B. Heath, & D. Lapp (Eds.), *Handbook of research on teaching literacy through the communicative and visual arts* (pp. 77–92). New York: Macmillan.

Reinking, D., & Rickman, S. S. (1990). The effects of computer-mediated texts on the vocabulary learning and comprehension of intermediate-grade readers. *Journal of Reading Behavior, 22,* 395–411.

Russell, M., & Plati, T. (2001). Effects of computer versus paper administration of a state-mandated writing assessment. *Teachers College Record.* Retrieved March 1, 2006, from *www.tcrecord.org*

Snicket, L. (1999). *The bad beginning.* New York: HarperCollins.

U.S. Department of Education. (2005). *National education technology plan.* Retrieved January 13, 2006, from *nationaledtechplan.org/*

12

Best Practices in Teaching Writing to Adolescents

DOLORES PERIN

Writing can be a satisfying and mind-expanding activity for the student who has acquired the necessary skills but a frustrating and even aversive experience when these skills are lacking. By the middle and high school years, it is necessary for students to possess a level of writing skill that will allow them to express increasingly complex thoughts and take a critical stance toward information. Secondary school teachers routinely assign writing assignments not for the purpose of teaching writing but in order to promote students' development of knowledge and ideas; however, many adolescents cannot engage in these higher-order thinking activities because they do not have an adequate grasp of the writing strategies needed for these endeavors. Further, low writing skills may mask a student's true state of knowledge, which confounds the assessment of his or her learning.

This chapter is addressed to middle and high school teachers to familiarize them with research-based techniques to teach writing and to use writing as a basis for learning. It starts with a theoretical framework for understanding the writing activity and continues with an overview of writing skills expected of adolescent students. After this introductory information, 11 teaching approaches are presented that are couched within recommendations supported by research with students in grades 4 through 12. (Although students in grades 4 and 5 are not technically adolescents, there is a wealth of research with these grade levels that applies to adolescent writing instruction.) Finally, some guidelines are offered for the use of these recommendations in school settings.

A THEORETICAL CONTEXT
FOR ADOLESCENT WRITING INSTRUCTION

Writing is an extraordinarily complex activity that incorporates thought processes, feelings, and social interaction. Hayes (1996) provides a comprehensive model of how people write, organized in two categories, the *task environment* and the *individual* (Fig. 1.3, p. 4). The task environment itself consists of a social environment and a physical environment. The social environment is the audience for a student's writing, the setting (such as the classroom), and texts that may be consulted for the purpose of writing. This part of the model relates to situations such as a 10th-grade social studies student researching slavery in the United States in the 18th century using primary historical documents and writing a persuasive essay addressed to her classmates arguing against the position that the United States was a true democracy at the time. Recognizing the use of source texts as a part of the writing process is an important aspect of the model as, in an academic setting, writing activities tend to be closely related to reading (Fitzgerald & Shanahan, 2000). The physical environment refers to the material a student has written so far (such as an organizational plan, a first draft of an essay, or a finished product that stimulates additional writing) and the modality of writing (such as a pen and paper or a word processor).

Components of writing relating to the individual include cognitive processes by which students can reflect on their work during the planning of writing, the actual production of text, and the interpretation of their text in the course of revising what they have written. To produce written text, the student must be able both to generate ideas mentally and to transcribe those ideas using spelling, handwriting (or keyboarding), grammar, punctuation, and capitalization. Another component of the individual aspect of writing concerns motivation and affect, which include goals for writing, predisposition to write, beliefs and attitudes about writing, and the writer's ability to weigh the advantages and disadvantages of engaging in a writing activity. Besides the cognitive and motivational aspects of writing, Hayes (1996) includes a category within the individual pertaining to different types of memory that are necessary in the act of writing.

While Hayes's (1996) aim was to characterize the writing processes of proficient writers, Bereiter (1980) described the development of writing.

For this purpose he proposed five overlapping phases, which combine cognitive and social processes. The first phase is *associative writing*, in which written messages are free associations that are hard for anyone but the writer to comprehend. The second phase is *performative writing*, in which the learner becomes able to adopt the conventions of style, punctuation, and capitalization. At this point, the writer is capable of producing full sentences, although, similar to the first phase, they are self-referential and may not have much meaning for another person. At the third phase, *communicative writing*, the writer is aware of an audience for what is being written. Thus, the writer understands that the reader has a need for certain information in order to understand the text. Writing becomes more sophisticated at the fourth phase, *unified writing*. Here, the writer can express opinions and otherwise evaluate information in logically flowing essays and reports. The fifth and last phase is somewhat elusive for many people, even adults. This is the *epistemic* phase, in which writing is used as a means of developing knowledge and extending ideas. Through the act of writing at this phase, a person's thought process itself changes, a phenomenon referred to as *knowledge-transformation* (Bereiter & Scardamalia, 1987, p. 6). This phase of writing development underlies the writing-to-learn approach, in which teachers assign writing activities in the course of teaching subject matter (Bangert-Drowns, Hurley, & Wilkinson, 2004).

It is useful when planning instruction to locate the performance level of individual students within Bereiter's (1980) developmental progression. The phases do not imply any particular age or grade level, although children of average and above-average writing achievement will probably accomplish all phases by adolescence. Many adolescents, however, may be operating at the lower phases of writing development. For example, a low-achieving adolescent student may be "stuck" at the communicative phase of writing and have difficulty planning and producing written work that expresses a coherent point of view, which becomes possible at the higher unified phase. Furthermore, many adolescent students cannot engage in learning-to-write activities possible when students are operating in the epistemic phase because of difficulties with spelling, sentence construction, and basic strategies for planning and producing a piece of written text.

ACADEMIC WRITING SKILLS
EXPECTED BY ADOLESCENCE

The National Assessment of Educational Progress (NAEP; Persky, Daane, & Jin, 2003) revealed that a large proportion of U.S. students in grades

4, 8, and 12 did not possess the competencies just described. The NAEP divided students' ability to compose text into basic, proficient and advanced levels for each grade (p. 8). For example, at the grade-8 level, basic writers are "able to produce an effective response within the time allowed that shows a general understanding of the writing task they have been assigned. Their writing should show that these students are aware of the audience they are expected to address, and it should include supporting details in an organized way. The grammar, spelling, punctuation, and capitalization in the work should be accurate enough to communicate to a reader, although there may be mistakes that get in the way of meaning" (p. 10). Proficient writers are "able to produce a detailed and organized response within the time allowed that shows an understanding of both the writing task they have been assigned and the audience they are expected to address. Their writing should include precise language and varied sentence structure, and it may show analytical, evaluative, or creative thinking" (Persky et al., 2003, p. 10). The study set the proficient level of writing as an acceptable goal for student performance, but as many as one quarter of students tested *below* the lowest (basic) level, and about half tested *at* the lowest level (Persky et al., 2003, p. 10). Only 22–26% tested at the proficient level across the three grades, and very few wrote at the advanced level.

Written expression as characterized by both Hayes (1996) and Bereiter (1980) is based on multiple component skills. Taking the literacy standards for eighth graders in New York state as an example (University of the State of New York, State Education Department, 2005) we see 11 writing competencies organized in four categories: spelling, text production, composition, and motivation to write. Within the category of composition, there are six competencies: "Compose mechanically grade-equivalent texts for a variety of student-selected and teacher-selected purposes; write with voice to address varied purposes, topics, and audiences across the curriculum; organize writing effectively to communicate ideas to an intended audience; compose arguments to support points of view with relevant details from single and multiple texts; work collaboratively with peers to plan, draft, revise, and edit written work; and produce written and multimedia reports of inquiry, using multiple sources" (p. 61). The student should be able to use each of these competencies for several purposes, expressed in the state standards as performance indicators of writing "for information and understanding," writing "for literary response and expression," writing "for critical analysis and evaluation," and writing "for social interaction" (pp. 61–62).

Another dimension of writing concerns its relationship to reading comprehension. Since writing and reading skills tend to be intertwined in practice (Fitzgerald & Shanahan, 2000), it is best that teachers view writing instruction within a larger reading–writing task. Fitzgerald and Shanahan (2000) proposed that, beginning in approximately fourth grade, students should be able to monitor their own understanding of text they read and write and repair errors they have made. Domain knowledge is expected to expand considerably from this time, with related growth in vocabulary knowledge for both reading comprehension and writing. Students are also expected to be aware of and utilize the structures of different types of text. For example, they should be able to write stories or personal narratives according to conventional story structures and informational reports following text structures such as compare and contrast, chronological sequence, and problem solution. Echoing the state standards described above, Fitzgerald and Shananhan (2000) indicate that adolescent students should be able to comprehend and write texts such as persuasive essays that convey multiple viewpoints.

LEARNING TO WRITE AND WRITING TO LEARN

In considering how teachers should address adolescent students' need to learn the many component skills that constitute written expression, it is important to distinguish between learning to write and writing to learn. Instructional activities that focus on learning to write provide explicit instruction in a variety of techniques that help students develop the competencies mentioned earlier. For example, teachers can teach detailed writing strategies made up of steps for planning, composing, and revising narrative, expository, and persuasive essays. In an approach of this type, Self-Regulated Strategy Development (SRSD), which is well supported by research, the teacher describes a strategy, models the steps, guides students as they practice it, and finally assigns independent practice (Graham & Harris, 2005, Chapter 6, this volume). Other forms of research-based writing instruction are described later in this chapter.

In contrast to activities such as SRSD that are designed to teach students component writing skills, teachers may utilize writing-to-learn activities within content-area instruction (Bangert-Drowns et al., 2004; see Newell, Koukis, & Boster, Chapter 4, this volume). For example, a math teacher may ask students to write instructions for solving a math problem, a social studies teacher may ask them to keep a journal of reactions to historical documents, or a science teacher may have them record the results of an experiment in a written lab report.

EFFECTIVE ADOLESCENT LITERACY INSTRUCTION:
EVIDENCE FROM A META-ANALYSIS

As a research field matures, more studies become available, and it is useful to summarize across studies to identify trends in benefits to students. The statistical technique of meta-analysis provides a summary of effects of instructional techniques that are tested using control groups and utilize research methodology that permits the calculation of an effect size. (There are other kinds of research that can also be valuable but cannot be included in a meta-analysis because, for one reason or another, their methodology does not yield effect sizes.) The effect size is a statistic that represents the difference between the test scores of a group that participates in a given instructional technique and another group that does not. If the group differences are sufficiently large, as expressed by the effect size, the technique is considered effective and teachers are justified in considering it for use. Generally, an effect size of 0.20 is considered to indicate only limited effectiveness, an effect size of 0.50 suggests a medium level of effectiveness, and 0.80 or above indicates that a technique is highly effective (Lipsey & Wilson, 2001).

Based on a wide-ranging search for research into adolescent literacy instruction, a set of studies was identified for a meta-analysis (Graham & Perin, 2006a). Studies that compared different types of writing instruction with adolescent students and yielded effect sizes were selected for the meta-analysis. The studies were categorized according to type of writing instruction, such as summarization and strategy instruction. Within each category in which there were at least four studies, an average weighted effect size was calculated to estimate the level of effectiveness across studies in the same category. For example, four different studies where teachers taught summarization strategies to adolescents were found, yielding an average weighted effect size of 0.82. This effect size indicated that the learners in the studies strongly benefited from engaging in activities that helped them summarize information in writing. From this we can propose that middle and high school teachers in general should consider teaching strategies for summarization in their classrooms.

The studies used in the meta-analysis were conducted with students from a range of grades between 4 and 12. Across all of the studies, 11 of the categories were found to demonstrate effective instruction according to two criteria: they were based on four or more studies and the average weighted effect size was significantly different from zero. These 11 categories were used to formulate recommendations for teachers.

RESEARCH-BASED RECOMMENDATIONS
FOR ADOLESCENT WRITING INSTRUCTION

The recommendations shown in italics below are quoted from Graham and Perin (2006) and ordered by magnitude of average weighted effect size, from large to small. For each recommendation, the average weighted effect size and the grade levels of the students who participated in the studies are given. Instructional examples are provided for the 11 recommendations, and the interested reader is referred to Graham and Perin (2006a) for references to other examples. Also, each example is intended as an overview of a technique tested in a research setting rather than a prescribed plan of action for the teacher. Specific details of how the instruction was delivered in the studies are available in the original articles referenced in Graham and Perin (2006a). A briefer description of the meta-analysis is provided by Graham and Perin (2006b).

Recommendation 1: Strategy Instruction

Teach adolescents strategies for planning, revising, and editing their compositions (mean weighted effect size = 0.82; grades 4–10).

- *Example*: De La Paz (2005), eighth-grade students, full range of ability.
- *Instructional steps*: A language arts teacher and a social studies teacher collaborate. The social studies teacher teaches a historical reasoning strategy using sets of primary and secondary historical documents for each of four different historical events related to westward expansion in the United States from 1800 to 1850. Using the historical reasoning strategy, the students learn to recognize and reconcile conflicting information or conflicting points of view in the documents. The language arts teacher teaches a strategy for writing argumentative (persuasive) essays. First, the students write in a journal about how to persuade a parent or peer about a particular topic, then review an essay presenting a point of view concerning voting rights for 10th graders. At this point, the students learn two mnemonics intended to help them plan to write an essay of their own. The first is STOP: *S*uspend judgment, *T*ake a side, *O*rganize ideas, and *P*lan as you write. The STOP mnemonic directs students to generate and organize ideas before writing. They then learn the DARE mnemonic: *D*evelop a topic sentence, *A*dd supporting ideas, *R*eject an argument for the other side, and *E*nd with a conclusion. DARE reminds students to include key elements of a persuasive essay and to consider the reader's informational needs when writing. The language arts teacher goes on to present the structure of a five-paragraph

persuasive essay on a historical topic and shows students essays arguing different views of this topic. This teacher then models planning and writing paragraphs of a persuasive essay on a topic related to westward expansion, using the mnemonics. The students work in small groups to plan a persuasive essay on another westward expansion topic. They proceed to work under the guidance of the language arts teacher, then independently compose essays on different historical topics.

- *Duration*: Historical reasoning: social studies class periods, 12 days. Planning and composing an essay: language arts class periods, 10 days.
- *Instructional materials*: Historical texts on westward expansion.

Recommendation 2: Summarization

Teach adolescents strategies and procedures for summarizing reading material, as this improves their ability to concisely and accurately present this information in writing (mean weighted effect size = 0.82; grades 5–12).

- *Example*: Bean and Steenwyk (1984), sixth-grade students, full range of ability.
- *Instructional steps*: Six rules for written summarization are taught. The first rule is "delete unnecessary material." The teacher shows the students two five-sentence paragraphs, and the students decide which words are unimportant to the overall meaning of each one. The second rule is "delete redundant material." The same two paragraphs are used, and the students are asked if too much information had been deleted. In this way, the teacher guides the students to grasp the nature of the deletion rules. The teacher then introduces the students to the third and fourth rules, "compose a word to replace a list of items" and "compose a word to replace the individual parts of an action," using different paragraphs. When the students have grasped these rules, the teacher works with the students to understand the fifth and sixth rules, "select a topic sentence" and "invent a topic sentence if one is not available," again using different paragraphs. When the teacher feels that the students have mastered all the rules, the students are asked to compose 15- to 30-word summaries of the paragraphs used in the instruction.

The teacher can vary this approach by showing the students one sentence from a paragraph and asking them to retell the information using 15 or fewer words. Then, the teacher presents two more sentences from the paragraph and asks students to write a 15-word sentence that summarizes these two sentences. The teacher repeats this process until the entire paragraph is summarized.

- *Duration*: Twelve 25- to 30-minute periods over 5 weeks.

• *Instructional materials*: Paragraphs on a range of topics from a published reading skills instructional package.

Recommendation 3: Peer Assistance

Develop instructional arrangements where adolescents work together to plan, draft, revise, and edit their compositions. Such collaborative activities have a strong impact on the quality of what students write (mean weighted effect size = 0.75; grades 4–high school). Two examples are provided below in which students collaborate according to clearly defined roles. The first involves the full writing process, and the second concerns revision.

• *Example 1*: Yarrow and Topping (2001), fifth- to sixth-grade students, full range of ability.

• *Instructional steps*: The teacher assigns students to mixed-ability pairs in which higher-achieving writers are "helpers" and struggling writers are "writers." The teacher presents a series of predetermined steps for writing, represented in a flowchart covering ideas, draft, read, edit, best copy, and evaluate. For example, in the draft section, the flowchart states that the writer should "look at the notes, start a rough draft, don't worry about spelling." The writer is directed to say a sentence and can choose between "Stage 1, Helper writes it all, Writer copies it all," "Stage 2, Helper writes hard words for Writer," "Stage 3, Helper writes hard words in rough, Writer copies in," "Stage 4, Helper says how to spell hard words," and "Stage 5, Writer writes it all." The flowchart indicates that the "Helper helps if Writer struggles on a word for more than 10 seconds, usually by going back a stage on that word" (Yarrow & Topping, 2001, p. 269). After the teacher explicates and discusses all the steps in the flowchart, the pairs of students write five compositions. The teacher monitors their use of the flowchart, provides prompts and praise to support their work, and solves any problems that may occur during the collaboration. The writing is of a personal nature, and the students select their own themes and titles.

• *Duration*: Four sessions per week for 6 weeks.

• *Instructional materials*: Flowchart of steps for peer-assisted writing.

• *Example 2*: MacArthur, Schwartz, and Graham (1991), fourth-, fifth-, and sixth-grade students with learning disabilities.

• *Instructional steps*: Peers collaborate to apply the *student editor strategy* to the revision of compositions on self-selected topics, usually personal narratives, that have been previously word-processed. The teacher begins by teaching pairs of students a peer-editing strategy. One student in each pair is the author, and the other is the editor. The author reads aloud a composition that he or she has written, and the editor listens and reads along. The editor tells the author what the composition is about and what he or she liked about it. The editor then reads it to him- or herself and makes notes on revisions needed, asking him- or herself whether there is anything that is not clear and where more details and information can be added. He or she discusses these points with the author. This is a reciprocal strategy—the students serve as author and editor for each other. When the discussion ends, each author revises his or her composition on a word processor in the classroom.

The teacher then introduces the student editor strategy to the whole class, describing it and emphasizing its importance. The teacher shows a videotape of two student actors using the strategy for class discussion. The students copy the steps in the strategy and are directed to memorize them. The teacher then models the strategy, and the students practice each step. Examples of essays are projected, and the students practice applying the strategies for revising, going on to practice with their own work. The students then collaborate in pairs. The videotape is shown again, and the pairs practice the strategies with teacher guidance until they can use the strategy without help. The teacher presents the strategy for independent use as well peer collaboration.

- *Duration*: 30–45 minutes per day, 4 days per week for 6–8 weeks.
- *Instructional materials*: Videotape, writing samples.

Recommendation 4: Setting Product Goals

Set clear and specific goals for what adolescents are to accomplish with their writing product. This includes identifying the purpose of the assignment, e.g., to persuade, as well as characteristics of the final product, e.g., addresses both sides of an argument (mean weighted effect size = 0.70; grades 4–8).

- *Example*: Page-Voth and Graham (1999), seventh- and eighth-grade students with learning disabilities.
- *Instructional steps*: This approach is designed for instruction in the writing of persuasive essays with individual students. The teacher asks the student to write essays answering three of the following four questions: Do you think boys and girls should play sports together? Do you think parents should give money for good grades? Should children have a say in where a family goes on vacation? Should schools have fast-food restaurants in them instead of cafeterias? The student writes three essays over four instructional sessions.

First, the teacher reviews the parts of a persuasive essay: statement of premise or belief, supporting reasons, refutation of claims that can be made against the initial premise, and conclusion. The teacher defines each part, then asks the student to provide an example and describe the parts until the teacher is sure they are set in the student's memory. The teacher makes especially sure that the student understands and can remember the nature of supporting reasons and the refutation of counterclaims. The teacher also defines and discusses the value of goal setting.

Three instructional sessions after this point comprise a prewriting conference, the writing of an essay by the student, and a postwriting conference. In the prewriting conference, the student receives an essay topic and is given the goal of refuting a specific number of claims that run counter to the initial premise stated in the essay. The student records this goal and discusses a six-part strategy to help accomplish it: (1) read the essay topic and state an opinion, (2) brainstorm and write down enough ideas to satisfy the goal, (3) write the essay, including the ideas brainstormed, (4) check whether all ideas are included in the essay, (5) modify the essay to add any ideas not included, and (6) check to see if the goal has been met and return to step 5 if it has not. At the end of the prewriting conference, the teacher asks the student to write the essay in such a way as to accomplish the goal, following steps they have discussed. The student receives a printed checklist containing the six strategies and space to note the brainstormed ideas. In the postwriting conference, the student reads the essay aloud, and the teacher provides feedback regarding the extent to which the goal was achieved.

- *Duration*: Four instructional sessions.
- *Instructional materials*: Essay prompts, printed strategy checklist.

Recommendation 5: Word Processing

Make it possible for adolescents to use word processing as a primary tool for writing, as it has a positive impact on the quality of their writing (mean weighted effect size = 0.55; grades 4–12).

- *Example*: Lowther, Ross, and Morrison (2003), fifth-, sixth-, and seventh-grade students.
- *Instructional steps*: The use of word processing is a general approach, in contrast to the instruction related to the other recommendations. Here, the intervention is simply that all children in the class are provided with personal laptop computers on which they do all writing assignments in all classes. Classroom instruction consists of a variety of approaches, including direct instruction, coaching by the teacher, student-centered activities, and independent seatwork. Where possible, the teacher leans toward student-centered approaches, including cooperative

learning, project-based learning, inquiry, and using the computer as a learning tool.

- *Duration*: One academic year.
- *Instructional materials*: Laptop computers in conjunction with routine materials.

Recommendation 6: Sentence Combining

Teach adolescents how to write increasingly complex sentences. Instruction in combining simpler sentences into more sophisticated ones enhances the quality of students' writing (mean weighted effect size = 0.50; grades 4–11).

- *Example*: Saddler and Graham (2005), fourth-grade students, both average and low-achieving.
- *Instructional steps*: Although the studies in the meta-analysis indicate that teaching grammar according to traditional methods is not effective, teaching sentence combining, an alternative approach to grammar instruction, had positive effects on student learning. The essence of the instruction is presenting small (*kernel*) sentences to learners, who combine the sentences into larger ones, including complex sentences at the advanced level. For example, early in the instruction, students learn to combine the sentences "The worm was squishy" and "The worm did not taste bad" to create the single sentence "The worm was squishy, but it did not taste bad." At the end of the instructional sequence, students should be able to combine the kernel sentences "Ralph stuck his head out," "Ralph was in Ryan's pocket," "Ralph looked around," and "Ralph did not know where he was," to form the single, complex sentence "Ralph, who was in Ryan's pocket, did not know where he was, but stuck his head out and looked around" (Saddler & Graham, 2005, p. 46).

The instruction is delivered to pairs of students. Sentence-combining instruction consists of five units of six lessons each. Unit 1 teaches the combining of kernel sentences into larger sentences using the "connectors" (Saddler & Graham, 2005, p. 46) *and*, *but*, and *because*. Unit 2 teaches students to embed an adjective or adverb in the newly combined sentence. Units 3 and 4 focus on combining sentences using adverbial and adjectival clauses. Unit 5 concerns embedding multiple items including adjectives, adverbs, adverbial clauses, and adjectival clauses. In each of the six lessons, the teacher first explains and models the combining of sentences. The pair of students practices the procedure, with the teacher writing down the students' responses until lesson 3 and then the students writing down their own responses. After a period of guided practice, the students work independently, alternately serving as coach and learner within the pair.

Instruction cards, charts and stickers, and planning sheets are used as instructional aids. In the later lessons in each unit, the students work collaboratively to write and revise stories containing the combined sentences and independently write a story based on a picture prompt. The teacher provides guidance and feedback at several points in each lesson. Highly detailed instructions for teaching the lessons are available in Saddler and Graham (2005). (See also Saddler, Chapter 8, this volume.)

- *Duration*: Thirty 25-minute lessons over 10 weeks.
- *Instructional materials*: Kernel sentences, story prompts, and instructional aids including charts, stickers, and planning sheets.

Recommendation 7: Process Writing with Training

Provide teachers with training in how to implement the process writing approach when this instructional model is used with adolescents (mean weighted effect size = 0.46; grades 4–12).

- *Example*: Pritchard and Marshall (1994), teachers of fourth- to twelfth grade students.
- *Instructional steps*: Teachers participate in professional development in the National Writing Project. The training focuses on the following elements of writing instruction: brainstorming, prewriting, free writing, journal writing, imitating writing models, use of peer groups, sentence combining, grammar and mechanics, spelling and vocabulary, use of reference sources, class publishing, evaluation rubrics, in- and out-of-class writing, and writing in the content areas. In professional development, the teachers demonstrate lessons they consider effective, engage in daily writing, participate in group discussion, and are guided to experience their own writing from the vantage point of prewriting, drafting, sharing, revising, sharing again, and self-assessing. Once back in their schools, the participating teachers read assigned journal articles, perform additional writing in varied genres, which is presented in subsequent training meetings, and plan their own professional development activities. Teachers collaborate across grade levels. Certain assumptions underlie the training, such as that writing instruction should focus on process, move in a sequence culminating in correctness, and include the use of writing-response groups and writing as a means to learn. (See Pritchard & Honeycutt, Chapter 2, this volume.)
- *Duration*: 1 week of professional development followed by 15 day-long workshops, school-based activities, and follow-up meetings, total time period required not reported.
- *Instructional materials*: Professional development materials designed by the National Writing Project; writing samples of the participants' students and other classroom artifacts.

Recommendation 8: Inquiry

Involve adolescents in writing activities designed to sharpen their skills of inquiry. Provide a clear goal, have the students analyze immediately available, concrete information using specific strategies, and have them apply what was learned from this analysis (mean weighted effect size = 0.32; grades 7–12).

- *Example*: Hillocks (1982), seventh- to eleventh-grade students, full range of ability.
- *Instructional steps*: The teacher presents several objects, such as an elastic bandage or a piece of onion, and leads a discussion about the objects' qualities. The students describe their sensory perceptions in spoken language and in written notes, lists of descriptive words, and sentences. The teacher draws on the students' observations to emphasize writing goals such as being specific in presenting information, narrowing one's focus, and addressing the reader's needs. The teacher then presents a model composition that provides a description and analysis of a specific object or place, which may be those discussed or may be different. The students examine the model composition either as a whole class or in small, student-led groups. The teacher organizes the discussion with the intention of promoting a high degree of student collaboration and response. In each class session, the students are asked to compose and revise an essay that is conceptually connected to the inquiry and the related collaborative discussion. Examples of writing prompts are "Write about a room at home or some other place. Be as specific as you can so that someone reading your composition will see what you see and understand the character of the room" and "Write a composition about a place. Give a physical description of the place, but focus on the sounds in that place. Be as specific as you can so that someone reading your composition will hear the sounds you hear or imagine the sights you see" (Hillocks, 1982, p. 267).
- *Duration*: Time ranges from four to ten class periods over 2–5 weeks.
- *Instructional materials*: One or more physical objects, model compositions, essay prompts.

Recommendation 9: Prewriting

Engage adolescents in activities that help them gather and organize ideas for their composition before they write a first draft. This includes activities such as gathering possible information for a paper through reading or developing a visual representation of their ideas before writing (mean weighted effect size = 0.32; grades 4–9).

- *Example*: Brodney, Reeves, and Kazelskis (1999), fifth-grade students, full range of ability.
- *Instructional steps*: The teacher shows students a videotape on a given topic (e.g., volcanoes) and the next day provides a related reading passage to the students (e.g., an eight-page report on volcanoes). The students are given 10 minutes to complete the reading. The teacher then asks them to use the next 10 minutes to think about the nature of volcanoes based on what they read and saw. During this time, the students are expected to organize their thoughts, choosing among listing their ideas, representing them in a web, writing an outline or notes, or free writing, all of which they have been previously taught. Finally, the teacher asks the students to write a one- to two-page composition in 30 minutes on the topic of the videotape and reading passage, using the material developed as they organized their ideas.
- *Duration*: Two class periods.
- *Instructional materials*: Videotape and reading passage on same topic, writing prompt.

Recommendation 10: Use of Models

Provide adolescents with good models for each type of writing that is the focus of instruction. These examples should be analyzed and students encouraged to imitate the critical elements embodied in the models (mean weighted effect size = 0.25; grades 4–12).

- *Example*: Knudson (1991), fourth-, sixth-, and eighth-grade student, full range of ability.
- *Instructional steps*: Students learn to write a persuasive essay based on exposure to well-written expository text. The instruction contains two elements: presentation of models of writing and opportunity to write. On one day, the teacher presents and discusses with the students a model of excellent expository writing, such as a persuasive essay that sets out to convince the reader that UFOs exist. The next day the teacher presents another well-written essay claiming the opposite. Then, the teacher asks the students to write a persuasive essay arguing for or against the position that girls are better in math than boys. This procedure is repeated a number of times during the instructional period with different texts and writing prompts. All of the models of writing are at readability levels below the students' grade placement, to ensure that students can focus on the characteristics of the writing without being distracted by text difficulty.
- *Duration*: 20 minutes per day for 14 days.
- *Instructional materials*: Models of excellent expository writing, expository writing prompts.

Recommendation 11: Writing to Learn

Use writing as a tool to facilitate adolescents' learning of content material. Although the impact of writing activity on content learning is small, it is consistent enough to expect some enhancement as a result of writing-to-learn activities (average weighted effect size = 0.23, grades 4–12).

- *Example*: Boscolo and Mason (2001), fifth-grade students, full range of ability.
- *Instructional steps*: This recommendation is different from the others because it addresses writing to learn rather than learning to write. An example of writing to learn is an activity conducted by a science teacher focused on the human circulatory system. The teacher's goal is to help students develop alternate conceptualizations of the role of the heart, blood, and circulation. Writing is assigned to further this goal, but writing skills themselves are not explicitly taught. Rather, the writing activity is a means to the end of learning content. The teacher asks the students to write summaries and answer questions in writing to increase their ability to explain information about the human circulatory system, elaborate knowledge leading to a deeper understanding of the topic, comment on and interpret information in assigned science text, communicate what they have not understood, and describe any change in belief they might be experiencing.
- *Duration*: Six sessions over 1 month.
- *Instructional materials*: Science text and any ancillary materials used to teach science, writing prompts.

HOW TEACHERS CAN
IMPLEMENT THE RECOMMENDATIONS

Given the writing difficulties of many U.S. adolescents, as described in the NAEP report (Persky et al., 2003), a surge of energy is needed in the middle and high schools to improve students' writing skills. One of the assumptions of this chapter is that teachers should base instruction on research to the extent that it is available and that the tested techniques are consistent with both the curriculum in use and the needs of the students being taught. Certain questions arise as teachers plan to implement the approaches recommended in this chapter. Should only the approaches with the higher effect sizes be used? What if the educational setting or student achievement levels are different from the conditions of the research study? Is the teacher justified in using approaches that have not been tested? In the language of Bereiter's (1980) framework, should students who have not completed the communicative or unified phases of writing development be assigned epistemic writing tasks? Should content-area teachers teach writing skills? How can low-achieving adolescents be motivated to write? These issues are discussed in this section.

Selecting Techniques Based on the Magnitude of Effect

All of the approaches recommended in this chapter have the support of research evidence, but the effect sizes are larger for some approaches than others. For example, teaching summarization (Recommendation 2) and teaching prewriting (Recommendation 9) are both effective, but the evidence is stronger for summarization than prewriting. Normally, this would not be a matter of concern to the teacher because each of these approaches has a different objective, so the teacher would rarely have to choose between them. Ideally, teachers of adolescents should incorporate all of the recommendations to the extent, as mentioned above, that they are appropriate for the particular instructional situation. If there are two approaches that address the same need, the teacher should choose the one with the larger effect size. In fact, this type of choice is a luxury at this time because of a lack of research.

Match between the Research Setting and the Classroom

The research leading to the recommendations varies considerably with regard to participants' grade levels, instructional tasks, and size of the learner group. Typically, a study of a given technique is performed only once, with a specified grade range, learner ability, and group size. For example, there is evidence in the meta-analysis for the effectiveness of summarization instruction with fifth through twelfth graders, but this evidence comes from several different studies, each of which tested a different summarization technique with different types of students in different learning conditions. Instructional characteristics vary across types of writing instruction research as well. For instance, the example for summarization was drawn from research with sixth-grade students of the full range of ability, while the example for setting product goals comes from a study by Page-Voth and Graham (1999) on individualized instruction for seventh- and eighth-grade students with learning disabilities. There is currently no study that tests the effectiveness of summarization with seventh- and eighth-grade students with learning disabilities. The very purpose of a meta-analysis is to capture effects across studies that have key aspects in common while differing in others.

Pending research into all the techniques with students at every achievement level and in whole-class, small-group, paired, and individualized settings alike, all of the recommendations in this chapter can rightfully be considered for use with all adolescents. Also, again because of a lack of research, it is suggested that any technique should be repeated as often as necessary, varying the types of materials used. For example, Brodney and colleagues' (1999) prewriting technique is of short duration, but the teacher can use it as often as necessary, varying the instructional materials to meet instructional goals.

Using Tested versus Untested Approaches

Only a fraction of all possible approaches to writing have been tested. It is important to recognize that the recommendations offered in this chapter do not constitute a writing curriculum. There is not a sufficient amount of controlled research available at present to propose such a curriculum for adolescents. Rather, the recommendations are for instructional approaches that various researchers have chosen to study. Teachers can best use the recommended techniques by incorporating them into their ongoing literacy curricula, which will have a larger scope than all the areas covered in the recommendations put together. What is important is that the teacher understand the nature of writing acquisition, for example through the conceptualization of writing offered by Hayes (1996) and Bereiter (1980), and incorporate the recommendations into ongoing practice to accomplish the goals suggested by these frameworks. In this view, teachers can combine techniques from the various recommendations, although such combinations have not been tested yet. Further, an approach consistent with the cognitive theory of literacy, although not directly tested to date, is that the teaching of writing should be systematically connected with reading instruction (Fitzgerald & Shanahan, 2000).

Relationship between Writing Instruction and Students' Developmental Level

If students have not completed one phase of writing development, should they be assigned tasks at a higher level? For example, should students whose writing is not easy for others to follow (Bereiter's communicative level) or students who have difficulty providing support for an opinion in a persuasive essay (Bereiter's unified level) be given epistemic, writing-to-learn tasks? Although at this time there is no controlled research on this issue with adolescents, research on writing instruction with younger children by Berninger, Abbott, Whitaker, Sylvester, and Nolen (1995) suggests that it is not necessary or desirable to wait for lower-level skills to be gained before higher-level tasks are assigned. Thus, in a single lesson, a teacher can provide explicit instruction in writing skills (such as sentence construction, audience awareness, or steps for presenting arguments and counterarguments) and assign a higher-level task such as writing an opinion with supporting evidence about a given topic. In this way, the low-achieving student can immediately apply the lower-level skills and receive the same opportunities as higher achievers to engage in meaningful writing.

An issue that complicates the planning of instruction for the many adolescents whose spelling and punctuation are very poor (Persky et al., 2003) is that there is little or no intervention research on these skills with adolescent participants. In this case, teachers should implement recommendations formulated for younger students (see Schlagal, Chapter 9, this volume) while retaining an approach that combines instruction in lower- and higher-level skills in the same lesson.

Relationship between Content-Area and Writing Instruction

Recommendation 11 in this chapter is that students be assigned writing activities as a way of promoting content learning. The emphasis in writing to learn is on writing practice rather than writing instruction, although it is possible to incorporate both. An example comes from a study (Keys, 2000) in which eighth-grade science students learned about erosion in an earth science unit. In this approach, the students observed the soil in an area near the school and recorded their observations in writing. They collected information about soil and, after returning to the classroom, created data tables, discussed findings, and wrote a scientific report. The teacher provided written guidelines with goals and subgoals that the students had to satisfy as they wrote their report, including a description of the procedure and an opinion statement about the erosion data supported by detailed evidence.

If schools accept the idea that writing-to-learn activities need to incorporate writing instruction, the teaching of writing skills will need to be distributed throughout the disciplines. Although some educators are tempted to confine writing instruction to the language arts and English classroom, it seems more beneficial to adolescents to teach writing within content-area instruction as well (Shanahan, 2004). Adolescents spend most of the school day in content-area instruction, in which they are expected to absorb and take a critical stance on information. Since writing difficulties are so widespread (Persky et al., 2003), it seems appropriate that the content-area teacher become involved in teaching writing, but content-area teachers have generally not been favorable toward this suggestion (Stevens & Bean, 2003). Further, even when teachers are interested in expanding the scope of content instruction to literacy skills, they run the risk of using instructional strategies as a superficial bag of tricks (Vacca, 1998, p. xvi, cited by Stevens & Bean, 2003, p. 190), rather than integrating them in a way that genuinely promotes learning of content.

Literacy instruction will be most meaningful if it is embedded in content (Biancarosa & Snow, 2004). Not only should content-area teachers teach writing skills, but language arts and literacy specialists should teach writing using tasks, vocabulary, and reading material drawn directly from discipline courses. Although instructional formats for accomplishing this goal have yet to be tested, adolescent outcomes may improve if language arts and content-area teachers collaborate to integrate writing-to-learn and learning-to-write activities.

Motivating Students to Write

Most of the studies of writing instruction that yield effect sizes concentrate on cognitive processes as theorized by Hayes (1996) but tend to neglect another of Hayes's elements, motivation. Affect is always present in learning, and the effects of feelings are perhaps most noticeable among adolescents, who are undergoing an emotionally intense period in their lives (Moje, 2002). The level of motivation to write is particularly important in interventions where collaboration is needed, such as in as peer assistance (Recommendation 3). Although different strategies for raising adolescents' motivation to write have yet to be tested rigorously, teachers can draw on literature reviews such as Bruning and Horn (2000) for practical suggestions. (See also Boscolo & Gelati, Chapter 10, this volume.)

For example, according to Bruning and Horn (2000), teachers should discuss the cognitive and social functions of writing, clarify students' beliefs about writing, and teach writing strategies to build students' self-efficacy for writing. Also, teachers can increase students' interest in writing by building topic knowledge and establishing authentic goals and contexts for writing. Further, teachers should express enthusiasm and positive opinions about writing. (A rarely discussed challenge arises when the teacher is not fond of or proficient in writing. This issue can be addressed in professional development efforts.) Bruning and Horn (2000) also recommend that teachers provide support, guidance, and feedback. Consistent with some of this chapter's recommendations, Bruning and Horn suggest that teachers help students set goals and monitor progress, offering comments and, where indicated, rewards for specific aspects of the students' work. Further, teachers should assign writing tasks that are as complex as possible within the students' instructional level. Finally, Bruning and Horn note the importance of creating a pleasant emotional environment for students as they write, letting them control as much of the writing task as they can.

Self-efficacy, or the level of confidence in one's ability to perform a difficult task, is a special challenge in teaching low-achieving adolescents. Such students tend to overestimate their performance, judging the quality of their work to be better than it actually is (Klassen, 2002). Teachers should find a balance between helping students maintain a positive attitude toward literacy instruction and providing realistic feedback on specific aspects of their writing performance.

CONCLUSIONS

Eleven research-based recommendations are offered to teachers in this chapter. On the assumption that instruction should be guided as much as possible by evidence from controlled studies, the recommendations represent best practices for teaching writing to adolescents. When implementing the recommendations, teachers should remain aware of the theoretical underpinnings of writing, be flexible based on curricular and student needs, and stay current with newly published research in order to adopt new approaches based on effect sizes as they become available.

ACKNOWLEDGMENTS

This chapter is based on a meta-analysis conducted with funding from Carnegie Corporation of New York, reported in Graham and Perin (2006a, 2006b).

REFERENCES

Bangert-Drowns, R. L., Hurley, M. M., & Wilkinson, B. (2004). The effects of school-based writing-to-learn interventions on academic achievement: A meta-analysis. *Review of Educational Research, 74,* 29–58.

Bean, T. W., & Steenwyk, F. L. (1984). The effect of three forms of summarization instruction on sixth graders' summary writing and comprehension. *Journal of Reading Behavior, 16,* 297–306.

Bereiter, C. (1980). Development in writing. In L. W. Gregg & E. R. Steinberg (Eds.), *Cognitive processes in writing.* Hillsdale, NJ: Erlbaum.

Bereiter, C., & Scardamalia, M. (1987). *The psychology of written composition.* Hillsdale, NJ: Erlbaum.

Berninger, V. W., Abbott, R. D., Whitaker, D., Sylvester, L., & Nolen, S. B. (1995). Integrating low- and high-level skills in instructional protocols for writing disabilities. *Learning Disability Quarterly, 18,* 293–309.

Biancarosa, G., & Snow, C. E. (2004.) *Reading next—A vision for action and research in middle and high school literacy: A report from Carnegie Corporation of New York.* Washington, DC: Alliance for Excellent Education.

Boscolo, P., & Mason, L. (2001). Writing to learn, writing to transfer. In G. Rijlaarsdam, P. Tynjala, L. Mason, & K. Lonka (Eds.), *Studies in writing: Vol. 7. Writing as a learning tool: Integrating theory and practice* (pp. 83–104). Dordrecht, The Netherlands: Kluwer.

Brodney, B., Reeves, C., & Kazelskis, R. (1999). Selected prewriting treatments: Effects on expository compositions written by fifth-grade students. *Journal of Experimental Education, 68,* 5–20.

Bruning, R., & Horn, C. (2000). Developing motivation to write. *Educational Psychologist, 35,* 25–38.

De La Paz, S. (2005). Teaching historical reasoning and argumentative writing in culturally and academically diverse middle school classrooms. *Journal of Educational Psychology, 97,* 139–158.

Fitzgerald, J., & Shanahan, T. (2000). Reading and writing relations and their development. *Educational Psychologist, 35,* 39–50.

Graham, S., & Harris, K. R. (2005). *Writing better: Effective strategies for teaching students with learning difficulties.* Baltimore: Brookes.

Graham, S., & Perin, D. (2006a). *A meta-analysis of writing instruction for adolescent students.* Manuscript submitted for publication.

Graham, S., & Perin, D. (2006b). *Writing next: Effective strategies to improve writing of adolescents in middle and high schools. A report to Carnegie Corporation of New York.* Washington, DC: Alliance for Excellent Education.

Hayes, J. R. (1996). A new framework for understanding cognition and affect in writing. In C. M. Levy & S. Ransdell (Eds.), *The science of writing: Theories, methods, individual differences, and applications* (pp. 1–27). Mahwah, NJ: Erlbaum.

Hillocks, G., Jr. (1982). The interaction of instruction, teacher comment, and revision in teaching the composing process. *Research in the Teaching of English, 16,* 261–278.

Keys, C. W. (2000). Investigating the thinking processes of eighth grade writers during the composition of a scientific laboratory report. *Journal of Research in Science Teaching, 37,* 676–690.

Klassen, R. (2002). Writing in early adolescence: A review of the role of self-efficacy beliefs. *Educational Psychology Review, 14,* 173–203.

Knudson, R. E. (1991). Effects of instructional strategies, grade, and sex on students' persuasive writing. *Journal of Experimental Education, 59,* 141–152.

Lipsey, M., & Wilson, D. (2001). *Practical meta-analysis.* Thousand Oaks, CA: Sage.

Lowther, D. L., Ross, S. M., & Morrison, G. M. (2003). When each one has one: The influences on teaching strategies and student achievement of using laptops in the classroom. *Educational Technology, Research and Development, 51*(3), 23–44.

MacArthur, C. A., Schwartz, S., & Graham, S. (1991). Effects of a reciprocal peer revision strategy in special education classrooms. *Learning Disability Research and Practice, 6,* 201–210.

Moje, E. B. (2002). Re-framing adolescent literacy research for new times: Studying youth as a resource. *Reading Research and Instruction, 41,* 211–228.

Page-Voth, V., & Graham, S. (1999). Effects of goal setting and strategy use on the writing performance and self-efficacy of students with writing and learning problems. *Journal of Educational Psychology, 91,* 230–240.

Persky, H. R., Daane, M. C., & Jin, Y. (2003, July). *The nation's report card: Writing 2002.* (NCES 2003-529). U.S. Department of Education. Institute of Education Sciences. National Center for Education Statistics. Washington, DC: Author.

Pritchard, R. J., & Marshall, J. C. (1994). Evaluation of a tiered model for staff development in writing. *Research in the Teaching of English, 28,* 259–285.

Saddler, B., & Graham, S. (2005). The effects of peer-assisted sentence-combining instruction on the writing performance of more and less skilled young writers. *Journal of Educational Psychology, 97,* 43–54.

Shanahan, T. (2004). Overcoming the dominance of communication: Writing to think and to learn. In T. L. Jetton & J. A. Dole (Eds.), *Adolescent literacy research and practice* (pp. 59–73). New York: Guilford Press.

Stevens, L. P., & Bean, T. W. (2003). Adolescent literacy. In L. M. Morrow, L. B. Gambrell, & M. Pressley (Eds.), *Best practices in literacy instruction* (2nd ed., pp. 187–200). New York: Guilford Press.

University of the State of New York, State Education Department. (2005, May). *English language arts core curriculum.* Available at *www.emsc.nysed.gov.*

Vacca, R. T. (1998). Foreword. In D. Alvermann, D. Moore, S. Phelps, & D. Waff (Eds.), *Toward reconceptualizing adolescent literacy* (pp. xv–xvi). Mahwah, NJ: Erlbaum.

Yarrow, F., & Topping, K. J. (2001). Collaborative writing: The effects of metacognitive prompting and structured peer interaction. *British Journal of Educational Psychology, 71,* 261–282.

13

Best Practices in
Writing Assessment

ROBERT C. CALFEE *and*
ROXANNE GREITZ MILLER

We begin this chapter with three snapshots to ground our discussion in the realities of practice. Each snapshot reflects several classroom experiences that we have shaped into an integrated portrait:

> Samuel had delivered his first show-and-tell report earlier in the morning. Now he sat beside Ms. Hancock as she reviewed the notes she had made at the time. Sam was small for his age and a bit shy, and talking in front of the entire class had been a challenge, but he had made it! His topic had been his new baby sister. After announcing that she had come home from the hospital, he was at a loss about what to say next. Ms. Hancock prompted him with a few questions. What kind of hair did she have? What kind of noises did she make? What did she do? Samuel had something to say about each of these matters. Ms. Hancock has written four sentences from Samuel's words: "Martha is my new sister. She is bald. She gurgles. She mostly sleeps." Samuel has completed his first academic project, which will appear in the upper lefthand section of the weekly parent newsletter. His parents show delight as reads his report to them, and it sets the stage for the upcoming parent–teacher conference.

> June has been a voracious reader since preschool and started a personal journal in second grade. As a fourth grader, she has already

written several brief papers, but now she faces a different challenge. Her teacher, Mr. Buchers, has announced that the March assignment will be a research paper. Students must first select a current events topic for background reading. Both the reading and writing will be expository rather than personal narrative. Mr. Buchers is enraptured by history and spent time during the fall and spring introducing students to historical analysis. Now the class is going to study history in the making! Mr. Buchers explains that he is pushing the class; this type of writing is generally introduced in fifth or sixth grade, but he thinks they are up to it, so he is giving them a head start. The assignment will take 2 or 3 weeks to complete; they will work in small groups. Mr. Buchers reviews some basics: how to find materials in the library and on the computer and how to take notes for the report. June is considering "Can a woman be President?" as her topic. Her parents have different positions; her father is inclined to support the idea, but her mother is less sure. June agrees with her father but knows that she must consider both sides of the issue. It will be a different kind of writing and reading for her.

Tom and Chizuko have been good friends since they met in ninth-grade math. As they near the end of high school, the SAT writing test looms large on the horizon. They both enjoy math and science but are less comfortable with composition assignments, and neither did especially well on the PSAT writing test. They now study together, using materials from the College Board website as a guide: "Brainstorm, collect information, organize, do a rough draft, revise and refine, read more, and write more" (*www.collegeboard.com*). Great advice, but how should one use it during an on-demand timed test? Math seems simpler to them—analyze the problem, work out the answer, and that's it. Writing is so mushy, with never enough time to make sure that everything is exactly right. And no one seems to teach writing! English class is about novels and plays, and their other teachers expect students already to know how to write.

These snapshots capture the range of writing scenarios that students experience during their school years. By the end of elementary school, students seldom write unless they have to and then only because it "counts." In high school, writing begins to count a lot, across the board and over the long run. The College Board advice about effective writing is certainly on target. Best practices should follow these guidelines, but too often neither students nor teachers can find the time. Standards have to be met, content has to be covered, and the textbook has to be finished. Writing is included in the standards, but the responsibility for acquiring skill rests largely on students' shoulders. In the elementary grades, reading has priority; in many classes, as much as half the academic day is devoted to the basal reader. By the middle school years, teachers deal with more than 100 students every day, which means little opportunity for individualization of any sort.

Our assignment in this chapter is to discuss best practices in writing assessment, a task that poses a twofold challenge for teachers—first, the task of providing authentic opportunities for students to acquire skill in writing while covering an ever-increasing array of other curriculum demands; second, the overriding pressures to ensure that students perform well on the standardized tests that have become the primary accountability index. As we complete this chapter, few state testing systems rely to any significant degree on performance tests for measuring student achievement. Multiple-choice tests dominate, and on-demand writing tests (including the SAT) generally contravene the counsel provided by the College Board.

We assume that we are writing for teachers who are writers and that you understand the importance of establishing both audience and purpose. We have framed our audience as "teachers who are writers" rather than "writing teachers." Ideally, every teacher, across all grades and subject matters, should incorporate writing as an integral part of instruction because writing reveals thinking (Miller & Calfee, 2004) and can serve as a critical source of information for both teacher and student. Writing takes time and patience, which can be a challenge in a daily curriculum packed with objectives and standards. We assume that our audience has some freedom, although it may be limited, to deviate from the official schedule and the patience required to help students reflect on their learning.

Our purpose is to survey assessment concepts and techniques supported by research and practical experience and to suggest ways to fit these ideas into the realities of policies that, although well intended, often conflict with best practices. The advice from the College Board illustrates this point; it captures many facets of best practices, but the real SAT assessment permits none of these elements. We have limited space for presenting how-to details, but we will provide selected references to help apply the ideas.

The chapter is organized around three topics. First, we describe the concept of embedded classroom writing assessments designed to inform instruction and provide evidence about learning. The bottom line here is the recommendation that writing tasks (instruction and assessment) be designed to support the learning of significant academic topics (Urquhart & McIver, 2005). Next, we present several contrasts that emerge from this perspective: process versus product, formative versus summative evaluation, and assessment versus testing. Finally, we review a set of building blocks that is essential to all writing assessments, especially those that are classroom-based: the prompt, the procedures, and the rubrics. As you have probably realized from the scenarios and the discussion thus far, our focus will be on *composing* more than *mechanics*. Attention to spelling and grammar is eventually important, but it helps if the writer has something to say and has learned how to organize his or her ideas.

WRITING TO LEARN

When and how should students learn to write? In reading, the contrast is often made between learning to read and reading to learn (Chall, 1995). A similar distinction can be made for writing, but we think that the basic idea is flawed in both instances. From the earliest stages, both reading and writing should be grounded in the purposes of literacy: to think and to communicate. To be sure, students need to acquire skills and strategies for handling print, which requires time (and patience) from both teacher and student, but learning is more effective when motivated by a clear purpose. In short, learning to write is generally best grounded in writing to learn.

In a world where student achievement is often gauged by the application of a pencil to a multiple-choice bubble, it is important to remember that writing is a performance task that requires substantial effort, motivation, persistence, strategic planning, and skill, as well as knowledge about the topic. If any of these ingredients is missing during an assessment, then the student's potential can be substantially underestimated. Valid assessment needs to tap into both product and process, with probes that gauge each of the preceding elements.

For all of these reasons, it makes sense that writing and writing assessment should be linked to meaningful academic outcomes. Given the substantial costs to everyone, writing activities are best focused on significant matters, rather than on writing for the sake of writing. This recommendation does not mean that writing must center around dull schoolwork. For Samuel, the kindergarten show-and-tell report demonstrates that he can focus on a topic (his new sister) and elaborate with a few sentences. He can now apply the strategy to the rock in his pocket, the snake in the terrarium, and (later) the causes of the Civil War. June and her classmates are acquiring new skills and strategies, including the mechanics of the five-paragraph essay, but the focus is the topic of their historical research. Tom and Chizuko have, in the best of worlds, spent more than a decade learning to write as laid out by the College Board. The reality is probably quite different. Instead of approaching the SAT with experiences that leave them confident and self-assured, able to adapt what they know to a broad range of situations, they suddenly confront a high-stakes task for which they feel poorly prepared. If they are lucky, their teacher (or tutor) will take this opportunity to help these two young people learn to deal with the SAT and to see the difference between SAT writing and real writing.

Best practices in writing assessment begin with an authentic task, where purpose and audience are clear and meaningful, where support and feedback are readily available, and where the final product has academic value for the student. Contemporary surveys of writing assessment (Black, Harris, Lee, Marshall, & William, 2003; Chappuis, Stiggins, Arter, & Chappuis, 2005; Harp, 2006; Stiggins, 2004) typically employ a conceptual framework with the elements shown in Figure 13.1.

Let us offer a few cautions before discussing the elements in Figure 13.1. The model suggests a fixed path not intended by the framers, but the basic elements generally make sense as a model of classroom assessment. The model needs to be filled in for a specific application, of course. In this instance, what is missing is "writing about what, and why?" At the risk of overstating the point, we recommend that you not teach writing for the sake of writing. Instead, think about ways in which writing can support learning of academic outcomes, including both content and process. From the lowly book report to the daunting research paper, subject matter provides opportunities for students to demonstrate learning at the same time that they acquire skill in communicating. For the teacher, the point is that writing (like reading) becomes an integral part of virtually every lesson. You may be asking yourself, "Who is going to grade all of this stuff?" We address this question later.

Three implications spring from embedding writing in subject-matter learning. First, this approach addresses issues of topic and purpose directly. Whether a check of background knowledge, a quick quiz to review an assigned reading, or an extended project, writing becomes an integral part of the learning process. Second, writing (like reading) varies substantially with developmental level and subject matter. What can be expected of a second grader describing a collection of fall leaves, a fifth

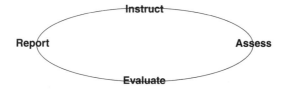

FIGURE 13.1. Conceptual model for classroom assessment.

grader preparing a report on why gas prices rise and fall, and an eighth grader developing an opinion piece about graduation ceremonies? Third, assessment techniques need to be shaped differently for each of these scenarios. In particular, valid and informative assessments must balance content with writing; to what extent does the composition reveal understanding of the topic, and how well written is the work?

Now a few words about each element in Figure 13.1. The action element is *instruct*, a word from the same root as *structure*, with the connotation of building, designing, framing, and completing. Teachers have the responsibility to help young people construct academic edifices during the school years—identifying essential parts of various structures, setting the stage for student projects, engaging them in the building task, checking the work along the way, and inspecting the final project. Literacy serves as an essential tool kit (or machine shop) for the construction process. Best practices for writing assessment check the status of the kit; the tools need to be in good shape, and the user must know how to use them effectively. Authentic curricular goals are the critical substance for the enterprise.

The joining of *assess* and *evaluate* is critical to best practices. We say more about *assess* in the next section, where we contrast it with *test*, but the core idea is the collection of evidence about student learning. *Evaluate* refers to the interpretation of the evidence. These two are interwoven, rather than sequential, but they require different activities and states of mind. When Ms. Hancock takes notes on Samuel's words during his report, these serve as evidence as does the scaffolding she provides along the way. Samuel was clearly eager to tell classmates about his new sister, but leading questions kept him going. He was still learning his ABCs and, from one perspective, was not able to read, but when Ms. Hancock wrote his sentences in the daily report, he could read them on his own. All these observations serve as evidence, which often takes shape as a story like Samuel's.

What does the story tell about what Samuel knows and can do? What might be the most useful next steps instructionally? Such questions exemplify the evaluation process, which requires reflection and debate. The point is not to decide whether the performance is good or bad but to consider alternative interpretations that suggest various instructional responses—to think like an experimenter (Calfee & Hiebert, 1990). The question is not "Can Samuel compose/write a show-and-tell report?" which implies a yes-or-no response. Rather, it is "Under what conditions can Samuel produce a show-and-tell report with particular characteristics?" (e.g., three ideas related to a central theme). The evidence in this case suggests that Samuel has not yet learned this task to the point where it has become automatic. On the other hand, with a bit of guidance he was able to complete the task reasonably well and seemed enthused about his accomplishment. He was engaged, he could talk about the results, and the event set the stage for his future learning activities and provided a model for the entire class.

Recommendations for best practices typically include completion of a *report* as an element. The basic idea is to document the activity. In fact, classroom assessment is often on the fly, with the results recorded mentally; where the evidence is oral, memory may be all that is possible. An important feature of written material is that one does not have to rely on memory—there is a concrete record. The question is how to make effective use of the information.

The most important assessment record is the one that serves the teacher in documenting student learning and steering instructional decision making. The student is clearly an important audience for such information, which can provide feedback, encouragement, guidance, and sometimes grades. Other audiences include parents, administrators, and other teachers. Reporting, except for formal mandates like report cards, tends to receive relatively little attention in educational situations, which is somewhat strange when you think about it. If you visit your doctor or auto mechanic, you expect assessment and evaluation to be part of the exchange, typically as a basis for action. You also expect a record of the entire process—what was checked, what was found, and what was done. Best practices for schooling should be documented to provide a basis for reflection on student learning, and to guide the teacher in shaping the curriculum in practice.

June's teacher, Mr. Buchers, appears tuned in to this principle. The class assignment is to write a research paper about a significant curriculum goal, the analysis of historical happenings. The task requires both reading and writing, but, most important, it requires thinking. June will report regularly to the class about her project, and Mr. Buchers will gently but firmly model and shape questions during these discussions. What evidence does June offer for her claims about a woman president? What about other interpretations? lessons from previous decades? possibilities for the future? June's written record informs Mr. Buchers about her progress in dealing with these questions. Tom and Chizuko, in contrast, often feel that they are working in the dark. Their English teacher administers biweekly practice exams and offers suggestions for self-assessment. The opportunity to practice helps, but it is up to the students to review their progress and decide what they need to do to improve.

CONTRASTS IN WRITING-BASED LEARNING

When writing becomes a commonplace of daily life in the classroom, the teacher confronts interesting contrasts. Evidence of student learning is everywhere, which allows assessment of both process and product. The teacher directly experiences the distinction between formative and summative evaluation, between growth and accomplishment. It clearly serves no purpose to grade every piece of student work, but neither can one ignore students' efforts; rather, the goal is to use compositions to guide growth. Students will eventually begin to take for granted the conditions of authentic writing, which allow time and offer support (from the teacher and other students), but they also need to learn about the realities of tested, on-demand writing. Each situation offers opportunities to review the distinctive features of best practices (or at least very good practices).

A student composition provides information about both *content* and *process*, about what students have learned and how well they can communicate it. One aim of this volume is to encourage teachers to consider writing as an integral part of learning for all curriculum domains, so the *what* is especially important.

We return to this matter shortly, but first we address the *how well* question, which centers on communicating, which is at its core a two-way process. Notice that, unlike reading and writing, schools do not schedule separate classes on listening and speaking. The point is not that students do not know how to listen and speak—they generally appear able to communicate informally with family and friends—but that virtually every student needs to learn about academic discourse (Heath, 1983). The usual assumption is that they will acquire this language register through participation in classroom conversations throughout the day. In fact, if you listen to such conversations, they frequently turn out to be rather one-sided, with teacher talk the dominant discourse and student talk rather sparse.

What are the alternatives to teacher talk? How can the teacher provide reasonable opportunities for students to engage in genuine academic discourse during classroom discussions? Time is limited. Only one student can hold the floor at any given time. Small-group techniques offer one option, but management poses a challenge, as does documentation (and, hence, assessment and evaluation). Writing provides a practical approach—students can all write at the same time, and the information does not disappear into the air—but (1) students must write well enough to capture what they have to say, and (2) someone has to handle evaluation tasks.

Separating content and process is an important first step for speaking as well as writing. A student may have produced a beautiful piece of writing (process), but the content may show little grasp of the topic or may simply be off topic. Another student may turn in a piece that is difficult to handle—poorly organized, misspelled, ungrammatical—but somehow one realizes that the student is deeply engaged with the message.

Surface features may stand in the way of appreciating what a student has to say. The challenge is to see beyond the mechanical flaws to an appreciation of the substance of the message.

We are not completely satisfied with our content and process labels. A contrast is also made between process and product, the difference between how a student writes a paper and the quality of the final work. Product often refers to organization and coherence, as well as mechanical details, all of which are important, but the substance of the composition is generally overlooked in product rubrics. Especially when writing is linked to subject-matter learning, it is important for assessment to give attention to the substance. Holistic approaches mush everything together, and most analytical approaches downplay or ignore substance. So we use process to refer to the student's activities in writing a composition as well as the characteristics of the written work, and product to refer to the substance of the work as a response to the assignment. Books and articles on writing and writing assessment deal generically with the writing part of the equation. Teachers are generally left on their own to figure out how to use a composition to judge student understanding of a topic.

Suppose, for example, that you have assigned eighth graders to write a paper explaining variation in the seasons. You emphasize that the work needs to be well crafted, and you have explained the rubrics for gauging coherence and conventions. How do you explain your plan for judging the substance of the papers? We assume that your instructional aim is something other than a collection of Web-based cut-and-paste pieces, that you expect students to go beyond a summary of resource materials to reconstruct or transform the ideas. In this case, you can expect individual variation in both structure and specifics. Within these variations, it is still possible to define the key concepts (e.g., the inclination of the earth on its axis) and essential relations (what happens at the North Pole as the Earth moves around the Sun). If these critical elements are missing or unclear, then the student presentation of the content is problematic, no matter how engaging or well structured the piece. In a study of Harvard graduates by Schneps (1989), students told enthralling stories about how the seasons changed as the Earth moved around the Sun. Unfortunately, the substance of their compositions (which were oral rather than written) was wildly wrong in many instances.

Assessment of content should allow writers considerable leeway, within reason, in how they approach the task. For example, suppose a student structures the essay as a narrative in which a space station crew recounts their observations as they circumnavigate the globe from 25,000 miles above the earth. This composition would be quite different from a more scientific piece that lays out the sequence of seasonal patterns in mechanical detail or a persuasive essay that describes how the shifting seasons play a role in the development of holes in the ozone layer. The goal in assessing content is to judge students' mastery of the essential information as they play with different styles and audiences. Suppose the assignment is to explain the seasons to third graders. What considerations come into play when the challenge is to explain the content to a genuine novice? The power of including compositions in subject-matter curricula is that students are called upon to demonstrate their understanding of a topic in a range of settings. The assessment challenge is to develop a set of principles that accommodate a wide range of topics in a consistent manner, so that the rules of the game do not constantly change. Notice that more is involved than getting the facts right. Facts are part of the puzzle, but concepts and relations among the facts are even more important.

The second contrast is between *formative* and *summative evaluation* (Bloom, Hastings, & Madaus, 1971), which often amounts to the difference between judging growth versus judging accomplishment (Calfee, 1997). Formative evaluation entails relatively informal procedures for obtaining information that can guide improvement in student learning. The primary goal in the classroom setting is to establish the degree to which the student is making progress—and, if he or she is not, to find out how to help the student begin to move ahead. Formative evaluation is experimental in the truest sense of the concept; under what conditions can a student perform the task at a level adequate to meet prescribed standards? A student may fail a task for many reasons. Formative evaluation searches for the conditions that support success, which can include helpful advice from the teacher, can also open the way to explore interest and motivation, opportunities to cooperate, and various accommodations. Notice that in the formative mode of assessment and evaluation, documentation of the scaffolding conditions is an important part of evidence, along with student performance. Formative evaluation is richly qualitative, creating portraits that can be viewed from different perspectives.

An example may serve to illuminate the point. Martin, who is repeating third grade, spends part of the day in a special education class. The diagnosis includes poor decoding skills, weak vocabulary, limited comprehension skills, and a total lack of motivation when it comes to reading. Martin cannot read and does not want to learn. During a school visit, one of us (Calfee) was asked to take a look at Martin, an invitation for formative evaluation. Martin, the teacher, and I met in the teacher's office, where a stack of textbooks had been placed on the table. The teacher asked Martin to pick a favorite book to show me how he could read. The aim was to give Martin a choice, which made sense. The problem, of course, was that Martin had little interest in any of the books, as evidenced by an uplifted eyebrow. I moved the books to the side and asked, "What do you think about them Bulls?" The school was in Chicago, and it was the heyday for the local basketball team. Martin brightened considerably and spoke at length about the team's exploits. The structure of his exposition was well formed, his vocabulary was rich and appropriate to the topic, and he seemed quite enthusiastic. When asked about his sources of information—"You must watch a lot of television?"—Martin responded that he watched the broadcasts, but was also an avid reader of the sports section in the local paper. How to evaluate this exchange? Formative evaluation pays attention to subtle clues such as raised eyebrows, tone of voice, and choice of words. Triangulation is critical; any single piece of evidence is limited, so the evaluator must put many pieces together. In Martin's case, I concluded that he could decode under certain conditions, that he exhibited significant capacity to handle complex vocabulary and comprehension tasks, that he was capable of constructing an engaging exposition, and that he was highly motivated. The obvious challenge was to move these capacities from the basketball arena to the classroom setting.

Summative evaluations address bottom-line issues, captured not by a rich portrait but by a few numbers or letters. Today's students must meet established levels of accomplishment on mandated tests at prescribed grade levels. The teacher needs to keep these requirements in mind for individual students, especially those who enter the school system at a disadvantage. The point is that the consequences of formative and summative evaluation are quite different; if a student fails a summative event, seldom does the evidence provide valid information about how to remedy the problem. In addition, summative assessments arise from external mandates and are beyond the control of the classroom teacher.

Which brings us to the third contrast, *assessment* versus *testing*. *Assess*, from French, means to "sit beside," to exchange thoughts, and so on—a positive context. *Test* is from Latin, and conveys the sense of pulverizing—less friendly. Most summative evaluations rely on a testing environment. The individual is placed under stress with no support and limited time. Assessment is critical for guiding instruction, but the teacher also needs to help students prepare for the demands of testing situations in modern life, from the SAT to the driver's license test.

As students move through the grades, it makes sense to help them manage a gradual transition from assessment to testing. Testing kindergartners is questionable practice and may even be unethical. It is probably reasonable to test most high school students to certify their capacity to demonstrate skill and knowledge in the academic arena and to provide evidence about work habits and the like. Test taking can and should be taught, including strategies for multiple-choice exams and for writing.

In today's high-stakes environment, it is especially important for young people to be clear about the distinction between testing and assessment and the gradations between these two points. Accordingly, the teacher needs to incorporate the distinction explicitly in classroom practice. Psychologists use the term *metacognition* to describe "thinking about thinking." It may be important to teach *meta-writing* to help students learn to describe how they approach various writing tasks, including their understanding of conditions, expectations, and criteria. Turning again to the College Board advice, we can imagine teachers leading their students through authentic writing exercises like those recommended but also introducing students to the realities of testing, such as how to apply skill and knowledge when taking the SAT. Older students are capable of handling these contrasts. They all know the difference between real driving and behavior on a driving test.

CONSTRUCTING EMBEDDED
WRITING ASSESSMENTS

This final section focuses on building an assessment protocol that provides valid evidence to support the model of curriculum-embedded writing sketched earlier (Calfee & Miller, 2005). The facets covered here are important for any writing assessment. The purpose is to place these facets within the context of the classroom teacher's daily work. It is one thing when a testing company or state develops a large-scale writing assessment. It can call upon its teams of experts, conduct pilot runs, calculate complex statistics, and so on. It is another thing when the classroom teacher sets forth to prepare a writing task that is relatively casual, intended for a one-time, low-stakes formative assessment. The second scenario may actually be more critical, in that the teacher can use the information to make judgments about student learning—the stakes are not high, but they are significant.

The facets required to construct a writing assessment are similar for virtually any scenario: the prompt, the procedure, and the rubric. Next, we explore each of these basic constructs, emphasizing the application to formative assessment in classroom settings.

The *prompt* sets the stage for the writing task. Rather amazingly, there is relatively little research on how variation in prompt design affects the quality of student writing, and we have accordingly spent considerable time on this facet in our research and practice with teachers.

Constructing a prompt is almost like writing a separate passage. In a brief amount of space, the teacher has to cover the following points:

- Develop a *focus statement* that directs students' attention to the key topic for the composition, activates prior knowledge (including the target text), and directs students in thinking about the task.
- Present, as clearly as possible, the *purpose* of the composition. Words like *tell*, *describe*, *explain*, *convince*, and *illustrate* serve this purpose, especially if students have received prior instruction on these terms.
- Identify the *audience* for the work. This is a challenge in school writing because everyone knows that the teacher is the real audience, but students can learn, to good advantage, to imagine various audiences. Indeed, for a good deal of authentic writing, we have to rely on imagination. Freedman (1997) gives a delightful and informative account of the ways in which high school students in San Francisco and London handled audience in writing to one another. With a little creativity, local audiences can be identified—the principal, the mayor, the editor of the newspaper. Writing for nobody can be discouraging.
- Where appropriate, specify the *form* of the product, such as a paragraph (or more) or a letter (a favorite because of the style).
- Tell the writers as much as possible about the *criteria* to be used in judging the work. How important are supporting details? If a text is provided, how should it be used? Is the work a draft, or should the student attempt a polished product? Ideally, for classroom assessments, criteria have been defined early in the school year and practiced (with feedback) regularly.

This advice means that the prompt becomes a mini-essay in its own right, and this is a problem because it takes a lot of work for the teacher to prepare and a lot of time for the student to digest. For classroom assessments, however, the investment in prompt preparation can be worth the effort because it provides an opportunity to teach students how to comprehend a prompt, including those instances when much of the information is missing.

Consider the following two prompts:

- Describe the differences between evergreen and deciduous trees. List at least three examples of each type of tree and describe what they are like.
- Explain the differences between evergreen and deciduous trees. Give three examples for each type of tree, and describe how these examples illustrate the differences.

These prompts are fairly typical of what we see in writing assessments developed by districts for classroom assessments. They are silent about audience and form. Both are roughly equal in length, but we suspect that the second question would pose the greater challenge. *Describe* and *explain* place quite different demands on the writer. Examples that "illustrate the differences" require more thought than random examples presented without a purpose.

Think about the possible *answer spaces* for each prompt, the content that students might generate in response to the prompt. Think about ways in which students might set out on productive paths or how they might be stalemated or led astray. For example, consider the following prompt:

- Describe the differences between evergreen and deciduous trees. Based on your personal experiences, what is your favorite kind of tree for each type?

When students are asked to build a composition around personal experience, which appears frequently in writing prompts, the way is open for them to move in any of a wide range of areas or nowhere, depending on the topic. We are not suggesting that prompts never invite students to draw on personal experience, but rather that the ground rules for such invitations require careful attention.

Of course, none of these prompts may provide a suitable starting point for students from urban areas, where trees are rare. The most effective starting point for a writing task often provides students with background about the topic—an experience, a discussion, or a passage, preferably with graphics. A basic contrast can be drawn between *stand-alone* and *text-based* prompts, and we recommend the latter, especially for classroom purposes. Stand-alone assessments, the prototype of a writing test, are cold-turkey scenarios. Students are given paper, pencil, and question and are then on their own. It is hard to imagine a more challenging situation! This approach makes sense only as a way to immerse students in the experiences they will encounter in large-scale testing, but the teacher should also try to build a ramp from a scaffolded situation to more spartan test environments.

A reference passage can provide a resource for the writing task. Even when students are writing on a topic that they have just studied, it often makes sense to include a target passage with the assessment procedure, as it lessens the demands on memory and ensures all students have a common starting point for the task. Selecting the reference text requires care, of course, much as for a comprehension test. Indeed, in this situation, comprehension and composition become interwoven.

The *procedure* for a writing assessment builds, in the ideal situation, on what we know about the writing process (Gray, 2000). Students need time, information about the topic, scratch paper, support and advice, and a strategy.

Time is the most precious commodity for the classroom—there is never enough time, even for basic writing. Then there is reading and scoring, discussing and reviewing, and handling the needs of individual students. No wonder many teachers assign writing a low priority. We offer two suggestions in this arena. The first is never to ask students to write about nothing. The second is to engage them in the assessment process. By "writing about nothing," we mean exercises (including district assessments) that are solely designed for writing. The result is akin to taking a driving test; you drive to show that you can drive, but you do not go anywhere! School subjects provide a plethora of openings for students to demonstrate knowledge, reasoning ability, and communicative capacity by composing, both orally and in writing. Especially when embedded in an authentic project, writing tasks evoke imagination and force that is otherwise totally lacking.

Information about *topic* was mentioned earlier in the distinction between text-based and stand-alone writing. Most readers can remember the closed-book exams of days past (they can still be found, of course). The contrast with writing tasks in life after school is striking. Seldom does a professional work on a problem (or write about it) with a closed book. Imagine a doctor, about to operate on you, announcing, "This is a closed-book operation!" We also suggest that information be made as public as possible. Walls in today's classrooms are often covered with papers full of notes, graphs, and pictures. What a writer needs most is words. Students will write more compelling and better organized papers when they can lift their eyes to the walls and find the words and phrases that jumpstart them. Those who write for a living depend on this approach, hence the need for *scratch paper* and room to spread it out.

Our high-tech colleagues are curious about how computers are used for writing in the classroom. They notice that students prepare a draft on paper, then use the computer for revision and publication, and ask, "Why don't they write on the computer from the beginning, like I do?" In fact, many of these colleagues rely on paper to get started. Pages can be spread out and scribbled and graphed on. It takes experience and practice with the computer screen to write exclusively on a computer.

Writing can be a lonely task. We have done a lot of writing together, and some of it has been lonely, but the joy of the experience comes from the collaboration, which takes many forms. Our point in mentioning *support and advice* is partly to encourage teachers to provide scaffolding, but the real message for assessment is to provide students with opportunities and counsel about how to work together in the construction of compositions.

Finally, the matter of *strategy*—a synopsis of the writing process can be captured by three two-part alliterative phases: (1) *develop* and *draft*, (2) *review* and *revise*, and (3) *polish* and *publish*. Not every writing assessment incorporates all of these elements, but best practices build on this design and lay out the specific assignment scenario for students.

We hope that, in ranging over this array of topics, you will consider the planning and management of a writing assessment as an organic exercise, where you begin with an overarching design but know that, much like an orchestra conductor, your role is not to tell the harpist when to pluck a particular string or the timpanist when to strike the drumhead with a particular force. We hope, in addition, to have sensitized you to the social aspects of writing.

So much for the soft side of assessment and evaluation. What about the bottom line? How should one judge how well the student did? What grade should one assign to the work? Grades have recently been complemented by a new concept, the *rubric*. Advice about appropriate rubrics for writing assessment can be found in a variety of sources (Arter, McTighe, & Guskey, 2001). The primary division is between *holistic* and *analytic*, or *trait*, strategies. In holistic scoring, which dominates large-scale assessment, the rater gives the composition a brief reading (a few minutes at most) and assigns it a single score. Raters undergo intense training for this task, during which they review *anchors*, prototypical papers in each of the score categories. To check consistency, benchmark papers are inserted during the scoring process, and raters are recalibrated as necessary. This process leads to reasonably high interrater reliability, which means that judges agree with one another, both overall and in judging individual students. The problem, of course, is knowing exactly what the ratings mean and what to do with the information. The strategy is poorly suited for classroom assessment.

Analytic or trait rubrics (Spandel, 2004) are designed around specific facets of a composition, mostly related to familiar writing features. The most popular system today is the "Six Traits" approach, which encompasses six features, with a plus-one facet added recently:

- *Ideas*: The composition includes a central focus or theme, which is elaborated with relevant details, anecdotes, and similar features.
- *Organization*: The order and layout of the paper are coherent, with a clear sense of direction in communicating the focus or theme.
- *Voice*: There is a sense that the writer is speaking directly to the

reader and communicating a sense of purpose and an awareness of audience.

- *Word choice*: Precision, appropriateness, and richness of vocabulary are present.
- *Sentence fluency*: One sees flow, connectedness, and variety in the construction of sentences; this aspect depends somewhat on grammatical conventions, but is not exactly the same as the next item.
- *Conventions*: Mechanical features, including spelling, grammar, punctuation, and paragraphing, are correct.
- *Presentation*: This new facet covers the appearance of the composition, including handwriting, effective use of layout, illustrations, and so on (partly reflecting the emerging use of computers for polishing a composition).

A wide range of resources is available to illustrate the use of the multitrait system for analytical assessment, including rubrics for each trait, along with examples of student writing that illustrate different levels of accomplishment for each facet. Best practices in writing assessment can clearly build on these features, which prepare the student for the practice of writing over the long run, through high school into college and on to the variety of professions where writing is either central (newspaper reporters, magazine and book editors) or essential (anyone who prepares memos or documents as part of his or her job).

A couple of the traits listed deserve special attention, and a few additional items are worth mentioning. Voice is both important and challenging in classroom writing. For serious writing in college and beyond and for secondary students, a clear sense of purpose and awareness of audience are critical requirements for any writing assignment. Unfortunately, most writing prompts address these two features weakly at best. The audience is either the teacher (implicitly) or an artificial entity ("write a letter to your parents"), and purpose is missing or made up.

All too often, the reality is that an assignment is just an assignment. Under these conditions, expecting students to infuse their composition with personal voice—with an authentic sense of purpose and audience—is unrealistic. An honest voice might lead the student to begin, "I'm writing this paper for Ms. Martin because I have to. I only need a B, so I'm not going to really do my best, but hope this is good enough." This matter can be handled at least partly in two ways. One is to call upon situations *within* the classroom that are as genuine and engaging as possible (some topics are more interesting and personally relevant than others). The other is to look for opportunities *outside* the classroom; with the arrival of the Internet, despite limited access in many schools, students can engage others from around the world in authentic dialogues.

The second point that we think deserves mention is length. Many writing experts are conflicted about this feature; indeed, many think it is a mistake even to mention it. More is certainly not necessarily better, but it should be possible to offer students advice and feedback about "not enough" and, in those rare instances when it becomes a problem, "too much." Teachers routinely include length as part of an assignment (five paragraphs, two pages, and so on). If length is not included, it often matters nonetheless. The fifth grader who hands in three sentences when everyone else is filling a page is likely to receive a low grade, even if the sentences are well crafted and on topic. Dealing with length is a complex matter, and we will not attempt to resolve it here, other than to encourage attention it in assignments. In the elementary grades, "more" is probably a positive outcome, certainly for a first draft. In the later grades, when it becomes critical for students to learn to manage their time, the nature of the assignment may be important. Even here, it is worth remembering that the best predictor of scores on most college entrance writing exams is not the content or style, but rather the length of the essay.

The third point centers on attention to genre, the type of writing called for by the assignment (Schleppegrel, 2004). Distinguishing between narrative and informational writing, between stories and reports, is an important first step, but in our review of the available resources, students could benefit from greater clarity in the distinction and from further distinctions within the informational genre. For example, we have seen rubrics for narrative writing that emphasize topical focus, introduction, conclusion, and so on. This language is a mismatch to the narrative form, which builds on concepts like theme, setting, and resolution (Lukens, 2002). For informational texts, planning a simple descriptive piece around the five-paragraph essay is quite different from laying out a compare-and-contrast analysis, a process explanation, or a persuasive argument (Chambliss & Calfee, 1998).

Our fourth point centers on the content or substance of a composition, which is absent from writing assessment systems with which we are familiar. Content was discussed earlier in contrast to process; for practical purposes, you can think of process as everything that the multitrait models cover. One approach to content uses topic as the criterion. If the assignment is about earthquakes, did the student stick with earthquakes? From one perspective, this point is simple, but staying on topic can take many forms. The student can reproduce material from various sources, from paraphrasing to outright cutting and pasting. A student can develop the topic as a story, recounting his experiences during the San Francisco

Loma Prieta quake. Other students can demonstrate understanding by transforming resources and experiences into a genuine composition—the building of something new from a collection of basic elements. Best practices in writing assessment should distinguish among these activities. Summarizing and note taking are important skills for students to learn to the point of fluency and as a context for practicing conventions. Storytelling is an engaging activity and provides another opportunity for practicing skills. To be sure, relatively few storytelling jobs are available for college graduates, but education should be about more than jobs.

At a practical level, we think that text-based writing assessments should include a rubric that gauges students' capacity to *transform* the substance of the topic. The challenge is to handle this task at a classroom level. Ideally, the teacher has led students through a topic like earthquakes (or a general domain like plate tectonics), and individuals or small groups have conducted additional reading and research, exploring the domain along paths that may be new to the teacher. Teachers cannot be experts on everything; how does one both offer students the freedom to explore and judge the quality and accuracy of diverse reports?

In a project on reading and writing about science (Miller & Calfee, 2004), we and our colleagues spent considerable energy wrestling with such questions. On the one hand, it is important for the student to include fundamental concepts and relations in his or her composition, what we refer to as *schemata* (Anderson, Spiro, & Anderson, 1978), or sets of ideas and words connected in particular ways, which can serve as a template for evaluating presentations. For instance, volcanoes, an engaging topic across the grades, take two wildly different forms in classrooms: (1) the vinegar-and-soda version in which these ingredients, along with red dye, are poured into a clay model to generate an eruptive fizz; and (2) the plate-tectonics account, which suggests that the earth is cracked into great chunks by the roiling of magma, where volcanoes emerge as "blurps," like a kettle of thick pea soup. However a student decides to treat the topic of volcanoes, a composition that captures the scientific content must include the pea-soup model in some form. A favorite example comes from a small-group project by students at a school near Honolulu, who prepared a lengthy project report on the difference between the vinegar-and-soda exercise in the weekly news magazine and what they had learned from reading about the volcanic terrain on which they walked. Their description of the contrast between the two models provided transformational evidence of deep learning.

Pursuing this assessment route poses a number of challenges, not the least of which is the demand on the teacher to read individual compositions thoughtfully. Addressing this matter can be tough, but here are a few words of advice. The first builds on the potential for computer-based text analysis to do some heavy lifting here. Programs like the Intelligent Essay Assessor (Ericsson & Haswell, 2006; Shermis & Daniels, 2003), while still in the prototype stage, provide students and teachers with a quick evaluation of the substance of a composition, including an analysis of the match to the content schemas. Which critical concepts and relations from the topic are found in the composition, and which are missing? If the idea seems far-fetched, remember that, not too long ago, calculating the readability of a particular passage required a fair amount of work.

The second point, one that applies to all facets of composition assessment, is the suggestion to give away grading—indeed, the entire writing system—to students. The teacher can accomplish this goal in a variety of ways, including cooperative learning. What could be more sensible than teaching students to collaborate on projects, including writing tasks, and to learn to critique their own work? The main advice here centers on teaching students about the concepts of genre, traits, and rubrics. This strategy brings at least two clear advantages. One is that students become independent learners in the fullest sense, responsible for handling all facets of communicating their mastery of a topic. The other is that the teacher no longer bears the entire responsibility for student learning; in particular, he or she does not have to read and review every piece of student writing in detail. Rather, his or her task is to monitor and discuss the students' reading of their work.

Two potential problems emerge from this advice. First, what if students do it wrong or cheat? Second, might it not be easier for the teacher to do the work than to spend the energy needed to teach students how to handle the task? The response to both questions is the same: Teaching students to become independent and responsible learners is difficult, but addressing this challenge is critical for reform of schooling in our country. These issues emerge with special clarity for content-area writing. When the conditions are right, writing reveals thinking with unusual clarity. The results show up partly as scores and grades, but more important are the portraits that students construct in demonstrating their understanding of a topic, revealing their capacity to "go beyond the information given" (Bruner, 1973).

MEETING THE CHALLENGE

Basic skills in reading and mathematics have taken center stage in recent years. Without questioning the need for attention to these fundamental areas, we believe that improving educational outcomes for students in the United States will require engagement with the challenges of helping students become proficient writers in the content areas. The principle here is that writing reveals thinking, that the capacity to lay out one's understanding in a clear, organized, and compelling fashion is an essential communication tool.

Effective and efficient formative assessment is a key consideration for this task. Writing assignments provide only limited benefit unless accompanied by informed and informative feedback on both the process and content of the compositions. The techniques for planning and conducting such assessments are not mysterious; we know a great deal about best practices from both research and practical experience.

It is tempting to try to assemble these techniques as a set of blackline masters, along with simple formulas to guide teachers and students. In reality, these accomplishments depend on classroom teachers who possess appropriate knowledge and skill for developing and implementing the best writing assessments that we can imagine from current research and practice. They need opportunities for professional dialogue around these matters, much as physicians have opportunities for medical rounds (time when they can discuss cases), and they need the benefit of institutional support that recognizes the validity of assessments that are grounded in genuine performance activities.

ACKNOWLEDGMENT

Support was provided by U.S. Department of Education Grant No. R305G050069.

REFERENCES

Anderson, R. C., Spiro, R. J., & Anderson, M. C. (1978). Schemata as scaffolding for the representation of information in connected discourse. *American Educational Research Journal, 15*, 433–440.

Arter, J. A., McTighe, J., & Guskey, T. R. (2001). *Scoring rubrics in the classroom: Using performance criteria for assessing and improving student performance.* Newbury Park, CA: Sage.

Black, P., Harris, C., Lee, C., Marshall, B., & William, D. (2003). *Assessment for learning: Putting it into practice.* Buckingham, UK: Open University Press.

Bloom, B. S., Hastings, J. T., & Madaus, G. F. (1971). *Handbook on formative and summative evaluation of student learning.* New York: McGraw-Hill.

Bruner, J. S. (1973) *Beyond the information given: Studies in the psychology of knowing.* Oxford, UK: Norton.

Calfee, R. C. (1997). Assessing development and learning over time. In J. Flood, S. B. Heath, & D. Lapp (Eds.), *Handbook for literacy educators: Research on teaching the communicative and visual arts* (pp. 144–166). New York: Macmillan.

Calfee, R. C., & Hiebert, E. H. (1990). Classroom assessment of reading. In R. Barr, M. Kamil, P. Mosenthal, & P. D. Pearson (Eds.), *Handbook of research on reading* (2nd ed., pp. 281–309). New York: Longman.

Calfee, R. C., & Miller, R. G. (2005). Breaking ground: Constructing authentic reading–writing assessments for middle and secondary students. In R. Indrisano & J. Paratore (Eds.), *Learning to write, writing to learn: Theory and research in practice* (pp. 203–219). Newark, DE: International Reading Association.

Chall, J. S. (1995). *Stages of reading development*. New York: Harcourt College Publishers.

Chambliss, M. J., & Calfee, R. C. (1998). *Textbooks for learning: Nurturing children's minds*. Oxford, UK: Blackwell.

Chappuis, S., Stiggins, R. J., Arter, J., & Chappuis, J. (2005). *Assessment for learning: An action guide for school leaders*. Portland, OR: Assessment Training Institute.

The College Board (2006). *The keys to effective writing*. Retrieved March 13, 2006, from *www.collegeboard.com*

Ericsson, P. F., & Haswell, R. (2006). *Machine scoring of student essays: Truth and consequences*. Logan: Utah State University Press.

Freedman, S. W. (1997). *Exchanging writing, exchanging cultures*. Cambridge, MA: Harvard University Press.

Gray, J. R. (2000). *Teachers at the center*. Berkeley, CA: National Writing Project.

Harp, B. (2006). *The handbook of literacy assessment and evaluation*. Norwood, MA: Christopher-Gordon.

Heath, S. B. (1983). *Ways with words*. New York: Cambridge University Press.

Lukens, R. J. (2002). *Critical handbook of children's literature*. Boston: Allyn & Bacon.

Miller, R. G., & Calfee, R. C. (2004). Making thinking visible: A method to encourage science writing in upper elementary grades. *Science and Children*, 42(3), 20–25.

Schleppegrel, M. (2004). *The language of schooling*. Mahwah, NJ: Erlbaum.

Schneps, M. H. (1989). *A private universe*. Cambridge, MA: Project STAR, Harvard University.

Shermis, M., & Daniels, K. E. (Eds.). (2003). *Automated essay scoring: A cross-disciplinary perspective*. Mahwah, NJ: Erlbaum.

Spandel, V. (2004). *Creating writers through 6-trait writing assessment and instruction*. Upper Saddle River, NJ: Pearson Education.

Stiggins, R. J. (2004). *Student-involved assessment for learning*. Upper Saddle River, NJ: Prentice Hall.

Urquhart, V., & McIver, M. (2005). *Teaching writing in the content areas*. Alexandria, VA: Association for Supervision and Curriculum Development.

PART III

~

SPECIAL
POPULATIONS

14

What Is Sound Writing Instruction for Multilingual Learners?

JILL FITZGERALD *and* STEVE AMENDUM

What can be done? Of the students in classrooms across our district, 15 to 50% are multilingual learners. One elementary school has two bilingual Spanish–English first-grade classrooms, but no other bilingual education program exists. We have English as a second language (ESL) pullout programs, but the ESL teacher only sees the students three times a week, in a group, for about 50 minutes each time. Some of the multilingual students have had no prior schooling, but others excelled in their homeland's schools and can read and write very well in their native language. How can we teach so that our multilingual students learn well? How can we help them read and write well? Can we, or should we, try to start reading and writing instruction right away? Can research help us know what to do?

Sound familiar? Educators' questions like these abound nowadays across the United States, as well as in some other countries. Often, literacy instruction is at the heart of multilingual students' learning, in part because reading and writing can be conduits to content-area academic achievement. In the present chapter, we focus on prekindergarten through 12th-grade multilingual writing, first characterizing multilingual writing research, then suggesting some instructional guidelines and activities that emanate from the research as well as from other sources.

We use the terms *multilingual writing* and *second-language writing* to refer to the writing process and products in two or more languages (Buckwalter & Lo, 2002). The terms are broad and include the meanings ESL, bilingual, and foreign language, among others.

HOW MIGHT RESULTS FROM MULTILINGUAL WRITING RESEARCH BE CHARACTERIZED?

In some arenas, multilingual writing is a hot topic. There are textbook and concept pieces galore about multilingual writing processes and theories in bilingual, foreign language, English language learner (ELL), and applied linguistics fields, but a good deal of what you will read involves college students and adults, where study of second-language learners is historically rooted.

A Research Review: How It Was Done

I (JF) recently reviewed multilingual writing research, asking: What research has been done on multilingual writing for preschool and school-age students? What issues have been addressed, and how thick is the evidence to support various contentions and theoretical positions about multilingual writing? (Fitzgerald, 2005). To address these questions, I examined published pre-K–12 research conducted from 1988 to 2003. I chose 1988 because before that date there were extremely few studies conducted with preschool and school-aged children.

I did a comprehensive review, attempting to locate all published research during the specified time period. I searched several databases: ERIC (for published research only), PsychInfo, and bibliographies provided in the *Journal of Second Language Research* (a regular feature). As I read articles and books, I scanned reference lists for additional pieces. Keywords used in searches were: English as a second language writing, L2 composition, bilingual writing, L2 writing, foreign language writing, English as a second language composition, bilingual composition, foreign language composition, L2 composition, Latino writing/composition, Hispanic writing/composition, and Spanish writing/composition.

Because the number of studies was limited, and I wanted to maximize the number of investigations under review, I applied very few criteria for inclusion of studies in the review. Research purpose or question had to be stated or easily inferred; data on writing had to have been collected; participants had to be of preschool through 12th grade age; the study had to have undergone editorial or peer review and been "published" (which excluded technical reports, ERIC documents, and the like); and I had to be able to identify the work as fitting my definition of multilingual writing. I selected 56 studies.

Next, I systematically analyzed the studies, looking for common themes and issues and ascertaining the extent to which study designs met common standards for rigor.

What the Studies Were Like

I examined the 56 studies in clusters by age/grade—preschool through primary grades, intermediate, and high school/secondary. There was a roughly equivalent number of studies in each of the three clusters. Most of the studies were done in the United States, but they were also done in 16 other countries. In 27 of the studies, the participants could be called English as a second (or third) language learners. In 13, they were English as a foreign language learners, in 13 bilingual, and in 3 French or Spanish as a foreign language learners. In all but 12 studies, investigators only examined new language writing.

A few of the studies were experiments with manipulation to form control groups. Most used designs that could be called *qualitative,* a term that includes case studies of one or some small number of students as well as studies to describe features about students' thinking processes or instruction. One significant conclusion was that few of the 56 studies demonstrated methodological rigor that might be judged sufficient. There were exemplary exceptions, though, in which investigators held their work to the highest standards.

Findings from the Research Review

I wanted to synthesize findings across studies, but it was difficult because many different issues were studied, many of which were narrow in scope, resulting in topic clusters that were not deeply researched. To make firm conclusions about a given topic, it is important to have findings from several studies, as any particular study may have atypical, or at least uncommon, results.

Only 18 studies were identified that involved some sort of writing *instruction* for multilingual students—again, making synthesis and summary difficult. Only 2 were done at the primary-grade level, 6 more at the intermediate, and 10 at the secondary level. Findings were:

- Book floods (i.e., buying a large number of new books) were found to assist new language writing.
- Initial instruction in native language writing tended to affect native language and new language writing more than new lan-

guage-only situations, but in one study, matching language of instruction to language used in essay writing was most effective in the matched language for ratings of text organization.

- Effectiveness of teacher feedback on writing varied across four studies.
- Ideas from interactive conversations during reading instruction reappeared in later new language writing.
- Structured writing instruction (teachers fixed purpose for writing and gave prompt feedback related to syntax, word choice, and ideational content) was associated with significant growth in composition topic development, organization, meaning conveyance, sentence construction, and mechanics, as well as overall writing quality.
- Using a process-writing approach had mixed effects.
- No partner talk about compositions was better than peer interaction for grammatical accuracy and complexity in composition.
- Explicit instruction in revision assisted new language writing quality.
- Computer use was better than pen-and-paper writing for some writing variables.
- A reading program affected new language writing speed, number of errors made, and writing style.
- Dialogue journals helped bilingual students improve their English and native language writing.
- Instruction targeting phonology and spelling effectively enhanced representation of phonology and spelling in new language compositions.

At the end of the review, I decided that only three dependable contentions could be asserted from the evidence, but even these were based upon small numbers of studies and participants. First, for preschool and primary-grades children, features of ESL writing may develop in ways that are similar to certain features of early writing development of native English-speaking young children (e.g., Buckwalter & Lo, 2002; Fitzgerald & Noblit, 1999; Neufeld & Fitzgerald, 2001). For instance, children's writing in several studies appeared to pass through phases of spelling development that were similar to commonly described phases for typically developing native English-speaking children, such as originally using drawings to represent meaning, then using any letters to represent words, then writing the correct first letter for a word, and eventually learning that many words have certain patterned appearances, such as words in which a final *e* affects the sound of a preceding vowel.

Second, for primary- and intermediate-grade students, knowledge/

skill can transfer between first- and second-language writing (e.g., Buckwalter & Lo, 2002; James & Klein, 1994; Lanauze & Snow, 1989; Zutell & Allen, 1988). For example, native language knowledge of print concepts (such as understandings about print directionality, or representation of sounds in print with letters) transferred to second-language writing.

Third, for intermediate- and/or secondary-level bilingual or English as a foreign language students, selected composing processes may be highly similar across native and second-language writing, though differences may also exist (e.g., Albrechtsen, 1997; De Larios, Marin, & Murphy, 2001; James & Klein, 1994). For instance, learners used similar prewriting and planning strategies and processes in native and new languages, and they used similar processes for formulating syntax and words in writing across languages.

SO WHAT *IS* SOUND WRITING INSTRUCTION FOR MULTILINGUAL LEARNERS?

In the following sections, we first lay out some premises for multilingual writing instruction and then illustrate selected writing instruction activities. In doing so, we use some inferences from the limited research base, selected features about what is known about sound native language writing instruction, and some research-based understandings about the role of language in learning.

Premises for Writing Instruction for Multilingual Learners

First, we assert an umbrella premise: that if young children's new language writing develops in ways similar to that of native language speakers (a dependable contention from multilingual writing research), then instructional contexts known to benefit early writing for native English speakers might also benefit children who are learning to write in English (see Coker, Chapter 5, this volume). Teachers might consider the sound evidence-based instructional practices they use for native English speakers to be sound instructional practices for multilingual learners. Representatives of the National Literacy Panel on Language Minority Children and Youth (August, 2003; August & Shanahan, 2006) tentatively suggested in two reports that literacy instruction practices known to be sound for native English speakers could also likely be sound practices for ELLs.

A corollary to the first premise is that if immersing native language students in writing instruction as early as possible is beneficial to their growth, then starting new language learners in writing instruction as soon as possible could greatly benefit their new language understanding, both in oral language and in literacy, with the caveat that early exposure to writing should be done carefully, slowly, and with deep consideration of the student's abilities (see Anderson & Roit, 1996; Gersten, 1996). On the other hand, results of one study with intermediate-level students (Carlisle, 1989) suggested that, in situations where native language writing can be done, providing native language writing first and following with new language writing may be beneficial. At least where native language writing instruction is not possible, early carefully modulated introduction to new language writing is likely to benefit multilingual students. Multilingual writers need to experience new language writing immersion gradually, and teachers should carefully scaffold their advancement.

A second set of premises arises from two findings from the multilingual writing research: that for primary- and intermediate-grade students, what a student knows about writing in his or her language is likely to be used in new language writing and that for older students, selected composing processes may be similar across languages. One implication of such findings is that native language writing instruction might indirectly facilitate new language writing. Where possible, writing instruction in students' native language could be highly beneficial both for native language maintenance and growth and for learning the new language, including learning about writing in the new language (see Gersten, 1996, and Klingner & Vaughn, 1996, for a similar position vis-à-vis reading).

Another implication is that, as teachers work with their multilingual students, they should be aware that such transfer of knowledge from one language to another may be happening on the spot. When teachers believe their students are either consciously or unconsciously using what they already know, they tend to support those students in positive ways. Moreover, through the ways in which they set up lessons, teachers can scaffold transfer of knowledge from native language to new language writing.

A third set of premises for multilingual writing instruction involves the belief that teachers should have some basic knowledge of how a second language is learned; how difficult and time consuming it is to become proficient in that second language; what the relationships are between first- and second-language orality and literacy; and important cultural sensibilities, many of which are symbolized in language. In the present chapter, it is not possible to elaborate much on the third set of issues. Instead, we simply make some brief key statements to provide a needed context for the writing activities that follow. (Interested readers may find further elaboration in Fitzgerald and Graves [2004].)

- Learning a new language is a complex process that requires consideration of many factors, such as phonological, semantic, syntactic, morphological, pragmatic, and social and cultural features (August & Hakuta, 1997). At present, no grand theory explains everything involved in oral or literate new language learning (Mitchell & Myles, 1998).
- On average, it may take about 2 years to learn conversational English at a level comparable to native English speakers and 8 years to learn more formal or academic language (Collier & Thomas, 1989).
- Culture and language are intertwined and inseparable. For instance, in some communities, adults routinely ask young children questions to which the adults already know the answer, such as "Where are your eyes?" or "Can you tell me what we did last night?" In other groups, such questions might seem silly or even rude. In our classrooms, we build and use all kinds of cultural routines, many of which may be unfamiliar, or even "wrong" in the multilingual learners' native cultures. Teachers who are sensitive to such cultural differences may be alert to bridging incongruencies between home and school cultures (see Jiménez, 2003).

Fourth, although the multilingual writing instructional research is scant, there were at least a few studies supporting the premise that multilingual students tend to learn what they are taught! For instance, instruction targeting new language phonology and spelling affected students' representation of phonology and spelling in new language compositions.

Illustrations of Multilingual Writing Activities

In this section we provide three examples of writing activities that are likely to be particularly beneficial for multilingual learners—Daily News, dialogue journals, and writing persuasive essays using a mnemonic strategy. Each activity emanates from one or more of the premises we have just discussed.

We think it important to say that while our examples may certainly be applied as-is to particular situations, our larger purpose is to illustrate a way of thinking about building writing lessons for multilingual learners. To construct the examples, we began with the premises about multilingual writing instruction, but the premises alone were not sufficient. Next, we had to consider students' background factors, such as age, degree of native language schooling, degree of schooling in the new country, length of time in the new country, native and new language oral levels, and, most important, native and new language literacy levels. For bilingual learners, new language literacy and oral levels are most often the primary consideration when teachers create activities. Some older new language learners may profit from modifications of activities that typically would only be used with younger native language learners. We also want to emphasize the word *modifications* because modifying lessons with the multilingual learner's particular abilities and background in mind is extremely important to successful learning.

We provide a common format for each of the following examples. First, we give a summary description of the activity. Then we suggest a range of multilingual students for whom the activity might be beneficial. Next, we enumerate which of our preceding multilingual writing premises the activity specifically is founded upon, explaining why the activity is likely to be particularly beneficial for multilingual learners. We then provide the writing purposes for the lesson. The activity is shown through a scenario or writing sample, and finally, possible adaptations for the activity are provided.

Activity: Daily News

Description. Daily News is a common event in native language primary-grades classrooms. It is a teacher–pupil or small-group shared writing experience about current news events using chart paper and markers. Students or a student and a teacher engage in interactive discussion about events that have happened in a school day. Students dictate information about the event, and the teacher records that information, sometimes with the students' help.

Multilingual Students for Whom the Activity Might Be Beneficial. Daily News is most likely to benefit students who are just beginning to learn a new language, whether they are younger or older. It could be used with students in regular education classrooms, pull-out ESL classrooms, foreign language education classrooms, or bilingual classrooms.

Multilingual Writing Premises. Daily News is founded upon all our four multilingual writing instruction premises. As you read the illustration, notice how Ms. García addresses the first premise, that ELLs might learn from sound evidence-based instruction used with native English speakers. Modeled writing activities of shared experiences are well-known instructional activities for beginning native language writers (Bromley, 2003). Ms. García also addresses the second premise when she draws out Julia's knowledge of sound-to-letter correspondence in Spanish and helps her understand that it is the same in English. Our example is also founded upon the third premise, that teachers should have some basic knowledge of how a second language is learned. Ms. García knows the importance of focusing on meaning construction while learning a new language. In Daily News, Ms. García provides the ELLs an opportunity to focus on meaning in the new language by talking about familiar daily events. She also knows that phonological awareness—hearing the separate sounds of the new language—is important for new language learners, so during Daily News, she manages asides where she emphasizes sounds in English words, such as when she stretches words orally while writing them. In doing so, she also demonstrates instruction based on our fourth premise, what you teach matters.

Setting in Our Illustration. Our activity takes place in a bilingual Spanish–English education kindergarten/first-grade classroom with students who are European American, African American, Latino, and Hmong. Approximately half the students are just beginning to learn English. Only the Latino students spoke Spanish before entering the class. Ms. García is fluent in both English and Spanish.

Writing Purposes. To understand that substantive issues can be recorded in writing, to learn about concepts of English print (e.g., directionality), to hear separate sounds in words, and to learn that specific English letters match specific English sounds.

Procedure. Ms. García begins her Daily News session by gathering the children around a large chart paper tablet in an area of the classroom where they can sit together on the floor.

Ms. García: Let's begin. What is today?

Luis: Tuesday.

Ms. García: Yes, good. Who can tell us something else? Maybe from our calendar?

Brittany: It's September 27th.

Ms. García: Yes, today is Tuesday, September 27th. We'll make that our first sentence. Let's write that. How do we write *today*? (*A student comes to the chart and writes the word while stretching it aloud.*) Julia, listen. *Septiembre*— /s/ /s/ /s/—what letter stands for /s/ /s/ /s/ in *Septiembre*?

Julia: *S!*

Ms. García: Yes. Listen: *Septiembre, September.* In Spanish, the sound is the same as in English, and the letter is the same. Watch me write *September.* (*She finishes writing the sentence, and the students recite it chorally. She points to each word as the students say it.*) Okay, let's think. What did we do today at school?

ALEXANDRA: We go to *música*, and we sing.

MS. GARCÍA: Yes, very good, Alexandra. We did go to music today. We will make that our next sentence. (*She writes, "We went to music."*) Now let's read it! Jorge, how many words are in that sentence? (*She models how to say the sentence word by word, while holding up a single finger for each word as she says it. Then she has Jorge join her in reading the sentence and counting the words.*) What was our first word?

JOE: *We.*

MS. GARCÍA: Yes, our first word was *we.* What do you hear in /w/ /ē/?

LETICIA: /w/.

MS. GARCÍA: Does anyone else hear /w/? (*Several students raise their hands.*) Good. What letter do we write for /w/?

LETICIA: *W.*

MS. GARCÍA: Where could we look to find out how to spell *music*?

ALEXANDRA: There (*pointing*). (*She refers to the daily schedule for Ms. García's kindergarten class, where "music" is posted as one of the scheduled activities for the day.*)

MS. GARCÍA: Good, Alexandra. (*She guides the students through the rest of the Daily News text, ending with the final text, "Today is Tuesday, September 27. We went to music. We had fun."*)

Adaptations. The Daily News activity can be adapted for other instructional purposes. Further direct instruction in English concepts of print can be incorporated once the text is written. For example, target English letters, sounds, or words could be searched and identified in the written text. Also, Daily News could be written using a more interactive writing process (McCarrier, Fountas, & Pinnell, 2000) in which the students and teacher share the pen, rather than the teacher-modeled shared writing activity described in the scenario above. Sharing the pen allows a teacher to further observe students' composing skills in order to plan for further writing instruction. The activity might also be more appropriate for older or more advanced new language speakers.

Activity: Dialogue Journals

Description. Dialogue journals are commonly used in elementary and middle-grade classrooms. They are written conversations in which a student and teacher talk with each other in writing, usually approximately two or three times a week. Students choose any topic and write as much as they want, and the teacher writes back to each student, responding to their topics. Teachers may also make comments, ask and answer questions, and give clarification.

Multilingual Students for Whom the Activity Might Be Beneficial. The activity is likely to benefit new language learners within a wide range of new language oral and literate levels because it helps the new language learner focus on meaning construction between writer and reader.

Multilingual Writing Premises. Dialogue journals are related to three of our multilingual writing instruction premises. As you read the illustration below, notice how Mr. López addresses the first premise—that multilingual learners might learn from sound evidence-based instruction for native language learners—by engaging students and supporting them with quality feedback through questioning and responses that aim to improve their written communication skills. Also, one researcher (Reyes, 1991) found that bilingual students who engaged in dialogue journaling in English and/or Spanish had positive self-concepts and increased control of English and/or native language writing.

Mr. López also addresses the third premise—that teachers should have some basic knowledge of how a second language is learned. Like Ms. García in our prior scenario, Mr. López chooses an activity that primarily focuses on authentic meaningful exchanges between student and teacher.

Mr. López also knows that some English syntactical structures are different from Spanish, and he tries to point out differences. Calling a student's attention to specific differences may encourage acquisition of the new syntactical form, which links to our fourth premise, that students learn what they are taught.

Students. The class includes two Latino students, one in fourth grade and one in fifth grade, who are said to be low intermediate-level oral English speakers. Their classroom teacher considers their English writing to be about 2 years below grade level. The students work with six other students three times per week in an ESL pull-out setting with a bilingual (English- and Spanish-speaking) teacher.

Writing Purpose. The main purpose is to assist the ELLs in understanding that the primary focus of composing is authentic meaning creation and conservation and that writers write with their audience in mind. A second purpose is to call attention to English syntactical structures that are different from those in Spanish. A third is to assist vocabulary embellishment by using English idioms.

Procedure. Mr. López uses dialogue journals twice each week. Below are dialogue journal samples from two students, Rafael and Gloria:

RAFAEL'S SAMPLE

RAFAEL: Tuesday, September 20. Mr. López, I like the story of Anansi we saw in class. I trick my brother little. I like to read it. Rafael.

MR. LÓPEZ: Wednesday, September 23. Rafael, I like the story of Anansi too. What kinds of tricks do you play on your little brother? (In English we say *little brother*. The adjective comes before the noun.) Are the tricks funny? Mr. López.

RAFAEL: Friday, September 25. Mr. López, I like to trick my brother. I play jokes on him. I tell him that it is *fin de semana* but it is school. He gets mad at me. I laugh. Rafael.

MR. LÓPEZ: Monday, September 26. Rafael, this sounds like a very funny joke. I like your trick on your brother! You know, the English word for *fin de semana* is *weekend*. I bet your brother would be mad at you. But it is fun to play a trick on someone (*hacer una broma a alguien*).

RAFAEL: Tuesday, September 27. Mr. López, I will go to the fair this weekend. I will eat candy. I will ride. My family will go to the fair this weekend. Rafael.

MR. LÓPEZ: Wednesday, September 28. Rafael, Are you going to the state fair? The state fair is a lot of fun! My favorite thing to do is to ride the ferris wheel that goes really high into the air. Don't eat too much candy! You don't want to make yourself sick! Next week I hope you will write about what you did. I hope you have a great time! Mr. López.

GLORIA'S SAMPLE

GLORIA: Tuesday, September 20. Mr. López, next month I will go to Mexico. I am going to see my family. I will be gone for a long time. It will be a long ride. From, Gloria.

MR. LÓPEZ: Wednesday, September 23. Gloria, wow! I didn't know that you were going to Mexico! That sounds interesting. Could you give me some more details? How long will you be gone? Who will you visit? Mr. López.

GLORIA: Friday, September 25. Mr. López, I will go to Mexico for 6 weeks. We will go visit my *abuela* and my cousins. I like to go to Mexico. I will get to speak Spanish. From, Gloria.

MR. LÓPEZ: Monday, September 26. Gloria, that sounds great. Will you go to school while you are in Mexico for so long? You are doing a great job with your English writing! Also, do you know the English word for *abuela*, or is that what you call her? Mr. López.

GLORIA: Tuesday, September 27. Mr. López, I know that *abuela* means *grandma*. I do not think that I will go to school. My mom says the school in Mexico is a very *escuela mala*. She means a bad school. From, Gloria

MR. LÓPEZ: Wednesday, September 28. Gloria, too bad you won't get to go to school. You are such a good student; I don't want you to miss out. Maybe you can read some English books and practice writing in English so that you won't forget all the English that you learned. Will you take your journal and write to me about what happens to you? Then you won't forget! I know you will have a great time in Mexico! Mr. López.

Adaptations. When teachers can speak a student's native language, they might begin dialogue journals by having students write in their native language and gradually transition them to writing in the new language. During the transition, teachers can make explicit connections between a student's written native language and written English, such as writing the new language word above the native language word in the journal. Another adaptation could be to reverse the process, with the teacher writing the inception thought and the student responding as reader.

Illustration: Writing Persuasive Essays with TREE[1]

Description. TREE is a four-stage mnemonic strategy used for writing a persuasive or opinion essay (Harris et al., 2002). Students plan their essay using a structured format: (1) Topic sentence—tell what you believe; (2) Reasons (several)—Why do I believe this? Will my readers believe this?; (3) Explain reasons—say more about each reason; (4) Ending—wrap it up right. (Additional methods for teaching planning strategies such as TREE are also covered in MacArthur, Chapter 7, this volume.)

---

[1] This section is adapted from Harris, Graham, and Mason (2002). Copyright 2002 by The Council for Exceptional Children. Adapted by permission.

*Multilingual Students for Whom the Activity Might Be Benefi-
cial.* This activity is likely to benefit new language learners with intermediate knowledge of a new language who are in the upper elementary
or middle grades. This activity extends writing beyond basic meaning
construction to writing with a specific purpose, to persuade. This activity could be used with students in regular education classrooms, pull-out
ESL classrooms, foreign language classrooms, or bilingual classrooms.

Multilingual Writing Premises. Writing persuasive essays with TREE
is related to the first, third, and fourth premises of multilingual writing
instruction. In our illustration, Mrs. Chen addresses the first premise—
that ELLs might learn from evidence-based practices that are helpful to
native English speakers. TREE has been shown to be beneficial for struggling writers with and without learning disabilities (Graham & Harris,
2005; Harris et al., 2002). It is likely to be particularly helpful for new
language learners because, for some students, learning the organizational structures in a new language can be challenging. Explicit teacher
guidance in such structures may be particularly useful for these students.

Mrs. Chen also addresses the third premise—that teachers should
have some basic knowledge of how a second language is learned. With
her emphasis on active student engagement, she reveals that she understands learning a new language involves active thinking and thinking
with peers and adults. Mrs. Chen engages the students by having them
actively participate in the creation of a persuasive essay. At the same
time, she scaffolds their active participation by modeling writing and
mnemonic strategy use.

Finally, she conducts the lesson based upon the fourth premise—that
students learn what they are taught. Structured lessons help teachers and
learners focus on specific targets for learning. New language learners are
especially likely to benefit from such focus because they can sometimes be
overwhelmed with all the factors that require their attention.

Setting in Our Illustration. Our illustration is set within a general
education middle school language arts class with students of several ethnic backgrounds: African American, Chinese, Latino, and European
American. Approximately 35% of the students are ELLs whose oral
English levels have been labeled intermediate to advanced. The teacher,
Mrs. Chen, speaks English as her first language, is also literate in Chinese, and has taught middle school language arts for 23 years.

Writing Purpose. Students learn a four-stage composing strategy
for writing persuasive essays in English. Mrs. Chen expects the students
to use the four stages in their independent essay writing.

Procedure. Mrs. Chen is teaching her students to write persuasive essays and is utilizing the TREE strategy. Previously, she introduced TREE when she described the strategy, discussed the mnemonic and each stage of TREE, and talked about how each stage might help students create strong persuasive essays. Mrs. Chen begins today's lesson with a review of the TREE strategy, then begins the activity.

MRS. CHEN: Let's continue our work on writing strong persuasive essays using the TREE strategy. Today we'll write a persuasive essay together using this strategy. Let's write an essay to Mrs. Henderson [the principal] persuading her to allow less homework. Using the TREE strategy, who can tell me the first thing we need to think about?

JOSH: *Topic sentence.*

MRS. CHEN: Good, Josh! What do we need to think about for our topic sentence?

XIAO: We need to tell what we believe about less homework. That's what we will try to persuade Mrs. Henderson with.

MRS. CHEN: Great! You are all remembering TREE! Let's see. I think that if we had less homework the students would be able to rest and recharge so that they could put forth their best efforts and get a lot of learning done at school. How can I make that into a topic sentence? Let's see. I'll write this. (*She writes, "With less homework, students will be able to rest and recharge and get more learning done in school.*) What do you all think?

THOMAS: That's pretty good. But I think we need more of a beginning. Maybe a different topic sentence at the beginning that says something like, "Too much homework can be a big problem for students in middle school."

MRS. CHEN: Thomas, I think that's a good idea. We need a more general statement here in the introduction for our topic sentence. Let's revise a bit. (*She inserts the sentence "Too much homework can be a big problem for students in middle school" and deletes the first sentence. Working together in this manner, she and her students complete an introductory paragraph.*) Next, we need to move on to the *R* in TREE. What does that stand for?

SHAKYA: It stands for *Reasons,* and we need several.

MRS. CHEN: Good. Okay, let's think of a few reasons that would support our topic sentence. What would be good reasons that too much homework is a big problem for students?

XIAO: Well, you say like you did in the beginning that we do not have enough time to rest. If we work all the time, we will always be tired.

MRS. CHEN: Good idea, Xiao. That sounds like one reason we can write about. Does anyone have another?

PAN: If we were not tired, then we would work better in school. If we could rest at home instead of doing so much homework, we would be better rested for school.

MRS. CHEN: Okay, Pan. That sounds good. Not only is it another reason to support our topic sentence, but it is related to the reason that Xiao gave. We have a couple of reasons so far. Does anyone have another?

JOSH: You'll like this one, Mrs. Chen—it would give the teachers extra time. If they didn't have to grade as much homework, they would have more time, too!

MRS. CHEN: (*Laughs.*) Nice one, Josh! Let's think about the next step in TREE. What do we need to think about next?

NAKIA: Next is *Explain your reasons.* We need to say more about each of our reasons.

MRS. CHEN: Good, Nakia. Let's see if we can write some paragraphs to explain each of these reasons. I would think we could write a paragraph for each of these reasons that we've come up with. I think I would begin this paragraph about our first reason with a sentence like "With less homework, students will be able to rest and recharge for the next day at school." (*She records the beginning of the next paragraph by writing the sentence she just stated, "With less homework, students will be able to rest and recharge for the next day at school."*) Let's think how we could support that statement in the first paragraph about our reasons. Any ideas? (*No answers from students.*) Okay, here's what I might do. See if you agree with me. I might use a sentence like, "If students did not have hours of homework, then they would be able to rest and recover from school." After that, I could add something else, like "Often students stay up late doing homework. If students were instead able to get a good night's sleep instead of doing homework, they would return to school the next day well rested and ready to learn." What do you all think?

THOMAS: That sounds good to me!

MRS. CHEN: (*Records the sentences that she said and creates a paragraph for the first reason the group decided on. After that, the group creates paragraphs for each of the other reasons given before the end of class.*) So, what is the last step in our TREE process in writing our persuasive essay?

XIAO: *Ending.* We need to wrap it up!

MRS. CHEN: Good! Let's see if we can wrap up this essay. Anyone have some suggestions?

JOSH: We could write "The End."
   (*Laughter*)

MRS. CHEN: We could . . . any other ideas?

NAKIA: We could restate what we said in another way to wrap it up.

MRS. CHEN: Good idea, Nakia! Let's see. I think I might word this by saying something like "Many middle school students have hours of homework to complete each night. By doing away with all of this homework, students will be able to get enough rest, recharge for the next school day of learning, and allow teachers more time for instructional planning." (*She writes the ending paragraph, making modifications as necessary with her students. Once the final paragraph is written, Mrs. Chen and her students review it for the continuity and structure of a persuasive essay.*)

Adaptations. Writing persuasive essays with TREE can be adapted for students who are just learning English. The teacher can support the second multilingual writing premise—that what a student knows about writing in his or her native language is likely to be used in new language writing—by encouraging students to write drafts of their persuasive essays in their native language. These drafts could be revised with native-language-speaking peers or with a teacher who speaks the students' native language. Additionally, the pace of instruction could be slowed considerably for multilingual students who are just learning English to allow them better understanding of the purpose of writing a persuasive essay and the instructional process.

CLOSURE

In this chapter, we provided a glimpse into the research findings on bilingual writing, posed some premises for bilingual writing instruction, and offered three illustrations that showcase ways in which teachers might think about bilingual writing instruction. As more and more teachers work with ELLs in their classrooms, it will become increasingly important that practitioners expand their understandings of new language writing and new language writing instruction. At the same time, it is equally important that teachers feel empowered to use what they already know about writing instruction as they work with new language learners.

Perhaps the two most important considerations for writing instruction with bilingual learners are not necessarily specific to writing but, instead, are strong principles of good teaching. First, try to see through the students' eyes. If you don't already have a background in the cultural specifics of the students' language(s), try to begin to learn about them. Assume that your students are doing their very best to understand you and the work of the classroom and that their efforts match or exceed others'. If you make such an assumption, not only will you have a better ability to locate the students' academic understandings, but you will also begin to build a strong relationship with your new language learners. That relationship is fundamental to the negotiations necessary to teaching and learning. Second, modulate, modulate, modulate instruction. In bilingual writing instruction, as always, it is crucial for students' progress that teachers locate a student's developmental writing level, know the critical writing process features for that developmental writing level, and teach *those* features. Lesson modulation is particularly important for older new language learners because they often are immersed or submersed in classroom settings where the concepts being taught are beyond their immediate reach.

REFERENCES

Albrechtsen, D. (1997). One writer two languages: A case study of a 15-year-old student's writing process in Danish and English. *International Journal of Applied Linguistics, 7,* 223–250.

Anderson, V., & Roit, M. (1996). Linking reading comprehension instruction to language development for language minority students. *Elementary School Journal, 96,* 295–310.

August, D. (Chair). (2003, December). *National Literacy Panel on Language Minority Children and Youth: Findings from the panel's research synthesis.* Symposium presented at the annual meeting of the National Reading Conference, Scottsdale, AZ.

August, D., & Hakuta, K. (Eds.). (1997). *Improving schooling for language-minority children: A research agenda.* Washington, DC: National Academy Press.

August, D., & Shanahan, T. (Eds.). (2006). *Developing literacy in second-language learners: Report of The National Literacy Panel on Language-Minority Children and Youth.* Mahwah, NJ: Erlbaum.

Bromley, K. (2003). Building a sound writing program. In L. M. Morrow, L. Gambrell, & M. Pressley (Eds.), *Best practices in literacy instruction* (2nd ed., pp. 143–165). New York: Guilford Press.

Buckwalter, J. K., & Lo, Y. G. (2002). Emergent biliteracy in Chinese and English. *Journal of Second Language Writing, 11,* 269–293.

Carlisle, R. (1989). The writing of Anglo and Hispanic elementary school students in bilingual submersion and regular programs. *Studies in Second Language Acquisition, 11,* 257–280.

Collier, V. P., & Thomas, W. P. (1989). How quickly can immigrants become proficient in school English? *Journal of Educational Issues of Language Minority Students, 5,* 26–38.

De Larios, J. R., Marin, J., & Murphy, L. (2001). A temporal analysis of formulation processes in L1 and L2 writing. *Language Learning, 51,* 497–538.

Fitzgerald, J. (2005). Multilingual writing in preschool through twelfth grade: The last 15 years. In C. A. MacArthur, S. Graham, & J. Fitzgerald (Eds.), *Handbook of writing research* (pp. 337–354). New York: Guilford Press.

Fitzgerald, J., & Graves, M. F. (2004). *Scaffolding reading experiences for English-language learners.* Norwood, MA: Christopher-Gordon.

Fitzgerald, J., & Noblit, G. W. (1999). About hopes, aspirations, and uncertainty: First-grade English-language learners' emergent reading. *Journal of Literacy Research, 31,* 133–182.

Gersten, R. (1996). Literacy instruction for language-minority students: The transition years. *The Elementary School Journal, 96,* 228–244.

Graham, S., & Harris, K. R. (2005). *Writing better. Effective strategies for teaching students with learning difficulties.* Baltimore: Brookes.

Harris, K. R., Graham, S., & Mason, L. (2002). POW plus TREE equals powerful opinion essays. *Teaching Exceptional Children, 34*(5), 74–77.

James, C., & Klein, K. (1994). Foreign language learners' spelling and proof-reading strategies. *Papers and Studies in Contrastive Linguistics, 29,* 31–46.

Jiménez, R. T. (2003). New directions in research: Literacy and Latino students in the United States: Some considerations, questions, and new directions. *Reading Research Quarterly, 38,* 122–128.

Klingner, J. K., & Vaughn, S. (1996). Reciprocal teaching of reading comprehension strategies for students with learning disabilities who use English as a second language. *The Elementary School Journal, 96,* 275–294.

Lanauze, M., & Snow, C. E. (1989). The relation between first- and second-language writing skills: Evidence from Puerto Rican elementary school children in bilingual programs. *Linguistics and Education, 1,* 323–339.

McCarrier, A., Fountas, I. C., & Pinnell, G. S. (2000). *Interactive writing: How language and literacy come together, K–2.* Portsmouth, NH: Heinemann.

Mitchell, R., & Myles, F. (1998). *Second language learning theories.* London: Arnold.

Neufeld, P., & Fitzgerald, J. (2001). Early English reading development: Latino English learners in the "low" reading group. *Research in the Teaching of English, 36,* 64–109.

Reyes, M. d. l. (1991). A process approach to literacy using dialogue journals and literature logs with second language learners. *Research in the Teaching of English, 25,* 291–313.

Zutell, J., & Allen, V. (1988). The English spelling strategies of Spanish-speaking bilingual children. *TESOL Quarterly, 22,* 333–340.

15

Best Practices in Teaching Writing to Students with Special Needs

SUSAN DE LA PAZ

Students with special needs comprise several heterogeneous groups of children and adolescents, including youth who are identified as having learning disabilities, attention-deficit/hyperactivity disorders, emotional and behavioral disorders, speech and language delays and disorders, and autism spectrum disorders; children who are bilingual with concomitant disabilities; and children who have mild to severe cognitive impairment with or without other handicapping conditions (e.g., cerebral palsy). We do not know how many children within each of these groups would be identified as having a writing disability; however, when considered as a group, children with special needs typically struggle when learning how to write (Graham & Harris, 2005). Nearly all of our available information on teaching writing to children with special needs is based on research involving children with high-incidence disabilities—that is, children with learning disabilities (LD), mild cognitive delays, speech and language delays and disorders, attention-deficit/hyperactivity disorder (ADHD), and/or emotional and behavioral disorders (EBD) who receive most of their educational services in general education classrooms. In addition, with only minor exceptions, the extant research has not revealed specific developmental trajectories or best practices for particular categories of disability.

What, then, should teachers know about teaching writing to students with special needs? The approach taken in this chapter is first to identify how children with special needs differ from their more capable peers in writing, keeping in mind the caveat that many children and youth without disabilities also do not write well (Persky, Daane, & Jin, 2002). I present detailed information about the writing abilities of particular subgroups of children with special needs when it is available and summarize results from exemplary studies in areas where we lack adequate information. Second, I include in this chapter best practices in writing assessment for children with special needs. Teachers may create their own assessments or call upon colleagues in school psychology or special education for assistance in implementing these ideas. Finally, I review several best practices in teaching writing to students with special needs.

DIFFERENCES BETWEEN STUDENTS WITH AND WITHOUT SPECIAL NEEDS

We know more about how children and adolescents with LD fare in their writing development than any other group of students with special needs. To begin, children with LD understand less about the recursive nature of the writing process than do children without special needs; they know less about the features of good writing, different genres, the role of audience in writing, and the purpose of writing (Graham, 2006). Students with LD also have difficulty identifying and using text structures and providing relevant details that support a given text structure (Englert, Wu, & Zhao, 2005); in addition, they write less than their peers (Wong, Graham, Hoskyn, & Berman, in press). Earlier work by Englert and her colleagues shows many students with LD possess far more information about topics than is reflected in their written compositions (cited in De La Paz, 1999b).

In addition, in comparison to their normally developing peers, students with LD fail to plan and organize their writing (Baker, Gersten, & Graham, 2003). To illustrate, whereas average sixth graders have been reported to plan in advance of writing for an average of 2 minutes, students with LD at the same grade have been observed to spend less than half a minute (Graham, 2006). Therefore, while inexperienced writers often start to write immediately after being given an assignment, converting it into what has been called a knowledge-telling tactic in which they respond to a writing prompt by recalling everything that is known about the topic, students with LD minimize the planning process even more than other children do. When explicitly taught, planning strategies are effective in improving the length, structure, and quality of papers written by students with and without LD (see Graham & Harris, Chapter 6, this volume); however, students with LD require more practice to gain mastery in their application of writing strategies (Wong et al., in press).

Another hallmark of the writing produced by children with LD is that they make considerably more spelling, capitalization, and punctuation errors than their normally achieving classmates, and their handwriting is less legible (De La Paz, 1999a). The importance of this weakness is highlighted by recent findings that individual differences in transcription skills correlate positively with overall writing quality. Graham and his colleagues found that transcription skills account for one quarter of the variance in writing quality and two thirds of the variance in writing output at the primary grades, and about 40% of the variance in writing quality and output at the intermediate grades (reported in Graham, 2006). Transcription affects the quality of writing for students with and without LD because having to attend to lower-level skills of getting language onto paper presumably interferes with higher-order skills, such as planning and content generation. For instance, having to stop to consider how to spell a word may cause the writer to forget plans and ideas already developed or may disrupt content generation (De La Paz, 1999a).

A second means by which the mechanical requirements of text production may interfere with writing involves speed of production. A person's rate of writing may not be fast enough to keep up with his or her thoughts. Slow writing may interfere with content generation and remembering ideas or text already planned and held in short-term memory. Students who struggle with transcription skills may also feel less motivated and show less persistence when composing. Finally, students with LD may use a more restricted vocabulary or syntax when producing text to avoid words they cannot spell or complex sentences (De La Paz, 1999a).

Students with LD also struggle with revising more than students without special needs, spending less time and making more superficial changes than their more capable peers (Graham, 2006). Their revising is often focused on correcting errors in punctuation and spelling and on making small changes in wording rather than on substantive changes that affect broader problems with their text. This is not surprising, given how problematic transcription problems are; moreover, it reflects the more general problem that students with LD understand less about the writing process. Fortunately, researchers and teachers have developed and validated successful revising strategies for students with and without LD (see MacArthur, Chapter 7, this volume).

What do we know about the writing of other populations of students who have special needs? As a group, the majority of children with ADHD are likely to be at risk for difficulties in learning to write (Reid & Lienemann, 2006). Children with ADHD have often been shown to have problems with the quality of their handwriting, and some research indicates that spelling is also a problem. Many children with ADHD also have LD; however, even for students who are diagnosed with ADHD alone, composition skills are problematic, as these children perform below peers without special needs in terms of word complexity, productivity, and general writing ability (Reid & Lienemann, 2006).

Students with EBD have chronic behavioral problems that interfere with their ability to achieve in school or emotional problems that interfere with their learning. We are only beginning to document how these problems affect academic outcomes. A recent study with a 155 students from kindergarten through grade 12 shows that both boys and girls with EBD struggle in reading, writing, and mathematics (Nelson, Benner, Lane, & Smith, 2004). Teachers rated the children's social adjustment to determine if internalizing or externalizing dimensions of their disorder were related to their academic achievement. The students' academic performance was based on an individually administered, standardized achievement test that is commonly used in special education. The results indicated that boys and girls with EBD had deficits in writing at all age levels and that students with externalizing problem behaviors (such as aggression) were more likely to struggle than children with internalizing behaviors (i.e., children who were withdrawn or depressed).

The writing produced by children with speech and language delays has not been well characterized, in part because the relationship between oral language and writing is difficulty to study (Shanahan, 2006). Another reason may be related to terminology, as researchers in the field of speech and language pathology refer to these children as having a *language-based learning disability*. Children who struggle to produce language orally are at risk for having problems in their written language even when their early oral language deficiencies are overcome (Shanahan, 2006). Moreover, if a study by Lewis, O'Donnell, Freebairn, and Taylor (1998) is representative, children with speech and language impairments may struggle with vocabulary, grammar, and overall organization. In this study, 7- to 14-year-olds with phonological and language impairments were compared to children with phonological disorders alone and to siblings without special needs. The results showed that students with speech and language difficulties scored lower than both comparison groups on a standardized writing test on subtests that measured their vocabulary, syntax, contextualized spelling, and development of a theme. Group differences were not found in usage of punctuation and capitalization, suggesting relative proficiency in at least some mechanical aspects of writing.

Finally, the writing of children with cognitive impairments is considered. This group includes children historically identified as having mild mental retardation (MMR), as well as children with Asperger syndrome (AS). While most literacy studies of students with MMR focus on reading, one published account by Katims (2000) provides evidence of writing achievement by 54 of 132 students who had an average IQ of 55. Most of these students were able to read and comprehend text at primer to first-grade levels and demonstrate the ability to write simple sentences from dictation with 25 to 70% accuracy (with higher levels seen in older students). Students were also able to generate about 10 words when asked to write as many words as they could in 10 minutes.

With respect to children with AS, Myles and her colleagues (2003) evaluated the writing of 16 students with and 16 students without AS who ranged in age from 8 to 16 years (children without special needs were matched on age, gender, and race and were neurologically normal). Standardized tests of writing and handwriting were given to all participants, and researchers analyzed students' writing samples along additional criteria to gain more information. The results indicated no differences between students with and without AS on the major subtests or overall score of the standardized writing test; however, informal analyses of the writing samples showed that the students without AS generated nearly twice as many morphemes and used significantly more t-units[1] in their sentences, a finding that has also been reported in comparisons of oral narratives by students with and without AS. The handwriting of students with AS was also less legible. Both results suggest subtle but real differences in the writing of students in this group; future research with additional students who are identified with this disorder is needed.

In summary, while heterogeneous, students with special needs typically struggle with several aspects of writing development. We know more about the writing of children with LD, but students who have been identified with other handicapping conditions often share many of the same difficulties. In fact, researchers who work with different subgroups of children with special needs do not advocate for different approaches for assessment or teaching (e.g., Katims, 2000). Therefore, the remainder of the chapter provides information regarding best practices in assessment and instruction for all children with special needs.

---

[1] A T-unit—standing for "minimal terminal unit"—is any independent clause with all of its subordinate clauses and modifiers. Basically, a T-unit differs from a sentence in that a compound sentence is one sentence, but it is more than one T-unit.

ASSESSMENT

In classrooms where teachers emphasize a process approach to writing, teachers and children often develop rubrics to judge written products. Well-constructed rubrics emphasize important traits of good writing and the processes (e.g., planning and revising) employed by the writer as he or she worked on an assignment (see Calfee & Miller, Chapter 13, this volume). Because the literature on rubrics is well described, I introduce two forms of assessment that meet different purposes and are less known: curriculum-based measurement (CBM) and dynamic assessment. The former is a type of curriculum-based assessment that is useful for monitoring children's progress in the curriculum over time, and the latter provides a way to understand the type of support an individual needs in the classroom. I then suggest ways to create an informal writing assessment and provide information regarding general testing accommodations.

Curriculum-Based Measurement

Whereas curriculum-based assessment is a broader, more generic form of assessment, including any approach that directly observes and records a student's performance in the school curriculum, CBM is a systematic approach for monitoring student progress that was developed to provide teachers with an efficient and useful means for assessing the effects of instruction (Espin, Weissenburger, & Benson, 2004). In writing,[2] CBM assessments are short probes administered to the entire class weekly or biweekly. CBM relies on writing fluency as the primary outcome measure due to its positive correlation with overall writing quality as well as its ability to differentiate students by grade level and status (i.e., students in general versus special education).

By examining each child's test, or probe, the teacher can focus on his or her progress during the grading period and compare the individual student's growth to the (average) growth of the class. Important benefits of CBM are that the teacher can (1) identify students who are at risk if they are not progressing at the same rate and level as the class average, (2) monitor each student's progress in the general curriculum, (3) identify a student's specific strengths and weaknesses, and (4) plan to make instructional changes whenever a student has less than satisfactory growth (Espin et al., 2004).

---

[2] CBM has also been developed for monitoring children's growth in spelling; however, due to space limitations, this aspect is omitted from this discussion.

At the elementary school level, recommended procedures for gathering CBM writing measures are as follows. Teachers first decide whether to use a story starter or topic sentence (e.g., "My ideal place to live would be very different from where I live now" or "One day, as I was petting my friend's dog, it started to . . . ") as the writing prompt and how frequently to administer tests. It is important to collect enough writing prompts for the entire year and to review them for similarity and interest for a given grade level. Teachers must administer the probes consistently: (1) instruct students to think about the story starter or topic sentence for 1 minute and then begin writing; (2) using a stopwatch or clock, after exactly 3 minutes, tell students to stop writing, or, if they are to finish writing their composition, to mark exactly where they are at 3 minutes; (3) students should spell independently.

According to Espin and colleagues (2004), teachers can choose to score the writing samples counting the total words in the passage (including misspelled words) or the total number of words spelled correctly. In the latter approach, each word is considered in isolation and counted if it represents a correctly spelled term in English. An advantage of the former measure is that older primary-grade students are able to score each other's papers. An advantage of the second method is that it provides additional information about the quality of the student's writing. Regardless of the scoring method, the results are graphed for each student, and a class average and standard deviation are determined.

Few research studies have been conducted with high school students, but modifications in CBM procedures appear necessary at the middle school level. First, the time for each probe is increased to 5 minutes. Second, teachers may administer story starters or descriptive or persuasive prompts; however, the writing genre is held constant across the entire year. Third, more complex scoring procedures are needed to be valid indicators. The scoring is based first on the number of *correct word sequences*, which requires the teacher to go beyond isolated words to consider how words relate to one another. Words are considered separate units. In addition to being correctly spelled, each two-word sequence must make sense within the context of the sentence be grammatically correct and accurately punctuated. The second scoring step is to subtract the number of *incorrect word sequences* from the first score, resulting in a final and more robust score, called *correct minus incorrect word sequences* (Espin et al., 2004).

Dynamic Assessment

The purpose of dynamic assessment is diagnostic. In contrast to traditional testing measures that capture students' skills and abilities at a particular point in time, this type of assessment provides insights about how students respond to instruction (Cioffi & Carney, 1997). Procedures during the evaluation lead to descriptions of not only how well the child writes, but also how individually designed changes in instruction, setting, and so forth influence a child's performance. To illustrate, consider how many writing tests require students to write in response to pictures or prompts. In contrast, in one form of dynamic assessment, the teacher compares the child's written essay under traditional conditions to his or her writing under one or more of the following conditions, in turn: (1) the child is given an opportunity to rehearse what he or she plans to write and is prompted to make notes before writing; (2) after the child composes a draft, he or she is asked to read it to the teacher; and (3) during revision, the child is asked to identify problems and suggest changes. The first instructional change isolates the effect that activating the child's background knowledge has on the resulting essay. The second instructional change provides an opportunity for the child to make self-corrections and allows the teacher to observe whether the child responds to errors or problems encountered in his or her writing. The final instructional change suggested here will not indicate the child's proficiency in making revisions per se; rather, it is designed to provide insight into whether the child can detect if his or her writing matches what he or she intended to say (Cioffi & Carney, 1997).

These instructional changes are not exhaustive and are determined by what the teacher knows (and wants to find out) about each child. For example, another instructional change in the above after-drafting situation might be for the teacher to ask the child to locate and then offer alternatives to misspelled words. The point of each instructional change is to help the teacher with what Cioffi and Carney call a kind of "if–then" thinking (1997). Rather than having an understanding of how well or poorly the child writes in the traditional assessment situation, the teacher is exploring the student's response to specific instructional changes (isolated to tease out exactly what is making the difference). *If* the teacher finds, for example, that a child can recognize differences between what he or she intended to write and the resulting words and sentences, *then* he or she might benefit from instruction in general methods for revising, such as moving ideas around, adding or taking away information, and changing words. Another student might be insensitive to major problems in his or her paper, believing that the original paper made sense when it did not, leading the teacher to understand that he or she will need to provide a far greater degree of scaffolding during the revision process. By exploring the student's response to changes in instruction, the teacher learns not only the level at which the child functions, but also the instructional interventions required for success (Cioffi & Carney, 1997).

To conclude, school psychologists and special education teachers may use other variations of dynamic assessment not described here, but these procedures will suffice for most teachers whose purpose is to gain information about an individual child that can be used in making educational decisions in the general education classroom. Through the use of brief interactions with different materials and methods, teachers can estimate children's response to instruction and learn how to modify instruction for students with special needs. The final analysis allows the teacher to contrast what the child can do independently with what he or she can achieve with adult mediation (which invokes Vygotsky's concept of the zone of proximal development). Measuring growth only in terms of what the child can do independently provides a static measure, whereas including what the child can do with mediation provides an estimate of the child's developing abilities, resulting in a richer representation of ability. Rather than viewing the more successful writing as an anomaly resulting from the instructional change, teachers might view it as an indication of the child's potential under appropriate instructional conditions.

Informal Assessment

The previous section on dynamic assessment may be understood better in the context of a teacher's existing informal assessment battery. That is, teachers may develop an informal writing assessment, use it with an entire class of students, and then modify it as needed for individual students using principles of dynamic assessment. Gregg and Mather (2002) suggest that teachers evaluate student performance across writing components (e.g., handwriting, vocabulary, text structure) and across different task formats (copy, dictation, spontaneous) to help clarify a student's strengths and weaknesses. A variety of tasks may be needed to fully explore relationships among the task, setting, and writer's experiences; however, daily work and attempted spellings from weekly tests can also provide a starting point for analyzing children's error patterns. While it is important to develop a full battery of assessments and administer whatever is most relevant for an individual child, due to space limitations I highlight three areas here: handwriting, spelling, and vocabulary.

With handwriting, two primary considerations are legibility and speed (Gregg & Mather, 2002). A child may be asked to copy a sentence containing different graphemes, such as "My cat jumped on the table.", using his or her best handwriting and to compare that version with writing the sentence as many times as possible in 1 minute. Other relevant tasks for young writers include writing the alphabet from memory as compared to copying it, which is intended to test the children's ability to formulate letters and words as well as ease and speed of production under different conditions. As children get older, they can be asked to copy a paragraph for 1½ minutes without making any mistakes. Repeating an informal testing procedure with successive classes of children over the years will allow teachers to quickly identify a child whose performance deteriorates given certain constraints.

Teachers generally know how to analyze children's invented spellings and how to view them within the context of developmental stage theories. Additional suggestions for informal spelling assessments include the following. First, ask the child to spell from dictation a list of nonwords that conform to English regularities (e.g., *vang*, *bibble*, *studge*) to determine his or her orthographic knowledge (Gregg & Mather, 2002). Second, create spelling assessments that include words with silent letters or letters with unpredictable grapheme–phoneme relationships, such as the *di* in *soldier*. Third, include words with different morphological endings for emerging writers (such as *walked*) and different word forms or derivational relations for older students (such as *critic* vs. *criticize*).

Vocabulary can be an added writing component to examine during an informal assessment. While we do not have much empirical research on the relationship between word knowledge and written expression in students with disabilities (Gregg & Mather, 2002), cognitive, linguistic, and metacognitive abilities as well as prior knowledge, text complexity, and social factors are all underlying influences on vocabulary knowledge and word learning. Suggestions for creating an informal assessment are to try to identify whether a student's problem is primarily receptive or expressive on a given task. To illustrate, teachers might ask students to identify or generate one of several verbs—*speak*, *say*, *talk*, or *tell*—in a specific context. Other vocabulary tasks worth mentioning focus on use of words with multiple meanings, labels such as *when* for understanding of time concepts, indirect requests, figurative language, and general word choice (Gregg & Mather, 2002). Children with expressive language problems such as word finding problems (i.e., they struggle to recall labels for concepts) will need general vocabulary instruction for both oral and written language.

Accommodations

Students with special needs are sometimes given specific accommodations to compensate for their primary area of disability. Two common forms of accommodation that have been evaluated with and without students with disabilities are the use of (1) dictation as a means to re-move challenges posed by difficulties with mechanics and (2) extended time. The purpose of such comparisons has been to determine whether the change in testing conditions can achieve two important outcomes: to remove a barrier to valid assessment based on a child's disability and to preserve the nature of the construct being assessed (MacArthur & Cava-lier, 2004). Formal evaluations with students from both general and spe-cial education are done to determine whether there is a specific benefit to the latter population; however, judging whether the accommodation changes the construct is a philosophical decision. If a teacher's purpose is to learn what students with disabilities can demonstrate regarding knowledge of a subject, then allowing him or her to dictate may be justi-fied.

In MacArthur and Cavalier's (2004) study, high school students with and without LD wrote a series of essays using handwriting, dicta-tion to a person, and dictation to a computer using speech recognition software (Dragon Naturally Speaking). In the second writing condition, an adult typed what the students composed on a computer so that the students could see the text on a monitor. In the third condition, students first spent several hours learning how to use the software. The results in-dicated that both dictation conditions helped students with LD and that their best papers were written to the adult scribe. Students without spe-cial needs were not affected by the different writing conditions. In addi-tion, while students without disabilities wrote better papers under all three conditions, the scores for papers composed by students with spe-cial needs approached their peers' scores in the dictation to a person condition. Composing orally to an adult while seeing one's text emerge may be an appropriate accommodation when students with LD are asked to demonstrate content knowledge.

The importance of extended time has also been explored experi-mentally. Typical comparisons involve students with and without dis-abilities writing on demand in a short (e.g., 30 minutes) and an extended (e.g., several days) period and comparing the performance of students in both groups. The primary assumption is that a longer time allows chil-dren to plan, draft, and revise their papers and that engaging in all stages of the writing process will lead to improved papers. A recent study by Crawford, Helwig, and Tindal (2004) compared the narrative writing of fifth- and eighth-grade students with and without LD when given 30 minutes and when given 50-minute sessions on 3 consecutive days. The results from this study were interesting but not altogether straightfor-ward: the older general education students did not improve given more time, although some improvement was found for students with LD; however, the younger children did benefit from the 3-day writing assessment, and this benefit was even more important for students with special needs. The authors noted that the scoring system valued conventions more than other aspects of writing, which may have lowered scores for writers who made more substantive revisions in lieu of fixing grammatical features. Perhaps the most important contribution that this study provided is a direct link between a writer's level of development and his or her need for extended time. Older students appear capable of engaging in the entire writing process in a short period of time, whereas younger students and those with disabilities are not.

ELEMENTS OF SUCCESSFUL WRITING PROGRAMS

Research from the past two decades has shown that students with special needs make significant improvements in their writing following explicit instruction in transcription skills (spelling and handwriting) and in strategies for planning, organizing, and carrying out writing tasks (Baker et al., 2003). Other chapters in this volume (Graham & Harris, Chapter 6; MacArthur, Chapter 7, this volume) discuss ways to implement instruction in writing strategies; thus, my explanation is limited and provides one illustration of their use with secondary students. Key elements include finding time for explicit instruction in specific skills such as genre conventions, transcription and revision (Baker et al., 2003; Fitzgerald & Markham, 1987; Graham & Harris, 2005), the use of self-regulated writing strategies for planning before composing (De La Paz, 1999b) that highlight the importance of self-regulation in instruction for students with special needs (De La Paz, in press), combining reading and writing (Berninger, Abbott, Abbott, Graham, & Richards, 2002; Shanahan, 2006; Wong, Kuperis, Jamieson, Keller, & Cull-Hewitt, 2002), and using technology to support writing (Englert et al., 2005; MacArthur, 2006).

Direct Instruction

In comparison to peers without disabilities, students with special needs require more intense and more explicit instruction. I provide examples of research-based methods for directly teaching revision (Fitzgerald & Markham, 1987) and transcription skills (Graham & Harris, 2005) because these particular methods exemplify instructional principles that are especially useful for students with special needs. In Fitzgerald and Markham's (1987) study, sixth-grade students learned four types of revisions (how to add, delete, rewrite, and move text) in a series of 3-day lesson cycles. The teacher defined, discussed, and modeled each revision on the first day. On the second day, after a review, students worked in pairs to revise a short passage that was supplied by the teacher. Students applied the same revision strategy to that passage. On the third day, students followed the same procedure but worked independently and ended the session by revising a story they had composed, again using the same revision strategy that had been modeled on day 1 of the teaching cycle. When compared to a control group, direct instruction in the revision process improved students' knowledge of that process, their efforts to make revisions, and the quality of their stories across drafts.

In a series of studies, Graham and his colleagues (reported in Graham & Harris, 2005) provided several hours of direct instruction in handwriting and spelling to first- and second-grade children who had either slow handwriting or poor spelling and generally poor writing skills. The handwriting instruction was designed to teach children how to write lower-case manuscript letters accurately and fluently. To accomplish these goals, children received 15 minutes of instruction three times a week for a total of 7 hours of instruction. Each lesson included four activities. The children first learned to name and identify letters of the alphabet. Next, they were introduced to and practiced sets of letters that shared common formational characteristics (e.g., *l*, *i*, and *t*). Three lessons were devoted to mastering each letter set; the teacher modeled how to form the letters, then students practiced tracing and writing the letters individually and in context. Third, students copied a short sentence that contained multiple instances of the letters being taught in that unit quickly and accurately for 3 minutes. Throughout these lessons, students evaluated their efforts (for example, by circling the best-formed letter), monitored their performance, and set goals to write faster. In comparison to children who received extra reading instruction, the children who received handwriting instruction not only improved handwriting, but also writing skills. They wrote better sentences and longer stories than children in the control group and maintained these gains on a follow-up probe 6 months later.

The second graders received 12 hours of extra spelling instruction, meeting three times a week for 20-minute sessions, in comparison to a group of children who received extra math instruction. There were six units in all, each containing five lessons. The focus of instruction was to teach children basic sound–letter combinations, spelling patterns involving long and short vowels, and common words that fit those patterns. In the first lesson of each unit, students sorted word cards into two or more patterns that were represented by keywords (e.g., *made*, *maid*, and *may* for the long-*a* sound) and discovered and learned rules for the patterns emphasized in each word sort. During the remaining four lessons, students examined eight new spelling words that matched one of the spelling patterns emphasized in that unit. Students used two basic procedures to study these words. The first activity involved self-recording the number of times that students correctly practiced the words during a traditional study session. The second involved studying words while playing a game with a peer. Students also practiced identifying sound–letter associations for consonants, blends, digraphs, and short vowels as well as building words by joining these combinations to rimes that fit the spelling patterns emphasized in the unit. Children who received the spelling instruction demonstrated improved spelling on words they practiced as well as on standardized tests; in addition, they showed improvement on word attack skills and sentence writing skills.

Self-Regulated Strategy Instruction

One reason the handwriting and spelling programs were so successful may be the way self-monitoring and goal setting were included in the instruction. These and other self-regulatory procedures help writers manage the process of writing (Graham, 2006). Although space does not permit a thorough review of the self-regulation strategies that successful writers use, they include planning (e.g., establishing rhetorical goals, brainstorming and recording ideas, organizing notes, and drawing on previously learned strategies to achieve goals), self-evaluating (e.g., reviewing text generated to see if it matches one's intended meaning or to see if goals are met), and revising (modifying text or plans for subsequent text). Therefore, in response to the instructional needs of students with LD, researchers from several universities have focused on teaching writing strategies and self-regulation procedures to elementary and secondary students with and without LD to help them develop more sophisticated approaches to writing and improve the quality of their compositions. Graham and Harris and their colleagues (cited in Graham & Harris, 2005) developed an approach referred to as the Self-Regulated Strategy Development (SRSD) model for teaching writing. In this approach, students learn specific strategies for accomplishing writing tasks, such as writing persuasive essays, along with procedures for regulating the writing process. Knowledge and skills students need to use the target strategies and write effectively are also taught. Teachers scaffold instruction so that responsibility for recruiting and using the target strategies, accompanying knowledge or skills, and self-regulation procedures gradually shifts from instructor to students (Graham & Harris, 2005). Additional hallmarks are that children actively collaborate with teachers and that feedback and instructional support are tailored to meet differing student needs.

In my work, I have applied the use of SRSD to the needs of secondary students, with and without LD (e.g., De La Paz, 1999b). One such strategy, identified to students by the mnemonics PLAN and WRITE, was used to teach middle school students to plan and compose expository essays on demand for a statewide timed writing assessment. The mnemonics were used to help students remember strategy steps and serve as a reminder to reflect on qualities of good writing while composing.

The primary focus of the first step, "Pay attention to the prompt," is to help students fully consider the topic. To illustrate, consider a previous writing prompt:

> Your class has been given an opportunity to go on a one-day educational field trip. In an essay, state where you think the class should go and give reasons explaining why you think the class should go there.

Students underline once what they are being asked to write about (i.e., their choice for a one-day educational field trip) and underline twice how they are to develop content (reasons, with details and examples as appropriate, explaining why you think the class should got here).

During the second step, "List main ideas," students first brainstorm and decide on the topic (field-trip destination) and then brainstorm at least three main ideas for the development of the essay (reasons for this destination). In the third step, "Add supporting ideas," students note three details or elaborations to support each main idea. The fourth step, "Number your ideas," reminds students to sequence the main ideas and details in a meaningful way (i.e., the most compelling reason for this destination becomes the first or last body paragraph in the essay).

Students follow steps identified by the second mnemonic, WRITE, to help them continue the planning process while composing by focusing their attention on additional features of good writing. The fifth step, "Work from you plan to develop your thesis statement," reminds students to incorporate ideas from their plan into a thesis statement. Either a basic or an advanced approach for introductory paragraphs can be used here. In the basic approach, the first paragraph begins with the topic sentence and provides an overview of the three body paragraphs. Students using an advanced approach start with a series of questions, statements, or a brief anecdote as a way to grab the reader's attention, concluding the introductory paragraph with their topic sentence.

The sixth step, "Remember your goals," serves as an additional reminder to continue planning as students compose. These goals reflect qualities of good writing and incorporate specific criteria from the state's holistic scoring rubric. Goals include maintaining control of the topic, providing clear organization, attempting to include mature vocabulary, and use of sentences that vary by form and function. Copies of these goals are provided to each student, and students select personal goals to strive for.

The last three steps of the strategy give specific suggestions for on-line planning. Students learn to "Include transition words for each para-graph," to "Try to use different kinds of sentences," and to include "Ex-citing, interesting, million-dollar words" in their compositions. Students are prompted to make revisions while writing. They reread their essays, check their use of transition words, make minor changes (such as creat-ing a compound sentence from simple sentences), and substitute syn-onyms for words that occur more than once in their essay.

In my first study with PLAN and WRITE, positive results occurred for students with LD as well as for low-, average-, and high- achieving writers (De La Paz, 1999b). Following instruction, students' papers be-came longer and more complex and improved in quality. Both writing performance and students' approach to the writing task remained im-proved 1 month after instruction was completed. The results were repli-cated in a subsequent study with middle school students without special needs.

Self-regulation appears to be especially useful for students with spe-cial needs. In general, the importance of self-regulation in a given task is likely to vary, not only with a student's ability in its management, but also depending on the relative difficulty of the task and setting demands. Incorporating self-regulatory procedures into writing programs contrib-utes to both transfer and generalization of learned strategies for students with LD (De La Paz, in press) and seems to be an essential component when students attempt conceptually difficult tasks.

Connecting Reading and Writing Instruction

Teachers have long held reading workshops in connection with writing workshops; in addition, empirical research provides other compelling reasons why it is beneficial to capitalize on connections between reading and writing (Berninger, et al., 2002; Shanahan, 2006; Wong et al., 2002). Of particular relevance here is the role that writing has in devel-oping children's reading and content knowledge. To begin, we know that reading and writing are not symmetrical activities (Shanahan, 2006) nor is writing the same as talk written down, but there is modest support for the belief that writing assignments can increase students' content under-standing (Shanahan, 2006) and reading comprehension (Wong et al., 2002). In addition, work by Graham and Harris (2005) demonstrates that, at least for second graders, spelling instruction can lead to improve-ments in word attack skills.

Berninger and her colleagues (2002) completed an evaluation of

600 children from first through sixth grade with findings that support and extend this data. Their work showed a reciprocal relationship between spelling and word recognition at all grade levels, suggesting that instruction in one should reliably affect the other. Teaching handwriting may also have a positive impact on word recognition skills, although this finding should be viewed as tentative. Additional research is needed to determine whether growth in word recognition is merely predicted from handwriting ability, rather than influenced by its development. Berninger and colleagues also examined the effect of compositional quality on reading comprehension. The results indicated that for students in the upper elementary grades (4–6), there was a direct link between the two. They interpreted the findings as a developmental outcome. In other words, students may need to reach an intermediate level of compositional proficiency before their compositional skills show reciprocal influences on reading comprehension (Berninger et al., 2002). Therefore, as students move into the intermediate grades and beyond, improvements in writing ability should affect their reading comprehension.

It should be obvious that I do not mean to suggest the best way to improve word recognition or reading comprehension is through writing activities, but they are interrelated constructs and instruction in one area may have unintended benefits. In fact, a more basic reason for combining reading and writing instructionally has to do with their shared knowledge and skills (Shanahan, 2006). For example, learning to be aware of an author's intent will have a positive impact on both reading and writing. In addition, revision requires children to have adequate reading comprehension to detect whether what they wrote matches what they intended to write. The better a child decodes words, the more likely he or she is to be able to spell words successfully. Children with special needs will benefit from instruction that combines reading with writing instruction just as their peers without special needs do.

Leveraging Technology to Support Writing

MacArthur (2006) provides a theoretical review of the use of technology for writing applications. With respect to students with special needs, he examines the utility of word processing and other computer tools, including spell-check, speech synthesis, and word prediction and speech recognition tools. One of his most significant findings was that using word processors as part of a writing instruction program improved the writing of students, especially for weaker writers, including students with LD. Appropriate instruction, however, such as combining word processing with instruction in revision, is needed to realize the benefits. In addition, although word processing removes the need to write by hand or to copy one's revisions, it places a new burden on students: they must learn to type efficiently. Finally, for some students with special needs, their underlying disability negatively affects both handwriting and learning to type (MacArthur, 2006).

Spelling checkers have been shown to help students with LD identify more of their errors (from below 10% to almost 40%); however, this still amounts to a failing grade. One difficulty is that spelling checkers do not identify a word that is spelled correctly but is not the word the student intended to write (MacArthur, 2006). It is also unable to suggest the correct spelling for severe misspellings (about 25% of the errors in the above sample of students). Finally, as would be expected, different versions of spell-check vary widely in their ability to suggest the correct word. Thus, teachers should teach students ways to manage its limitations.

Speech synthesis and word prediction software are other tools that can help writers with special needs. Speech synthesis, or text-to-speech software, allows the user to listen to what he or she has written. Students who have relatively strong oral skills may be able to decide if their text "sounds right" and make revisions based on what they hear. Word prediction programs were originally developed for individuals with physical disabilities; however, they also offer potential for students with spelling problems (MacArthur, 2006). The software predicts the user's intended word based on its initial letters—a list is provided after the user types in a few letters. If the intended word is on the list, the student can select it rather than typing it, thus avoiding some spelling problems. Research on the effectiveness of speech synthesis and word prediction software indicates that it is important to tailor the vocabulary to the writing task (e.g., include words that students use regularly or for specific purposes) and make sure the pool of words is not so large that it becomes difficult for students to search.

Speech Recognition

With speech recognition software, students can generate text orally without the assistance of another person and can read the emerging text at the same time (MacArthur, 2006). Composing to a machine may be beneficial for students with LD as human transcribers tend to prompt students rather than wait for them to express their ideas. There are some disadvantages to current speech recognition systems. Current programs merely translate an utterance or execute oral commands (e.g., *delete that* followed by a word or phrase that the speaker wants to cut); they do not understand speech and have limited capabilities for interpreting a speaker's message even after being trained to understand a speaker's voice (De La Paz, 1999a). Second, students must learn to speak clearly, avoid extraneous vocalizations (such as breathing deeply, which is recognized by the system as nonsensical words), and use explicit punctuation (MacArthur & Cavalier, 2004). Third, users must recognize and correct mistakes—they are required to spell (orally or by keyboard) the correct word when the system remains unable to recognize the target item. Based on the difficulties that students with special needs have in detecting and fixing errors when using spelling checkers, efficient use of speech recognition systems will require a significant amount of training.

Englert and her colleagues (2005) recently demonstrated the utility of a new form of technological support for writing. They developed a web-based software system that combined word processing and speech synthesis with a series of prompts (e.g., topic sentence) to cue text structure. The system offered brief reminders from the teacher that appeared in pop-up windows whenever students clicked on the word *Prompts*. Spell-check was also built into the system. Finally, the teacher communicated a general set of instructions in a box at the top of the screen to students for the specific task at hand. Although the sample size in this study was small (12 fourth- and fifth-grade students with LD), the results indicated that students who used the system generated more details related to their topics and had better overall organization of their texts. In addition, students were observed using spell-check and the speech-to-text tools to support their efforts at revision. Finally, the technology integrated procedural facilitators directly within the word-processing environment, which presumably allowed students to concentrate more on their content and less on remembering what they needed to include. Future developments in software applications similar to this program are likely to provide additional support for students with special needs, especially when they are combined with instruction in basic writing processes.

CONCLUDING COMMENT

In conclusion, teachers whose classrooms include students with special needs will benefit from knowing what to expect, in general, about these children's writing, how to plan for different types of assessment and accommodations, and how to incorporate successful teaching approaches into their existing writing programs. Some teachers may be hesitant to try approaches that appear to benefit only a small segment of the classroom, but many of the suggestions in this chapter are likely to benefit a wide range of learners, not just those identified with special needs, because they are based on sound instructional principles. Future research on writing instruction with and without students with special needs should document the extent to which several populations of students without special needs (e.g., English language learners) use and benefit from similar instruction.

REFERENCES

Baker, S., Gersten, R., & Graham, S. (2003). Teaching expressive writing to students with learning disabilities: Research-based applications and examples. *Journal of Learning Disabilities, 36,* 109–123.

Berninger, V. W., Abbott, R. D., Abbott, S. P., Graham, S., & Richards, T. (2002). Writing and reading: Connections between language by hand and language by eye. *Journal of Learning Disabilities, 35,* 39–56.

Cioffi, G., & Carney, J. J. (1997). Dynamic assessment of composing abilities in children with learning disabilities. *Educational Assessment, 4,* 175–202.

Crawford, L., Helwig, R., & Tindal, G. (2004). Writing performance assessments: How important is extended time? *Journal of Learning Disabilities, 37,* 132–142.

De La Paz, S. (1999a). Composing via dictation and speech recognition systems: Compensatory technology for students with learning disabilities. *Learning Disability Quarterly, 22,* 173–182.

De La Paz, S. (1999b). Self-regulated strategy instruction in regular education settings: Improving outcomes for students with and without learning disabilities. *Learning Disabilities Research and Practice, 14,* 92–106.

De La Paz, S. (in press). Managing cognitive demands for writing: Comparing the effects of instructional components in strategy instruction. *Reading and Writing Quarterly.*

Englert, C. S., Wu, X., & Zhao, Y. (2005). Cognitive tools for writing: Scaffolding the performance of students through technology. *Learning Disabilities Research and Practice, 20,* 184–198.

Espin, C. A., Weissenburger, J. W., & Benson, B. J. (2004). Assessing the writing performance of students in special education. *Exceptionality, 12,* 55–66.

Fitzgerald, J., & Markham, L. R. (1987). Teaching children about revision in writing. *Cognition in Instruction, 4,* 3–24.

Graham, S. (2006). Writing. In P. A. Alexander & P. H. Winne (Eds.), *Handbook of educational psychology* (pp. 457–478). Mahwah, NJ: Erlbaum.

Graham, S., & Harris, K. H. (2005). Improving the writing performance of young struggling writers: Theoretical and programmatic research from the Center on Accelerating Student Learning. *Journal of Special Education, 39,* 19–33.

Gregg, N., & Mather, N. (2002). School is fun at recess: Informal analyses of written language for students with learning disabilities. *Journal of Learning Disabilities, 35,* 7–22.

Katims, D. S. (2000). *The quest for literacy: Curriculum and instructional procedures for teaching reading and writing to students with mental retardation and developmental disabilities.* Reston, VA: The Council for Exceptional Children.

Lewis, B. A., O'Donnell, B., Freebairn, L. A., & Taylor, H. G. (1998). Spoken language and written expression—interplay of delays. *American Journal of Speech-Language Pathology, 7,* 77–84.

MacArthur, C. A. (2006). The effects of new technologies on writing and writing processes. In C. A. MacArthur, S. Graham, & J. Fitzgerald (Eds.), *Handbook of writing research* (pp. 248–262). New York: Guilford Press.

MacArthur, C. A., & Cavalier, A. R. (2004). Dictation and speech recognition technology as test accommodations. *Exceptional Children, 71,* 43–58.

Myles, B. S., Huggins, A., Rome-Lake, M., Hagiwara, T., Barnhill, G. P., & Griswold, D. E. (2003). Written language profile of children and youth with Asperger syndrome: From research to practice. *Education and Training in Developmental Disabilities, 38,* 362–369.

Nelson, R., Benner, G., Lane, K., & Smith, B. (2004). An investigation of the academic achievement of K–12 students with emotional and behavioral disorders in public school settings. *Exceptional Children, 71,* 59–74.

Persky, H., Daane, M., & Jin, Y. (2002). *The nation's report card: Writing.* Washington, DC: U.S. Department of Education.

Reid, R., & Lienemann, T. O. (2006). Self-regulated strategy development for written expression with students with attention-deficit/hyperactivity disorder. *Exceptional Children, 73,* 53–67.

Shanahan, T. (2006). Relations among oral language, reading, and writing development. In C. A. MacArthur, S. Graham, & J. Fitzgerald (Eds.), *Handbook of writing research* (pp. 171–183). New York: Guilford Press.

Wong, B. Y. L., Graham, L., Hoskyn, M., & Berman (in press). Writing. In B. Y. L. Wong, *ABC's of learning disabilities* (2nd ed.). San Diego: Academic Press.

Wong, B. Y. L., Kuperis, S., Jamieson, D., Keller, L., & Cull-Hewitt, R. (2002). Effects of guided journal writing on students' story understanding. *Journal of Educational Research, 95,* 179–191.

Index